Vanessa Evans, Mita Banerjee (eds.)
Cultures of Citizenship in the Twenty-First Century

Culture & Theory | Volume 292

Vanessa Evans is a settler scholar and assistant professor of Indigenous literatures at Appalachian State University. Her current research focuses on the ways diverse and distinct Indigenous novels from North America, Oceania, and South Asia represent Indigenous resurgence. She is also an associate managing editor for the *Journal of Transnational American Studies*.

Mita Banerjee is a professor and chair of American studies at the Obama Institute for Transnational American Studies at Johannes Gutenberg-Universität Mainz. Her research interests include postcolonial literature, issues of naturalization and citizenship, and medical humanities. She is the author of six monographs, a Principal Investigator in the research unit "Human Differentiation" and co-speaker of the research training group "Life Sciences, Life Writing: Boundary Experiences of Human Life between Biomedical Explanation and Lived Experience," funded by the German Research Foundation.

Vanessa Evans, Mita Banerjee (eds.)

Cultures of Citizenship
in the Twenty-First Century

Literary and Cultural Perspectives on a Legal Concept

[transcript]

This publication was supported by funds from the Publication Fund of the Johannes Gutenberg University, Mainz.

Bibliographic information published by the Deutsche Nationalbibliothek
The Deutsche Nationalbibliothek lists this publication in the Deutsche Nationalbibliografie; detailed bibliographic data are available in the Internet at http://dnb.dnb.de

This work is licensed under the Creative Commons Attribution 4.0 (BY) license, which means that the text may be remixed, transformed and built upon and be copied and redistributed in any medium or format even commercially, provided credit is given to the author.
https://creativecommons.org/licenses/by/4.0/
Creative Commons license terms for re-use do not apply to any content (such as graphs, figures, photos, excerpts, etc.) not original to the Open Access publication and further permission may be required from the rights holder. The obligation to research and clear permission lies solely with the party re-using the material.

First published in 2024 by transcript Verlag, Bielefeld
© Vanessa Evans, Mita Banerjee (eds.)

Cover layout: Maria Arndt, Bielefeld
Cover illustration: Photo by Tom Barrett on Unsplash
Printed by: Majuskel Medienproduktion GmbH, Wetzlar
https://doi.org/10.14361/9783839470190
Print-ISBN: 978-3-8376-7019-6
PDF-ISBN: 978-3-8394-7019-0
ISSN of series: 2702-8968
eISSN of series: 2702-8976

Printed on permanent acid-free text paper.

Contents

Cultures of Citizenship
An Introduction
Vanessa Evans and Mita Banerjee... 9

Fluidity in Space and Time

Citizenship in Time
Temporality and Time-Reckoning in Jamaica Kincaid's *A Small Place*
Mitchell Gauvin.. 23

John MacKenzie's *Letters I Didn't Write*
Rewriting Home, Homeland, and Citizenship
Kristen Smith.. 43

Transnational Citizenship and Dreams of Belonging
in Imbolo Mbue's *Behold the Dreamers*
Sonja Georgi.. 57

Citizenship and (State) Violence

"Present Absentees, Weak-Kneed Nobodies"
Exile, Airport, and Non-Citizenship in Abdourahman Waberi's *Transit*
Nasra Smith... 79

"You've Heard It Now"
Storytelling and Acts of Citizenship in Cherie Dimaline's *The Marrow Thieves*
Vanessa Evans..111

"Clean Body, Clean Mind, Clean Job"
The Role of Penal Voluntary Sector Organizations
in Constructing "Good" Carceral Citizens
Kaitlyn Quinn and Erika Canossini 131

Between Imprisonment and Citizenship
Jessica Kent's Navigation of Carceral Citizenship
Nina Heydt 155

Performing Citizenship

Paragon of Aging, Paragon of Voting
Centenarians and the Imaginary of a Model Citizen
Julia Velten 177

Making Material Borders
Petro-Cultures and Modern Citizenship
Scott Obernesser 195

Citizenship of the Dead
Antigone and Beyond
Marcus Llanque and Katja Sarkowsky 217

"We had to control the narrative"
The Innovations and Limitations of Youth Citizenship
Anah-Jayne Samuelson 233

"To Couple the Beauty of the Place and the Harsh Realities of Its Racist History"
Piecing Together African American Citizenship
in Faith Ringgold's *Flag Story Quilt* and *Coming to Jones Road*
Malaika Sutter 251

Citizenship, Science, and Medicine

"What the Eyes Don't See"
Medical Citizenship and Environmental Justice in Mona Hanna-Attisha's Medical Memoir
Mita Banerjee 271

Foreign Relations
Utopian Fictions and the Birth of Scientific Citizenship
Jessica Hanselman Gray 291

"You're My People Now"
The Last of Us Series on the Question of Human Belonging
and Citizenship during the Age of Pandemics
Amina Antonia Touzos...311

Appendix

Contributors 335

Cultures of Citizenship
An Introduction

Vanessa Evans and Mita Banerjee

> "Assimilation is not a precondition for either unity or belonging; indeed, it is a deep and irreversible impoverishment."
> *James (Sákéj) Youngblood Henderson, "Sui Generis and Treaty Citizenship"*

Ours is a time when the concept of the citizen has become more urgent than ever. While some argue that the nation state is obsolete given the transnational flow of both goods and capital, the question of being a citizen of a particular country nevertheless continues. In an era when entire populations are forced to relocate as a result of wars, climate change, and economic precarity, the concept of the citizen comes to be further defined by its opposite: the non-citizen. What does it mean, in other words, not to have citizenship? What does it imply for someone to be "undocumented"? At this crucial juncture, literary texts and other cultural representations can give a different meaning to legal concepts. As Jason De Léon has argued, these texts and representations can translate the language of border policing back into the language of humanity; they can illuminate the violence of state-sanctioned belonging hiding in plain sight (3–4).[1]

In recent years, the debate over the "status" of (climate) refugees, asylum seekers, and undocumented migrants has thus continued to challenge our understanding of citizenship, citizens, and non-citizens. One needs little more than a Google search to be reminded of citizenship's material realities in 2023: US-bound migrants continue to be held at the Mexico-US border in inhumane conditions ("Photos"); the Coastal Gaslink Pipeline in what is currently British Columbia, Canada, has been completed despite Wet'suwet'en nation Hereditary Chiefs not giving consent to the project;

---

1 For De Léon, the United States's strategic plan regarding immigration is a "killing machine that simultaneously uses and hides behind the viciousness of the Sonoran Desert [of Arizona]" (3–4).

nearly nineteen million people have left Ukraine for European countries since Russia's invasion in February, 2022 (Sharma); thousands of refugees and migrants continue to flee to Europe from countries such as Côte d'Ivoire, Guinea, Syria, and Egypt ("At least"). Further, as thousands of refugees lose their lives crossing the Mediterranean Sea each year, a number of questions emerge that lie at the heart of citizenship. How do we mourn the lives lost? Does the concept of "undocumented migration" affect or even determine whether we mourn for these lives? As Judith Butler forcefully argues in *Precarious Life*, we have come to make a distinction between deaths we mourn and those that have become "ungrievable" (xiv). The difference between the citizen and the non-citizen has thus become more vital than ever; and, as we argue in this collection, it is increasingly urgent to interrogate this distinction. With this focus, we consider how the alterity of citizenship "does not pre-exist, but is constituted by [the citizen]" (Isin *Being Political* 4). In her recent work, Lily Cho articulates this reality in no uncertain terms: "Non-citizenship is the verso of citizenship, and the existence of one depends on the other ... because citizenship emerges only in relation to non-citizenship, the latter functions as citizenship's perpetual other. Non-citizenship haunts citizenship" (*Mass Capture* 8). The shifting climates and developing histories of our contemporary worlds require constant vigilance within citizenship studies and its intersecting disciplines as cultures of citizenship shift and harden in response to the lines drawn and redrawn between citizen and non-citizen.

The connection between culture and citizenship is one of citizenship studies' earliest points of interest (Rosaldo; Turner, *Orientalism*; Pakulski). In addition to social, political, and civil rights, early citizenship studies scholarship saw a focus on the term *cultural citizenship* as a means of expressing membership beyond the confines of state-sanctioned citizenship (Turner, "The erosion of citizenship"; Stevenson; Ong; Rosaldo). Cultural citizenship, as Renato Rosaldo contends, is "a deliberate oxymoron" referring to "the right to be different and to belong in a participatory democratic sense" (402). Cultural citizenship means belonging—group membership and self-determination—regardless of one's class, gender, sexuality, religion, or race (402). Cultural citizenship, however, has proved a somewhat amorphous concept, and while the chapters in this edited collection undoubtedly contribute to its further theorization, they also consider what it might mean to think about cultures *of* citizenship.

In 2006, responding to the robust focus on cultural citizenship, Nick Couldry called for scholars to further investigate these culture(s) *of* citizenship. In so doing, Couldry suggests that there are essential contributions to be made beyond continued theorizations of cultural citizenship which "may obscure a more interesting set of questions" about what a culture of citizenship might look like, and what new cultures of citizenship might be emerging (321–23). Surprisingly, Couldry's call has received very limited attention. Our edited collection responds to this gap, asking: what cultures emerge when we focus on the cacophony at the intersection of the citizen and non-citizen? What norms, expectations, and understandings appear or are challenged by the friction between citizen and non-citizen? To begin answering these questions, the chapters in this edited collection attend to the tension between the citizen and its spectral others, centering the latter to reveal the tensions determined by how countries define difference at a given moment. In doing so, *Cultures of Citizenship in the Twenty-First Century* is interested in citizenship's conceptual realm where a lack of consensus still hovers (Bosniak, "Being Here," "Citizenship and Bleakness"; Cisernos; Clarke; Gauvin). By investigating the cultures of citizenship conjured in this cacophony, we seek to illuminate the affective and conceptual space where non-citizens can also be theorized as future citizens. Here we follow Cho, who considers non-citizens as future citizens whose anticipation of citizenship can be just as important as citizenship itself: "anticipation is an affect, but also a mode of agency" (199). Consequently, our chapters theorize cultures of belonging in an array of contexts including post-apocalyptic communities, the penal voluntary sector, early modern science, among the living and the dead, or in post- and decolonial contexts. In thinking this way about citizenship, our edited collection embraces "citizenship's elastic cultural purpose" to consider the multiplicative ways that cultures of citizenship can be theorized toward a more robust understanding of citizenship's processual nature and heft (Gauvin 7; Macklin).

Importantly, cultural productions have long contended with the affective and conceptual space between citizen and non-citizen. For example, in Sophocles' *Antigone*, the princess Antigone demands that her brother Polynices—who attacked his own city—be buried according to custom rather than left to decay. In doing so, Antigone questions the culture of citizenship surrounding the dead, their rights as citizens or non-citizens, as well as their agency (Llanque and Sarkowksy). Illuminating the sustained relevance of *Antigone*'s concerns, Kamila Shamsie's 2017 novel *Home Fire* reimagines *Antigone* through contemporary British Muslim siblings Aneeka and Parvais. When Parvais joins ISIS and is killed, the British Home Secretary refuses to repatriate Parvais's body: "the only story here was that of a British citizen who had turned his back on his nation" (191). When Aneeka tries to return her brother's body to Britain, she is also killed in a terrorist attack. With this reimagining, *Home Fire* demonstrates the sustained importance of citizenship's conceptual realm and its cultures across temporal and state borders, demonstrating the urgent need in citizenship studies for further consideration of how cultures of citizenship are theorized, sustained, and expressed.

More recently, cultural productions have proven to empower citizens facing the curtailing of their rights. Specifically, we are writing this introduction at a time when abortion is once again being banned in many states across the US after the US Supreme Court overturned the constitutional right to an abortion, reversing *Roe v. Wade*. In Washington, DC, in 2021, protestors against these abortion bans—anticipating the threat to Roe v. Wade—took to the streets wearing the handmaid uniform envisioned by Margaret Atwood in her dystopian novel, *The Handmaid's Tale*. Speaking with *The Guardian* about the costume being adopted by women protestors, Atwood notes that the handmaid's costume is a symbol of visual protest (Beaumont and Holpuch). For our purposes, this symbol demonstrates how cultural productions such as literary texts can provide citizens with powerful blueprints through which they can try to resist legal realities and shift cultures of citizenship.

As our edited collection demonstrates, cultures of citizenship are responding to current climates and developing histories that require constant vigilance in citizenship studies and its intersecting disciplines. All too often, legal and state-bound conceptualizations of citizenship occlude and even eclipse citizenship's cultural dimensions, its multiplicative modes of expression, severely limiting our understanding of citizenship's performance. As Mitchell Gauvin has rightly noted, "overemphasis on statutory conditions unjustifiably obscures how citizenship is not monolithically a legal status" (27). Cultures of citizenship, then, may be those cultures created through and by the anticipation and enactment of belonging. Ultimately, citizenship studies has had an enduring focus on the ways in which the citizen and its others contest, constitute, and converge to form diverse and distinct cultures to which our collection is especially attuned.

The last three decades have seen a large outpouring of scholarly interest in the subject of citizenship, coalescing in a rich interdisciplinary field. Writing on the relationship between the citizen and its others is a constant thread. Notable works on this connection have paid attention to how spatial technologies of the city have shaped the citizen and non-citizen (Isin); the principles and practices for incorporating refugees, immigrants, and asylum seekers under just membership rather than just distribution (Benhabib); problematic invitations of statutory citizenship that erase and deny the legitimacy of sui generis and treaty citizenship (Henderson); the ways birthright citizenship in affluent societies can be theorized as a form of property inheritance that entrenches global inequality (Shachar); and more recently, how Chinese head tax in Canada functioned as a form of mass capture surveillance that results in the making of non-citizens (Cho). The chapters in this collection are concerned with new perspectives on this relationship, the interdisciplinary locations within which it is being negotiated in the twenty-first century, and the potential these perspectives hold for broader considerations of citizenship's transit across disciplinary boundaries. More specifically, our edited collection is interested in the cultures of citizenship produced by this relationship.

Citizenship has been explored across a variety of disciplines in the edited collection form, further demonstrating its importance. These collections have considered citizenship's intersections with geography (Kallio et al.), sociology and social anthropology (Gonzales and Sigona), political science (Bianculli and Hoffmann; Brooks; Henderson et al.), sociology and childhood studies (Baraldi and Cockburn), migration studies (Dobrowolsky and Tastsoglou; Proglio), and cultural studies (McCosker et al.). Remaining critical of the borders and boundaries that delineate scholarly fields, our edited collection takes an interdisciplinary approach to its interrogations of the cultures that emerge from the relationship between the citizen and non-citizen. In doing so we contribute to the burgeoning tide of interdisciplinary research on citizenship in works such as *Die Politik Der Toten: Figuren und Funktionen der Toten in Literatur und Politischer Theorie* ("*The Politics of the Dead: Figures and Functions of the Dead in Literature and Political Theory*"), edited by Marcus Llanque and Katja Sarkowsky, and *Democratic Citizenship in Flux: Conceptions of Citizenship in the Light of Political and Social Fragmentation* by Markus Bayer et al. By bringing citizenship studies into contact with fields not typically in dialogue with citizenship (e.g., literary studies, medical humanities, video game studies), our contributions explore how cultures of citizenship are expressed at new and exciting intersections. They ask: what is the affective power of, for example, literary narrative for describing what it feels like to be excluded from (or in anticipation of) national belonging and legal protection? These chapters explore, for example, undocumented migrants or economically disenfranchised groups who may have little access to health insurance and criminalized individuals who are deprived of their right to vote after their release from prison. The chapters revisit concepts, discourses, and scenarios that have often been associated with citizenship but whose cultural expressions require greater attention. How, for instance, might the concept of citizenship be infracted differently with regard to old age, the history of science, environmental justice, or resource extraction? How might the tension between citizen and non-citizen relate not only to the living, but also to the dead? In these and in many other instances, the present edited collection aims to probe what the concept of the citizen conveys as much as what it may obfuscate.

In this vein, our collection gathers its contributions into four thematic sections: (i) citizenship's fluidity in space and time, (ii) citizenship and (state) violence, (iii) performing citizenship, and (iv) citizenship, science, and medicine. The first section comprises chapters focused on the cultures of citizenship that emerge when we consider citizenship's endurance and fluidity in/across space and time, as well as the effects and affects of that endurance. In "Citizenship in Time: Temporality and Time-Reckoning in Jamaica Kincaid's *A Small Place*," Mitchell Gauvin explores the intersection between citizenship, time, and temporal variability in Kincaid's famous work. This intersection presents stark temporal fissures that are wed to geographical location in a way that serves as allegory for the distinction between the local and the global. Subverting traditional views of citizenship as an emancipatory status, Gauvin reads citizenship as a neo-imperialistic and neo-capitalist cudgel against transgressive identities. In "John MacKenzie's *Letters I Didn't Write*: Rewriting Home, Homeland, and Citizenship," Kristen Smith considers how home, through a transnational transposition, can become a mobile and fluid concept. To do so, she examines how MacKenzie critiques Eurowestern arbiters of citizenship by reconsidering (and destabilizing) the relationship between national belonging and textual ownership through the concept of transposition. For Smith, MacKenzie's act of transposition is one of absolute deterritorialization with implications for the conceptual realm and culture of citizenship. Finally, Georgi's "Transnational Citizenship and Dreams of Belonging in Imbolo Mbue's *Behold the Dreamers*" examines how migration narratives can challenge the concept of the American Dream and the immigration policies that illuminate its fictions. Mbue's characters ultimately emerge as agentic transmigrants who, initially motivated by the American Dream, come to understand its fiction and ultimately build a better life for themselves in Nigeria.

In the collection's second section on citizenship and (state) violence, scholars examine the cultures of citizenship that emerge in response to various forms of (state) oppression, control, and disciplinary power. In "'Present Absentees, Weak-Kneed Nobodies': Exiles, Airports, and Non-Citizenship in Abdourahman Waberi's *Transit*," Nasra Smith centers Achille Mbembe's post-Foucauldian concept of biopolitics to critically analyze how recent citizenship discourse challenges "technologies of control" (airport) and "exclusion" (deportation) as the sovereign, militarizing power of the host-state, theorizing the role of the new, normalized refugee who is between death, detention, and deportation—the citizen Other's Other (Nyers 1069). Through Fanon, Smith suggests that the modern airport is a colonial space of control and coercion—the novel's silent character that wields the power of the French nation-state. In "'You've Heard it Now': Storytelling and Acts of Citizenship in Cherie Dimaline's *The Marrow Thieves*," Vanessa Evans investigates how Indigenous characters respond to the violent control and oppression of Indigenous Peoples through the extraction of their bone marrow in post-apocalyptic North America by enacting resurgence. In focusing on how a return to Indigenous ways of being and knowing cultivate belonging (and actively destroy settler infrastructure), Evans's reading of *Marrow Thieves* illuminates the novel's interrogation of the unsustainable nature of western citizenship and its theorization of a decolonial set of rights and responsibilities rooted in storytelling and reciprocal relations with land. The final two chapters in this section contend with carceral citizenship and its implications. In "'Clean Body, Clean Mind, Clean Job': The Role of Penal Voluntary Sector Organizations in Constructing 'Good' Carceral Citizens," Kaitlyn Quinn and Erika Canossini contend that criminal justice non-profit organizations respond to state violence by offering (re)integrative services and support to former prisoners, actively participating in the construction of "good" carceral citizens. Quinn and Canossini thereby examine the cultures of citizenship produced in non-profit organizations that have both inclusionary and exclusionary effects—spaces that comprise an important, but underexamined site for the production and consumption of ideas about carceral citizenship. Lastly, Nina Heydt's "Between Imprisonment and Citizenship: Jessica Kent's Navigation of Carceral Citizenship," positions the prison survival guide found on Jessica Kent's *YouTube* as a response to the state's curtailing of her political and economic belonging following her imprisonment. Heydt thus extends Quinn and Canossini's considerations of carceral citizenship to prison survival guides that aim to help people navigate the process of community re-entry after imprisonment.

Our collection's third section considers how citizenship's performance produces cultures of citizenship that critique and reimagine the relationship between citizen and other. Julia Velten, in "Paragon of Aging, Paragon of Voting: Centenarians and the Imaginary of a Model Citizen," argues that because centenarians are regarded as the paragons of positive aging with their exceptionally long lives, narratives about voting centenarians elevate them to a status of paragons of citizenship. Velten interrogates the cultural norms and implications of idolizing how centenarians perform citizenship toward a better understanding of the complex arguments put forth in their (auto)biographies and the media's representations. In "Making Material Borders: Petro-Cultures and Modern Citizenship," Scott Obernesser focuses on oil as a material criterion of citizenship which equates national ideologies with socio-cultural obligations to petro-capitalism. By examining (con)texts that span sovereign borders, Obernesser illustrates how modern citizenship is steadily becoming less about imagined geographies and more about one's ability to perform the requirements of an oil culture membership that shapes and reshapes human interiority. Marcus Llanque and Katja Sarkowsky's "Citizenship of the Dead: Antigone and Beyond" draws on examples from both political debates and literary texts to reveal how the dead continue to perform the role of citizen-actors. Llanque and Sarkowsky work to understand how such an extended notion of membership and belonging, and the practices that potentially follow from it, question and challenge the self-conception of contemporary liberal democracies. Similarly, Anah-Jayne Samuelson's "'We had to control the narrative': The Innovations and Limitations of Youth Citizenship," examines expressions of youth citizenship with a focus on activism. As a method of youth citizenship, activism allows American youths to perform and negotiate their uncertain and fraught relations with the state and its hegemonic criteria of belonging. Malaika Sutter's "'To Couple the Beauty of the Place and the Harsh Realities of Its Racist History': Piecing Together African American Citizenship in Faith Ringgold's *Flag Story Quilt* and *Coming to Jones Road*" analyzes Faith Ringgold's story quilts, which trace and re-imagine the incomplete genesis of African American citizenship in hegemonic white US culture. Ringgold's depictions of Black identities and histories as well as white men's violence in the US remain pressing to today's conversations on African American citizenship and its performance.

In the collection's final section, Mita Banerjee, Jessica Hanselman Gray, and Amina Touzos consider what cultures of citizenship might exist in the tension between the citizen and its others where medicine and science are concerned. In "'What the Eyes Don't See': Medical Citizenship and Environmental Justice in Mona Hanna-Attisha's Medical Memoir," Banerjee asks what happens to belonging when the nation-state fails to ensure the health and well-being of its subjects. Her investigation draws on Hanna-Attisha's memoir to consider the breach of citizenship rights that occurred during the Flint, Michigan, water crisis. In "Foreign Relations: Utopian Fictions and the Birth of Scientific Citizenship," Hanselman Gray turns to Margaret Cavendish's seventeenth-century entrance into the Royal Society of London to investigate how such a border crossing rendered her an alien outsider to science and what such a rendering can tell us about gendered politics of inclusion. In her analysis, Hanselman Gray considers two works of seventeenth-century fiction: Francis Bacon's *The New Atlantis* and Cavendish's *The Description of a New World, Called the Blazing World*, both of which narrate border-crossing adventures in which travelers enmesh themselves in new scientific worlds. Finally, Touzos's essay "You're My People Now': *The Last of Us* Series on the Question of Belonging and Citizenship during the Age of Pandemics" takes readers into the post-apocalyptic world of *The Last of Us* video game series where medical status—infected and uninfected—overtake traditional arbiters of citizenship. Touzos looks at how representations of citizenship are made ambiguous by the medicalization of civic rights and their intersection with trauma, unearthing disconcerting truths about our own (post)pandemic lives.

With these sections in mind, we remain aware of the limitations of our collection's focus, especially regarding questions of sexuality, gender, reproductive rights, or the rights of people with disabilities. We hope these limitations encourage other scholars interested in citizenship studies to consider what cultures of citizenship have yet to be theorized and to continue the work done in this edited collection. Future research might, for instance, investigate how the cacophony at the intersection of citizen and non-citizen could be further illuminated through analyses of cultural responses to the Respect for Marriage Act or the introduction of bills across the US that aim to prevent trans people from receiving basic healthcare and legal recognition. Alternatively, future research may ask what cultures of citizenship can be observed through the dialogue between dystopian literary texts such as Atwood's *The Handmaid's Tale* and Louise Erdrich's (Chippewa) *Future Home of the Living God* and contemporary restrictions on reproductive rights. We see the potential of these future interventions as indicative of the openness and mutability inherent in cultures of citizenship, an openness inviting of further exploration.

As we move through the second decade of the twenty-first century, this edited collection underscores how the concept of the citizen is far from obsolete. As each of the chapters that follow will demonstrate, it is essential to probe not only into the legal specificities of how citizenship is bestowed and on to whom, but to also inquire into the social and cultural underpinnings of the citizen. In this vein, literary and cultural texts can provide alternative representations of what the citizen is or what they might be. These texts vividly demonstrate what it may mean to be excluded from citizenship and from the rights and benefits that it bestows. In dialogue with the field of law and literature studies, then, this collection argues that literary and cultural texts are indispensable commentaries without which the material, emotional, and psychological consequences of legal concepts cannot be fully grasped. Seen from this perspective, we hope, the notion of *cultures of citizenship* may be vital not only for understanding the literature and culture of the twenty-first century, but also the legal assumptions through which this century is currently defined. At a time when the relevance of the humanities and social sciences is increasingly being questioned, the issues foregrounded in this edited collection are all the more significant.

Works Cited

"At least 951 died trying to reach Spain by sea so far this year." *Aljazeera*, 6 Jul. 2023, https://www.aljazeera.com/news/2023/7/6/at-least-951-died-trying-to-reach-spain-by-sea-so-far-this-year?traffic_source=KeepReading.

Atwood, Margaret. *The Handmaid's Tale*. Emblem, 2011.

Baraldi, Claudio and Tom Cockburn, editors. *Theorising Childhood: Citizenship Rights and Participation*. Palgrave Macmillan, 2018. https://doi.org/10.1007/978-3-319-72673-1.

Bayer, Markus, et al., editors. *Democratic Citizenship in Flux: Conceptions of Citizenship in the Light of Political and Social Fragmentation*. transcript, 2021.

Beaumont, Peter, and Amanda Holpuch. "How the Handmaid's Tale dressed protests across the world." *The Guardian*, 3 Aug. 2018, https://www.theguardian.com/world/2018/aug/03/how-the-handmaids-tale-dressed-protests-across-the-world.

Benhabib, Seyla. *The Rights of Others: Aliens, Residents and Citizens*. Cambridge UP, 2004.

Bianculli, Andrea and Andrea Ribeiro Hoffmann, editors. *Regional Organizations and Social Policy in Europe and Latin America: A Space for Social Citizenship?* Palgrave Macmillan, 2016.

Bosniak, Linda. "Being Here: Ethical Territoriality and the Rights of Immigrants." *Theoretical Inquiries in Law*, vol. 8, no. 2, 2007, p. 389–410.

—. "Citizenship and Bleakness." *Citizenship Studies*, vol. 26, no. 4–5, 2022, pp. 382–86. *Taylor & Francis Online*, https://doi.org/10.1080/13621025.2022.2091217.

Brooks Thom, editor. *Ethical Citizenship: British Idealism and the Politics of Recognition*. Palgrave Macmillan, 2014.

Butler, Judith. *Precarious Life: The Powers of Mourning and Violence*. Verso, 2006.

Cho, Lily. *Mass Capture: Chinese Head Tax and the Making of Non-Citizens*. McGill-Queen's UP, 2021.

Cisernos, J. David. "Rhetorics of Citizenship: Pitfalls and Possibilities." *Quarterly Journal of Speech*, vol. 100, no. 3, 2014, pp. 375–388.

Clarke, John. "Reconstructing Citizenship (again)." *Citizenship Studies*, vol. 26, no. 4–5, 2022, pp. 411–17. *Taylor & Francis Online*, https://doi.org/10.1080/13621025.2022.2091221.

Couldry, Nick. "Culture and citizenship: the missing link?" *European Journal of Cultural Studies*, vol. 9, no. 3, pp. 321–339. *SAGE*, DOI: 10.1177/1367549406066076.

De León, Jason. *The Land of Open Graves: Living and Dying on the Migrant Trail*. U of California P, 2015.

Dobrowolsky, Alexandra and Evangelia Tastsoglou, editors. *Women Migration and Citizenship: Making Local National and Transnational Connections*. Taylor and Francis, 2016. http://public.ebookcentral.proquest.com/choice/publicfullrecord.aspx?p =4414700.

Gauvin, Mitchell. *The Rhetoric of Citizenship, Slavery, and Immigration: Fashioning a Language for Belonging in English Literature*. 2021. York U, PhD dissertation.

Gonzales Roberto G and Nando Sigona, editors. *Within and Beyond Citizenship: Borders Membership and Belonging*. Routledge, 2018.

Henderson, James (Sákéj) Youngblood. "Sui Generis and Treaty Citizenship." *Citizenship Studies*, vol. 6, no. 4, 2002, pp. 415–40. *Scholars Portal Journals*, https:// resolver-scholarsportal-info.ezproxy.library.yorku.ca/resolve/13621025/v06i00 04/415_sgatc.xml.

Henderson Ailsa et al., editors. *Citizenship After the Nation State: Regionalism Nationalism and Public Attitudes in Europe*. Palgrave Macmillan, 2014.

Isin, Engin F. *Being Political: Genealogies of Citizenship*. U of Minnesota P, 2002.

Kallio, Kirsi Pauliina et al., editors. *Politics Citizenship and Rights*. Springer, 2016. htt p://rave.ohiolink.edu/ebooks/ebc/9789814585576.

Llanque, Marcus and Katja Sarkowsky, editors. *Die Politik der Toten: Figuren und Funktionen der Toten in Literatur und Politischer Theorie*. transcript, 2023.

McCosker Anthony et al., editors. *Negotiating Digital Citizenship: Control Contest and Culture*. Rowman & Littlefield International, 2016.

Nyers, Peter. "No One is Illegal Between City and Nation." *Acts of Citizenship*, edited by E. F. Isin and G. M. Nielson, Zed Books, 2008, pp 160–181.

Ong, Aihwa. "Strategic sisterhood or sisters in solidarity-questions of communitarianism and citizenship in Asia." *Indiana Journal of Global Legal Studies*, vol. 4, no. 1, 1996, pp. 107–35.

Pakulski, Jan. "Cultural citizenship." *Citizenship Studies*, vol. 1, no. 1, 1997, pp. 73–86.

"Photos show US border facility crowded with migrant children." *Aljazeera*, 22 Mar. 2021, https://www.aljazeera.com/news/2021/3/22/biden-administration-faces-new-crutiny-on-unaccompanied-minors.

Proglio Gabriele, editor. *The Black Mediterranean: Bodies Borders and Citizenship*. Palgrave Macmillan, 2021.

Rosaldo, Renato. "Cultural citizenship and educational democracy." *Cultural Anthropology*, vol. 9, no. 3, 1994, pp. 402–411.

Shachar, Ayelet. *The Birthright Lottery: Citizenship and Global Inequality*. Harvard UP, 2021.

Shamsie, Kamila. *Home Fire*. Riverhead Books, 2017.

Sharma, Gouri. "West still welcoming Ukrainian refugees, but challenges lie ahead." *Aljazeera*, 10 Mar. 2023, https://www.aljazeera.com/news/2023/3/10/she-is-family-ukrainians-fleeing-war-find-refuge-in-germany.

Sophocles. *Oedipus the King / Oedipus at Colonos / Antigone I*. Translated by F. Storr, Harvard UP, 1981.

Stevenson, Nick. *Culture and Citizenship*. SAGE, 2001.

Turner, Bryan S. *Orientalism, Postmodernism, and Globalism*. Routledge, 1994.

—. "The erosion of citizenship." *The British Journal of Sociology*, vol. 52, no. 2, 2001, pp. 189–209.

Fluidity in Space and Time

Citizenship in Time
Temporality and Time-Reckoning in Jamaica Kincaid's *A Small Place*

Mitchell Gauvin

Jamaica Kincaid in *A Small Place* recounts "sitting across from an Englishman" who, as a result of the collapse of the British empire, looked "so sad, sitting on the rubbish heap of history" (30–31). In likening the historical contribution of the English to the accumulation of trash, Kincaid portrays the past as an accretion of stuff or a reservoir of pollution, rather than something that is simply elapsed and unrecoverable. The metaphorical rubbish of history that the English have discarded onto their former colonies is literalized by Kincaid in her attention to the actual waste-disposal problems that Antigua faces from crumbling public infrastructure—a consequence of both domestic corruption and a globalized economy that has privatized the country's resources in the aftermath of colonial rule. The Englishman's view of history, which conveniently overlooks the garbage they have produced, contrasts with the local Antiguan whose sense of the past, present, and future are compounded, revealing in stark relief the accretion of waste over time. As opposed to the "present day of timetables and fashion" which has "rendered the past anachronistic" (Fritzsche 2), Kincaid's depiction recognizes the debris that constitutes history's often amorphous and unignorable presence, to the extent that distinguishing where the present starts and where the trash heap of history begins becomes exceedingly difficult, if not impossible. Indeed, such an exact sequestering of time seems hubristic when analogized to the accumulation of rubbish—an image that connotes environmental disaster. Unlike the Romantic reverence of the castle or church ruins that constitute British national pride, the Englishman when confronted with the "rubbish heap of history" cannot recognize the continuity between their rubbish and the old buildings that evoke sentiments of belonging or sublime. Kincaid hints at something of a contradiction in the Englishman's historiography, which involves a discrepancy in notions of ruination: reverential towards church ruins and relics, they simultaneously ignore the trash they have similarly produced and which they have accumulated in places that were as much a part of the British empire as Scotland or Wales.

Kincaid's metaphor of history as a rubbish heap offers a departure point for interrogating the interaction between literature, time, and citizenship. Time in this context means durational time, such as that "embodied in the various rituals, routines, calendars, discourses and devices which provide a sense of regularity and rhythm and which orientate human collectives towards an accepted source of temporal authority, whether they be the celestial motions of the stars or the mechanical ticking of clocks" (Nanni 6). In using a spatial reference (a heap) as a point for distinguishing the past, Kincaid does what perhaps anyone would in attempting to comprehend the nebulous metaphysics of time: grounds it in something concrete and recognizable. But this maneuver potentially obscures what is distinct about time that cannot be captured by analogy, especially in the context of time's political value. Yet Kincaid's *A Small Place* also engages with forms of time-reckoning that underwrite localities disrupted or destabilized by forces not adequately addressed by simplistic categories of "foreign" or "outside" in a strictly geographical sense. The spatiotemporal is an unnecessary compounding of two distinct realms that must be wrenched apart to see how both may connote in markedly different ways. I concentrate on the moments throughout *A Small Place* where Kincaid deepens her representation of Antigua through reference to local senses of time and temporal rituals and their discrepancy with global time embodied by the white tourist. While certainly the cartographic dimensions of Antigua as the titular small place directs our reading of the work, I focus more exclusively on Kincaid's representation of time as a corrective to the abundance of analysis that have focused on her exploration of globalization and colonial inscriptions in the Caribbean in mostly geographical terms. In particular, I focus on how a portrait of Antiguan citizenship constituted by local temporal practices emerges alongside a global imposition of time that binds locals in an antagonistic relationship between forms of time-reckoning. In sum, *A Small Place* offers an avenue for interrogating citizenship as a form of temporal valuation.

The historical growth in time-consciousness and the technological capacity to measure time has been reflected in literature for centuries. As Adam Barrows notes, the "history of modernity is in part a history of the global management of spatial and temporal relations" (5), and Giordano Nanni calls the clock the "internationally spoken language of hours, minutes and seconds" which "has become so familiar that an alternative consciousness of time seems scarcely conceivable" (1). In pursuit of understanding time's cultural centrality, literary scholars of the contemporary period have concentrated on both the portrayal of mechanisms for time-telling (timepieces such as the clock or the wristwatch) and the rhetoric of temporality (analogies, allusions, descriptions of time) in literary works. Marcus Tomalin, for example, has explored how the depiction of watches in the long-eighteenth century text "never acquired a stable set of symbolical connotations" (303). The ornate pocket watch "provided excellent opportunities for ostentatious ceremonies involving the melodramatic extraction of the watch from the fob pocket" (Tomalin 306), serving as a signal of wealth that was intimately tied to the public ritual of telling time. Yet alongside this exotic display were watches specifically crafted for the puritanical, who would have detested the flaunting of "superficially ornate adornments" (306). This disjuncture in the connotation of watches was in turn reflected in the literary works of the period. With Kincaid, we have a more stable set of connotations with which to unravel the representation of time, specifically in the context of the disjuncture she depicts between the incursion of a global standard for time and the local sense of time of Antiguans.

Of course, we must not forget that literature itself is a spatiotemporal practice, though the inertness of the page may exaggerate the thingness of literature to the detriment of its temporal dimensions. My focus on *A Small Place* reflects the capacity of literary works to capture what Barrows calls the "rhythmic density of space in its complexity" in contrast to the "powerfully simple cartographic construct" of coordinated standard time that manages our spatial and temporal relations (11). Literature can capture "the vast and the microscopic, the slow and the fast, the planetary and the local, the continuing, repetitive rhythms of the planetary and the fugitive temporal rhythms of random experiences" (11). As Barrows elaboration makes clear, time is more than just empirical measurement practice or intimate social ritual, it possesses political value that is inseparable from imaginings and enactments of citizenship.

Linda Bosniak notes how "some version of *citizenship* is now vital to the intellectual projects of scholars across the disciplines" (1), including literary studies, where the enduring legacy of citizenship on imaginings of personhood have infiltrated how characters and communities are configured in literary representation. In focusing on the specifically temporal dimension of citizenship in literature, I do not propose a new form of political belonging called "temporal citizenship"—such a phrase is redundant. Every practice of citizenship requires time, and political subjects have encountered "myriad ways in which their time is structured, valued, and appropriated" (Cohen 1). Time's political value is reflected in numerous political procedures, such as age restrictions on voting, the duration of prison sentences, the conditions of naturalization, the designated length of stay for work visas, the office terms for politicians and so on.[1] However, if time occupies such an essential role in the functioning of the state or the practice of citizenship, then a trusting relationship be-

---

1   For more on how some of these procedures interact with and complicate citizenship as a concept and status, see: Anah-Jayne Samuelson's "'We had to control the narrative': The Innovations and Limitations of Youth Citizenship"; Kaitlyn Quinn and Erika Canossini's "'Clean Body, Clean Mind, Clean Job': The Role of Penal Voluntary Sector Organizations in Constructing 'Good' Carceral Citizens"; and Nasra Smith's "'Present Absentees, Weak-Kneed Nobodies': Exile, Airport, and Non-Citizenship in Abdourahman Waberi's *Transit*," in this volume.

tween state and citizen becomes dependent on the state's capacity to justly regulate and keep time. As Elizabeth Cohen notes, the "clocks of an affluent and poor person will operate identically but the way in which either person must 'spend' their time is a product of social class and circumstances that are not themselves often figured into temporal rules" (15). A carceral system that, for example, "misappropriates the time of entire classes of people delegitimizes a democratic state" (5). The mismanagement of time or the failure of equitable time-provisioning can sow mistrust and skepticism among a citizenry. The assumption that time, specifically durational time, is a great equalizer—insofar as we all hold equal quantities of time, unlike money—misses how time is valued, compensated, and delineated as a political good. On the other end of things, temporal deviancy among groups or individual persons may factor into either their exclusion from a community of citizens or coerced assimilation into a dominate temporal culture. Even though experiences of time can vary considerably, the danger that temporal variability among persons can pose to "institutional authority and moral law" may motivate this variability being "projected onto exilic figures who are forced to bear the burden of temporal instability through physical segregation and mortification" (Barrows 13). Durational time's seeming neutrality makes it an idyllic standard by which to legitimate authority over people's lives, and those who misalign with prevailing methods of time management may be deemed a threat to national cohesion or community safety. Time is "crucial to the formation and maintenance of communal and national identities," most evidently seen in how particular "historical narratives of origins and futures" configure nationhood (McCrossen 221), but also evinced in the expectations surrounding who constitutes a citizen and how those citizens should spend their time (i.e.: singing a national anthem, pilgriming to sites of national significance, adhering to moments of silence, etc.). Additionally, anxiety over time discipline has arguably solidified in the hyper-capitalist world of hourly wage work and ever shorter durations in delivery-based consumerism (see, for example, the notion of time theft,[2] something I was accused of while working a former customer service job), which have in turn robbed people of the time to participate in basic political activities, such as voting.[3]

---

2   Henle, Reeve, and Pitts (2010) define time theft as the "time that employees waste or spend not working during their scheduled work hours," which they suggest constitutes unethical behaviour because "they are intentionally stealing time rightfully belonging to their company" (53). This definition is explicit in framing time itself as something owned by ("belonging to") an employer, a pernicious aspect of contemporary ideologies of work that harkens to time-discipline standards inured by industrialization.

3   In addition to the economic toil, certain countries like the United States have also used state power to intentionally shorten the amount of time some persons have to vote, compounding the problem further. For example, in the aftermath of President Joe Biden's election victory in 2020, Republicans in multiple states proposed stricter voting laws aimed at disenfranchising Black voters (though they defend the laws as a matter of "election integrity"). These

Citizenship as a normative assessment is a type of temporal valuation, not exclusively a marker of geographic belonging, and this condition endures despite the multiple ways citizenship's definition has been negotiated over the last two decades by scholars who can no longer ignore the presence of citizenship in their own disciplines or who find citizenship a resourceful critical well. As such, I seek to emphasize significations already latent within citizenship's function and experience. Subverting traditional views of citizenship as an emancipatory status, I offer a new intervention that reads citizenship as a neo-imperialist and neo-capitalist cudgel by focusing on Kincaid's depiction of time in Antigua, where the combination of domestic politics and a voracious global market are compounded to configure an Antiguan citizenship constituted by exploitative labour practices and public corruption (embodied in the unrepaired library, for example). Far from this being a bespoke condition of Antigua, Kincaid offers a mirror to citizenship regimes in ostensibly liberal democracies where similarly exploitive and corruptive practices rob persons of the political value of their time.

My methodology for this approach derives from the so-called "spatial turn." The spatial turn in literary, cultural, and postcolonial studies has resulted in a resourceful critical debate regarding the extensive meshwork shared between literature and spatiality. Multiple scholars have shown that landscapes and architectures are readable cultural mediums not only represented in literature but also constituted *by* literature.[4] The production of space involves the texts, images, and motions that imbue these geographies with significance or remind us of the "rhythmic density" of time and space against the backdrop of global systems of management. Architecture, for example, embodies narrative content through the way structures occupy and organize time and space, such that a "discernable shift in the form and structure of language are reflected in both literary and architectural production" (Charley 3). As such, changes in the representation of political and racial belonging effect the production of spaces for preferred identities to occupy. Lucienne Loh, for example,

---

new laws would "limit mail, early in-person and Election Day voting with such constraints as stricter ID requirements, limited hours or narrower eligibility to vote absentee" (Gardner, Rabinowitz, and Stevens). For more on how the relationship between voting and citizenship is conceptualized and complicated, see Julia Velten and Nina Heydt's chapters ("Paragon of Aging, Paragon of Voting: Centenarians and the Imaginary of a Model Citizen" and "Between Imprisonment and Citizenship: Jessica Kent's Navigation of Carceral Citizenship") in this volume.

4   Important texts for the inauguration of a spatial turn include Raymond Williams *The Country and the City* (1973) and Edward Said's *Orientalism* (1978) as well as *Culture and Imperialism* (1991); other selected texts include the essay anthology *Landscape and Power* (1994), edited by W. J. T. Mitchell, and David Harvey's *Spaces of Hope* (2000); more contemporary analysis can be found in *Geocritical Explorations: Space, Place, and Mapping in Literary and Cultural Studies* (2011), edited by Robert Tally Jr., and Lucienne Loh's *The Postcolonial Country in Contemporary Literature* (2013).

has shown how Britain in the 1980s, in response to defensive attitudes regarding the collapse of empire, instrumentalized their heritage industry to revive English nationalism by framing the rural countryside as a racially coded space, naturalizing "Englishness around the discourse of whiteness" (10). George Lipsitz has similarly noted that the "lived experience of race has a spatial dimension, and the lived experience of space has a racial dimension" exemplified by the segregationist housing policies and lending discriminations in the United States (12). The result has been a "national spatial imaginary" bifurcated by race (Lipsitz 10).

The spatial turn, however, has tended to emphasize discourses of landscape and place while overlooking the role of time in the exercise of state power or the experience of temporality in underwriting forms of political belonging. Edward Said, for example, in *Culture and Imperialism* argues that:

> To think about distant places, to colonize them, to populate or depopulate them: all of this occurs on, about, or because of land. The actual geographical possession of land is what empire in the final analysis is all about. [...] Imperialism and the culture associated with it affirm both the primacy of geography and an ideology about control of territory. (78)

Time measurement and regulation are implicit parts of both imperial conquest of physical land and coerced assimilation of populations into particular labour regimes, such as factory or (in the case of Antigua) plantation work, particularly in the nineteenth century when advancements in the technology for timekeeping coincided with the peak of industrialization. But an analysis of time as a "tool and a channel for the incorporation of human subjects within the colonisers' master narrative" is missing from Said's examination of geography and its projections (Nanni 4).

This essay aspires to be a corrective to this imbalance by focusing on a work of contemporary non-fiction where time configures the relationship between locality and globality in politically significant ways, and in doing so seeks to think through time as a variable that has and will continue to inflect citizenship. While often imagined as geographic markers, I will instead emphasize locality and globality as temporal distinctions, most evidently seen in the international measurement of standard time versus the local particularity of time. Temporal variability emerges not simply from personal experience but also in popular historiography, often seen in neo-imperial assessments of countries as "behind the times," which mark these locations as strange, asynchronous regions. We must also recognize scholarship's complicity in these neo-imperialist imaginings of non-European persons as deficient in timekeeping or time-discipline. Johannes Fabian, for example, has detailed how the origins of anthropology as a discipline are couched in depictions of non-European societies as asynchronous or allochronic with European societies. The "allochronic relegation of the Other," as Matti Bunzl in the preface to Fabian's *Time and the Other* puts it (xxv), underwrote European claims to modernity alongside portrayals of Indigenous societies as pre-modern. Popular imaginings of history continue to evince notions of linear progress that find resonances with early anthropological and ethnographic depictions of non-Europeans, most evidently seen in the distinction of first, second, and third worlds. The perniciousness of these categories derives precisely from Western claims that supposedly second or third worlds are asynchronous with the first, insofar as the former have not achieved a level of development already reached by the latter—in the context of anthropological study, Fabian terms this phenomenon a "denial of coevalness." Scholars from other disciplines, and this includes literary studies, are certainly not immune from treating their subjects in similarly asynchronous or allochronic ways.

1.

L. P. Hartley's 1953 novel *The Go-Between* opens with an aphoristic observation about time: "The past is a foreign country: they do things differently there" (9). Hartley, in likening time to a foreign country, has perhaps committed an error in analogizing the past to a cartographic projection. "Time cannot be mapped," Barrows remarks in reference to Henri Bergson, who suggests, far less pointedly, a problem with the way we represent "time by space and a succession by a simultaneity" (180). This problem of projecting time into space, according to Bergson, involves confusing the "value of a description" for a symbol and to ascribe "inertness" to something that is fundamentally "a *progress*" (181). Of course, as Barrows goes onto mention, the ostensible disjuncture between space and time has not stopped writers like Marcel Proust from interrogating the relationship between them, and certainly our ways of speaking, thinking, and writing about space and time involves some conceptual interchange. In some respects, time is just too expansive and tenuous a concept to convey in any way *other* than by concretizing it through cartographic projection or metaphors of spatiality, and certainly an analysis of imperialism will involve examining the spatialization of time for the purposes of domination. However, the risk of overcorrection where time and space are compounded threatens to erase, as Barrows explains, "the kinds of political and cultural connotations that adhere differently to time than to space, as well as potentially ignoring the ways in which time and space have been uncomfortably wed in particular ways in the histories of scientific development, economic imperialism, and globalization" (3).

Analysis is thus required to address the implications of discrepancies between time and space, such as those present in Kincaid's work. The phrase "Antigua is a small place" can easily be read cartographically (56). After all, Antigua on a map certainly seems small relative to the ocean that surrounds it, or the countries in its geographical proximity. Yet Kincaid also configures the notion of smallness around conditions of temporality. "In a small place," Kincaid writes, "people cultivate small events" which are "isolated, blown up, turned over and over, and then absorbed into the everyday"; for "the people in a small place, every event is a domestic event; the people in a small place cannot see themselves in a larger picture, they cannot see that they might be part of a chain of something, anything" (53). The eventfulness of experience for people from a small place is fed through the prism of locality, which dislodges self-perception from grander mechanisms of history or globalization and transforms future events into burdensome enterprises which are eventually dissolved into the quotidian, and then "the process begins again" (53). The local or domestic is not precisely equivalent to a small geographic place, as intuitive as that conflation might be. Popular configurations of the local and global will read the country village or parish town as paradigmatically local, while the large metropolitan centre is aligned with or analogical to the global, fostering a rather clear visual separation between these two realms. Such a distinction will not quite work for reading Kincaid. The localness of the small place is not exclusively embedded in the relationship between the metropolitan centre and village that defines the relationship between the urban and rural or between Great Britain and her colonies, because an operative condition of locality cannot be geographically mapped. It is partially embedded in the amorphous relationship people of a small place have with time. In *A Small Place*, the depiction of Antigua as exposed to the hegemonic forces of globalization appears alongside a description of local Antiguans who have not entirely assimilated to a global culture of time rooted in punctuality, productivity, and a selective historical amnesia. Even though Kincaid appears to critique Antiguans for their sense of time, this critique simultaneously outlines a form of collective resistance to an imposed temporality.

Kincaid's emphasis on the temporal invites us to rethink the content of our distinctions between locality and globality that occupies global literary studies, and to identify where such a distinction borrows from imperial imaginings of the planet as sequestered into mappable time zones. This rethinking is critical if we are going to overcome insufficient readings of *A Small Place* that have dismissed the text as a "sniveling attack on the sins of the nasty—and long departed—colonial power," as one early reviewer put it (Maja-Pearce 40). These sorts of critiques read Kincaid narrowly as a disgruntled victim of history and geography, and whose resulting narrator is thus always to be positioned as the periphery biting back against the centre. These reviewers have scrutinized *A Small Place* with a restricted, geographical and historical vision of colonial margins, and that Antigua's or Kincaid's peripheral location accounts for the work's tone and target. Maria Boletsi, for example, reads the work as part of an "ongoing process [...] to create one's own place in the world not *despite*, but *through* and with *boundaries*" (232), in turn suggesting that the narrator is "too angry to celebrate mobility and the alleged liberating potential of the dissolution of boundaries within our cosmopolitan world" (234). Such an assessment emphasizes the presence of the geographically or historically peripheral, and frames Kincaid as stuck in a discourse of postcolonialism that she cannot acknowledge the liberating effects of globalization. Morten Hansen, in response to these critiques, suggests that the cold critical response to *A Small Place* "should alert us to the fact that Kincaid's text was not simply an angry screed from the global periphery towards the center," arguing instead that the text's "multidirectionality allows us to glimpse the contours of a unified global space as they are refracted through a small place like Antigua" (32), emphasizing how multiple corruptive and exploitative currents have passed through the country in a way that captures the totalizing influence of the global economy.

Other relatively positive critiques of Kincaid have similarly stressed the spatial or geographical as the prism through which to assess her work. Suzanne Gauch, for example, suggests that Kincaid "reveals Antigua as a *place*—no matter how small—in its own right," reframing the country from one "perceived as an extension of English and American space into a place that is occupied, lived, and dwelt in" (910). Part of this approach may derive from postcolonialism itself which, as Jenny Sharpe elaborates, sometimes seeks to "reconstitute the margins in the metropolitan center" so as to invert them and in turn displace the "center/periphery binarism belonging to colonial systems of meaning" (185). Under such a reading, Antigua is not necessarily portrayed as peripheral—not least because Kincaid has made the country the centre of her text—because globalization has reframed the sort of imperial nucleuses that defined empire. Countries are instead refractions and flows of capital, although the routes for commerce may still follow those inured under colonial or imperial rule. Kincaid acknowledges this relationship between colonialism and globalization in *A Small Place* with the presence of Japanese automobiles, Syrian and Lebanese financing and land ownership, American hospitals, and British tourists—phenomena that are dependent on, firstly, integrated networks of exchange developed during the transatlantic slave trade and, secondly, a vision of the global world where there are no edges, just areas served or underserved by capital.

By engaging the temporal in the text, we may avoid overemphasizing the notion of spatial peripheries or centres, along with the neo-imperial imaginings of global space that are so easily smuggled into discussions of geographic margins. Part of this is a necessary corrective. As Paul Giles explains, the very idea of exile has shifted from an "epic narrative of the journey involving a difficult quest for knowledge and liberation, [towards] more recent configurations under the rubric of globalization" (365), which involves "narratives of traversal, a two-way process involving reciprocal interactions between different territories" and which in turn puts "the near and the remote into closer proximity" (365, 368). The advent of the Internet has allowed inhabitants to occupy one country while connected to another in a meaningful enough way that "they might in many cases be said to live concurrently in two places at once" (368). While geographically we cannot read this suggestion too literally, temporally we can meaningfully address how persons in a fiber-optically connected world can spend their time either digitally traversing between two places or occupying both in a mix of physical and digital ways—not enough to upend established citizenship regimes, but enough that we require frameworks for comprehending new forms of hybridity. As Giles continues, postcolonial "conditions in the twenty-first century" have complicated "the spatial and temporal mapping which formerly preserved colonial and postcolonial zones as discretely bounded geographic zones and academic territories" (368).

There is an additional reason for addressing *A Small Place* on a temporal plain that concerns the second-person point of view that defines Kincaid's narrative technique. The accusatory tonality of the narrator's address to the reader has quite universally been assessed as a "short and angry account" (Boletsi 231). While anger or rage are palpable features of the narrator's tenor, Kincaid is also fashioning an audience with recurrent references to "you," which is not exclusively a geographical positioning but a compounding of the temporal proximity between the narrator and reader, and between the past and present. As opposed to the anthropologist's "denial of coevalness" as elaborated by Fabian, Kincaid positions the narrator and reader in a synchronous relationship. The narrator accomplishes this by interpolating the reader as an English tourist in the midst of their vacation in Antigua, detailing their quotidian tasks, such as taking a taxi or using the washroom, and putting these tasks in the context of corruption, wealth inequality, and the transatlantic slave trade:

> You must not wonder what happened when you brushed your teeth. Oh, it might all end up in the water you are thinking of taking a swim in; the contents of your lavatory might, just might, graze gently against your ankle as you wade carefree in the water, for you see, in Antigua there is no proper sewage-disposal system. But the Caribbean Sea is very big and the Atlantic Ocean even bigger; it would amaze even you to know the number of black slaves this ocean has swallowed up. (13–14)

The seamless transition between contemporary tourist activity and the historical grand systems of racial exploitation collapses the temporal distance between these events, implying a continuity between the naïve English tourist and the purveyors of the transatlantic slave trade. The totalizing structure of the global economy in which both tourist and Antiguan participate (as well as its continuity with historical world systems like slavery) are obfuscated by colonial histographies that fracture the past into convenient, enclosed epochs discontinuous with the lives and actions of the contemporary. Kincaid's interpolation restores continuity, which in turn dissolves the crude linearity of Western history and situates the narrator and reader in an expanded temporal relationship that is synchronous with the global economy that underwrites the situation in Antigua and from which the text of *A Small Place* emerges.

2.

Bergson's suggestion that time cannot be mapped could perhaps be dismissed as unnecessarily restrictive when it comes to our everyday uses of the term, when the physics of time's function arguably do not matter. In the context of Kincaid, though, Bergson's critique of conflating time and space is also an invitation to work in the opposite direction of Hartley's grounding of the past in the cartographic imaginary towards an understanding of foreignness and belonging embedded in the chronometric—an approach that acknowledges the points where time and space cannot be compounded but must be analyzed as separate phenomenon with separate implications for the twenty-first-century citizen. While traditional political boundaries like nations or cities continue to bear heavily on how we think of community and affiliation, we have also been drawn into temporal neighbourhoods that impress on daily life just as strongly as state borders, such as time zones. The lines that distinguish time zones are imaginary and imperfect, along with the international date line or Greenwich Mean Time that cleave the planet into temporal halves.[5] The notion of a uniform fissure between today and yesterday is itself an enduring fiction upon which global networks of finance, labour, and travel depend, along with the seven-day week, "a ritual which silently affirms and reactualises the underlying master narrative of Judeo-Christian mythology [...] whilst synchronising the rhythms of capital and labour (Nanni 6).[6] Prior to the late-nineteenth-century, however, time was a local issue like many other forms of measurement practice, such as for distance or weight. Time was a regional particularity invested in local ritual and not necessarily a value of chief concern for the state or nation. It is no coincidence that more modern versions of citizenship bounded to a national context were developed and hardened with the advent of technologies that could track and manage time to previously impossible levels of exactness. The accuracy of clocks and their symbolic expression of scientific rationality made them instruments for the exercise of state power, "for punctuality effectively embodies the site of authority that ensures a collective sense of social regularity and wellbeing" (Nanni 6). "Anthropologists, political theorists, and historians," Alexis McCrossen notes, "have made it clear that assertions of state-centered power often take the form of time-reckoning technologies" and that clocks in particular, such as those elevated in towers high over public spaces, were "instruments through which the state laid claims to ownership of time" (221).

---

5   Dan Thu Nguyen refers to GMT as a "mathematical fiction which signals the collapse of the human experience of space and time into a mathematical formula of space-time" (33).

6   Nanni explains how the ordering of days into groups of seven, "a ritual that was unique to Europeans in the colonies," constitutes one of the key temporal practices preached by Christian missionaries in their traversal of the British Empire (7).

As such, the capacity and authority to track time has likewise involved exercises of institutional power over time's provisioning in a national context.

On a more global scale, marks of imperialism are evident in the imposition of a world standard for time that configured global space into time zones, which had its meridian conveniently intersecting a European metropolitan centre and which positioned its anti-meridian in the Pacific Ocean—indeed Nanni labels the introduction of Greenwich Mean Time (GMT) "temporal imperialism" and "one of the most significant manifestations of Europe's universalising will" (2). Though local struggles also defined shifts in cultures of time, the official deployment of GMT in 1884 at the height of the colonial era is not mere coincidence. Regions already represented as geographically distant could be exoticized as temporally distant, and local rhythmic practices were replaced with standardized time-discipline that aligned with increased emphasis on the Christian calendar and labour productivity. Time zones were an essential imaginative framework for imperial cultures to justify their dominance over other regions. Sandford Fleming, for example, proponent of standard time, saw time regulation as a means of transcending race and "petty regionalisms" (Barrows 34), which resulted in Indigenous forms of timekeeping being erased by imperial projects for global time.

Fleming's attack on "regionalisms" was an unapologetic admonishment of locality as an obstacle to industrial and imperial projects. His work as a Canadian railroader who "took to massive projects with an eye scaled to empire" clearly suggests his promotion of a global unification of time went hand-in-hand with the physical conquest of land embodied in the large national projects he promoted (Galison 116), such as a Canadian transcontinental railroad.[7] Though his engineering work was centred on Canada, his concerns were sensitive to the interests of a British nation in search of new methods for controlling the extent of its empire. As Nanni elaborates, "there is little doubt that the globally interconnected society to which colonialism gave rise by the end of the nineteenth century necessitated a common discourse of time – a temporal *lingua franca*" (1). More intuitive methods of determining time invested in the visual recognition of the sun's position were replaced with convoluted methods of measurement that made time—seemingly one of the most intimately known variables—a specialized knowledge practice regulated by the educated and political elite. The positioning of standard time as a "cosmopolitan 'placeless' toll of scientific rationality" cast the local practices of time measurement and management as outmoded, unreliable, and barbarous (Barrows 35). While attentiveness to time was practiced in different ways, "it was partly by *imagining* itself as a time-conscious civilization in opposition to a time-less Other, that Western Europe staked its claim

---

7   Fleming is present in the famous photograph "The Last Spike," which captures the symbolic completion of the Canadian Pacific Railway linking the east and west coast of the country—by extension an important event in the history of Canada as a single, unified nation.

to universal definition of time, regularity, order" (Nanni 3). Over time, the "temporal measures devised by human beings above and beyond 'natural' cycles'" have been taken as "not only our natural experience of time, but more the ethical measure of our very existence" (Nguyen 29).

Despite Fleming's envisioning of standard time as exceeding local disputes—and instead of outright eliminating what he saw as relics of local placeness—the imposition of global time also contributed to resistances to globalization that have sought to re-emphasize the particularities of regional existence against the overbearing presence of a planetary or cosmic time. Kincaid in *A Small Place* depicts local Antiguans whose time-consciousness displaces the imposition of global time and a Westernized historical practice. In the opening section where the reader is positioned as a white English tourist, the narrator ostensibly paraphrases from an unnamed economic history book (conveyed into the country by the tourist) that says Western wealth derived from the "invention of the wristwatch [...] for there was nothing noble-minded men could not do when they discovered they could slap time on their wrists just like that" (10). The presence of physical timepieces in the personal possession of Europeans underwrote their self-perception as purveyors of a universal standard for time and productivity. In referencing the English specifically, Kincaid acknowledges the fervent capitalist mindset of the English gentlemen seeking to convert whatever they can into a commodity, which in this case involves turning time into money. The presence of timepieces returns later in the work: "The Swiss are famous for their banking system and for making superior timepieces. Switzerland is a neutral country, money is a neutral commodity, and time is neutral too, being neither here nor there, one thing or another" (60). Here again the salient connection is not so much time and space, but time and money, which Kincaid's stereotyping of the Swiss as neutral are imminently skilled at acquiring. The ephemerality of time, however, (it is "neither here nor there") contrasts with European obsessions with courting and counting it.

European timepieces and their representation of scientific objectivity and wealth through the exploitation of other people's time is also contrasted with the "strange, unusual perception of time" among the Antiguans (9), or so the English tourist must be thinking. How else will they explain the sign on the library building destroyed by The Earthquake that announces pending repairs—a sign that has been there since 1974? The Earthquake stands as both a tectonic event and a temporal fissure from which the "old" library emerges. The library itself is a concrete artifact of English occupation, "one of those splendid old buildings from colonial times" (9). Much like the English tourists themselves, their enduring presence in Antigua marks out legacies of previous epochs that are still felt as present or overlapping, or which emerge in how Antiguans spend their time catering to white wealthy travellers. In turn, a distinction between past and present is largely evacuated of significance and cast as ineffectual temporal markers that cannot account for the endurance of exploitative practices like slavery or colonialism, or capture their presence in contemporary globalization. Hansen notes, for example, the impact of the International Monetary Fund, an arguably neo-imperialist organization insofar as "[l]ike England centuries earlier, the agencies in charge of managing the global flows of capital attempt to remake the small places of the world in their own image, from the kinds of trees planted in botanical gardens to the arrangement of the local economies" (39). The subsequent regulations imposed by organizations like the IMF extends to the standardization of time and coerces Antigua to assimilate to global standards for borrowing and spending, and which also leads to the physical reconstruction of the island to appeal to monied tourists.

As Kincaid writes, however, the imposition of a global standard for time has not been as successful in displacing Antiguans from cultivating their own sense of temporality. In a "world that is twelve miles long and nine miles wide (the size of Antigua) twelve years and twelve minutes and twelve days are all the same" (9). Durations are compounded; linearity between past, present, and future are dislodged. Indeed, because "people in a small place cannot give an exact account, a complete account, of themselves" they also cannot give the "hour in the day" or "the day of the year some ships set sail" (53). There is little interest in punctuality, because such an interest would

> demand the invention of a silence, inside of which these things could be done. It would demand a reconsideration, an adjustment, in the way they understand the existence of Time. To the people in a small place, the division of Time into the past, the Present, and the Future does not exist. An event that occurred one hundred years ago might be as vivid to them as if it were happening at this very moment. (53–54)

On the one hand, the proximity between the past, present, and future can collapse entirely and make an event that is technically beyond direct memory endure as an unrivalled intimacy. On the other hand, Kincaid describes how Antiguans have failed to internalize the rhythm of an imposed temporal arrangement and are in turn incapable of fulfilling the level of punctuality that underwrites the global economy. However, rather than this being a harsh critique of Antiguan's sense of time, Hansen suggests that Kincaid in this passage outlines how an "exact account" is not just difficult, "it would be impossible" (41). On display in Kincaid's distinguishing of the local Antiguan perception of time is the recognition of how claims to universality and objectivity in time-reckoning—embodied in Greenwich Mean Time and Western horology—are hubristic. Such precision is aspirational, and to think otherwise is to merely pretend to an authority and exactitude over temporality that is not actually possible in practice. Kincaid thus implies a disjuncture between the experience of time, which is often amorphous and disjointed, and the numerically precise representation of time in Swiss watchmaking or in the wristwatch worn by the Englishman, which, no matter how innovative, cannot achieve the promise of perfect time-reckoning.

Moreover, Kincaid's critique of Antiguan time practices must be read in light of her description of the white tourist, whose journey to the country is predicted on a boring, miserable existence inured by an inescapable ideology of work that prioritizes punctuality and productivity:

> From day to day as you walk down a busy street in the large and modern and prosperous city in which you live, dismayed, puzzled (a cliché, but only a cliché can explain you) at how alone you feel in this crowd, how awful it is go unnoticed, how awful it is to go unloved... (15)

This experience leads you, the tourist, to spend time and money vacationing in a country with unrivalled beauty but which is populated by people who hate you:

> Still, you feel a little foolish. Still, you feel a little out of place. But the banality of your own life is very real to you; it drove you to this extreme, spending your days and your nights in the company of people who despise you, people you do not like really, people you would not want to have as your actual neighbour. (17–18)

The culture of time that the British have imposed upon the world is implicated in the "ugly, empty thing" that the white tourist becomes in travelling to Antigua. The harsh levels of time-discipline that underwrite global finance rob life of meaning and lead the tourist to travel elsewhere in order to forget their troubles, something "every native" would similarly like to do, namely to rest, to take a tour, to go anywhere (18). The relationship between the native Antiguan and tourist is thus configured by a global time culture that undervalues the time of the Antiguan and locks them in cycles of low wage work while coercing white tourists into peddling their time for money, which they then can spend on Caribbean vacations as a means of forgetting their miserable existences back home.

As such, Kincaid is not merely offering a reductive portrayal of the English but offering an incisive depiction of global capitalism since the advent of industrialization and its dependence on time measurement and regulation. As Dan Thu Nguyen explains:

> the successful mobilization of labour within the factor system was achieved by a simultaneous imposition on and acceptance by workers of a new understanding of the nature of work as time and money, within the context of a temporal regime based on the universalization and standardization of metric time. (34)

Fluidity in Space and Time

The interests of factory owners paired well with a burgeoning international community looking to impose a globally recognized yardstick for counting time, which helped to redefine the notion of work itself. Workers were expected to surrender their own organic or intimate rhythm in favour of the imposed cadence and regularity of the workspace:

> The factory clock of modern industrial capitalism, owned and controlled by private interests, rested on and brought forth a radically new understanding of the nature of the working day as well as that of the day itself. This is to say that the working day (=*labourtime*) now belongs to the capitalist as fully and undeniably as do the warehouses and machines (=*labourspace*). (35)

The transformation of time itself into a countable variable with an equivalent monetary value arrested the capacity of workers to function as custodians of their own time in exchange for wages. Time when conflated with currency "is not passed but spent" (Thompson 61).

3.

Critics who dismiss colonialism as a "long departed" past risk misunderstanding Kincaid when she writes that the "Antigua that I knew, the Antigua in which I grew up, is not the Antigua you, a tourist, would see now" (24). While that Antigua "no longer exists" because of the "passing of time, and partly because the bad-minded people who used to rule over it, the English, no longer do so" (24), legacies of exploitation fostered under the old Antigua have relocated under the guise of the contemporary citizenship regime, in which the shine of liberal democracy obscures governmental mismanagement and clandestine networks of financing. We can respond to critics with Kincaid's own words: such temporal distinctions of past, present, and future upon which the critic depends—and which conveniently protect descendants of colonizers by implying an expiry date on legacies of colonization—are redundant and narrow methods of regulating and managing time. Locally derived forms of time-reckoning capture the presence of past events without succumbing to Westernized configurations of history or the sense of durational time that runs networks of travel, finance, and labour. Giles suggests that it is "the memory of this circumscribed colonial condition" in Antigua that lends Kincaid's work "its peculiar iconoclastic resonance" (371)—which includes a temporal iconoclasm, I might add. We receive in turn a configuration of Antiguan citizenship grounded in temporal practices distinguishable from other citizenship regimes evinced by the white tourist, which, crucially, Kincaid does not appraise as a superior form of time-reckoning. Instead, Kincaid notes how this opposition between practices of time-reckoning reverberates into the configuration of and the movement across space. Early on in *A Small Place* the reader is conveyed into Antigua via the narrator's explicit puppeteering:

> You disembark from your plane. You go through customs. Since you are a tourist, a North American or European—to be frank, white—and not an Antiguan black returning to Antigua from Europe or North America with cardboard boxes of much needed cheap clothes and food for relatives, you move through customs swiftly, you move through customs with ease. Your bags are not searched. (4–5)

While white tourists have their passage into Antigua eased, Black Antiguan citizens have their return slowed—in other words, the tourist's time is expressly valued more than the citizen's.

For the white portion of Kincaid's audience, this circumstance will seem contradictory. Citizenship is ostensibly supposed to guarantee free (or at minimum smoothed) entry and exit from the home country. But that view belies the way citizenship functions as, firstly, documentary surveillance and, secondly, as an instrument for regulating the provisioning of time—a function disproportionality imposed upon racialized and Indigenous persons. This regulation and provisioning displays inheritances from colonial rule when time was a tool for "conscripting human subjects within the matrix of the capitalist economy" through a process of "cultural curfews" and "collective reorientation in the understanding of what constituted the permissible time for each and every activity, even including movement across the land" (Nanni 4). Citizenship regimes in Europe and North America continue to maintain this prerogative of undervaluing the time of racialized persons by slowing their movement across physical space, and not just at airports or ports of entry but in public places generally. The white tourist's eased movement into Antigua directly confronts the undervalued time of the Antiguan citizen when the tourist takes a taxi driven by a local. Time and money come to define the experience: confusion over which currency the driver is to be paid in transforms into a concern over his "reckless" driving as he attempts to hurriedly deliver the tourist to their hotel and presumably acquire another fare (5).

What we receive in this intimate encounter are the fruits of an unjust system of time management that overvalues the political and economic time of the white tourist relative to the Antiguan. Far from being an emancipatory condition, citizenship does not protect the local Antiguan from exploitive practices inured by the global economy but functions as a tool for regulating and managing their time.

Works Cited

Barrows, Adam. *Time, Literature, and Cartography After the Spatial Turn: The Chronometric Imaginary*. Palgrave MacMillan, 2016.

Bergson, Henri. *Time and Free Will: An Essay on the Immediate Data of Consciousness*. Translated by F. L. Pogson, Dover Publications, 2001.

Boletsi, Maria. "A Place of Her Own: Negotiating Boundaries in Jamaica Kincaid's *A Small Place* and *My Garden (Book)*." *Tamyris/Intersecting*, no. 19, 2008, pp. 229–246.

Bosniak, Linda. *The Citizen and the Alien: Dilemmas of Contemporary Membership*. Princeton UP, 2006.

Charley, Jonathan. *The Routledge Companion on Architecture, Literature and the City*. Routledge, 2018.

Cohen, Elizabeth F. *The Political Value of Time: Citizenship, Duration, and Democratic Justice*. Cambridge UP, 2018.

Fabian, Johannes. *Time and the Other: How Anthropology Makes Its Object*. 1983. Columbia UP, 2014.

Fritzsche, Peter. *Stranded in the Present: Modern Time and the Melancholy of History*. Harvard UP, 2004.

Galison, Peter. *Einstein's Clocks, Poincaré's Maps: Empires of Time*. W.W. Norton & Co., 2003.

Gardner, Amy, Kate Rabinowitz, and Harry Stevens. "How GOP-backed Voting Measures Would Create Hurdles for Tens of Millions of Voters." *Washington Post*, 11 Mar. 2021, https://www.washingtonpost.com/politics/interactive/2021/voting-restrictions-republicans-states/.

Gauch, Suzanne. "A Small Place: Some Perspectives on the Ordinary." *Callaloo*, vol. 25, no. 3, 2002, pp. 910–919.

Giles, Paul. "Narratives of Traversal: Jamaica Kincaid and the Erasure of the Postcolonial Subject." *Recharting the Black Atlantic: Modern Cultures, Local Communities, Global Connections*, edited by Annalisa Oboe and Anna Scacchi, Routledge, 2008, pp. 365–378.

Hansen, Morten. "'A World of Something': Jamaica Kincaid and the New Global Epic." *Comparative Literature*, vol. 68, no. 1, 2016, pp. 31–45.

Hartley, L. P. *The Go-Between*. 1953. *The New York review of Books*, 2002.

Harvey, David. *Spaces of Hope*. Edinburgh University Press, 2000.

Henle, Christine A., Charlie L. Reeve, and Virginia E. Pitts. "Stealing Time at Work: Attitudes, Social Pressure, and Perceived Control as Predictors of Time Theft." *Journal of Business Ethics*, vol. 94, no. 1, 2010, pp. 53–67.

Kincaid, Jamaica. *A Small Place*. Farrar, Straus and Giroux, 1988.

Lipsitz, George. "The Racialization of Space and the Spatialization of Race: Theorizing the Hidden Architecture of Landscape." *Landscape Journal*, vol. 26, no. 1, 2007, pp. 10–23.

Loh, Lucienne. *The Postcolonial Country in Contemporary Literature*. Palgrave MacMillan, 2013.

Maja-Pearce, Adewale. "Corruption in the Caribbean." *New Statesman and Society*, 7 Oct. 1988, pp. 40.

McCrossen, Alexis. "'Conventions of Simultaneity': Time Standards, Public Clocks, and Nationalism in American Cities and Towns, 1871-1905." *Journal of Urban History*, vol. 33, no. 2, 2007, pp. 217–253.

Mitchell, W. J. T., editor. *Landscape and Power: Space, Place, and Landscape*. University of Chicago Press, 2002.

Nanni, Giordano. *The Colonisation of Time: Routine, Ritual, and Resistance in the British Empire*. Manchester UP, 2012.

Nguyen, Dan Thu. "The Spatialization of Metric Time: The Conquest of Land and Labour in Europe and the United States." *Time and Society*, vol. 1, no. 1, 1992, pp. 29–50.

Said, Edward. *Culture and Imperialism*. Vintage Books, 1994.

—. *Orientalism: Western Conceptions of the Orient*. 1973. Penguin Classics, 2003.

Sharpe, Jenny. "Is the United States Postcolonial? Transnationalism, Immigration, and Race." *Diaspora*, vol. 4, no. 2, 1995, pp. 181–199.

Tally Jr., Robert T., editor. *Geocritical Explorations: Space, Place, and Mapping in Literary And Cultural Studies*. Palgrave MacMillan, 2011.

Tomalin, Marcus. "The Intriguing Complications of Pocket Watches in the Literature of the Long Eighteenth Century." *The Review of English Studies*, vol. 66, no. 274, 2015, pp. 300–321.

Thompson, E. P. "Time, Work-Discipline, and Industrial Capitalism." *Past & Present*, no. 38, 1967, pp. 56–97.

Williams, Raymond. *The Country and the City*. Oxford University Press, 1973.

John MacKenzie's *Letters I Didn't Write*
Rewriting Home, Homeland, and Citizenship

Kristen Smith

Often in discourse of poetry, a divide abides between the aesthetic and the political. This division is a false one because, whether overtly referencing politics or not, poetry is political. There are many critics including David Orr and Stu Watson who discuss the political nature of poetry and how political poetry can be categorized.[1] In *Prelude Mag*'s article "Political Poetry," Watson breaks down two types of political poetry. One is the overtly political: "the poetry of protest that seeks to address, through its content or the radical form it takes, society's perceived ills. It can emanate from an alienated voice crying in the wilderness, or from a laureate standing beside a newly anointed king." Critical to this type of poetry is its direction and its intended audience: the people (the *polis*). This type of political poetic discourse emanates from a locus of morality; either arguing for or against the status quo, a political poem necessarily asserts a stance. The second kind of political poetry, Watson contends, is "one that seeks not so much to marshal forces but to dramatize society's forces as they are marshaled; to reveal, not through subject matter but through a manner of approach, the affective ramifications of living-in-the-world—ramifications almost always truncated, foreclosed upon, by the didactic turn of the first type of overtly political poetry." This second type of political poetry is a less idealistic one because it demonstrates the effect of the structures upon the people who inhabit that society and is "a tallying of our human indemnities" (Watson).

Falling under Watson's first category of political poetry, some poems deal directly with the complex relationship between home, homeland, and national borders. Whether it be a poetic discourse of war, protest, or witness in relation to citizenship and belonging, some contemporary poets who deal with these themes directly include Caroline Bergvall, Carolyn Forché, Allen Ginsberg, Denise Levertov,

---

1   In "The Politics of Poetry", Orr highlights a significant connection between poetry and politics: engagement in verbal persuasion. Considering rhetoric as a commonality, Orr insists that political poetry "like all speech, it exists at the mercy of time, history, and other people. But that doesn't mean poetry itself is passive" (418). Instead, Orr insists that a poet is actively engaged in battle (stakes unknowable) each time they write.

and Brian Turner. Some poets even critique the construct of nationality and a "national literature." In Canada, there are many established poets such as Margaret Atwood, Octave Crémazie, E. Pauline Johnson (Mohawk), Lee Maracle (Sto:lo), Erín Moure, John McCrae, and Émile Nelligan who grapple with nationalism and national identity. Poetry and written literature has often been used in the national/nation-building project. National or Provincial Poet Laureates have an obligation to use their artform for the promotion of their country or province. Yet, the complications of classifying and categorizing a Canadian "national" literature are still debated contemporarily. In her essay "Toward a National Literature", Maracle references the *Oxford Canadian Dictionary*'s definition of literature ("a body of writing") and emphasizes that the study of "literature" today eschews the true (and more significant) *body of written materials* that counter imperialism (band council resolutions and grant applications, etc.) for an "elevated" literature that prioritizes colonizing voices. Moreover, in a recent collection, *Refuse: CanLit in Ruins* edited by Hannah McGregor, Julie Rak, and Erin Wunker, the editors elucidate the recent public controversies in Canadian Literature and demonstrate how this cultural formation and industry has institutionalized injustices. Categorizing art by national identity is problematic because it often draws false borders and boundaries while privileging power structures that have institutionalized colonialism, racism, and genderism.

How does one decide what is "Canadian" in terms of literature? Such a designation made by physical and political boundaries complicates the positions of Indigenous Peoples who have lived in these places long before settler borders were established. Indigenous people have nation-specific, reciprocal relations with the physical land that colonizers are so often praised for describing in "early Canadian literature." Indigenous poets such as Kenzie Allen (Oneida), Jordan Abel (Nisga'a), Billy Ray Belcourt (Driftpile Cree), Joy Harjo (Muscogee), Johnson, Maracle, and Thomas King (Cherokee) grapple with the intersections of settler and Indigenous identities in their poetic discourse and examine the mischaracterizations of their cultures. Moreover, the Canadian experience is one of immigration. So, would not writers of the diaspora such as Dionne Brand, Roy Miki, Michael Ondaatje, M. NourbeSe Philp, and Fred Wah be one of the closest representations of the Canadian experience?

How does one decide who is Canadian? Citizenship is intricately tied to considerations of national identity because nationality through birth or parentage is often a determining factor of citizenship. Regarding the "The Rights of Non-Citizens," the Office of United Nations High Commissioner for Human Rights defines citizens as:

> persons who have been recognized by a State as having an effective link with it. International law generally leaves to each State the authority to determine who qualifies as a citizen. Citizenship can ordinarily be acquired by being born in the country (known as *jus soli* or the law of the place), being born to a parent who is a

citizen of the country (known as *jus sanguinis* or the law of blood), naturalization or a combination of these approaches. (5)

Therefore, even if poets are not discussing citizenship explicitly, their contemplations and criticisms of home, homeland, and national identity connect with considerations of citizenship. Moreover, there are poets whose creative works enter into the interstitial space where they do not discuss these politics directly but instead implicitly describe personal and societal identity in connection with home and homeland. In their *Handbook of Citizenship*, Engin Isin and Bryan Turner outline the problem of national citizenship "in relation to human rights, the question of the obligations and virtues of the citizen, and finally the problem of globalization and territoriality" (5). This essay does not focus specifically on human rights or its citizens' particular obligations; instead, this essay illuminates the nuances of the third issue: the problem of globalization and territoriality. "The third issue," Isin and Turner delineate, "concerns the place of citizenship in the dynamic relationships between region, state, and global society in the modern world" (8). As an exemplar of Watson's second form of political poetry and a rumination on themes of belonging, this paper focuses on the contemporary Canadian poet John MacKenzie as he addresses the themes of home and homeland to challenge the constructs of national borders, especially for Canada—a nation constructed from and through other nations. As a whole, the collection *Letters I Didn't Write* (2008) critiques authorship and ownership, which illuminates the problem of being claimed by a settler state and by extension the issue with citizenship as a form of belonging to a particular state, of being owned/possessed/authored by that state. MacKenzie's poetry further illuminates the divide between homeland and home in a country like Canada, where so many of its residents call Canada their home but another place their homeland. Moreover, through his act of "transposition" in the composition of the poem "Georgetown Memories," MacKenzie problematizes the roles of authorship and ownership; this act of *absolute deterritorialization* through the creative act of "transposition" expresses a person's individual agency in redefining their sense of belonging and their effort in constructing a place they call "home."

In an age of global diaspora, MacKenzie calls for a reconsideration of home and homeland via the experience of belonging. Isin and Turner similarly note that these shifting definitions problematize our understanding of citizenship: "As the globalization process produces multiple diasporas, we can expect very complex relationships between homeland and host societies that will make the traditional idea of national citizenship increasingly problematic" (9). MacKenzie's chosen method of a "transposition" in "Georgetown Memories" is an act of *absolute deterritorialization* which incites and informs this essay's discussion of citizenship. In *Anti-Oedipus*, Gilles Deleuze and Félix Guattari generate the term "deterritorialization." In short, "deterritorialization" is the separation of particular social or political practices from the populations and places that adhere to those practices. In a subsequent translation of *Anti-Oedipus* by Brian Massumi entitled *A Thousand Plateaus* (1987; 2004), Deleuze and Guattari discuss the process of translation as a "deterritorialization": "the temporal linearity of language expression relates not only to a succession but to a formal synthesis of succession in which time constitutes a process of linear overcoding and engenders a phenomenon unknown on the other strata: *translation*" (69; emphasis original). Deleuze and Guattari further expand the idea of "deterritorialization," differentiating between "relative deterritorialization" and "absolute deterritorialization." In his book *Deleuze and Guattari's A Thousand Plateaus*, Eugene W. Holland provides an accessible example for "deterritorialization," describing it in musical terms: "jazz musicians de-territorialize a tune by improvising on or around it" (9). Holland, through the example of jazz musicians, effectively differentiates "relative" and "absolute deterritorialization": "What Deleuze and Guattari call **relative** deterritorialization entails improvising on a familiar tune's chord sequence (or 'chord chart') in a specific key" (9; emphasis original). Holland goes on to explain "absolute deterritorialization": "But it can also happen that jazz musicians will unexpectedly change keys, or indeed suddenly switch from one tune to a completely different one … in the middle of an improvisation: these are instances of **absolute** deterritorialization" (9; emphasis original). In "Georgetown Memories," MacKenzie works as a jazz musician moving the piece from one key (a specific time and place) to another (different time and place). This act, even in the world of music, is called by the same term that MacKenzie uses: transposition.

The composition of MacKenzie's *Letters I Didn't Write* as a whole is a dialogue of voices. Throughout this collection of poems, MacKenzie overtly references and responds to the creative work of Hank Williams, Fernando Pessoa, Eugenio Montale, and Federico García Lorca. Interspersed between these named voices, some unnamed speakers give first-person accounts of their struggle to understand their place in the world. While some critics could argue that MacKenzie's rhetorical and compositional style is appropriative, I argue that these poems work intentionally against that very interpretation to complicate our understanding of contemporary *belonging* in Canada. I present four ways in which MacKenzie actively engages with these other poets and destabilizes conventional expectations of authorship and ownership of creative works that map onto the relationship with the nation state. MacKenzie disrupts assumptions of authorial ownership over texts at the same time that he destabilizes notions of belonging as singular in terms of place; by re-imagining the relationship between national belonging and textual ownership through transposition, MacKenzie critiques traditional arbiters of citizenship. Consequently, one could argue that a citizen can define their own sense of citizenship by navigating and reimagining home, homeland, and belonging.

This critical examination of the book as a whole is necessary to understand the context of the particular poem, "Georgetown Memories," which bears the epigraph:

"Transposed from Li Bai's Changgan Memories into the voice of a 19th-century Prince Edward Island woman." This poem's content elucidates the meaning of belonging as it relates to home and homeland. In response, I address the established critical considerations of home and homeland while also demonstrating how MacKenzie destabilizes those constructs. Furthermore, this poem is one of MacKenzie's self-proclaimed acts of transposition, in which he responds to and transforms a separate author's poetic work into a different work of poetry. I suggest that MacKenzie's act of transposition is one of absolute deterritorialization, and I emphasize the musical undertones evident in the term and act of transposition that also resonate with the other poems in the collection. Such an act of absolute deterritorialization calls for a re-examination of borders of all kinds—including boundaries and conditions of citizenship. MacKenzie's *Letters I Didn't Write* and the individual poem, "Georgetown Memories," both demonstrate the power of the written word to respond to conventions of authorship and ownership while simultaneously subverting those conventions through absolute deterritorialization, which suggests the power of critical writing and engagement to re-imagine and re-envision a new sense of citizenship. MacKenzie's *Letters I Didn't Write* demonstrates through its many voices, speakers, and transpositions that writers can rewrite contemporary understandings of home and citizenship.

John MacKenzie's *Letters I Didn't Write*: Voices Destabilizing Conventions

MacKenzie was born on Prince Edward Island (PEI) in Canada in 1968. Without finishing high school, he set off working jobs that took him across Canada—all the while writing poetry. He found his way back to PEI, and he currently lives in Charlottetown. His first book of poetry, *Sledgehammer and Other Poems*, was shortlisted for the Atlantic Poetry Prize and the Gerald Lampert Award. His second book of poetry, *Shaken by Physics*, blends mythmaking and science. *Letters I Didn't Write* is MacKenzie's third published book of poetry. As described in the book's cover material, *Letters I Didn't Write* is "imbued with a sense of longing for opportunities lost and lives unfulfilled." As the title suggests, the narrative voice shifts from poem to poem—almost as if the narrator inhabits different experiences—with an undertone of loss. The book is divided into three sections: "The Moon Just Went Behind a Cloud (lost Hank Poems)," "Letters I Didn't Write," and "The Book of Hours." The first section, "The Moon Just Went Behind a Cloud (lost Hank Poems)," presents a vivid portraiture of the country music star Hank Williams. Each poem in this section is titled with key and time signature—highlighting the musical resonance in both form and content. Written in third-person narration (describing the life and impact of Williams) as well as first-person narration (where the narrative voice is that of Williams, himself), these poems grapple with the grief, alcoholism, and untimely death of Williams at

48   Fluidity in Space and Time

the age of 29. The second section, "Letters I Didn't Write," has poems in first-person narration that muse upon the passage of time and loss of innocence while threading musicality throughout. This section has songs ("Sparrow Song," "Crows Calling in the Evening," "Midnight Song of the Seasons"), laments ("To Sorrow"), and notes ("Notes in a Diminished Minor"). The poem "Georgetown Memories" appears in this middle section of the book and contains the themes that resonate throughout the collection: music, voices, loss, and belonging. The final section, "The Book of Hours," dialogues with the poets Pessoa, Montale, and (especially) Lorca. Each of these twentieth-century poets has radically different lived experiences and cultural backgrounds (Pessoa is Portuguese, Montale is Italian, and Lorca is Spanish). Referencing and engaging with these poets, MacKenzie makes connections between diverse backgrounds while also demonstrating shared experiences. The poets' poetic discourses relate to the themes of loss and belonging throughout *Letters I Didn't Write*, as they each demonstrate these themes in their poetry while they struggle with this reality in their daily lives. Interspersed between these poetic conversations in the final section of *Letters I Didn't Write*, other first-person poems reveal a speaker grappling with loneliness, loss, and solipsism.

MacKenzie's engagement with these specific creative writers is significant, especially that of Pessoa. One critical aspect of the poet Pessoa concerning authorship should be highlighted: Pessoa wrote under various personae, which he called "heteronyms." Instead of a pseudonym (a different name), a heteronym is a persona created by an author, and it is a separate person with their own history. A writer taking on a heteronym is an act of deterritorialization, itself. In *The Dictionary of Literary Terms and Literary Theory*, J. A. Cuddon attributes the creation of the term "heteronym" to Pessoa and defines it as: "a kind of creative *alter ego*: a separate character and personality who produced poetry and prose" (331).[2] Writers at the Poetry Foundation explain even though Pessoa would write under his own name, he considered that identity separate from himself: "Pessoa published under his own name as well, but considered that work the product of an 'orthonym,' another literary persona." In his creation of heteronyms, Pessoa separates himself from his creative output by engendering various personae and imbuing their lives with complex experiences. Pessoa ardently argued that he did not write those works written by his various heteronyms. In creating these personae and attributing the creative agency to them, Pessoa breaks down preconceived notions and traditional expectations that yoke

---

2   Cuddon also adds that Pessoa "invented three main personalities, namely Alberto Caeiro, Ricardo Reis and Álvaro de Campos, on whom he bestowed lives and histories of their own. In effect, one may conclude that they represented different facets of his own many-sided personality. For him, they had a real existence; they were not pseudonyms (q.v.). In a letter to Adolfo Casais Monteiro (13 Jan. 1935), he describes in detail how they came to exist and how they tended to take over in the creative process (331–332).

authorship to ownership. Ahead of his time in his progressive thoughts on authorship and ownership, "Pessoa's insistence on identity as a flexible, dynamic construction, and his consequent rejection of traditional notions of authorship and individuality, anticipated the concerns of the post-Modernist movement" (Poetry Foundation). MacKenzie similarly shares this flexibility of identity and authorship in *Letters I Didn't Write*, and this dynamic understanding of authorship should shape the way the reader interprets the poetry therein. This same reevaluation of authorial ownership maps onto those arbiters—gatekeepers—of citizenship; MacKenzie's subversion of authorship can be read as a critique of those arbiters of citizenship who seek to exert power and "ownership" over people by determining the parameters of their identity as citizens.

One could read MacKenzie's *Letters I Didn't Write* and claim that the book is one of cultural appropriation and elision of other writers; however, this interpretation lacks the contextualization necessary to appreciate the complexity of this book of poetry. There are four significant aspects of *Letters I Didn't Write* that highlight MacKenzie's intention and care for fellow poets: 1) acknowledgement, 2) dialogue, 3) transpositions / versions, and 4) destabilizing conventions. Firstly, MacKenzie acknowledges the other authors in the titles or epigraphs of the poems he writes; MacKenzie intentionally names and highlights the authors that inspire the works within *Letters I Didn't Write*. Secondly, this whole collection is comprised of letters (as the title suggests), which implies a dialogue. In his epistolary collection of poems, MacKenzie responds to the creative works of these poets by writing responses. Thirdly, MacKenzie writes transpositions and versions of other poets' artistic work.[3] With these designations, he is suggesting that these "letters" exist as iterations of previous poems—not as poems that supersede the works that inspire him. Fourthly, MacKenzie challenges conventions of both "high" and "low" art by responding to Chinese poetry as well as songs (and the life) of Hank Williams. Through the many compelling creative writers he cites, MacKenzie demonstrates they should be given consideration—regardless of artistic categorization that may be attributed to those artists and their medium. Another way in which MacKenzie destabilizes convention is his consideration of authorship. As previously mentioned, MacKenzie challenges the conventions of authorship in a similar way to Pessoa; MacKenzie acknowledges the fluidity and flexibility of authorship. MacKenzie builds this fluid understanding of authorship into the text itself—in its form, content, and even its title. The title *Letters I Didn't Write* suggests that the poet abdicates ownership or authorship of these works. Throughout this paper, I continue to attribute the poems in this collection to MacKenzie because no other crediting seems veracious. But one may ask: if MacKenzie did not write these letters—as the title suggests—then who did? With

---

3   I will address the complexity and significance of this term transposition (and the differences between transposition and translation) when I closely examine "Georgetown Memories."

50 Fluidity in Space and Time

each transposition and each poem's speaker, the "letters" take on different authors. While MacKenzie may not be the speaker of these letters—he is the author of this work as a whole. Throughout the collection, it is difficult to ascertain the distance between the poem's speaker and that of the writer himself. But that distance (or lack thereof) seems to be precisely an area of inquiry for MacKenzie, the poet. *Letters I Didn't Write* is not a book that attempts to elide other poetic voices or speak for underrepresented experiences; instead, it reads like a series of carefully worded letters in conversation with other complex and compelling works of poetry—attempting to navigate the world and the speaker(s) place within it. Further, the polyphony of voices and abdication of ownership suggest that readers find areas of shared experience—belonging—and understand how each individual's navigation of this experience may be different but that each person shares the opportunity to define their own sense of belonging. By extension, people have an agency in defining their place in the world and this should extend to notions of citizenship.

"Georgetown Memories": A Transposition

> I've heard that even atheists will pray and pray
> in fair weather near the Cape of Good Hope,
> and you sailed in the changeable springtime
> with its litany of names of lost ships. (45.31–4)

In this brief excerpt from MacKenzie's "Georgetown Memories," the poem's speaker describes her experience as a sea merchant's wife, a reality experienced by many women in nineteenth-century Prince Edward Island. Appearing in the second section, "Letters I Didn't Write," the poem "Georgetown Memories" is compelling and quixotic. As the epigraph notes, this poem was originally written in eighth-century China by Li Bai (also known as Li Po), and MacKenzie rewrites the content to make it a representation of the life of a nineteenth-century PEI woman through a self-described act of transposition. Through this transposition, MacKenzie challenges the concepts of "home" and "homeland" in "Georgetown Memories." MacKenzie questions home through the actions of the characters in the poem. MacKenzie presents an idealized version of home and subsequently problematizes it; consequently, this work prompts a reinterpretation of home. Instead of home as a place defined by four walls and physical boundaries, home is a metaphysical construction experienced through emotional and spiritual connections with others. In addition to questioning home, MacKenzie challenges the notion of homeland in his self-described act of transposition. In "Georgetown Memories," MacKenzie aligns two distinct female characters: an eighth-century female narrator in China with a nineteenth-century female narrator in Prince Edward Island. By breaking down temporal and spatial boundaries between these women, MacKenzie performs an absolute deterritorialization. The dissolution of these boundaries through MacKenzie's creative act of transposition presents a new understanding of homeland. Homeland is not just defined by one location with physical boundaries; instead, homeland is constructed through community—through relationships. This reimagining of homeland is similar to Isin and Tuner's discussion of the changing concept of citizenship which is in the locus of "the dynamic relationships between region, state, and global society in the modern world" (8). Home, homeland, and citizenship are constructed by both social and political forces; however, the intersection of relationships and belonging is the nexus for these negotiations.

Finding Home (Heim)

MacKenzie first challenges notions of home in "Georgetown Memories." The actions of the narrator in this poem suggest that home is a construction dependent not on the state or parameters of citizenship but defined through emotional and spiritual connections. Eric Hobsbawm, employing the German term "heim," describes home as an "essentially private" space (67). Contrastingly, in *Home Territories: Media, Mobility, and Identity*, David Morley challenges such ideals of privacy: "I am concerned to explicate a number of senses of what it might mean to be 'at home' in a world where the sitting room is a place where, in a variety of mediated forms, the global meets the local" (2). Morley explores a conception of home infiltrated by the public, and as such, he questions whether home is indeed an essentially private space. Similar to Morley, MacKenzie in "Georgetown Memories," challenges the private sphere of home within the plot of the poem by presenting an idealized home and problematizing it.

MacKenzie begins with the poem's narrator describing her budding romance with her childhood friend:

> When I first began to care
> about how my hair would look, I sat
> one day near the apple trees by our gate
> picking and arranging flowers.
> A boy came by on a high-necked horse
> he made from a branch of white birch—
> You rode round and round me as if I were a sun,
> and apples the small green moons of your thoughts. (44.1–8)

MacKenzie fashions an idealized marriage and home: one of companionship, love, and faith shared by two lovers. These two lovers had even known each other as children, as the poem reads: "We were not really strangers to each other; / both of us born and raised in the same village" (44.9–10). The beginning of the marriage, especially for the woman narrator, is characterized by shyness. The speaker describes this, saying: "as a wife I was too shy / to dare open my face in a smile" (44.15–6). However, the trust that they shared in their marriage and the warmth of their home was transformative: "I learned again / that laughing with you was a thing I loved. / I knew that day life with you was good" (44–5.21–3). The emotional and spiritual connection they share defines home for them. The narrator speaks of this powerful bond: "I wanted us to be together even as ashes and dust" (45.24). This illustrates the speaker's recognition that home is defined by her connection with her husband.

MacKenzie complicates this connection with a plot development: the husband's business takes him away from his wife to travel on the dangerous seas that have claimed many lives; his departure gives rise to conflict. MacKenzie highlights that the husband's absence tears their home asunder. She says:

> It is August already. Already August,
> and the butterflies are yellow.
> In pairs, like slow, hesitant suns, the butterflies
> dance the west meadow's grass towards yellow.
> Your absence is the hard, long axis
> my heart turns around, wearing and wearing.
> Every day adds a line to my lament. My colour fades.
> tears score my cheeks the way rivers etch the earth. (46.45–52)

For the narrator, the absence of her husband is equated with the loss of home itself. The speaker claims that she will leave that physical space once called home. She is willing to overcome all barriers to seek her love and be at home with him—wherever he may be.

The speaker of the poem seeks home in emotional and spiritual connection and thereby evidences home characterized by fluidity. Similarly, Morley addresses these fluctuations: "... various forms of mediation, displacement, and deterritorialization are generally held to have transformed our sense of place, their theorisation has often proceeded at a highly abstract level, towards a generalised account of nomadology" (3). While the poem's narrator is compelled to leave her private sphere to search for home, she does not intend to seek a life of nomadology; instead, she has a clear idea of where home can be found:

> If company business ever brings you
> as near as Halifax, Boston, or New York,
> please write as soon as you know
> to tell me when you will be there.
> Discomfort of travel, distance from the Island
> mean nothing. I will board the first train

or ship bound for that city
and come directly to meet you. (46.52–59)

Although MacKenzie's poem is set in the nineteenth century, the question of home still resonates with a twenty-first-century readership. (And it must not be forgotten that the poem's readership originally was an eighth-century audience, which further evidences the enduring significance of the meaning of home.) In *Routes: Travel and Translation in the Late Twentieth Century*, James Clifford portrays the twentieth century as an age of rapid mobility: "... crucial community 'insides' and regulated traveling 'outsides.' What does it take to define and defend a homeland? What are the political stakes in claiming (or sometimes being regulated to) a 'home'?" (36). The actions of the narrator in this poem suggest that home is defined through emotional and spiritual connections instead of "the state" or definitions of citizenship. As evidenced by MacKenzie's poetic discourse, home, experienced in these connections, produces a plurality of manifestations, resisting a singular definition. Poetic discourses, like MacKenzie's, demonstrate that the broadening of narrow definitions allows for greater diversity, and ideally, greater compassion. Individuals have the agency to define their own sense of home and belonging; by extension, they become arbiters of their own citizenship by identifying themselves with a place and defining it as their home.

Finding Homeland (Heimat)

In addition to questioning the construction of home, MacKenzie also challenges the concept of homeland. In *Banal Nationalism*, Michael Billig also addresses the term "heimat" or homeland: "Heimat ... is the place of 'our' personal homes—my home, your home—and, as such, it is the home of all of 'us,' the home of homes, the place where all of 'us' are at home. In this sense, the homeland is imagined as a unity.... Each homeland is to be imagined both in its totality and its particularity" (75). In "Georgetown Memories," MacKenzie makes a self-proclaimed transposition by shifting from eighth-century China to nineteenth-century Prince Edward Island. By exposing similarities between these entities, his transposition challenges the constructs of history and nationhood. By aligning two disparate time periods and countries—revealing their similarities—MacKenzie effectively troubles those boundaries, performing an absolute deterritorialization.

The first question to consider is: why is MacKenzie's "Georgetown Memories" not considered a translation? In *Performing Without a Stage*, Robert Wechsler describes the art of translation as "an active way of reading something closely, critiquing it, and writing it, all at the same time" (13). MacKenzie's re-envisioning of "Changgan Memories" fits these parameters. But MacKenzie does not seek to translate; he does not wish to put the poem from one language to another. He *changes* the poem's details: the age of the narrator, the names of important places, the degree of the marriage's description, and later the intensity of the pain the absence causes. While he makes these small changes, he makes this text align with a different time period, a different geographical location, and a different audience. Making these changes to the text is what situates MacKenzie's act as a transposition instead of a translation.

The second question to consider is: if MacKenzie does not translate but instead transposes, what type of activity is he performing? As previously explained, this act of transposition is one of absolute deterritorialization because MacKenzie moves the piece from one key (a specific time and place) to another (different time and place). The subsequent question to consider then is: what is the significance of the act of transposition? MacKenzie, through his act of absolute deterritorialization, removes the boundaries between seemingly disparate nations, time periods, and individuals. He evidences that concepts of nationhood and historicity are constructs, a theoretical development with which we are familiar in the twenty-first century. But more significantly, MacKenzie demonstrates that constructs can be challenged and destabilized through creative acts, in this case through transposition. In *Out Of This World: Deleuze and the Philosophy of Creation*, Peter Hallward discusses Deleuze's emphasis on the creative act: "Purely creative thought will proceed on the model of what Deleuze calls an 'abstract line,' a line that traces a trajectory whose development or becoming is indifferent to any already constituted forms or shapes, whose creative flight is free from any territorial constraint" (2). MacKenzie puts into action what Deleuze describes in theory. MacKenzie, through his creative act of transposition, allows the reader to recognize territorial boundaries but not be constrained by them. Instead of merely removing boundaries, MacKenzie also elucidates connections. MacKenzie, in his creative act, illustrates that connections can be found between individuals, nations, and time periods. This is not to say that individuals, nations, and time periods are all the same; the differences between these groups are often significant foundations of a culture. MacKenzie's transposition illustrates that cultural groups, despite their differences, should not be considered as another's "opposite" or "other," because each share connections and are not completely alien from one another. Canada, in particular, is a country that so clearly is constructed by and comprised of many cultures and nations. In this act of transposition, MacKenzie demonstrates that humans share experiences that elucidate connections that extend beyond political, cultural, spatial, and temporal boundaries. MacKenzie highlights the shared human experiences of finding home, coping with loss, and seeking belonging that bind people together by restoring agency and power to individuals in being authors of their own identity and citizenship.

Writing Citizenship

MacKenzie's *Letters I Didn't Write* destabilizes preconceived notions of authorship regarding creative or artistic works. This subversion of ownership critiques the assumed power of the state to author an individual's identity, personhood, and citizenship. Also, at the level of the individual poem, MacKenzie's "Georgetown Memories" challenges established ideals of both home and homeland. Initially questioning the role of home by employing the plot of the poem, MacKenzie creates an ideal home, problematizes it, and provides a new interpretation of it. MacKenzie reveals that home is not a physical, bounded entity; instead, home is experienced in emotional and spiritual connections. This presents a fluid concept of home; as a result, this problematizes a strict definition of home as being only a private sphere defined by physical boundaries and separated from the public sphere. MacKenzie also tests the construction of homeland. MacKenzie demonstrates that homeland is experienced in connections—through relationships and community. Such spiritual, personal, and yet communal re-imaginings of home and homeland remind us of the shared experience of belonging. The act of belonging to a place is an integral part of being a citizen of that place. MacKenzie's transposition is an act of absolute deterritorialization which speaks to the power of the creative act and the agency of the individual to delineate their sense of belonging and where they fit in the world.

This discussion of the creative act and the role of contemporary authorship is paramount to us as scholars and critics. As Hallward says: "Almost every aspect of Deleuze's philosophy is caught up with the consequences of this initial correlation of being, creativity, and thought" (2). We seek and study the result of creative acts, each time attempting to gain a greater understanding of how we function in the world of which we are a part. We are in a constant state of pursuit: the pursuit of knowledge, the pursuit of our place in the world, and even the pursuit of home and belonging. MacKenzie's "Georgetown Memories" subverts traditional definitions of home and gestures toward new interpretation, inundated with a plethora of manifestations. And regarding the search for home, it remains to be said: if you can experience home and homeland in connections and community, then perhaps you are closer to home than you originally thought. These desires link to our understanding and our definition of citizenship. Isin and Turner suggest that citizenship and its definition are fundamental to global governance: "Citizenship must be a central component to whatever answers and policies emerge towards global governance" (9). Considering the significance of citizenship and its definition, as critics, we ought to consider our role in writing critically about citizenship, even as we engage with and examine the work of authors or other creative thinkers. Isin and Turner declare the vital role of citizenship studies: "Citizenship studies is about producing analytical and theoretical tools with which to address these injustices with the depth, sensibility, scope and commitment that they demand and deserve" (3). Isin and Turner demonstrate the valiant undertaking of an ethical approach in citizenship studies, and they illustrate how sensible and nuanced thinkers/writers are central to producing analytical and theoretical tools to generate positive change. Poets like MacKenzie demonstrate the power of the written word and creative forms (of transposition) to remind us of the agency we have in personal expression to define our personhood, determine our home and homeland, and to designate our citizenship.

Works Cited

Billig, Michael. *Banal Nationalism*. Sage, 1995.

Clifford, James. *Routes: Travel and Translation in the Late Twentieth Century*. Harvard UP, 1997.

Cuddon, J. A. *A Dictionary of Literary Terms and Literary Theory*. 5th ed., Wiley-Blackwell, 2013.

Deleuze, Gilles, and Félix Guattari. *Anti-Oedipus: Capitalism and Schizophrenia*. Translated by Robert Hurley, U of Minnesota P, 1983.

—. *A Thousand Plateaus: Capitalism and Schizophrenia*. Translated by Brian Massumi, Continuum, 2004.

"Fernando Pessoa." *Poetry Foundation*, Poetry Foundation, https://www.poetryfoundation.org/poets/fernando-pessoa.

Hallward, Peter. *Out of This World: Deleuze and the Philosophy of Creation*. Verso, 2006.

Hobsbawm, Eric. "Introduction." *Social Research* Spring 1991: 65–68.

Holland, Eugene W. *Deleuze and Guattari's A Thousand Plateaus*. Bloomsbury, 2013.

Isin, Engin F., and Bryan S. Turner. *Handbook of Citizenship Studies*. Sage, 2002.

MacKenzie, John. *Letters I Didn't Write*. Nightwood Editions, 2008.

—. *Shaken by Physics*. Polestar, 2002.

—. *Sledgehammer and Other Poems*. Polestar, 2000.

Maracle, Lee. "Toward a National Literature: A Body of Writing." *Across Cultures / Across Borders: Canadian Aboriginal and Native American Literatures*, edited by Paul Depasquale et al., Broadview Press, 2009, pp. 77–96.

Morley, David. *Home Territories: Media, Mobility and Identity*. Routledge, 2002.

Office of the United Nations High Commissioner for Human Rights. *The Rights of Non-Citizens*. United Nations, 2006.

Orr, David. "The Politics of Poetry." *Poetry*, vol. 192, no. 4, Poetry Foundation, 2008, pp. 409–18. JSTOR, http://www.jstor.org/stable/20608250.

Watson, Stu. "Political Poetry." Edited by Stu Watson and Armando Jaramillo Garcia, *Prelude Mag*, 2016, preludemag.com/issues/1/political-poetry/.

Wechsler, Robert. *Performing Without a Stage: The Art of Literary Translation*. Catbird Press, 1998.

Transnational Citizenship and Dreams of Belonging in Imbolo Mbue's *Behold the Dreamers*

Sonja Georgi

"Understanding migration within a global scope helps us observe fundamental differences—legal, political, and cultural—as well as shared elements around the world," writes Dohra Ahmad in the introduction to *The Penguin Book of Migration Literature* (xix). In immigration literature and its related disciplines of multicultural and ethnic studies, the immigration process of people to the US is often thought of as being "permanent and unidirectional" and as finding its destiny in the integration of immigrants into mainstream US American society and culture (xviii). However, recent narratives about immigration to the US from African countries—for example novels by Taiye Selasi, Chimamanda Ngozi Adichie, and Imbolo Mbue—depict the migration experience to the United States from Ghanaian, Nigerian, and Cameroonian perspectives and challenge in significant ways common tropes of immigration and integration discourses and the legal, cultural, and political conditions of migrants in the US.

Imbolo Mbue's 2016 debut novel *Behold the Dreamers* depicts the lives of Jende Jonga, his wife Neni, and their six-year-old son Liomi, who migrate from Cameroon to the US in search of better living conditions and job opportunities. When Jende is hired as chauffeur by Clark Edwards, a high-ranked manager at Lehman Brothers, the family's American Dream of gaining financial security, finding a stable home, and integrating into mainstream American society seems within reach. However, when Jende loses his job in the wake of the 2008 financial crisis and is unable to apply successfully for a permanent residence permit, he decides to return to Cameroon and a more secure middle-class existence in his hometown Limbe rather than staying in the US illegally. The family's assessment of their situation—no prospect for a legal permanent residence in the US paired with a bleak financial situation during the economic crisis—and their return to Cameroon counter a common trope of immigration literature. Namely, that migration "automatically leads to a better life; and that the ultimate goal of migration is to assimilate to a new place" (Ahmad xviii). The novel's outsider perspective on the multicultural US-American society thus extends the point of view on immigration literature from within the US to a transnational perspective on the mobilities of migrants in a globalized world.

58   Fluidity in Space and Time

Multiculturalism has traditionally located migration discourses within the realm of the "borderland and the contact zone as ... mythological sites" to be "negotiat[ed] with the multicultural domestic society" (Pease, "How Transnationalism" 51). While multicultural studies within the US acknowledge the experiences and perspectives of ethnic minorities and immigrants as part of US-American social discourses and cultural productions, in my understanding of the debate, much of the discourse nonetheless focuses on the geographical and cultural territory of the US and describes immigration as "permanent and unidirectional" (Ahmad xviii). Popular cultural and literary tropes of immigration narratives in the US, such as the American Dream, cultural assimilation, and self-reliance inform cultural productions on migration and immigration despite their recognition as myths, and they reflect the hegemony of an Exceptionalist paradigm of the US American nation state and its cultural and social foundation.[1] Heike Paul identifies these tropes as "core foundational myths upon which constructions of the American nation have been based and which still determine contemporary discussions of US-American identities" (*The Myths That Made America* 11).

The shift in American Studies to a transnational framework extends the genre of immigrant literature beyond the geographical and discursive boundaries of the US and recognizes narratives that open the perspective beyond the national borders of the US and the nation-state's social, cultural, and legal discourses. Echoing Ahmad's call for a global perspective on migration, Alfred Hornung and Nina Morgan proclaim that "all transnational approaches are necessarily comparative" ("Introduction" 2). *Behold the Dreamers* is thus a transnational immigration novel that presents this comparative perspective when the main characters contemplate their living conditions as soon-to-be illegal immigrants in the US to those that await them as returnees from the US in Cameroon, and then decide for the latter. And while the novel begins as a narrative about the American Dream that Jende and Neni Jonga hope to realize—a permanent residence permit for Jende, a degree in pharmacy for Neni, and a down payment for a home in the lower Hudson Valley region—it emphasizes the legal conditions of immigration to the US when Jende's asylum application is not approved.

---

1   The concept of American Exceptionalism is based on the ideas that the US as a nation is politically, socially, and morally distinctly different from other nations, especially from those of the so-called Old World in Europe, because this new nation is founded on democratic documents like the Constitution and the Bill of Rights and thus a model for other countries. This exceptionalism's foundational moment is rooted in John Winthrop's declaration: "We shall be a city upon a hill. The eyes of all people are upon us," delivered in a sermon onboard the Arabella to a group of Puritan migrants in 1630 (qtd. in Pease, "American Exceptionalism"). The so-called Founding Fathers of the Republic in the late eighteenth century announced the US as the future champion of universal rights of humankind (Pease, "American Exceptionalism").

In *Contesting Citizenship: Irregular Migrants and New Frontiers of the Political,* Anne McNevin introduces the term irregular migrants for people who do not have a legal, documented, or permanent status in their country of residence. The economies of North America and Europe, as well as other countries in Asia and Africa, often rely on the labor of immigrants with indeterminate legal status (132). However, "irregular migrants are more than passive victims shuttled from one place to another. They are also active agents in the transformation of political belonging," writes McNevin (viii). Immigrants' political belonging to and partaking in the society and economy of their country of residence as asylum seekers, green-card holders, or naturalized citizens contrasts and seems to be at odds with notions of mobility and fluidity of borders, nations, concepts, and people that the transnational approaches of American Studies as well as of citizenship studies at times emphasize. It is this tension that will be discussed in this chapter.

Narratives like *Behold the Dreamers,* however, depict the hard facts of the legal conditions of mobile laborers as the prerequisites for immigrants' social and political participation. My reading of Mbue's novel *Behold the Dreamers* thus analyzes the protagonists' intertwined narratives of belonging and citizenship and argues for the centrality of the legal conditions on which all other moments of and chances for their cultural, economic, and political participation in the US ultimately depend. This approach extends the idea of migration as the movement from one place to the US, and as typically ending in integration, to a multi-perspectivity on migration when it shows how migrants turn their back on discriminatory practices in the US that perpetuate their status as illegal or irregular migrants who are exposed to criminalization and exploitation. The transnational lens applied in this chapter thereby foregrounds the central yet often neglected role that citizenship discourses hold in literary reflections about immigration processes and social and economic participations of immigrants in US-American society. Additionally, this comparative perspective on US-citizenship which the protagonists of Mbue's Cameroonian American novel present is analyzed as what Taiye Selasi has coined an "Afropolitan" view that further challenges the centrality of the United States in literary, cultural, and legal discourses on migration from the perspective of contemporary writers from African countries. Depicting the characters not so much as the global young professionals of the Afropolitan community but as irregular immigrants in the US, *Behold the Dreamers* ultimately locates current transmigration discourses around issues of cultural and, most importantly, legal citizenship.

Transnational Approaches in Literary Studies and Citizenship Studies

The Transnational Turn has shaped much scholarship in American Studies in the past few decades. Prominently introduced by Shelley Fisher-Fishkin in her presidential address to the American Studies Association in 2004, this turn seeks to counter the idea of American Exceptionalism and views the United States and US American culture as "a crossroads of cultures" located both inside as well as outside its national borders and calls for a comparative study of social movements and cultural productions (Fisher-Fishkin 28–32).[2] Sharing ties with multicultural and ethnic studies in its conception of the US as a multicultural nation, Transnational American Studies understands immigration no longer primarily from the point of view of immigrants leaving their "home" to make a new one in the US. Rather, migration is seen as a "process of comings and goings that create familial, cultural, linguistic, and economic ties across national borders" in which America is less seen as a "static and stable territory and population" (24).

In this context, globalization plays a significant role in the critical and scholarly recharting of the United States in transnational terms. Generally, the term globalization describes "[t]he process by which the world is becoming increasingly connected through access to global markets, technology and information, but at the same time homogenized by the very forces of globalization which are still located in the capitalist societies in the West" (Cuddon 304–305). The increasing connectivity between regions and people, which are made possible in large part by recent developments in information technologies, communication technologies, and modes of travel, led to the destabilization of cultural boundaries and geographical borders. At the same time, globalization increases the homogenization of products and modes of consumption that "mask older forms of Western imperial domination" (Cuddon 305). This increasing connectivity encompasses economic, social, and individual spheres. As social critics of transnationalism observe, economic changes in the US that transformed the industrial and manufacturing economy of the early and mid-twentieth century to a service economy in the late twentieth and early twenty-first centuries on one hand and that disintegrated local economies in the global South on the other, brought forth migrants with what Nina Glick Schiller, Linda Barsch, and Cristina Blanc-Szanton term a "transnational existence" (9). This transnational existence is caused by "economic dislocations in both Third World and in industrialized nations ... yet made it difficult for the migrants to construct secure cultural, social or economic bases within their new settings" (Glick Schiller et al. 9). This "new and different phenomenon" (9) of "transmigrants" who "build fields that

---

2   Robert Gross describes the development from American Exceptionalism to Transnationalism: "In the 1960s and 1970s, a new generation of scholars set out to demolish the myth of exceptionalism. Variously inspired by the New Left and looking at American history 'from the bottom up,' they scoured the past for proof that the United States was no different from other Western nations. Its working class had fought militantly against the bosses; its farmers could behave like peasants the world round. Patriarchy oppressed women on both sides of the Atlantic. War and conquest dominated the nation's history. And slavery and racism were the original sin. The biggest deception was the myth of American innocence" (Gross 387).

link together their country of origin and their country of settlement" (1) cannot only be attributed to "the invention of rapid transportation and communication systems" but also must consider "the current state of the world social and economic system, as the reason why modern-day migrants are more likely to maintain ongoing ties to their societies of origin" (Glick Schiller et al. 9). In a similar line, Donald E. Pease describes the complex and contested role of globalization and its social, economic, and technological processes for transnational studies and its related disciplines of literary and cultural studies:

> Transnational American studies can valorize deterritorializations that serve the interests of the world marketplace and transnational corporations. It can also endorse movements that advance concerns of antiglobalization activists, nongovernmental organizations (NGOs), environmentalists, social movements, migrant laborers, refugees, and stateless peoples. ("How Transnationalism Reconfigured the Field of American Studies" 40)

Transnationalism is thus "a highly contradictory concept" and considers effects of economic globalization and the global mobility of people (Pease 40).

Charting the conceptual potentials of analyzing migration, immigration, and citizenship in a global space that goes beyond the limits and borders of the nation-state of the US, a transnational perspective redefines immigration discourses when the geographical area of the nation-state "is no longer synonymous with the interests of U.S. citizens" (Giles 16). Related to transnationalism is a planetary approach in multicultural literature that focuses on global influences on a given culture and community in a specific historical moment (Fisher-Fishkin; Hornung). "Evaluating the fate of displaced migrants and their unstable places of residence, cultural critics of ethnic writers moved away from the national frame of reference to an analysis of local factors of migrants' lives and their potential construction of a sense of place," writes Hornung in "Planetary Citizenship" (39). He continues, "[w]hile America represented the locus of global economic structures, which expressed itself in the superficial equation of globalization and Americanization, academic disciplines concerned with national literatures and cultures moved beyond these borders" (39). Globalization changes the roles and constituents of nation-states and invites new interpretations of citizenship that emphasize the mobility and fluidity of concepts and people in a globalized world.

Citizenship studies has likewise debated a transnational turn in the field of states, polities, citizens, and migrants and stresses the "boundary crossing practices, rights, identities and statuses" in political, social, and philosophical discourses on citizenship (Bauböck 2). In the introduction to *Transnational Citizenship and Migration*, Rainer Bauböck gives a detailed definition of the term transnational and its application in citizenship studies: If citizenship describes the "legal and political status" of individuals in relation to a given nation-state and primarily distinguishes citizens from non-citizens in that state, the concept of transnational citizenship seems to be a paradox as one can either be a member or citizen of a given nation state or not (1). Emphasizing immigrants and their movements and mobilities, transnational citizenship studies postulate that "migrants are simultaneously rather than sequentially engaged in citizenship relations with at least two states and, ... the crossing of territorial borders by migrants generates also a blurring of membership boundaries" (3). What follows from this observation is that immigrants may find themselves in

> ... a membership relation between an individual and several independent states that is articulated through legal statuses, rights and duties, as well as informal practices and identities, and that extends across the territorial borders and nationality boundaries of the states involved. We have seen that there is nothing paradoxical about the concept if we take into account the dual nature of state jurisdiction and consider citizenship as involving not only a singular relation between an individual and a state, but a triangular one between a person and different states connected through individuals' multiple ties across borders. (Bauböck 4)

Transnational turns in both American Studies and citizenship studies emphasize the mobility and fluidity of concepts like nationality, ethnicity, and culture as well as of people as migrants, immigrants, and citizens. Concepts like citizenship, the nation-state or the polity of a given country are perceived as flexible and permeable. Recent migration literature, such as Mbue's novel *Behold the Dreamers*, however, applies this transnational perspective when it portrays the trope of the American Dream and its impact as pull factor for people worldwide vis-a-vis the legal—and most often solid—conditions of granting and gaining citizenship, and of belonging not only metaphorically but also legally to the US.

Behold the Dreamers: A Transnational Immigration Narrative

"Anyone entering this country can make up any story about what their life was like back in their country. You can say you were a prince, or someone who ran an orphanage, or a political activist, and the average American will say, oh, wow!" (*Behold the Dreamers* 226). These are the words of Winston, a successful associate lawyer, to his compatriot Jende, a recent immigrant from Cameroon and the protagonist of Imbolo Mbue's novel *Behold the Dreamers*. The quote encapsulates the novel's plot that depicts the immigration experience and attempted naturalization process of Jende and his wife Neni, who move from their hometown Limbe to the United States of America in hope of better social and economic prospects in the wake of the Obama

Presidency and the global financial crisis of 2008.[3] Jende, a low-skilled man in his thirties, leaves his home in Cameroon and migrates to the United States, applies for asylum, holds precarious jobs, and saves as much money as he can to bring his wife Neni and son Liomi to the US two years later.

Although in the first few chapters of the novel the Jonga family seem on their way to settling in New York City financially and socially, Jende's asylum application and his hope to acquire a legal permanent residence permit in the US are ill-fated, as attentive readers soon find out. Even though immigrants may reinvent the stories of their past lives and the average American listener may believe them, the novel shows that even if immigrants are able to keep up with the fast pace of the precarious branches of labor for unskilled newcomers and earn enough money to partake in American society, the legal conditions of asylum and naturalization processes in the US ultimately decide the fate of immigrants like the characters Jende and Neni. In Jende's case, the exaggerated story of personal prosecution at the hands of his father-in-law does not meet the formal conditions of asylum eligibility as defined by the United States Citizenship and Immigration Service: people who are expecting to or have "suffered persecution ... due to: Race, Religion, Nationality, Membership in a particular social group, Political opinion" ("Asylum").[4]

The novel introduces the sub-plot of Jende's asylum application in the first chapter when Jende answers a question about his legal status in the US in the job interview with Clark Edwards. Answering correctly—albeit only vaguely—he says he has an Employment Authorization Document, and that he is "very legal, sir ... just ... still waiting for my green card" (*Behold the Dreamers* 7). A few pages later the narrative depicts him reminiscing in free indirect and free direct thought about his first two years in the US and the early meetings with his lawyer Bubakar and his own hope for "claim[ing] his share of the milk, honey, and liberty flowing in the paradise-for-strivers called America" (19). "Bubakar ... was not only a great immigration lawyer with hundreds of African clients all over the country but also an expert in the art of giving clients the best stories of persecution to gain asylum" (19). Although Jende and his cousin Winston doubt Bubakar's skills as immigration lawyer

---

3   For a detailed discussion of the post-9/11 and pre-Obama context in the novel see Elizabeth Toohey "9/11 and the Collapse of the American Dream: Imbolo Mbue's *Behold the Dreamers*."

4   In the "The Year of Living Nervously" in *The New York Times*, Emily Brady portrays the story of Njoya Hilary Tikum, an immigrant from Cameroon who successfully applied for asylum in the US in 2006 on well-founded grounds of having endured torture during imprisonment for his political activism for the secession of the English-speaking provinces from Cameroon. During his four months in prison, Jende suffers inadequate food and lack of medical treatment, conditions that he describes as "far more horrendous than he's imagined," but the narrative does not depict him as having experienced any physical violence or torture (*Behold the Dreamers* 245). The novel thus refrains from giving Jende a political background that would justify his asylum application.

after their first few meetings, they follow his advice and file the asylum application for "persecution based on belonging to a particular social group" due to class differences between Jende's family and Neni's parents, who do not allow their daughter to marry him (23–24).

Like Jende's stagnating asylum application, in the first half of the plot the naturalization process remains rather vague and looms in the background. Instead, the novel explores in more detail the settling-in phase of the family and their hopes and dreams for a secure future in New York, which seems to be at hand when Jende is hired by Clark Edwards. Thus, in line with its title, *Behold the Dreamers* at first evokes the ethos of the American Dream and invites readers to observe the move of the Jonga family from their bleak (albeit not endangered) existence in Limbe, Cameroon, to their new home in Harlem. Exploring the trope of the American Dream and its pull-factors, the story starts with a moment of success that catapults Jende from "dishwasher in Manhattan restaurant[s and] ... cabdriver in the Bronx" to his imminent employment as chauffeur of a high-ranking executive manager at the investment bank Lehman Brothers (*Behold the Dreamers* 3). Correspondingly, the novel introduces readers to the main character Jende when he is high above the streets of midtown Manhattan for his job interview in Clark Edward's office in the Lehman Brothers building. Jende is holding the résumé that was stitched together and jazzed up a few days before by a career counselor in the public library in sweaty palms envisioning his future in the US. The success story continues when Neni receives good grades in college and is hired by Clark's wife Cindy as domestic help in the Edwards' summer house in the Hamptons. Together, the couple can save up a lot of money and the possibility of a financially stable future seems at hand.

What is at stake for the Jonga's realization of their American Dream—a "down payment for a two-bedroom in Mount Vernon or Yonkers" and a college education for their son (*Behold the Dreamers* 30)—are the legal conditions of their existence in the US. As the story unfolds, Neni's and Jende's experiences as immigrants in the US counter common tropes of immigration discourses. For example, that migration "automatically leads to a better life; and that the ultimate goal of migration is to assimilate to a new place" (Ahmad xviii). Juxtaposing the Jonga family to the white, rich family of Clark Edwards, his wife Cindy, and their sons Vince and Mighty, the unravelling of Jende's job situation halfway through the novel could easily be related to the conflicts between Clark and Cindy and their failing marriage due to which Jende loses his job as Clark's chauffeur. The economic recession during which Jende finds himself jobless certainly adds its share of challenges. However, the ultimate obstacle for Jende to succeed in the US is his unsuccessful application for asylum. Unlike Winston's exclamation above suggests, Jende did not reinvent his vitae beyond describing his miscellaneous jobs in Limbe and Manhattan in terms of more serious professions like "farmer," "street cleaner," "dishwasher," and "cabdriver" when he applies for asylum but takes the advice of his—as it turns out—clueless immigration lawyer to tell a weak story about alleged threats of violence and imprisonment at the hands of Neni's father to prevent their marriage were he ever to return to Cameroon (3; 23–24).

The migrant Jende endorses a "relational view of citizenship" when he compares his situation in the US to that of Barack Obama, the son of an African immigrant like Jende, who at the time is competing against Hillary Clinton for the Democratic Party's nomination as candidate for the presidential election of 2008 (Bauböck 2). Whereas in Cameroon Jende does not see any chances of social standing and financial security for himself and his son because his family neither has a lot of money nor a social reputation, explaining to Clark that "Cameroon has nothing" (Behold the Dreamers 40), in the US he identifies similarities between Obama, his father Onyango Obama, and himself and his son Liomi. He thus concludes that since Obama "is a black man with no father or mother trying to be president over a country, … America has something for everyone" (40). For Jende, Obama's rise as the son of a Kenyan immigrant to Harvard Law School graduate, Illinois state legislator, United States senator, and Democratic presidential candidate symbolizes the promise of "cultural mobility and cultural sharing" accessible to all those who are willing to work hard, as entailed in the trope of the American Dream (Paul 261). Toohey summarizes Jende's conception of the American Dream: "For Jende the American Dream is a meritocracy in which neither race nor nation are an obstacle and Obama naturally symbolizes and promises all of that through his own ascendance to what appears as the pinnacle of both American and global power" (394). Conclusively, Obama gives voice to Jende's belief in the possibilities for success that the US holds for African migrants when he says in his 2008 nomination address:

> I am the son of a black man from Kenya and a white woman from Kansas. I was raised with the help of a white grandfather who survived a Depression to serve in Patton's Army during World War II and a white grandmother who worked on a bomber assembly line at Fort Leavenworth while he was overseas…. I have brothers, sisters, nieces, nephews, uncles and cousins, of every race and every hue, scattered across three continents, and for as long as I live, I will never forget that in no other country on Earth is my story even possible. (Obama)

Obama's vita symbolizes and represents the very notion of transnational mobility and identity not only for Jende but also for transnational American Studies. Inaugurating Obama as a prime example of a transnational life constitutive of much scholarship in contemporary American Studies, Hornung has analyzed and discussed the autobiographical writings of the former US President as representative of this notion of transnational citizenship. This representation favors shared experiences of "multiple migrations, repeated efforts of adjustment and acculturation in different places of residence and problematic political allegiance to a loose concept of nationality" that are reflected in life writings like Obamas and, as I assert, in recent fictional migration narratives like *Behold the Dreamers* (Hornung 40).

While the narrative of the American Dream as the success of the individual regardless of their cultural and familial background and of the US as a "crossroads of cultures" where encounters between people from various cultural and ethnic backgrounds are not only possible but enable and encourage understanding is reflected in some of the encounters between the families of Jende and Clark, *Behold the Dreamers* does not present the legal conditions of immigrants in the US as flexible, mobile, and fluid. The solid legal definition of citizen, permanent resident, and asylum seeker as described by US federal law ultimately defines the status of and re-territorializes the location of the immigrant. This seems to be the fallacy in Jende's comparison between Obama's rise as the son of an unknown Kenyan immigrant to renown lawyer, senator, and president, from which he infers the hope for his son "to become a respectable man," in the US (39). The decisive—and deciding—difference between Jende (and by extension Liomi) and Obama is that while his father was an immigrant student from Kenya, his mother was a US citizen and Obama was born in the US and is thus a US citizen, too. Jende and Liomi on the other hand have little, if no, chances for permanently staying in the US legally, as it turns out. Jende's comparison with Obama may also rest on a misunderstanding of the conditions of citizenship: understanding citizenship as "a person's allegiance to a government in exchange for its protection at home and abroad" and understanding allegiance as "the obligation of an alien to the government under which the alien resides" ("Using 'Citizen' and 'Resident' Legally"; "Allegiance"), Jende identifies himself semantically as a citizen of the US. Having verbally rejected his Cameroonian citizenship when exclaiming that "Cameroon has nothing" (*Behold the Dreamers* 40), Jende has pledged allegiance to the US when he professes a few pages later, "I thank God, and I believe I work hard, and one day I will have a good life here.... And my son will grow up to be somebody, whatever he wants to be. I believe that anything is possible for anyone who is American" (46). In this sense, the exchange between Jende and Clark in the quotes above reflects Bauböck's statement that "migrants should always be understood as being both emigrants and immigrants" (3). Transnationalism's idea of fluent and permeable borders and concepts thus finds its equivalent in the conflict that Jende faces when he feels that he must disavow his Cameroonian citizen identity to proclaim allegiance to the US:

> If we transfer this banal but widely ignored insight from migration studies to citizenship studies we become aware, first, that migrants are simultaneously rather than sequentially engaged in citizenship relations with at least two states and, second, that the crossing of territorial borders by migrants generates also a blurring of membership boundaries. (Bauböck 3)

This blurring of membership boundaries, however, is not part of the legal process of Jende's asylum and naturalization process. Still, he will find a way to reconcile this transnational understanding of citizenship with his legal situation in the US toward the end of the narrative, as I will discuss below.

As slowly as the asylum application process started in the beginning, the faster it unravels once Jende must appear in court before an immigration judge. Shortly after Neni and Jende's daughter is born, Jende receives a letter from the US Citizenship and Immigration Service that his asylum application is not approved:

> On the basis of being admitted to the United States in August of 2004 with authorization to remain for a period not to exceed three months and staying beyond November 2004 without further authorization, it has been charged that he is subject to removal from the United States, the letter said. He was to appear before an immigration judge to show why he should not be removed from the country. (*Behold the Dreamers* 224)

Immigration lawyer Bubakar and Neni urge Jende to prolong deportation and exhaust all legal and financial means to stay in the US for as long as possible. "We're going to buy you a whole lot of time in this country," Bubakar promises (224). From the perspective of the lawyer, asylum applications are a business, and the process of gaining a green card or an American passport is a business transaction and an investment. "It's going to cost good money, my brother. Immigration is not cheap. You have to do what you gotta do and pay it," says Bubakar to Jende (224–25). However, taking up the legal battle would happen at the same time when the family is facing financial difficulties. Not only does Jende's rejected asylum application coincide with the birth of their daughter Timba, who is *jus soli* a US citizen, but this is also the winter of the economic recession and the moment when Clark lays off Jende as his chauffeur at the insistence of Cindy, who feels ashamed that Jende knows about their marriage crisis. Jende must work three jobs at the same time but still does not make enough money to cover the family's living expenses, and he soon suffers from health problems.

The novel leaves open to interpretation the causality of the sequence of events around Jende's job situation and the rejected asylum application. It remains open to speculation if Jende and Neni's situation would have been different were this not the year of economic recession in the US or the period of post-9/11 immigration policies.[5] However, the bleak job opportunities bring Jende to assess his situation more realistically and he begins to accept the fact that they will have to return to Cameroon eventually, because he understands that even if he were able to prolong his legal case,

---

5   For a detailed discussion of *Behold the Dreamers* as post 9/11 fiction see Toohey.

68 Fluidity in Space and Time

the family's financial situation and the country's economic state would make it impossible for them to lead a safe and self-reliant life in the US:

> In America today, having documents is not enough. Look at how many people with papers are struggling. Look at how even some Americans are suffering. They were born in this country. They have American passports, and yet they are sleeping on the street, going to bed hungry, losing their jobs and houses every day in this...this economic crisis. (307)

This quote encapsulates the intricate situation of many immigrants in the US in the early twenty-first century and shows that reading the immigration narrative of Jende and Neni in terms of metaphorical belonging would fall short of considering the legal and economic foundations on which concepts like self-reliance and the American Dream rest. A reading that focuses on the legal and economic backgrounds of the immigration narrative then brings to the fore dire conditions of poor and working-class immigrants in the US, because for many of them, as for Jende and Neni, their legal situation very much depends on their financial situation:

> Even if Jende got papers, Winston went on, without a good education, and being a black African immigrant male, he might never be able to make enough money to afford to live the way he'd like to live, never mind having enough to own a home or pay for his wife and children to go to college. He might never be able to have a good sleep at night. (322)

Thus, social and cultural participation in the US is not so much about welcoming immigrants, as the liberal protestant pastor and immigrant Natasha preaches at the church Neni joins (364–65).[6] Rather, for immigrants and many US citizens alike, social and cultural participation is more a matter of who can *afford* to partake in American society.

The legal situation of Jende and Neni is grounded in their financial situation, which is one that cannot be changed through hard work and diligence. This means that the aspirational goal of immigrant cultural integration into US-American society that is entailed in the American Dream is one that is only attainable for those immigrants that have the financial means to afford living in the US. As Clark says to Jende, thinking about the future of his son Vince, who wants to quit law school, but encapsulating Jende's situation quite well, too, "unless you make a certain kind of money in this country, life can be brutal" (147–48). Jende and Neni Jonga's legal and financial situation in the US is, according to Clark and Cindy Edwards, also accompanied by cultural difference.

---

6   For a detailed discussion of Natasha as an example of a "white savior" see Toohey.

The car in which Jende drives Clark and his family through Manhattan and Long Island symbolizes the transnational space in which Jende, Clark, Cindy, and their sons Mighty and Vince communicate with each other about their different cultural backgrounds, their shared life experiences as parents on a mostly friendly, attentive, and at times personal level. These conversations contrast the "quasi-Babel in a New York City livery cab" created by the interactions between people from various cultural, social, and national backgrounds in the microcosm of the globalized world that New York City is a trope of in popular discourses (16). Shortly after Jende becomes Clark's chauffeur, Cindy hires Neni as help in their summer home in the Hamptons, and the interactions between the Jongas and the Edwards can first be read as an example for a successful intercultural understanding and transnational "contact zone" as envisioned by transnational and multicultural literary studies (Pratt). Although a certain cultural curiosity and skepticism or distance remains on both sides, Cindy and Clark (for example) think of Jende and Neni's hosting of a Cameroonian evening in their home in Harlem as an intercultural contact "experience" for their children (345). Differences in family traditions, social customs, or way of life do not seem to be the characteristics on which differences between the American and the Cameroonian family are based. On the contrary, familial similarities and conflicts between fathers and sons, mothers, parents, and siblings of the Jongas and the Clarks appear in conversations throughout the novel.

Thus, it is almost ironic that in the moment in which Jende emancipates himself from the tropes of the immigrant desiring to integrate into mainstream society at all costs and without choice, his legalization and naturalization process essentializes his cultural "otherness." Leti Volpp points out the legal and cultural construction of citizen and non-citizen and explains the reciprocal relationship between these constructs and the role that cultural "othering" plays in this binary:

> The citizen is assumed to be modern and motivated by reason; the cultural other is assumed to be traditional and motivated by culture. In order to be assimilated into citizenship, the cultural other needs to shed his excessive and archaic culture. Citizenship emerges through its distinction from the cultural other, who is measured and found wanting for citizenship. We should therefore understand that the cultural other is constitutive of the citizen. (574)

The moment Jende acts not as the culturally "other" "backward" or "irrational immigrant" stereotype is when he acts and decides "rationally" and "self-determinately"—at least to the point that he rejects a life as an irregular migrant—that he will not be able to become the "respectable man" he had hoped for but will have to enter the vast undocumented and unregulated immigrant work force were he to stay in the US. Unlike how the stereotype would have him behave, he is "motivated by reason," to use Volpp's formulation quoted above, and returns to Cameroon. The moment he would thus culturally and mentally qualify as US citizen, he leaves the US, albeit as a "transmigrant" and "self-made" man who uses the money he has earned in the US to open his own business in Limbe (Glick Schiller et al. 1). Jende, Neni, and their children return to Limbe to their own house and business.

The transnational lens on the concept of citizenship prevents a reading of the migrant's return as defeat because it compares Jende's position in the US after his job loss and rejected asylum application to the prospects that he will have in Limbe after his return from the US. Reflecting the semantics of the citizen of Volpp's quote above, in a conversation with Winston Jende reasons, "Cameroon did not have opportunities like America, but that did not mean one should stay in America if doing so no longer made sense" (*Behold the Dreamers* 322). It is here that Jende can eventually emancipate himself from the "grotesque being created by the sufferings of an American immigrant life" that he has become to Neni and his children as well as from the demeaning behavior that he assumed while working for Clark Edwards (237). Visiting Clark shortly before the family's departure, Jende can now explain his situation to his former boss clearly and rationally. When Clark asks Jende why he returns to Cameroon, he answers:

> No, sir, I'm not being deported. But I cannot get a green card unless I am granted asylum, and for that to happen I will have to spend many years and a lot of money going to immigration court. And then maybe the judge will still decide to not give me asylum, which means the government will deport me in the end. It's not how I want to live my life sir, especially when you add the fact that it's just not easy for a man to enjoy his life in this country if he is poor. (372–73)

At the end of the novel, Jende can comprehend his years in the US in the context of his life and what it means for his future in Cameroon when he says, "because of that job I was able to save money and now I can go back home to live well" (372). Due to his changed financial situation and the business experience, Jende is "no longer afraid of [his] country the way [he] used to be" (373). The emancipation process that Jende experiences as the plot progresses is an example of the "complex and multilayered" context of migrations and their narratives that Ahmad describes when she writes that "migration would be better understood as effect rather than cause" (xviii).

Although Jende quickly adapts to ways and customs of US-American society and the pace of his tight work schedule in New York, he also maintains financial and emotional ties to his family and community in Nigeria when he sends money to his parents and extended family and cannot forgive himself for not being able to attend his father's funeral (304). Despite what can be called his symbolic disavowal of his Nigerian citizenship in favor of expressing allegiance to the US in the scene quoted above, Jende participates in the social and material flows across nation states and borders that mark globalization. Jende's situation as transnational migrant is marked by the reconciliation of these complex and at times even conflicting characteristics of his identity, which Glick Schiller et al. attribute to transmigrants. "Through these seemingly contradictory experiences, transmigrants actively manipulate their identities and thus both accommodate to and resist their subordination within a global capitalist system" (Glick Schiller et al. 12). For Jende, the reconciliation of his Nigerian citizenship and his loyalty to the US eventually enable him to emancipate himself from oppressive US-American labor conditions and to exit voluntarily the regularization process that he started with an ungrounded asylum application before facing detention and deportation.

Afropolitan Transmigration

This transnational perspective on migration narratives presents an outside, and outsider's, perspective on immigration discourses in the US. The immigrant Jende emancipates himself from the myth of the American Dream and its narratives of metaphorical belonging that sidetrack the story of legal and economic realities of immigrants like him. Echoing the figurative language of this myth, Jende summarizes the labor conditions of immigrants in New York during the financial crisis when he says, "[t]his country no longer has room for people like us" (332).[7] And although Jende and Neni are in the beginning of the novel certain that they will stay permanently in the US since this country has so much to offer them, the juxtaposition of Manhattan and Lagos—not only metaphorically in the memories of the characters but also as concrete localities and cultural spaces—extends the tropes of the traditional immigrant novel in the US to a transnational context. Reflecting this new-found independence, Jende declines Winston's offer as hotel manager in Limbe and uses the money he earned in the US to start his own agricultural business with his family's plot of land, applying the skills he acquired while working for Clark to "diversify and conglomerate and acquire as many competitors as possible" (353). As transnational migrants, Jende and Neni no longer see the necessity to disavow US society and the so-called American way of life to reintegrate into their communities in Nigeria. Rather, they can put their skills and experiences as well as their material goods to use in Limbe when they exhibit Wallstreet smartness and fake and original Gucci and Versace outfits (11).

At the end of the novel, Jende resembles the "fair number of African professionals" who are returning to African countries from American, British, Canadian, and European metropoles and whom Taiye Selasi describes as Afropolitans in her 2005

---

7   This "like us" also includes American citizens such as his middle-aged co-worker Leah at Lehman Brothers, who is unable to find a new job after the bank's collapse in the ensuing economic crisis.

essay "Bye-bye Babar." The term Afropolitan refers to young artists, writers, musicians, and business professionals who live in globalized urban spaces across the world and have ties to the African continent. In Selasi's words, this new generation is a "funny blend of London fashion, New York jargon, African ethics" at home in one or more "G 8 cities" and in "at least one place on the African Continent," who "choose which bits of a national identity (from passport to pronunciation) [they] internalize," and who are "not citizens, but Africans of the world" (Selasi). Foregrounding their creative work, she emphasizes that they "refus[e] to oversimplify" Africa and its pasts and presents: "Rather than essentializing the geographical entity, we seek to comprehend the cultural complexity" (Selasi). The essay sparked and rekindled a heated debate in artistic, academic, and media circles about representations of generalized and often stereotyped images of Africa and Africans in Western, that is US-American and European, discourses on one hand and about the positions and roles of contemporary creative professionals with roots and links to African countries and cultures on the other.[8]

Mbue's *Behold the Dreamers* does not obviously adhere to the understanding of Afropolitan/Afropolitanism as outlined in Selasi's essay. Firstly, the novel's main characters Jende and Neni do not belong to the sophisticated, intellectual, and worldly community that characterizes Selasi's Afropolitan (Selasi). Secondly, it foregrounds the migration story of Jende and Neni in the tradition of the immigrant novel popular in the US when it sets out to depict the couple's efforts to partake in the American Dream as the self-made success story of the integrated, industrious, and enduring immigrant worker. What the so-called one percent at the top of the social ladder and the immigrant worker share is their belief in the American Dream, which they find out is a "very tough challenge achieving," as Imbolo Mbue describes the commonalities of the two families who inhabit the top and bottom steps, respectively, of the social ladder in a *CBS: This Morning* interview ("Oprah's Book Club"). Thirdly, it applies the idea of "not citizens but Africans of the world" quite literally to the legal situation of its protagonists (Selasi), who cannot choose from a set of privileged nationalities but preempt deportation by voluntarily returning to their country of national origin.

---

8   In "Cosmopolitanism with African Roots: Afropolitanism's Ambivalent Mobilities," Susanne Gehrmann contextualizes and summarizes the popular, digital, and academic controversies around the concept. Analyzing two key novels that engage the discourse, Teju Cole's *Open City* (2012) and Taiye Selasi's *Ghana Must Go* (2013), Gerhmann concludes, "These novels open up a fruitful literary landscape for the uncovering of contemporary Afro-diasporic identity politics traversing America, Africa and Europe" (69). Donald Morales points out in defense of the concepts as formulated by Selasi, "Afropolitanism should not be dismissed as a commercial or pop-culture movement but a future-leaning way of moving African literature and art forward" ("An Afropolitan 2017 Update" 229).

However, what *Behold the Dreamers* and the Afropolitan discourse share is the comparative point of view on US-American society and its "monopoly on the idea of being a 'nation of immigrants'" (Ahmad xix). The transnational lenses of both Afropolitanism and *Behold the Dreamers* call into question the assumption that "the ultimate goal of migration is to assimilate to a new place" and foreground the movement and mobility of transmigrants (Ahmad xviii). Speaking about the evolution of the concept Afropolitanism several years later in an interview with Bhakti Shringarpure, Selasi relativizes the critique of her essay as elitist and stresses travel as necessity rather than luxury:

> The essay describes, very specifically, a group of people in movement. But they are not—or not mostly—in movement toward luxury packaged vacations. They're going from Storrs to Nairobi to see their family, from London to Lagos on on-sale flights, they're counting their pennies to pay inflated prices at Christmas, they're trying to get home (from home). (Selasi qtd. in Shringarpure)

The young professionals of "Bye-bye Babar" are thus to be understood as the result of their parents' "obsession with upward mobility" who are raised and trained internationally with the aim to enter the "global middle class" (Selasi qtd. in Shringarpure). On a similar note, Madhu Krishnan identifies contemporary African novels that portray the returns of their protagonists, so-called narratives of return (144), as "departing from the more market-driven image of the African subject as a mobile, free-floating consumer of culture" that is represented in the image of the Afropolitan (145). Thus, Jende and Neni's return to Cameroon and the comparison of the living and precarious working conditions of immigrants in the US challenge both the myth of the American Dream as global master narrative of a successful life and the centrality or dominance of the transnational discourse of migration. Jende gives voice to this "monopoly" when he reasons that "Columbus Circle is the center of Manhattan. Manhattan is the center of New York. New York is the center of America, and America is the center of the world" (*Behold the Dreamers* 96). For Neni and Jende, Columbus Circle presents a microcosm of a global, transnational world where people from all over the world cross but do not necessarily interact.[9] Neni, for example, observes that "most people were sticking to their own kind. Even in New York City, even in a place of many nations and cultures, men and women, young and old, rich and poor, preferred their kind when it came to those they kept closest" (95). Columbus Circle thus symbolizes the promises and opportunities of the US

---

9   Toohey describes the symbolism of the statue of Christopher Columbus in post-9/11 narratives like *Behold the Dreamers* as follows: "Columbus as the arrival of the new and the symbolic starting point for Europeans' possession of the land and claim of racial superiority, and subjugation of enslaved Africans in the new world—these two sides of the man and his myth blend in the Jonga's experience of New York" (392).

74 Fluidity in Space and Time

and the American Dream. But these promises come with a price for Afropolitan transmigrants and their families and communities, as Selasi points out:

> Travel was how we kept our family together. We didn't have a choice. We did have the means. And that is, undoubtedly, a privilege. But the fracturedness of the family unit, its multi-locality, is a post-colonial outcome. To re-write that multi-locality in capitalist terms is to erase the human cost, the heartbreak." (Selasi qtd. in Shringarpure)

Globalization and the free flow of capital, goods, people, and ideas enables the Jongas to first migrate to the US without cutting ties with their families and friends at home. When they return to Cameroon it then allows them to stay connected to their friends and associates in the US. Jende's business will connect him to the US and if not Neni's education then the education of their children will take them to the US, or Canada or Great Britain. At the end of the narrative, Jende can act on the reasoning that he expressed already in the first half of the book when still being one of the dreamers:

> So they sat beneath the statue of Christopher Columbus, side by side, ... In his first days in America, it was here he came every night to take in the city. It was here he often sat to call her when he got so lonely and homesick that the only balm that worked was the sound of her voice. During those calls, he would ask her how Liomi was doing, what she was wearing, what her plans for the weekend were, and she would tell him everything, leaving him even more wistful for the beauty of her smile, the hearth in his mother's kitchen, the light breeze at Down Beach, the tightness of Liomi's hugs. The coarse jokes and laughter of his friends as they drank Guinness at the drinking spot; leaving him craving everything he wished he hadn't left behind. During those times, he told her, he often wondered if leaving home in search of something as fleeting as fortune was ever worthwhile. (*Behold the Dreamers* 95–96)

It is from the core of the US-American cultural and social monopoly on immigration, legalization, and naturalization that Columbus Circle symbolizes, that the Jonga's departure from New York destabilizes the notion of the US as the center of a globalized world and the standard for measuring and judging a successful life. A transnational novel, *Behold the Dreamers* foregrounds the economic and legal conditions of transnational migration and transnational citizenship and questions the price tag attached to the American Dream for working immigrants. The characters emerge as transmigrants who compare their life and prospects in the US to those of their hometown in Nigeria. Although they may not have much of a choice in legal terms, they nonetheless are able to choose their future and reconcile the transcultural markers of their identity within transnational locations that encompass the US and Nigeria—the global North and the global South—simultaneously.

Works Cited

"Allegiance Definition & Meaning." *Merriam-Webster*, 23 July 2023, https://www.mer riam-webster.com/dictionary/allegiance.

"Asylum." *U.S. Citizenship and Immigration Services*. U.S. Department of Homeland Security. https://www.uscis.gov/humanitarian/refugees-and-asylum/asylum.

Ahmad, Dohra. "Introduction." *The Penguin Book of Migration Literature*, edited by Dohra Ahmad, Penguin Books, 2019, pp. xv–xxix.

Bauböck, Rainer. "Introduction." *Transnational Citizenship and Migration*, edited by Rainer Bauböck, Routledge, 2017, pp. 1–17.

Brady, Emily. "The Year of Living Nervously." *The New York Times*, 5 Dec. 2008, https://www.nytimes.com/2008/12/07/nyregion/thecity/07asyl.html.

CBS This Morning. "Oprah's Book Club: *Behold the Dreamers* by Imbolo Mbue." *CBS News*, 26 Jun. 2017, https://www.cbsnews.com/news/oprahs-book-club-be hold-the-dreamers-imbolo-mbue/.

Cuddon, J.A. "Globalization." *The Penguin Dictionary of Literary Terms and Literary Theory*, edited by J. A. Cuddon, 5th ed., Wiley-Blackwell, 2013, pp. 304–305.

Fisher-Fishkin, Shelley. "Crossroads of Cultures: The Transnational Turn in American Studies." Presidential Address to the American Studies Association. *American Quarterly*, vol. 57, no. 1, Mar. 2005, pp. 17–57. *JSTOR*, https://www.jstor.org/stable/40068248.

Gehrmann, Susanne. "Cosmopolitanism with African Roots: Afropolitanism's Ambivalent Mobilities." *Journal of African Cultural Studies*, vol. 28, no. 1, 2016, pp. 61–72.

Giles, Paul. *The Global Remapping of American Literature*. Princeton UP, 2011.

Glick Schiller, Nina, et al. "Transnationalism: A New Analytic Framework for Understanding Migration." *Annals of the New York Academy of Sciences* 645, 1992, pp. 1–24. Reprinted in *Transnational Citizenship and Migration*, edited by Rainer Bauböck, Routledge, 2017, pp. 77–100.

Gross, Robert A. "The Transnational Turn: Rediscovering American Studies in a Wider World." *Journal of American Studies*, vol. 34, no. 3, Dec. 2000, pp. 373–93, doi:10.1017/S0021875851006437.

Hornung, Alfred. "Planetary Citizenship." *Journal of Transnational American Studies*, vol. 3, no. 1, 2011, pp. 39–46.

— and Nina Morgan. "Introduction." *The Routledge Companion to Transnational American Studies*, edited by Alfred Hornung et al., Routledge, 2019, pp. 1–8.

Krishnan, Madhu. "Reading Space, Subjectivity, and Form in the Twenty-First Century Novel of Return." *African Migration Narratives: Politics, Race, and Space*, edited by Cajetan Iheka and Jack Taylor, U of Rochester P, 2018, pp. 143–59.

McNevin, Anne. *Contesting Citizenship: Irregular Migrants and New Frontiers of the Political*. Columbia UP, 2011.

Morales, Donald. "An Afropolitan 2017 Update." *Journal of the African Literature Association*, vol. 11, no. 2, 2017, pp. 223–237.

Obama, Barack. "A More Perfect Union." Sen. Barack Obama Addresses Race at the Constitution Center in Philadelphia, 18 Mar. 2008, Philadelphia, Penn., The Washington Post Company, 2008. https://www.washingtonpost.com/wp-dyn/content/article/2008/03/18/AR2008031801081.html?sid=ST2008031801183.

Paul, Heike. *The Myths that Made America: An Introduction to American Studies*. transcript, 2014.

Pease, Donald E. "How Transnationalism Reconfigured the Field of American Studies: The Transnational/Diaspora Complex." *American Studies as Transnational Practice: Turning Toward the Transpacific*, edited by Yuan Shu and Donald E. Pease, Dartmouth College P, 2015, pp. 39–63. *Project MUSE*, https://muse.jhu.edu/book/43328.

—. "American Exceptionalism." *Oxford Bibliographies*. 27 Jun. 2018. doi: 10.1093/obo/9780199827251-0176.

Pratt, Mary Louise. "Arts of the Contact Zone." *Profession*, 1991, pp. 33–40.

Selasi, Taiye. "Bye-Bye Babar." *The Lip Magazine*, 3 March 2005. https://thelip.robertsharp.co.uk/2005/03/03/bye-bye-barbar/.

Shringarpure, Bhakti. "Revisiting Afropolitanism: An Interview with Taiye Selasi." *Brittle Paper*, 9 Sep. 2020. https://brittlepaper.com/2020/09/revisiting-afropolitanism-an-interview-with-taiye-selasi/.

Toohey, Elizabeth. "9/11 and the Collapse of the American Dream: Imbolo Mbue's *Behold the Dreamers*." *Studies in the Novel*, vol. 52, no. 4, (Winter) 2020, pp. 385–402.

Volpp, Leti. "The Culture of Citizenship." *Theoretical Inquiries in Law*, vol. 8, no. 2, 2007, pp. 571–602.

"What's the Difference between a 'Citizen' and a 'Resident'?" *Merriam-Webster*, 2023, https://www.merriam-webster.com/words-at-play/what-is-the-difference-between-a-citizen-and-a-resident.

Citizenship and (State) Violence

"Present Absentees, Weak-Kneed Nobodies"[1]
Exile, Airport, and Non-Citizenship in Abdourahman Waberi's *Transit*

Nasra Smith

> Borders are no longer sites to be crossed but lines that separate.
> *Achille Mbembe, Necropolitics*

> Structures kill and maim, not individuals or collectives.
> *Donald Black, The Geometry of Terrorism*

> France is not Fanon's Other; he is *France's* Other.
> *Lewis R. Gordon, Fanon and the Crisis of European Man*

> The settler-native relationship is a mass relationship.
> *Frantz Fanon, The Wretched of the Earth*

In Abdourahman Waberi's *Transit* (2012), L'Aéroport de Roissy-Charles de Gaulle is an international transitory zone separate from, yet part of, France's territorialized border. As a heterotopic space,[2] Roissy underscores the imperial epoch of *Fortress Europe*. Its stringent immigration policies and mobility control[3] overwrite the air-

---

1   Harbi's comment about his exilic presence at the Roissy airport in France (Waberi 134).

2   In "Of Other Spaces," Foucault states a "heterotopic site is not freely accessible like a public space" (25). I argue the airport is not a public place but a heterotopic space.

3   I borrow this term from Robert Pallitto and Josiah Heyman: their article argues that mobility control underscores how the extensity of checkpoints are, not only an effect of post-9/11 securitization but challenges to our theorizations about citizenship and identity (316).

port[4] to underscore the "official assimilationism accompanying the French idea of citizenship"[5] (Sekyi-Otu, *Left* 58). Complicit of France's colonial legacy, Roissy is the modern, globalized site of the French empire. It marks itself as a "confessional" complex that monitors and differentiates the movements and identities of bodies in a post-9/11 milieu (Salter 49). Reinforced by America's War on Terror, the Paris aéroport is a panopticon that militates technologies of surveillance over citizens and non-citizens[6] alike (Foucault, *Discipline* 195; *Left* 58). As an autonomous state apparatus, the airport legitimates the national citizen, enacting a permanent partiality towards the Other. Thus, by carefully mapping, surveilling, and inspecting the non-status, the airport naturalizes its imperial vocabulary of territorial control to expel the refugee—whom Ato Sekyi-Otu quips as the "catastrophic return of the repressed" (*Left* 58).

Transit fictionalizes the effects of transnational migration and globalization on the East African migrant from the coast. By questioning how racial-colonial-capital inequalities reproduce hierarchical power through a geographically defined site, the novel challenges any obscuring of the connection between racism and capitalism. Given the mobility of global accumulation has produced the underdevelopment

---

4   I want readers to integrally note the airport as a port, like a seaport, or an inland port, etc. While not all ports are surveilled, the airport is regulated border. As a transportation site of people, goods, and services that has, overtime, turned into a securitized zone of the nation-state, where territoriality is key in instituting its national sovereignty, the modern airport inscribes the limits of travel for the non-status claimant.

5   I agree with Ato Sekyi-Otu's analysis of the 2005 Paris Riots, where he critiques a visiting French scholar to Canada who applauded Canada's stance against Islamic Sharia courts and other faith-based cases as a welcoming retribution. This scholar rebuked Canada's tradition of multiculturalism as inherently unsustainable. In this chapter, Sekyi-Otu addresses the scholar's remarks by analyzing the young history of Canada's multicultural policies, while admonishing France's *mission civilisantrice*. In short, Sekyi-Otu argues the scholar's argument is couched in assimilationist rhetoric that has governed the French polity since colonization.

6   As terms used in Citizenship Studies, I interchange asylum seeker, refugee, and non-status to describe the migratory status of claimants in a host country. In the field, the terms alien and non-citizen are used interchangeably, often denoting the legal precarity of entrants. In the past, terms like foreigner and stranger often evoked an exilic existence in travel narratives, where some were privileged or carried forms of social status (émigré as Edward Said and stranger/expatriate as per James Baldwin), and others were forced or differentiated. Engin Isin uses the terms foreigner, stranger, and outsider to inculcate how dominant forms of citizenship in the Roman and Greek metropolis were formed. As well, the term non-status has recently been theorized in Indigenous Studies, where borders, through European map-making, have shifted to exclude and/or impose on Indigenous communities the loss of their territorial sovereignty. I do differentiate between the non-status and the immigrant, for the latter usually denotes the acceptance into a country and the waiting process for citizenship of that country. But I use both terms to discuss the issues that plague the refugee at the airport and the immigrant in France. .

of the global South, mass migration not only augments the airport as a space of modernity, but replicates the colonial relations between the colonizer and the colonized (Davidson 5). Ato Quayson would agree the airport mimics forms of "colonial space-making" as the (im)migrant (unwillingly or willingly) consents to "forms of subversive complicity" as would the colonized in the context of imperial-colonial dominance (16; 17). Thus, colonial power is evident, not only through territorial control, but in relations of the "cultural and symbolic ... [and the] political and spatial" (16). As a result, "the postcolonial nation-state, the ex-colonial metropolitan centres and predatory multinational corporations are all taken to be inheritors and beneficiaries of colonial space-making in the modern world" (17). In the context of migration and diaspora, Waberi articulates the failures of Djibouti's anti-colonial struggle, instantiating the metropolitan as a hyper-colonized space where racial difference, particularly France's vehemence towards the post-colonized migrant, is a division waged both materially and ideologically.

As such, the novel ties two formerly colonized subjects to Roissy to politicize a terrorizing post-civil war nation caught in the never-ending conflicts of the Greater Horn region. Migrating from Djibouti to the French metropolis, Harbi and Bashir are the globalized littoral subjects from the Indian Ocean. As *apatrides*, they centralize the "very real histories" of colonization, decolonization, and global capitalism (Treacy 64). Their transit, their mobility, does not erase Djibouti's postcolonial crises, but stresses it as "consequence of the colonial legacy" (64). In fact, Harbi's acknowledgement of Bashir, (while they are on French soil), heightens the dawning possibility of a post-dictatorial Africa (64). Given a "new and inventive language of resistance," Waberi delegitimizes France's *mission civilisantrice* via the non-status refugee (Treacy 64, 65; Sekyi-Otu, *Dialectics* 119; *Left* 58; Fanon, *Wretched* 147). By centering the migrant—who is between detention, deportation, and death—, the novel decenters the annihilating power of France's sovereignty. For if the 'act' of constituting oneself as a citizen is akin to the act of liberating oneself from the colonizer, Harbi's acceptance of Bashir—his fight for another's freedom—subverts their subalterned predicament. Roissy is a post-imperial setting complicated in *Transit* to question the legacies of French coloniality against the existence and survival of its *former* East African colony.

In the displaced refugee-emplaced citizen dyad, the novel synoptically creates a tension between the airport and citizenship to inscribe the migrant as the only recourse against Europe's absolute subjection of the Other. Rather than reiterate the perils of transnational migration, *Transit* reflexively integrates a critical, collective consciousness to challenge normative frameworks of national citizenship. The novel connects, through a mistaken identity, Bashir, a young, foul-mouthed ex-sol-

82   Citizenship and (State) Violence

dier, and Harbi,[7] a placid, anti-regime intellect, to arrive at Roissy's *zone d'attente* (holding area, cell, detention center). While in a state of liminality, their internalized monologues augur the tropes of migrant surveillance and the (im)mobilities of exile from a war-torn country (Treacy 73). Roissy arguably shapes their non-status identification, yet Harbi and Bashir "seize the silences, the refusals, and [their] flight as something active" (Moulier-Boutang 227). They counter the airport as an authorial site that territorializes citizenship, and in that "moment" that they assert themselves, regardless of "status and substance, [they] constitute themselves as citizens—or better still, as those to whom the right to have rights is due" (Isin 276, qtd. in Nyers 161–62). Insisting non-citizens are political actors rather than threatening *immigrés* when they assert, realize, or "act" on their rights, Engin Isin adds "becoming political is that moment when one constitutes oneself as being capable of judgment about just or unjust, takes responsibility for that judgment, and associates oneself with or against others in fulfilling that responsibility" (276). Peter Nyers also states, "to self-identify as a non-status person is to engage in an act of citizenship" (163). To be clear, Harbi or Bashir do not protest nor are forcibly abused at Roissy, but the fear of deportation is always imminent for the migrant. The very idea of deportation engenders Harbi's acceptance of Bashir as his son. Essentially, it validates the "principle of equality" often undone by the laws of "pure citizenship" (native born) versus "borrowed citizenship (one that, less secure from the start, is now not safe from forfeiture)" (Mbembe, *Necro* 3). If Harbi's act is a counter-discourse that critiques the link between imperial violence and modern democracies today, then in that "moment" where "freedom becomes responsibility and obligation becomes a right," Harbi and Bashir become agentic mediators (*Necro* 23; Isin 276; 275; Salter 49). As a non-citizen, Harbi's concealment of Bashir's false identity becomes "the only courageous act" against his homeland's terrifying present and the host-nation's colonial stance (Waberi 141).

Full of tensions, the novel interrogates the ways in which African geographies of war and uneven development manifest the displacement of the African subject. Since Waberi challenges all forms of borders—the colonizer versus the colonized, the global North versus the global South, the developed world versus the under-developed, etc.—Achille Mbembe and Frantz Fanon's theories of the border and colo-

---

7   Harbi in *Transit* might be an invocation of Mahmoud Harbi, an Issa-Somali who advocated against French rule, forming the Union of Republicans (UR). As a resistance party, they withdrew their support from Somali and Arab communities (in Djibouti) to gain independence from France and unify instead with Somalia. Winning their first election over territory in 1958, UR divested the support of France, conditioning national politics in the parliament towards a Pan-Somali movement. Yet in the second referendum in 1959, the Afar, for fear of the alliance of the Issa-Somalis with Somalia, joined forces with the colonial government and eventually cemented the path towards French control. Despite another uprising for independence in 1966, France held power in Djibouti till its independence in 1977.

nial space helps translate the racist/fascist phantasmagoria of *Fortress Europe*. In this paper, I center the airport as a global, transnational space, where its technologies of control complicate any easy readings of colonial mimicry. I explore how Harbi and Bashir's restorative act(s) of citizenship illuminate the airport as an apparatus of territorial power almost analogous to a 'carceral archipelago.' At the heart of my argument is the plight of the East African subject caught in the racial-colonial-capital modes of global circulation that wields a "planetary renewal of colonial relations" to continuously immobilize coastal East African nations (Mbembe, *Out* 4). For these reasons, this paper is divided into two sections: a theoretical inquiry of the postcolony through various concepts—citizenship, airport, and the (im)migrant as enemy—and a textual analysis of *Transit*.

Acts of Citizenship

Harbi's "courageous act" is a very complex act of citizenship (Waberi 141). As a political act, it is not neutral, nor linear or simple, but spiral and circuitous in its transgressive power. That is, the novel arrives at this "act" through the subject's dialectical struggle against globalization. As a migrant narrative, *Transit* infers the precarity of the African immigrant navigating the brutal realities of alienation and displacement in a foreign land. Although the subjects are conditioned by the loss of home, Harbi's decision, and Bashir's willingness to go along with it, involves change. It signifies action, not only in the taking back of power (i.e., speaking back to the empire), but in the totality of the 'act,' the refugee's praxis signifies their heterogeneous narratives, not their migration or citizenship status. In so doing, Waberi circumvents the flow of migration to disrupt the France-Djibouti corridor. However, Roissy's immigration policies can curtail Harbi and Bashir's 'moment of entry' into metropolitan France. In fact, the aéroport strategically regulates a myriad of surveillance assemblages to make "resistance such a challenge" (Salter 63). Salter asks: "what are the politics of resistance at the airport, beyond the romanticism of the global nomad or the protest of specific policies?" (63). Notwithstanding Salter's critique, I argue Harbi's act, his *resistance*, already counters Roissy in his refusal to 'compromise' at the colony (*Wretched* 62). Harbi's act and Bashir's determination transform the embassy and the airport into contested spaces where the refugee can counter, negotiate, and redefine relations of power.

Is Harbi's "courageous act" a decolonial act? I ask this possibility because Harbi constitutes himself and Bashir as 'citizens,' and by this virtue, absolves Bashir as the

84   Citizenship and (State) Violence

product of post-independence failure.[8] By countering Djibouti's failed decolonial struggle, Harbi's 'immediate' act, then at the colony, and now at the white man's border, at the settler's place, is *his fight for recognition*. According to Jean Khalfa, any act of liberation is an "antagonistic process of recognition," and as consciousness gains recognition of itself in opposition with the another, it becomes an "Other (*autrui*) and not simply the other" (45, emphasis original). Noting Fanon's discourse of de- colonization, does Harbi's act challenge the hierarchies of power at Roissy? Perhaps not fully, but it does confront—quietly—the lure of France for Djiboutis. To some extent, Harbi's act propels him to shape his reality and counter the colonizer, so one truly "*exists*" (Khalfa 45, emphasis original). However, a true act of liberation, Foucault would argue, is only possible when the "*practice of freedom*" is "grounded on and arises out of the self-formative ethos of a people" (*Ethics* 2, emphasis original). That is, freedom is only possible when the collective action of the people wields a process of becoming (Serequerberhan 68; 89). Harbi and Bashir's acts of courage do not propel the young nation towards decolonization, but they do confront Djibouti's colonial heritage. By countering France's dominance over the postcolonized, Waberi illuminates the underbelly of Djibouti's underdevelopment and political corruption is a result of its "neocolonial independence [which is] a *de facto* extension of [French] colonialism" (89).

Harbi and Bashir's presence at Roissy not only conjures France's colonial past, but its racial present. Achille Mbembe argues the politics of racism in the metropolis "is the driver of necropolitical principle" (*Necro* 38). If so, then Europe's crisis against the immigrant Other is based on racial difference—what Fanon called "negrophobia" (*Necro* 38; *Wretched* 183). Harbi and Bashir's difference then, their "fact of blackness," leaves them doubly alienated, subjected, and viewed through a process of "projective non-seeing" (*Black Skins* 109; Gordon 24). According to Lewis Gordon, "projective non-seeing" proffers a racist ontology that is wholistically conditioned by historical consciousness and (colonial/white) identity— "*In Europe, the black man is the symbol of Evil*" (24; *Black Skins* 189, emphasis original). Gordon writes, if "perception is a function of an historical condition," then the dominant gaze sees the black for his "blackness," or his "darkness," thus conditioning his struggle for ontology (24). Therefore, a difference exists between the black non-citizen from the "dominated, stigmatized, oppressed, marginalized, and disenfranchised" non-citizen as per Isin (276). By their existential inferiority—race and the persistence of (colonial) racism—the African, worse than the brown or Arab immigrant from a former French colony, is considered a "plague" (*Discipline* 195). According to Foucault, if "measures are to be taken when the plague appeared in a town," then like the brown

---

8   Although Bashir is considered a symbol of postcolonial failure, Fanon would have called him an "honest intellectual" whom might have led to a "healthier outlook for the nation" (*Wretched* 177).

or Arab immigrant, the black endures symbolic violence at the metropolis (195). As a result, the formerly colonized black can *never* be French, nor can the formerly colonized Arab *ever* be French. To put it another way, the non-status at the airport can *never* or *ever* have rights. As such, Isin observes that while there are "always spaces for becoming political [by] ... transversing strategies and technologies of citizenship inventively and imaginatively," they cannot be interpreted as "continuous or 'revolutionary'" (279). Rather, citizenship is acquired when "time and again groups establish their rights ... as direct inheritors of historical forms of citizenship" (279). As airports exercise greater surveillant practices, Roissy becomes the border of racial tension and the "dividing line" regulated by "the language of pure force" (*Wretched* 38; 38). The non-status/immigrant, then, is considered, like the colonized native, an "absolute evil," a *negation* and an "enemy of values" (41). Consequently, Harbi and Bashir's acts counter the neocolonial subterfuge of France's anti-immigration policies but also call into question the formation of the Other as enemy (Isin 275; *Necro* 48). The "desire of the enemy," Mbembe argues, goes beyond the social desire to differentiate the citizen from the Other, but becomes the ontological crisis of the (French) citizen (48).

Earlier, I argued Harbi's "courageous act" is a political act, but Isin would add any "act of citizenship" grounds the non-status to be "implicated in the strategies and technologies of citizenship as otherness" (275). Constituted as outsiders, aliens, and strangers, the non-status must contest those who have inculcated their political belonging, agency, and community (282; 275).[9] Though citizenship has always succumbed to a "logics of exclusion and enclosure," Isin reminds us that dominant groups were hardly "revolutionary in the sense of being spontaneous, radical, and rapid overthrows," and since the "moments of being political were polyvalent, multiple, minor ... ," it signifies no act of citizenship is too small (282). This means Harbi's act is not nominal nor can be considered void of mobilization, because its effect was self-affirming to him and life-affirming to Bashir. In other words, if 'becoming political' are those moments where the status quo is "reversed, transvalued and redefined," then we can say Harbi's acceptance of Bashir (when questioned by an immigration official) is the very act of being political—his immediate act of speaking up

---

9   In in his final chapter, Isin emphasizes that groups that politically conscripted their rights not only became "direct inheritors of historical forms of citizenship," but their ascendency naturally eroded and thwarted the autonomy of other groups in the civitas (279). However, their mobilization was circumstantial because they self-prescribed to gain political participation (280). In other words, those who gained access befitted themselves not only as those "capable of being political," but also endowed themselves "with the capacity to be governed by and govern other citizens" (280). Isin establishes the dominant groups were not revolutionary nor radical in their ascendency, but they "certainly wished to present it that way" (280). Therefore, we must critique the "grand narratives" of historical citizenship as it is no longer the "game of the dominant few" (281–282).

(276). As a non-citizen, Harbi performs a subversive act that embodies or "provokes acts of speaking against injustice and vocalizing grievances as equal beings" (277). Isin adds that "when the natural order of domination is interrupted by ... those who have no part," and as they confront and defy dominant discourses, then these forms of mobilizing, assembling, or becoming an ally with others, automates change (277). It is in these activistic reversals that the vision for citizenship is enacted to counter whose who are privileged and accustomed to benefits.

Since citizenship naturally produces modes of Othering, it is contradictory in its social and semantic formations. Acts of non-citizenship politicize the non-status to contest formal citizenship. Nyers argues that "claim making" and "right taking" by non-citizens legitimize these groups *"without* any mobilization" from other established organizations (160; 161). Adumbrated by their precarity, these "moments" catapult non-citizens to publicly frame their "rights, membership, freedom and equality" in social spaces where they were historically excluded, and still are in our contemporary world (161). Nyers asks, "what kinds of acts of citizenship would allow for no one to be illegal?" (162). By publicly engaging their "political act" to constitute their citizenship, not by moral plea, nor by defying conceptual and legal ramifications of citizenship do these persons or groups claim 'non-status,' but by *action*, they take to task institutions of power (162). Nyers establishes that the non-status centralize these contradictions—between law and necessity, between reason and reality—to acquire freedom. It follows that Nyers connects agency to "voice," arguing that "to act is to put something into motion, to create something new" (163). According to Isin, to act then is to verily subvert historical citizenship, and whether it is "authored or anonymous, intended or accidental, individual or collective," the non-status refugee has challenged their social, political, and legal realities (qtd. in Nyers 163). That "moment" of the act, transcendental yet veritable in destabilizing the status quo, produces these "actors/subjects," and as Isin reminds us, "acts produce actors that do not exist before acts" (qtd. in Nyers 163).

The Airport and Non-Citizenship

Modern airports totalize their institutional power, thus conditioning the *desire* for citizenship. The geometries of security and policing legitimize the French airport as an exemplary, sovereign world beyond "the limits of the political," thus, fraternizing its codified language of enmity, racism, and death against the Other (*Necro* 70). It is an *excess of power* that "continuously refers and appeals to the exception, emergency, and a fictionalized notion of the enemy" (70). As a port of entry that accepts, confines, or denies entrance to the traveler/migrant/claimant, the airport inscribes the judicial power of the nation over the Other. For instance, the border officer—mercifully or mercilessly—substantiates entry through its legal statures, yet can also discriminately impose "the laws of autochthony and common origin" over the new claimant (*Necro* 3). For these reasons, the airport is a contentious, intersecting space that marries the governmentalities of the state with the contemporary realities of its site as a national border of citizenship. While it is a global port of transnationalism and a *de facto* international zone of travel, it is also a real, physical space that maps itself into a modern, federalized security system (especially after 9/11). As an active geographic site of differentiation, it implicates the (im)migrant subject. Robert Davidson calls airports "spaces of immigration" because they wield their totalising power over the "global migration regime" (3; Salter 50).[10] As such, the airport grounds its carceral logics of discipline and punishment to produce a "strict spatial partitioning" that encloses some, while opening others to feelings of joy, adventure, and homecoming (*Discipline* 195; Lisle 3). Foucault presents the basic formula of an enclosure: it is a "segmented, immobile, frozen space," where the gaze is "everywhere" and "functions ceaselessly" (*Discipline* 195). Surveillance is not only centralized and operates through a "permanent registration" where individuals are "observed at every point," but the subjects are ordered and regimented, for "visibility is a trap" (195; 197; 200). Given the hidden, disciplinary practices of the prison, Foucault argues its major effect on the subject is "to induce in the inmate [insert *deportee*] a state of conscious and permanent visibility that assures the automatic functioning of power" (201, emphasis added). While the panopticon conditions, "automatizes and disindividualizes power," Salter would argue the airport disperses power by surveilling "dangerous objects, not dangerous individuals" (202; 51). Airport surveillances are decentralized as they calculate risk based on "frequency and impact," and requiring a "balance between mobility and security," there is usually an "incompleteness" of control that leads to its "unreliability"—an issue starkly

---

10 Harbi and Bashir, as visible bodies occupying the airport, presuppose the dialogue between space, place, and citizenship, in what Robert Davidson calls the "spaces of immigration" (3). As interdictive spaces, Davidson would argue the airport is conditioned by pre-emptive and post-emptive practices of border control, regulation, and management (5). If interdiction is the "act of prohibiting, intercepting ... [and] deflecting unauthorized movement," then the state exercises absolute control despite the 1951 Convention Relating to the Status of Refugees which mandates signatory nations to grant asylum (Nyers 5). Certainly, in the novel's prologue, Harbi and Bashir narrate the deportation of African refugees by articulating a set of interdictive practices in which state authority displaces refugees, and how, ultimately, these exercises of power psychically affect them. Interdictive methods, some anticipatory and others insidiously legitimized, raise questions about how much a state aggressively creates "migration zones where the rights of asylum seekers are lessened or eliminated" (Davidson 5). Roissy, as a fixed and recognized border, serves as an example of France's "national environment" (5). Thus, the airport maps out "a state's outright excision of its own national space" (6). Davidson notes how state authority "perforates itself by selectively leaving areas of its space exposed to international jurisdiction," and ultimately, it only functions to detain and deport refugee claimants (6).

clear between the rhetoric of unacceptability (of terrorism) and its "unavoidable" reality (51). In other words, this "disconnect" between control and risk does and can lead to a rhetoric of the claimant as dangerous (51). Quoting Bigo, Salter writes "mobility control has shifted 'from the control of and hunt for individual criminals... to the surveillance of so-called risk groups, defined by using criminology and statistics'" (qtd. in Salter 51).

For these reasons and more, the airport is a heterotopic, deviant space. It is a "curious property" because it can "suspect, neutralize, or invert the set of relations that they happen to designate, mirror, or reflect" (Foucault, *Other Spaces* 24). As it doubly "trac[es] the power relations that are continually forged and broken between subjects, objects, spaces, and meanings," Debbie Lisle claims power is produced at the airport (4). She asks, "what is *political* about the airport?" suggesting airports are spaces where "new forms of mediated power" emerge (3). In other words, the airport's interdictive practices emerge and re-emerge "in spaces that exceed the modern distinction of here/there, inside/outside, citizen/alien" (Davidson 5; Lisle 4). Marc Auge also theorized the airport is a "supermodern" site;[11] it is a 'non-place' that inscribes a trinary process of alterity, precarity and temporality (qtd. in Lisle 6; Auge 25). It represents "an overload of signs" and through a "combination of excessive meaning and compressed space," its overfamiliarity encourages our passivity (6). For this reason, it cannot sustain a dialectics of meaning for the traveler visiting, the citizen, or the non-citizen, due to its "hypersignification" (7). According to Lisle, airports are "sites of destabilization, ambiguity, and constant movement," for "just as people never stay at airports, neither does power" (4). Not a public place, nor a space of centralized power, but as a "negative space of banality," Lisle argues Auge's theorization evacuates power, overlooking moments where "significations and spaces coalesce to form an oppressive hegemonic formation" (7).

For the refugee, citizenship begins at the airport. Therefore, it is a scary border because it can consent the terrorizing of the (im)migrant Other. In the epilogue, Harbi explains migrants are "terrified by the administrative mess inherent in the European, my brothers discovering some legal refinement their colonial education had never touched on" (Waberi 134). Earlier, I called the airport a 'carceral archipelago,' in part due to the post-9/11 rhetoric that demands an accommodationist language of policy and strategy in their naming of the Other. In another, the border is a critical geography that imposes the imperial-sovereign rights of the West to be circumspect of the migrant from politically charged countries. Since Somalia is a geographical substrate of the troubling Greater Horn, Djibouti's proximity to it inheres the accretions of the region's regimes of political corruption and Islamic fundamentalism.

---

11   Noting its various spatial configurations, the airport is not a "place of memory" (anthropological), but a "frequented place," "a geometric space," and "an existential space" where "the scene of an experience of relations with the world" are observed (Auge 25).

Despite arriving from one of France's strongholds, the Djibouti (im)migrant is examined through a quasi-military "sovereign right to kill," where the airport invariably acts as a heterochrony[12] to carry out "a set of obscure policies and practices" for the "containment of deviant, mobile subjects" (*Other Spaces* 23; *Necro* 70; Salter 49; 52). To examine this another way, given the excesses of globalization have broadened and diversified our migratory pathways, the "new swarming" from populations of the south—"the planet's centers of poverty"—to the metropolitan have passed from the "*human condition*" to the "*terrestrial condition*" (*Necro* 13; 12; 13, emphasis original). In the novel, the deportation of other Africans from Roissy signifies the (im)migrant is not only conceived as a terrorist but also as the bestial Other. The vague, indifferent notion of the Other is further produced by the "security assemblage{s]" that regulate the border (Salter 50). Mbembe concedes that borders are now a detonating zone of biopower in our late modernity, not between the citizen and the terrorist, but between the citizen and the non-citizen seen as a terrorist because of their claimant status (*Necro* 71). For "in the calculus of biopower," the airport divides people "into those who must live and those who must die" (71). While Foucault nor Mbembe directly critique the airport, Mbembe asserts the border is determined by a nocturnal politics that delimits democratic ideals in lieu of the militarization of the nation-state. In other words, the airport functions as a critical site of hegemony that expedites, through design and function, the "constitutive elements of state power" (Salter 53; *Necro* 71).

Harbi and Bashir's observations of Roissy are never neutral nor objective, and their narratives are compartmentalized into two worlds of the citizen and the non-citizen. Reading Fanon's concept of space in the colony, I suggest the modern airport is a colonial zone/space of control and coercion. As the colony spatially separated the colonized from the colonizer, the airport, in its transplantation of power in our contemporary world, adheres to a form of colonial division (*Wretched* 36). Divided into compartments, the colonial system is a world cut into two, as a "dividing line" is between the "established order" and the Other, in order to create in the "exploited person," an "atmosphere of submission" (38). The colonial border, therefore, is lineated through "frequent and direct action" by an intermediary, who "does not lighten the oppression" (38). By following the "principle of reciprocal exclusivity," this dividing line is a chasm, "two zones" that are not complementary to each other, nor in service towards one goal, but diametrically and ontologically

---

12   I want to add that the airport is an empty space of architectural and technological wonder until a mobile population flows into discrete and separated zones of entry and exit according to time and destination: "the heterotopia begins to function at full capacity when men arrive at a sort of absolute break with their traditional time" (Salter 53; *Other Spaces* 26). Therefore, the competing relations of power, consumption, and competition make visible or invisible the plethora of bodies present: staff, travelers, and the law (53).

opposed (38). One zone is superior to the other, the settler's town (read: the citizen) is "brightly lit ... well-fed, ... an easy-going town; its belly is always full of good things" (39). The other zone is "hungry," "a place of ill fame, peopled by men of evil repute" (39). The division between the colonial and native zones is demarcated by its panopticon design: "they have surrounded the native city; they have laid siege to it. Every exit ... opens up on enemy territory" (Fanon, *Dying* 50). If the vocabulary of colonial division—i.e., the history of imperial subjugation—inhabits modern institutions of power (the nation-state, the carceral state, the global economy), then the colony is the genesis of the "sovereign right to kill" (*Necro* 78). Mbembe warns: the sovereign right to kill "is not subject to any rule in the colonies," and because of this, it reserves the right to "kill at any time or in any manner" (*Necro* 78).

The airport is border policing par excellence. In *Fortress Europe*, the border is akin to the guillotine in the desire to exterminate the immigrant Other. Fortified by the state's anticipatory and expansive methods of exclusion against potential refugees, a separation wall keeps the "swarming" of migrants from these nations at death's door—i.e., *the border* (*Necro* 13).[13] *Transit* avows the border emerges and remerges to strangle the migrant. It signifies the total negation of the subject, as Roissy coalesces France's imperial past and neocolonial present into a new proverbial anxiety—the extraction of the immigrant Other. Corbin Treacy prescribes Roissy as "a site of paradox"—a "gateway," a transnational space created by the global flow of capital, labour, and communication that legislates the territorialization of the nation-state while legitimizing a homogenized, deterritorialized place for those with "the right passports from the right countries" (63; 64). A "*gate*" that arrests and punishes those outside the purview of the national citizen exposes its own arbitrary power in defining (and redefining) the non-citizen (64, emphasis original; Isin 276). Treacy explains it well: "the immigrant's very presence is a challenge both to the relics of *la veille Europe inquiéte* ("old and worried Europe") and the newly designed structures of control and surveillance (*Zones d'attentes, Centres de retention administrative, Centres de detention administrative*, "les lois et les policies")" (73, emphasis original). By suppressing, containing, and regulating "the incoming wave of immigrants from the former colonies," Treacy contemplates "if its capacity for bureaucratic triage is pushed to a breaking point, it may have to rethink the (il)logic of attempting to determine one group of people as "regularized" 'normalized' and another as "cladestins" 'illegal' (especially when these arriving migrants come from the former colonies)" (74). Neither French citizens nor Djibouti residents, Harbi and Bashir are transit subjects. Racialized and marginalized, they are "border-artists ... hoarder[s] of hyphen" (Kumar 34). Governed by their temporality, they are spatialized subjects. As they occupy

---

13   In *Discipline and Punish*, Foucault numerates these "physical," punitive penalties: "imprisonment, confinement, forced labour, penal servitude, prohibition from entering certain areas, deportation"—which have occupied so important a place in modern penal systems.

real, physical borders such as the airport, they become mediators caught between a struggling Djibouti and a racially charged France. By this extension, Harbi and Bashir's exilic, yet "arrested nomadism" derides France's protection of its territory while it historically annexed other territories in the global South (Treacy 64).

The Immigrant as Enemy

The postcolony weighs heavily in *Transit*. With the protagonists trapped in France yet psychically bound to Djibouti, the novel's setting is a colonial aperture that hinders their mobility. Not only does it challenge France's denial of its colonial past, it underscores its continuity. In *Out of the Dark Night*, Mbembe asks: "why does France stubbornly refuse to critically think about the *postcolony* [?]" (90, emphasis original). As such, *Transit* ignites a rethinking of France and its former colonies. Precisely, France's inability to think about the postcolony is a result of its republican model (*Out* 90). In its assent, it has underwritten out those difference from the white, French citizen, and "its originary capacity for brutality, discrimination, and exclusion" now makes France *exit* from an affective vocabulary of humanity towards those they consider the Other (*Out* 90; 91; *Necro* 9). In much the same way the American republic constitutionally relegated the Other—the enslaved, the Indigenous—outside of its logics for liberty, the French republic adheres to its repressive colonial-assimilationist model. In its reluctance to extend representation to its formerly colonized subjects, the border is instituted to hold them out as the enemy (*Out* 90; *Necro* 48). In other words, in the somatics of migration, the airport legitimizes national identity and discourse, what Davidson describes as the "shifting coordinates of the 'national'" (3). Mbembe explains its social effect in France: "the figure of the 'Muslim' or the 'immigrant' that dominates public discourse is never the figure of a full-fledged 'moral subject,' but is based on devaluating categories that treat 'Muslims' and 'immigrants' like 'an indistinct mass'" (*Out* 104). "This way of dividing people," explains Mbembe, is a result of the French civic model, where the "racial question" and the "question of Islam" are already codified in its national rhetoric (104). Newcomers, therefore, are duty-bound to "integrate into an identity that already exists and that is offered to them like a gift, in return for which they must show recognition—'respect for our own foreignness'" (104).[14] Mbembe notes how calling into question France's "ethnic and racializing foundations" inheres the difficulty of a modern nation-state to move beyond its inaugural elucidations of a French citizen (104).

Precisely, Mbembe argues France has advanced its resistance to the (historical) veracity of colonial violence on autochthonous societies, thus reproducing its current mobilization against the non-Western Other (112). By placing this crisis as

---

14   Mbembe quotes Julia Kristeva (*Strangers* 154).

a "disease," a matrix of separation and extermination to rid of the Other through forms of disappearance, expulsion, and differentiation, Mbembe situates the *desire* for the border as part of the anxiety of the loss of fantasy in dominating the Other, the *master-desire* (*Out* 131; 132; *Necro* 43, emphasis added). In *Necropolitics*, Mbembe describes the *master-desire* or simply "*desire* (master or otherwise)" as the master-slave relation that is brought into a multiplicity of differences from one object to the other—from the colonized/enslaved to the immigrant/refugee (43). For instance, Mbembe relates that "Negro" and "Jew" were oft the favoured names in the past, and today, they are known by other names: "*Islam, the Muslim, the Arab, the foreigner, the immigrant, the refugee, the intruder, to mention only a few*" (*Necro* 43, emphasis added). As a result, the citizen's desire is to "protect itself from external danger ... to conquer this terrifying object," despite the "object" never actually existing (43). These intensely driven fantasies, what Mbembe collectively signals as "the desire for an enemy, the desire for apartheid (for separation and enclaving), [and] the fantasy of extermination" are all states of abstraction that translate fantasies of separation into realistic action (43). A border wall can be sufficient "enough to express such [a] desire": "a separation wall is supposed to resolve a problem of excess of presence, the very presence that some see as the origin of situations of unbearable suffering" (43). Therefore, the need to expel the enemy, *a.k.a.* the immigrant, helps to regain *this* loss (of domination). By grounding the difference between the citizen and the migrant, mass fantasies reduce the immigrant to a *thing* and thereby gain absolute control. Mbembe explains the extensity of this psychoanalytical crisis: "To regain the feeling of existing henceforth depends on breaking with that excess presence, whose absence (or ... disappearance pure and simple) will by no means be felt as a loss" (43). The *loss* here simultaneously reveals the irrational dependence on the prejudice or the object of that prejudice. It also reveals the fear of their internalized hatred towards a pro-immigration nation-state. In practice, this schema not only weakens the immigrant in their quest for citizenship but reinforces the meta-discourse about the Other as a beast, as an animal, and as a spectacle.

As Mbembe observes, French patriotism ignites the desire for borders. In turn, it actualizes neorevisionist policies that severely regulate ports of entry—air, land, and sea—through pre-emptive and post-emptive interdiction practices (*Out* 131; Davidson 5–6). By standardizing "pure" (native-born) citizenship through a normative, absolutist inversion of law and equality, for instance, the building of "security barriers"—checkpoints, enclosures, watchtowers, trenches, and other random and permanent structures—imposes "a regime of separation" while waging a "proximate intimacy" with the Other (*Out* 131; *Necro* 44). As an elementary system, the border is the most "primitive form of keeping at bay enemies, intruders, and strangers—all those who are not one of us" (45; 3). Thus, the desire for apartheid through the border systematizes the repressed discourse of the Other through social language and political practice. In other words, it revives the "French disease of colonization," bent on evoking the "very identity of France" to stand for the salvation of *Fortress Europe* (*Out* 131). Contemptuously, this disease "arises out of the confrontation between two antagonistic desires: "the *desire*—supported by a nebulous neorevisionist movement—for borders and for the control of identities, and ... the desire for symbolic recognition and expansion of a *citizenship in abeyance*, [that is] defended ... by minorities and those who support them" (131–2, emphasis original). At the metropolitan center, the dispossession the immigrant feels is a process mired by the "severe policing of identities" and the extensity of interdictive practices on all French border sites (133).

The desire for the border, and its function for dominative mass fantasies, requires an understanding of the enemy as one who exists concretely, not conceptually—essentially as "the other that I am" (*Necro* 48-49). This drive or need, Mbembe details, is no longer a "social need" but a projection of militarized, fascist, racist, and nationalist forces of enmity, what he calls "the society of enmity" (42). Mbembe admonishes an adherence to concepts over the reality of racial fantasy, arguing, psychoanalytically, this reality derives from the "discrimination between friend and enemy" (48–49). He stresses the distinction: "the concept of the enemy is to be understood in its concrete and existential meaning, and not at all as a metaphor or as an empty and lifeless abstraction" (49). In other words, the desire for an enemy is always present and serves as a vector for the racial intolerance of the Other. The enemy is not a rival nor a competitor, but one who endures the "supreme antagonism" of the dominant citizen—especially those who ascribe to the nostalgic fantasies of racial domination (49). By exteriorizing these fantasies, "in both body and flesh, the enemy is that individual whose physical death is warranted by his existential denial of our own well-being" (49). For immigrants, the many gradations of intolerance rise from the facile certainties of racial hierarchy. While visible and non-visible minorities, at times, are both referred through this simple schema of racial fantasy, the enemy, often, is identified with "accuracy" (49). For as intolerance thrives in secrecy, suspicion, and conspiracy, the "desire to destroy" is usually activated when an arena of nationalist hostility is present (49). Mbembe reminds us that the enemy *at once* has a face and does not have a face: "A disconcerting figure of ubiquity, the enemy is henceforth more dangerous by being everywhere: without face, name, or place. If the enemy has a face, it is only a *veiled face, the simulacrum of a face*" (49). Whether under the "aegis of the state" or through a singular deployment of physical extremity, the "hatred of the enemy" requires a need to "neutralize" at best, and at worst, to define them as a "permanent threat" (50). In other words, the immigrant Other is akin to a terrorist because our contemporary world is now a battlefield of the enemies of the state: "We have, it is true, always lived in a world deeply marked by diverse forms of terror ... of squandering human life" (34). The immigrant Other is the new terrorist, and is, not only a threatening outsider, but a *thing* to be eradicated. Mbembe implores: "[c]an the Other, in light of all that is happening, still be regarded as my fellow creature?" (3).

94   Citizenship and (State) Violence

Transit: **The Novel**

Transit is a series of monologues by Bashir Assoweh (a protagonist and an antagonist who knowingly calls himself Bashir Binladen), Mahmoud Harbi, and his deceased family: his father, Awaleh, his French wife, Alice, and his son, Abdo-Julien. The narratives vary from detailing a desert landscape replete with the contrive climate of a civil war, to the departed souls signifying the affairs of the spirit/body difference through a simulacrum of issues: French colonial policies, the history of Djibouti, and the political corruption of a small, arid nation on the Gulf of Aden. Perhaps motivated by the legal case, *Amuur v. France*,[15] or the eighteen-year stay at the Charles de Gaulle airport by Iranian immigrant, Merhan Karimi Nasseri (who died recently),[16] *Transit* might be an intertextual nod to their lives[17]. Either way, the

---

15   *Amuur vs. France:* The legal case relates the story of four Somali nationals from Damascus on March 9, 1992. They were refused entry to France on the basis that their passports were falsified and were subsequently detained at Hotel Arcade. Adjacent to the Roissy airport, the Ministry of Interior rented a section of the hotel as a "waiting area" for the airport and the four claimants were detained there (Davidson 10; *Amuur v. France*). On March 25, the men were denied refugee status because they did not have temporary residence permits, and thus do not qualify for protection from the state. Despite applying for release of confinement from Hotel Arcade on March 26, the men were deported back to Syria three days later. The case was brought before the European Court of Human Rights, which ruled for "the contention that people in international zones had not technically entered the country and thus could not fall under Article 1 of the European Convention of Human Rights had no merit in respect to "jurisdiction" is defined [Mole 35]" (Davidson 10). According to the Court, an expulsion under Article 3 from the state is valid only when the state acts [35]. The Amuur case focused on the men's detention at Hotel Arcade, and as an "appended *de facto* to the international zone," the state's ruling was unlawful due to its rendering of the hotel in providing a transit zone for claimants and visitors.

16   Merhan's death was announced on November 12, 2022. He died of a heart attack.

17   In their writing of Merhan Karimi Nasseri, Soguk and Whitehall centralized the airport as a "transit area," a metaphor for "the transversal condition of our being and becoming" (8; Soguk and Whitehall 678). Nasseri's exilic story, as told to four different newspapers, was detained for eleven years at Roissy Airport, from 1988 to 1999, because he could not provide a passport upon entry to United Kingdom, nor to France. According to Nasseri, his one-way ticket to London was upended by the passport being stolen at a Paris train station, yet Paris airport authority released him to travel to England. Upon arrival at Heathrow, British immigration officials rejected his entry and deported him back to Charles de Gaulle airport and he has remained here for eleven years (Daley). *New York Times*'s Suzanne Daley called Nasseri's story one of the most "bizarre stories in immigration history," while citing Merha's adaptation to the airport now makes it difficult to leave after his papers were finally processed (Daley). According to Soguk and Whitehall, Nasseri's (whom they refer to by his first name, Merhan) detention was due to the bureaucratic mistakes of passport and immigration officials. Forced to live, sleep, and eat at the airport, Nasseri survived on the kindness of airport workers and strangers.

novel's setting complicates *Transit*: it centralizes the French airport as an interstitial space of non-/citizenship, while scrutinizing the regional conflicts of the Horn of Africa. Roissy is the novel's physical setting, not Djibouti. Yet Djibouti is the novel's center, the space in which the characters reflect on their exilic existence, not France. In so doing, the novel prefigures the modern, global port—*the airport*—as the hyper-surveilled, securitized, and enforced border while the local port—*the coast*—is the novel's dialectical struggle of war and strife.

The novel concentrates on the Djibouti civil war (1991–1994) to show the country's rapacious colonial history is still, and always will be, its present. Indeed, the culmination of a one-party rule since 1977 produced a disastrous war between the Issa-led government and the Afar militia group FRUD.[18] Exacerbated by the 1991 fallouts of dictator Siad Barre in Somalia and Mengistu Haile Mariam in Ethiopia, the secession of Eritrea and Somaliland, and the continuing skirmishes between the two tribes, the civil war not only underscored severe ideological differences, but the nation's arrested development. Notwithstanding the legacy of French imperialism and its continuation of power in Djibouti ten to twenty years after the independence of many African nations, Hassan Gouled Aptidon's government became the final blow of the colonially sanctioned Issa-Somali dominance. Historically, the fallout between the colonial administration (French Somaliland) and the Afar over territory in 1882 (which solidified moving its colonial headquarters from the port of Obock on the Red Sea (Afar territory) to Djibouti City (closer to the Issa-Somalis) eventually led to no conceivable exit from Issa rule. Furthered by Djibouti's referendum to remain under French rule in 1966 and now with a weakened Horn region, the Afar insurgency was the degeneration of ethnic restructuring, colonial authority, and the assertion of territorial legitimacy and sovereignty. Needless to write, the civil war was a bitter reminder of the severity of inter-clan warfare and political corruption, but also the overt violence caused by decades of imperial-capital legacy. As Bashir states, "City says war no good, no good...But I don't agree. I say war too too good for sure," the novel institutes the enculturation of colonial genocide in Africa (Waberi 25).

The aftermaths of a civil strife is interweaved through the everyday, social spaces of Djibouti City as a capital. The "City," as Bashir unwittingly calls it, is a representational zone that incubates the ever-present French military base, an inter-dependent nation-state, an autarchic and dictatorial one-party ascendency, and a civil population teeming under the surface, almost vertiginous to the slightest political unrest. In Bashir's account, the city maps the intensely spatial corridors of a militarized state, often citing the technologies of war and the horrifying crimes committed by crooked generals and violent warlords. Certainly, Bashir's narrative navigates the aggressive modes of control over civilians—murder, hunger, destitution,

---

18 FRUD is an abbreviation of *Front pour le Restauration de l'Unité et la Démocratie.*

96   Citizenship and (State) Violence

and rape—but it also mocks the idiocy of politicians so much that the translators of the novel, David Ball and Nicole Ball, consider his satiric chronicle "upbeat" and "funny" (xiii). Bashir's impressions of a war-torn society, replete with vernacular, broken French, much like Ken Saro-Wiwa's "incorrect, broken English" in *Sozaboy*, write the translators, is a "spoken" rather than a "written" language (xii). Though, unlike *Sozaboy*, Bashir's narrative is a "faux-naif," a technique in satire used to "deflate political pretense" (xiii). Nonetheless inspired by Saro-Wiwa's first-person narrative of (civil) war, *Transit* both illuminates and complicates Bashir as an ex-soldier, whose wit, charm, and ignorance is juxtaposed by Harbi's intellectual transfiguration of French colonialism and East Africa's postcolonial malaise.

As a political asylum seeker to France, Harbi represents the old world mired by imperial-colonial hegemony yet teeming at the birthing promise of liberation: "In 1977, Djibouti was stepping down from the high solitude of being the last colonial stronghold. My country was brought into the world in its flag (blue, green, white, and red star), and I was in my prime, hardly thirty" (Waberi 7). Harbi's monologues offer a somber acknowledgment of Djibouti as a neocolonial potentate. His Western education and returnee status (a *'been-to'* educated in France) makes him, according to Fanon, a native intellectual (*Wretched* 209). The educated native, trapped between two worlds, defends their national culture, and "takes up arms to defend [the] nation's legitimacy," for "the native intellectual who decides to give battle to colonial lies fights on the field of the whole continent" (211). For Fanon, political power is substantive when coupled with a call-for-arms on the battlefields of liberatory justice that profoundly corrects the condemnation of colonial rule (211). Harbi's exhaustion with East Africa is obvious, and while his determinate experience counters Bashir's, it is the young ex-soldier who sublimates the failures of the region's ideological and cultural decolonization. Bashir chronicles the psycho-existential woes of the continent's many crises—civil discontent, famine, poverty, Western aid, and foreign military bases—to starkly remind us of the situated lives of Djiboutis. For it is Bashir who aptly chides, "there was war back home, the war kind of over now cause the Big Foreigner they say, better stop that war right away or no foreign aid" (Waberi 10). In so doing, his vivid animation about corruption disrupts Harbi's nationalist stance, despite the absence of Harbi's monologues from the novel's body.

Bashir's imperative liberty to spin off, without any categorical structure, the empire's never-ending presence makes the reader aware of the extensive chasm—physically and psychically—between the two characters. At the holding cell, the lack of interaction between the two represents the chasm present in the postcolony—liberatory praxis versus its subsequent fall—to come full circle. By writing monologues, Waberi builds on this structural disunity/unity between the reader and the speaking subjects. For example, Waberi complicates the role of the *"modern griot,"* varying between Awaleh (pre-modern ancestor), Abdo-Julien (New Age), Alice (foreigner), Bashir (post-modern), and Harbi (modern). Indeed, *Transit* can be situated as

Waberi's "griotic project"(Bouchard 50).[19] The *modern griot*," the storyteller (the oral traditionalist Awaleh), is no longer a "premodern ancestor," but "the harbinger of a new culture of knowledge and action yet to be planted and harvested" (*Dialectical* 204). In *Transit*, the reality of a post-war society obliterates any reconciliation to a national identity and as such, the modern/national subject (Harbi) is questionable. Without disqualifying the national subject, Waberi invites the hybridized, cosmopolitan griot (Abdo-Julien) equally as he invites the foul-mouthed ignoramus—the fool (Bashir)—who speaks of irreconcilable truth, intimating a bitter, yet honest account of the colonial condition in present-day East Africa! Given Bashir's extraordinary virtue lies in his ability to speak the truth of his condition, is he the preferred griot rather than Harbi, Abdo-Julien, Alice, Awaleh? Sekyi-Otu explains: "like the Gramscian archetype, the modern griot is for Fanon the 'incarnated voice' of popular national requirements than the civil servant of the ruling class" (204). This assertion argues the griot shepherds the nation in a way "radically free from the ancestral complicity of the [premodern] griot's craft and epic knowledge in 'systems of 'power and domination'" (204). One clue to help us is the veritable containment of Harbi's narratives in the prologue and epilogue: powerful yet still contained. While Harbi admonishes Djibouti's bouts of violent unrest, and is compellingly Fanonian in necessitating Africa's future, he is the past. To put this another way, while Harbi recognizes justice and truth as politico-ethical imperatives, he must impart to the new subject: Bashir. Either way, Waberi evokes three deceased tritagonists—Alice, Abdo-Julien, and Awaleh—to lay out the historical context of the region's shifts and changes. Their monologues, written in a stream-of-consciousness mode, provide an excess of real and metaphysical borders. Written almost as spectral appendages between the human and non-human worlds, their stories connect the existential realities of a war-torn society. Perhaps or not, Waberi complicates Jacques Derrida's spectral of the ghost in the postcolonial world. Rather than adhering to 'living with the ghosts' as per Derrida, their phantom presence mark their deaths as part of Africa's legacy of violence—as victims of war and crime (Alice and Abdo-Julien), and of assassination (Awaleh). Since their ghostly existence cannot be analyzed as empty abstractions, their presence indicts Djibouti's perpetual calamities. As

---

19   Writing on Sembene Ousmane's oeuvre, Bouchard claims the iconoclastic filmmaker and writer engages with the griot as a "self-reflexive commentary on his own role as an artist in contemporary society" (50). While Waberi's work also engages with, quite consistently, the griot, the griot's power is questioned. That is, African literature has long centralized the power of the singular, powerful griot, who is political. Rather, Waberi diversifies this role to imply its former fixation on a singular character can no longer explain our contemporary world. In *Transit*, there are multiple griots, multiple roles, multiple goals. While Bouchard argues that Sembene advanced the "new griot" as a political one more acutely through film and word, Waberi's "new griot" is the unenlightened and the uneducated, but still has the capacity to fight for autonomy by questioning the uneven relations of power.

98   Citizenship and (State) Violence

an ephemeral being, Abdo-Julien's magic lies in his evocation of the dialectical as critical engagement ("every man bears witness for humanity") while his mother criticizes colonial partition ("who cut up the land of the Son of Samaale") (Waberi 38; 49).[20]

The novel begins with Bashir's declarative, "I'm in Paris, *warya*—pretty good, huh?" (Waberi 3; emphasis original).[21] Compulsively, yet comically, Bashir admits, "Ok, it's not really Paris yet but Roissy. That the name of the airoport. This airoport got two names, Roissy and Charles de Gaulle" (3). Bashir's initial outburst outlines the spatial difference between the border and the city—the airport as an international zone of transit, and Paris, as the imperial capital of French power and contemporary reverence. Juxtaposing Roissy against Djibouti's Ambouli, with its one name, Bashir offers a spatial description of the airport as "tinier" (3). Arriving on a Boeing 747, Bashir speaks like a bandit who is "discovering travel," falsely claiming he was "scotched-taped-in the last row ... where the cops tie the deportees up tight when the plane goes back to Africa" (3). Aware of his precarity, the narrative echoes Bashir's antics: "Act dumb to the cops ... Main thing, don't show you speak French. Don't mess things up, so shut your trap" (4). As Treacy quips Bashir "is the exemplary par excellence of the newly globalized subject," he is also a keen observer (66). He concedes an African migrant is observed differently: "OK I don't say anything cause Roissy's danger, *they might say Africans, pains in the ass*" (Waberi 4; emphasis added). Despite France's anti-immigration policies— "Roissy's danger"—Bashir is happy to be there. His hackneyed, riddled vocabulary, full of ironies and macabre humor, presents *Transit* as a novel that refuses to be easily defined, assimilated, and receded into the background. Bashir's pace is quick, taciturn, and only comprehensible as a spoken language. Through his gusto, vulgar speech, Bashir is intent on making history, and this "act of self-fashioning," his street credo, challenges the European gaze (Treacy 68).

Starkly different is Harbi's narrative. It begins with his itinerary, and with contempt for Air France, France's contemporary sins are heightened. Despite Harbi's previous travels to Roissy, it is now different: it is a "new type of border—one that is mobile, portable or omnipresent," where the migrant is regulated by "an exercise of disciplinary power" (*Discipline* 198). At Roissy, Harbi observes "the boarding time for the Africans being deported 'of their own free will.' A dozen or so scheduled to be transported the usual way; three male individuals will be locked up in the cramped

---

20   Sab and Samaale are the founding lineages of the Somali culture. As such, there are several major tribes, clans, sub-clans, and families that make the extensive and complex genealogy of the Somali people. Waberi's mention of the "Samaale" is because the Djibouti people are descendants of the *Dir*, which makes them the cousins of the descendants of the *Ishaq* (Northern Somalia), whom both are from the Irir, then from the Samaale.

21   Warya means guy or man in Somali.

space of the restrooms, piled in and immediately incarcerated quick as two whiffs of a cigarette" (Waberi 5; *Necro* 101). Escorted by PAF agents (*Police de l'Air et des Frontieres*), the (African) refugee undergoes a processional removal: "each time, the unfortunate deportee tries squealing like a tortured whale just to stir the consciousness of the ordinary passenger, usually a tourist" (Waberi 6). The deportee's "extreme state of agitation" is juxtaposed by the impotence of any sympathetic passenger and an irate pilot malformed by the exasperating cry of the African (6). The intensity of his accursed fate, this Congolese shopkeeper, Harbi observes, defines him as the "savage of the colonial world"—the visible link between modernity and terror often found "in the political practises of the ancien régime" (*Necro* 72). A spectacle, the deportee exists between the state and the people and is condemned through various interdictive tactics at the border. Resisting arduously, the "troublemaker" is taken off the plane and returned to the holding cell, "the retention center in the waiting zone of the airport" (Waberi 6). Like the mark of the beast, the detention of the African deportee continues to incarcerate him. Harbi describes this deportee's fate as "luckier than the ones who die of dehydration in the Arizona desert or freeze to death inside the carriage of some cargo plane" (6). As Mbembe exclaims, "Where are the most deadly migrant routes? It is Europe! Who claims the largest number of skeletons and the largest marine cemetery in this century? Again, it is Europe!," the border is the ultimate confrontation that provokes fear and enforces death, not the (im)migrant (*Necro* 101).

Interestingly, Bashir's praise of Roissy airport, with him being "in front of the paradise of Whites" is countered by Harbi's memory and present disgust: "lost in the bowels of Roissy airport" (Waberi 9; 6). Bashir's utterances, hardly reflective and mostly projecting, are clear: "I'm talking all alone to buck myself up, I look overhere or overthere and I can't see nothing...gotta keep cool, act like professional military. I stare everywhere and name everything I see in the rush and crush of voices an lives" (9). Young, immature, and exhibiting a false consciousness, Bashir's rapaciousness weaves an intricate web of survival and subsistence. His adaptive skills serve him well at Roissy, as following Moussa, his inconspicuous expert guide, allows him to navigate the "poured-concrete labyrinth of late-'60s brutalism" many must cross before entering the French territory (Treacy 64). Bashir always stirs trouble, always the antithesis: His mischievous slights such as introducing himself as 'Bashir Binladen' is a heightened exemplar of inversion. Treacy argues that Bashir "authors a double counter-narrative" where his infamous nickname undermines Western hegemony in an increasingly securitized post-9/11 site such as the airport (68). Equally bright yet duplicitous, Bashir never utters his nickname to the French officials. Amusing teaser, he knows his reader is the West: "Calling yourself Binladen, the most *wanted* man on the planet, the biggest rich-killer. His big head with fine-fine beard, most expensive in the world. Worth five million dollar" (Waberi 23, emphasis original). Admonishing himself on the one hand, "it's too-too much, right?" yet a few minutes later declaring, "I am mini-Binladen, like Madonna dolls, Michael Jackson dolls," Bashir is the apt consumer of Western capitalism, and his contradictory impulses counter his adherence to Islamic fundamentalism (23). Bashir's comparison to Bin Laden offers the reader a set of competing signs, where his symbiotic relationship to the world's notorious killer becomes a national symbol of identity and pride. Like Bin Laden, he is "wicked and pitiless. I suicided men, enemy Wadags and other men not enemies. I trashed houses, I drilled girls, I pirated shopkeepers. I pooped in the mosque, but don't shout that from rooftops cause I was pickled. I done it all" (23).[22] Yet unlike Bin Laden, his warrior ethos is not funded by "rich fat-cat Saudis," whom along with Bin Laden's family abandoned him, "afraid to catch big American revenge" (23). Bashir's bombastic exhibition of Osama Bin Laden's notoriety is to satirically tease out an irreconcilability between his childish venality and the acerbic reality of 9/11 for the global community. Indeed, Bashir mocks America's ignorance of Bin Laden's backstory: it's not "Gaudy Arabia," because "before he got rich an smart he was living out in the sticks in Yemen" (37). Similarly, Abdo-Julien's warning also activates the haunting danger of the "inevitable victory of the Great Bearded One," with school posters commemorating "Long Live Osama," as well as protests, and the "aggressive sympathy in strategic points in the capital," the Greater Horn is broadcasted as a supposed hiding spot—"have located him in the nakedness of nearby Somalia"—much to the chagrin of the unbelieving peasant (108).

As French speaking subjects, Harbi and Bashir are distinctly the Other, or as Mbembe informs us, part of the "indistinct mass" at Roissy's *zone d'attente* (to paraphrase Fanon, the relationship between the settler and the native is always a 'mass relationship') (*Out* 104; *Wretched* 53). The novel's inception implies a treacherous history of anti-immigration in France, and as Harbi and Bashir become indelibly linked, the desire to acquire citizenship in a post-Cold War era trigger "the residual nerves" of a post-September 11 context in Western Europe (Roman 73). In her article, Leslie Roman reflects on the facile discussions of global citizenship, insisting the dominant rhetoric of the "official we" is based on the interests of the "original citizens" of the West (73). With 9/11 as the "defining catastrophe" of the US and other terrorist attacks in Europe have stirred anxieties and insecurities, Harbi's advocacy for the (im)migrant Other is a juxtaposition (74). By defending the immigrant, not only is Harbi disturbed that the airport is a special zone that excises the influx of the Other, for the nation-state's capacity for "refoulement," risk of return for the refugee is always greater, but the disavowal of the immigrant's history:: "I have an old debt to settle with France; people think migrants arrive naked in a new land at the end of their odyssey; yet migrants are loaded with their personal stories and heavier still with what is called collective history" (Roman 5; Waberi 6). Part of this "collective history" is Harbi's portraiture as a living vestige of post-independent East Africa.

---

22 Wadags means male religious leaders.

As Waberi connects Djibouti's colonial legacy to the migrant's plight, Harbi's "final" exilic journey has shattered him, and all memories of Djibouti devastate him. In a flashback to his childhood, he recalls passing a military patrol and asking, "Who are those people? (Waberi 7). His aunt replies, "'the French, our colonizers,'" and as he questions their validity, he is silenced, "because they're stronger than we are" (7).

As a French colony, Djibouti is at Roissy's door. By withstanding colonial domination, *Transit* augments the devastating effects of civil war in post-colonial societies are rooted in a myriad of differing cleavages. This complexity—the duality between internal and external factors—has sequestered Africa into a media-informed frenzy of political corruption and economic subsistence. The result is the mass exodus of its inhabitants: "that shrinking land of ours is crisscrossed with people in perpetual motion," says Harbi, sympathetic of the African's plight (6). Forcibly removed from the colony to the mothercolony, the (im)migrant displays the psychic wounds of a brutal, violent (recent) past that suspends any reconciliation towards nationhood. For instance, Harbi is troubled by the extensity of African migration, like the African football players who shamelessly seek refuge elsewhere after an event. Ashamed to receive political asylum in France, his *return*, produces his *death desire*: "I've accepted the idea that I am going to die like everyone else and I'm not about to change my mind" (7). By reconciling his "morbid, incongruous ideas," "snickering little voice," and "dislocated body," Harbi contends this process produces the new immigrant: "In short, get used to my new identity" (7). Like the colonized, the immigrant is "absolutely fixed in this space," separated from others and "compelled to renounce the 'self'" (*Dialectical* 83). In Harbi's case, migration to the metropolis is a process of re-colonization helped by OFPRA,[23] "the open sesame for any aspiring candidate for exile" (Waberi 7). Harbi's exile offers the airport as a conflicting context, thereby enforcing the dismemberment of belonging and memory: "it's like the silence of the desert here; the hours go by in neutral. Nothing to do except think, rehash the past, obsess over it endlessly" (7). Equally, Bashir's new awareness of the airport is edged as a space of difference, further tabling his prideful assertions: "I'm not afraid of nothing, not even foreigners (oh no! am I off my rocker or what? the foreigners, that's us now, the natives here, its them)" (9).

Signifying Djibouti's independence, Bashir's birthdate is a post-colonial crisis: "I was born yesterday. ...I mean I was not born too long ago, even for this little chick of a country...we're the same age" (9). Correspondingly, in 1977, Harbi was thirty—"I was young, handsome, and strong"—an eager nationalist, a cosmopolitan *évolué*, and faithfully, the son of Africa's future (7). If Bashir is a symbol of the new regime, a "neocolonized subject," then Harbi's return from France at the exact moment of flag independence enacts a conditional *ethos* of liberation in Djibouti (Treacy 66). Waberi's hesitance—his crisis of difference—is because Djibouti's path to national

---

23   OFPRA : Office de Protection des Refugies et Apatrides. See Waberi, page 7.

102   Citizenship and (State) Violence

consciousness exacerbates the limits of liberatory struggle. A late bloomer, "colonialism's exit," so to speak, in Djibouti never fully matriculated with the rest of Africa's national fervour (66). In other words, the birthing of a 'true' national consciousness in Djibouti has been a contrived process. The armed struggle by FLCS against French targets,[24] the impossibility of a successful third referendum, and French colonial power at its tethering ends by the 70s has led to the young nation's somewhat piecemeal process—rather than a complete revolutionary overthrow—further securing France's imperial power forever. France never left and given the proximate hotbeds of the Middle East and Greater Horn region, the two permanent bases—the French Foreign Legion and US's Camp Lemonnier—and at least eight other military bases and several operative agencies, adumbrates Djibouti's compliance (and its continual allegiance) with the "official machinations" of the global North (66). So much so, Waberi situates this existential reality in Bashir's prologue to show France's imperial stronghold. The reader is made aware of the colonizer's grasp, as Bashir notices a soldier's return from Djibouti when picking up his baggage at Roissy: "My bag blocked between two boxes of French military, label it says: 'AD 188,' I know what that is, it Air Detachment 188, navigation base right next to airoport in Ambouli as a matter of fact" (Waberi 3–4). This 'matter of fact' is a presage to the novel's crisis with Roissy, enacting a spatial dynamic between France's imperiality and Djibouti's postcoloniality. Although not mentioned in the novel, the US base is also situated near Ambouli, heightening its spatial proximity as the product of post-independence failure—one demonstrative of Djibouti's gradual indeterminacy.[25]

Transit avers the Djibouti civil war has revitalized the devastating effects of colonial partition and oppression by the ascendant ethnic group. Notwithstanding the political legitimacy of the Afars versus the Issa-Somalis, Waberi mocks Djibouti's post-conflict reconstruction by detailing its crises at Roissy. By inversing the dynamics of French oppression through Bashir's volcanic outbursts, the narrative is quick, fast, and gives the reader no pause, no moment for reflective truth. Mocking Africa's failed leadership, Bashir references his president's popularity versus Binladen's: "our new president, old camel pee compared to that" (23). Bashir's indictment of Djibouti's leaders as neocolonialists, and by extension, African political leaders with their minted resumes of *coup d'etats*, assassinations, and corruption, is fateful: "they say president he don't give a damn about anything, homeland, fatherland, population. He too-too old. He left for vacation in Parisian hospital after rest in private villa-chateau" (40). The president, like other leaders, Bashir explains, "rest in Paris, Switzerland, Washimton" while "we famished an languished on bald mountain there" (40). Bashir is remarkably aware of the extensity of political greed that fuels economic subsistence and food security: "Restoration is very

---

24   FLCS is an abbreviation of Front for the Liberation of the Somali Coast.

25   See my paragraph earlier on Djibouti's political history of French rule.

correct word too, they even say in real French from France. Politicians, they never stop eating, stuffing their face, gobbling, suffocating on the leftovers" (10). Presidents, wounded rebels, to the drafting of soldiers, the Djibouti war has exacerbated corruption in the region: "Me I say all that business shady-shady" (41). However, the permanent hostility between the Walals and the Wadags is complexly intermeshed with family and network relations from both groups: "half the government Wadags" (30). Interclan, intercommunity, and interethnic fighting and feuding, argues Bashir, is further splintered by political cleavages: "Wadags or not Wadags, not the problem. It's all politics" (31). The challenge for post-war peace requires an active conscription against the colonial legacies of divide-and-rule embedded in modern African institutions. Violent clan conflicts "cannot simply be wished away," and since they operate in a "defensive manner," Hussein M. Adam (speaking of the Somali civil war) argues, to harness the affected parties towards reconciliation requires a "consciousness of shared oppression," which is different from "forms of 'false consciousness' artificially manufactured by a cynical elite" (189). Bashir, though, refutes interclan conflict as the impetus for political fractions, he argues, "Wadags, tribes an all that, not a problem. Problem is dirty tricks, corruption an politics. You know, Restoration" (Waberi 31).

Mocking the president's willingness to abide by the "Big Foreigners," Bashir does a translation play on the name Moi (former Kenyan president Daniel Arap Moi) to "moi": "I'd call myself *Moi* like the president of that Kenyan-there. *Moi*, its best president name I know. *Moi*, its simple—beautiful too, right? Ok, close parenthesis" (10, emphasis original). Given the president, who "said ok before anybody else," signed peace with FRUD 1,[26] and after two years, its now FRUD 4 ("Frud 1, Frud 2, Frud 3, Frud 4, all the same and one"), Bashir cements 'restoration' as another term for political opacity (11). Bashir notes the diversity of national and international players: the soldiers, political wheeler-dealers, and international interferers as "real foreigners," the "*Gallos*—you know, Whites. Poles, Lebanese, or Albanese, Czechoslowhatians an all that," are not only "mercenaries," but are "*top military secret*" (25, emphasis original). The plethora of actors in the civil war from Europe, Asia, Africa—the war-lovers like Eritreans, Ethiopians ("from Mengistu's army"), and Somalis ("plenty cousins")—challenge the West of their ill-informed understanding of international politics and networks (25). Indeed, both Abdo-Julien and Bashir cite Djibouti's authoritarian regimes and its coterie of corrupt politicians to morally question a colonial-induced civil war. Democracy, for Bashir, is "that hot air of politicians who take bread from whoever giving it" (11). From Siyad Barre ("real blood thirsty one, that guy. Holy Shit! ... He gobbled little kids not to die old-old"), to Haile Selassie ("bigger kid-eater than Siyad Barre with his wife-there, Queen Menem. She liked flesh

---

26   FRUD: In English, Front of the Restoration of Unity, and Democracy. In French, *Front pour le Restauration de l'Unité et la Democratie.*

and fresh blood of children too-too much"), to the "Morning Hyena, the Ministry of Police," to Mohammed Farah Aidid ("the Somalian general who screwed the American soldiers. Aïdid, champion in battle, Platini of war"), to the "asshole general" who hid in the French base (because he "screwed up his military coup"), to the Djibouti president who had to come out of hiding from Camp Sheikh-Osman military camp, Bashir notes the virility of the Wadag rebels and the Walals government against military power did not lessen their mobilization efforts (25; 13; 24). While the bombing of DRT (Djibouti Radio Television) and other notable institutions signaled the battle against Djibouti's colonial legacy, the French base was not bombed, nor "did they shell the police base of the asshole general" (12). Defeating the "asshole general," who does not deserve a "capital G," Bashir informs of the president and his entourage, "Morning Hyena, Stuffed Hyena, Pushy Hyena, Toothless Lion, etc. all there. Still shaking with fear," announced on TV the general's withdrawal (13;12). With the help of the French, the "asshole general" received a "fair trial," and the president is happy as a "clam," as the general with his lieutenants were sentenced to "terriblific Gabode prison" (12–13). Bashir adds: "The motherfucka now with the little Ethiopian thieves he used to bust himself, I say little cause the big ones they still out there, making restoration with the president's wife" (13).

From "restoration" to Roissy, Harbi and Bashir are the visible reminders of postcolonial failure: the inability of African presidents to enact peace in war-torn East Africa. Bashir laments, "politicians useless losers who don't know how to do anything," while informing the reader of the political charades underway: "the three chiefs, they gonna hug the president," get official positions, attend events, declare "Peace day," while the soldiers are "out there on the mountain facing enemy" (46; 45). Citing the number of civilian deaths to the government's bureaucratic abuse ("[they] put 27 percent of pay direct into its pocket to support the war"), the viciousness of national conflicts, replete with guerilla militia tactics, attacks from criminal groups, and unresolved regional tensions, signals Djibouti as a frontier that is ungovernable in part due to the legacies of Islamization and European imperialism, and the other, East Africa's continuing violence (57). Indeed, the connection between war and colonialism is evident in Bashir's mercilessness as a soldier: "So, kill, destroy the other side, eat enemies' hearts, ok. By who? Why? That none of my business. I get my orders, chief say kill that fat rebel sonofabitch, I kill without fear or fault cause you gotta obey chief" (24). Bashir is the equivalent of the Askari for the colonizer. His recruitment, mistreatment, and disregard as a soldier, from drafting to demobilization—"On the front, lot of us didn't have no uniform. Draftees cruited quick-quick like me" because "war into overtime...president brought in a lot-lot draftees to replace the dead"—cements his despair: "Draftees, they like that old camel the family gonna kill to eat him cause he's too-too old" (24; 80). Bashir's monologues, now grotesque and disturbing, illustrate the cruelty of warfare on women and girls: "we drilled the girls" (12); "We killed Wadags, screwed their daughters (11); "all the girls, they're for us, they gotta show their ass, that simple" (50); and "they say: I wanna stay with soldiers, there's army food" (50). Seen as traitors, the Wadags "would knock them off quick-quick...You traitors, you cooked for soldiers, you screwed all the time. Bitches, I'm gonna fuck up your life: here: take that in the ass and bang!" (50–51). Bashir recalls his post-traumatic disorder, the damage of seeing the atrocities and realities of war: "after that you go crazy," he cries, and as a result, he would go on killing women, children, elders, and animals without mercy (51).

By evocating all spatial and temporal borders Harbi and Bashir occupy, Waberi utilizes the incorporeal to question how the infrastructures of Western hege-monies—colonialism, the border, migration—have eroded African systems of survival. These spectral figures are, according to Treacy, "potential figures of hope and stability" (69). They represent the collective identities of a vibrant, thriving post-colonial Africa: tolerance (Alice), cooperation (Abdo-Julien) and tradition (Awaleh). Yet, they are all dead! In so being, they are a reminder of the failures of postcolonial Africa. For one, as these dead subjects are borderless figures, Harbi and Bashir are stateless figures. Hence, Waberi deliberately placates the psychoexistential realities of the living to accentuate their internal worlds. Through Abdo-Julien, Alice and Awaleh's narratives, Waberi complicates the connection between the living and the dead, the refugee and the citizen, and between the traditionalist and the mod-ernist. For instance, Awaleh is a "transmitter of tradition," espousing how African philosophies of communitarianism subvert the legacy of European colonialism (xiii). Waberi recognizes Awaleh's counter-narrative—i.e., via tradition and Indi-geneity—as a great critique of migratory exile. Equally, the novel utilizes Harbi's deceased wife, Alice, a French woman, as a traditional modernist, a contrast to her husband's modernist leanings. Her monologues, caught between lamentations of Djibouti's potentiality, her marriage, and her birthright crisis, underscores her crises with France's continual disavowal of Africa—"nothing here to worry about as far as our interests are concerned, the same old stories of bloodshed, poisoned wells, kidnapped fiancées, raids on ze-bus, and vendettas between rival clans"—versus her *jus soli* citizenship, which solidifies Harbi's eventual asylum to France (48).

It is Abdo-Julien's monologues that counter Bashir's rough language of war, death, and migration. Correcting how others see refugees as homogenous vic-tims, Abdo-Julien informs us that "real creators are stateless wanders, like the nomads of the desert—and they have only one function," they are "guides" (Waberi 43–44). The beloved son of Harbi and Alice, is hybrid in name, race, and religion. Knowledgeable, interesting, avant-garde—the opposite of Bashir's brutish per-sonality—, Abdo-Julien is the consummate young man. Almost with as many monologues as Bashir, his monologues are full of ancient knowledge and tidbits of European, African, and other mythologies. He is the cosmopolitan *émigré*, yet by his death, his space on earth has been succumbed by the un-educated, ex-soldier—his twin, Bashir. As such, the narrative embodies a multiplicity of modes, codes, and voices that struggle with the postcolonial nation in the advent of transmigration. Abdo-Julien, dead by the hand of the postcolony, is very much the spirit guide of Djibouti. Though it is in Alice's penultimate monologue that we discover his worth or his mother's worry. Informing Awaleh her son's "just as old as Independence," Awaleh also recalls his birth on "the night of Miraj" (119). Translating Abdo-Julien's destiny in the footsteps of Islam's prophet, Waberi enacts a world of tolerance and forbearance, marrying secular, religious, and national sentiments. Abdo-Julien himself states: "I'm the product of love without borders; I'm a hyphen between two worlds" (35). Signaling his cosmic fate, Waberi is implying Africa is not ready for those like Abdo-Julien. Not ready for the native is still under control, as per Fanon.

Bashir's mobility as a migrant is differentiated because of his orphan status: "in city-there, I got no more house, see no more family. The others they went home" (102). Hurt and resting at the embassy, "I'm dead, I'm almost dead," Bashir has no "demobilization money," and if he leaves the embassy, he must face "Operation Dead Town" (127). In Bashir's last monologue, the reader finds out his last trick—his ticket out of Djibouti (102). Recalling the flurry of arguments, the "gentleman was saying: he cant escape in that crazy city with those drugged policemen and all ... France has to protect him and his son, an there he pointed to me with his intellectual finger, clean an all," while demanding an investigation into his wife's death, securing a flight, and a "permit for urgent repatriation" (127; 128). Perhaps Bashir's presence cemented an opportune plot for Harbi, but the novel complicates this simple gesture of convenience. Earlier Bashir noted his "last card": "an me, I didn't play my last card. Not so dumb, Binladen, right?" permits the reader to understand Bashir's adaptiveness is not necessarily consciousness of self, but the self-certainty of his sly resistance—a commitment to surviving. (102). In the prologue, Bashir observes Harbi as "the intellectual genleman who lost his French wife and his rich-son," signifying Bashir's awareness of Harbi's political history (15). While Harbi is torn and distraught by his nation's and his family's predicament: "we describe ourselves as present absentees, weak-kneed nobodies who have a lot to say about their previous life, but the traffic jam of words in our throats makes us more silent than a regiment of Buddhist monks," Bashir tries to survive (Waberi 134). Indeed, driven by necessity from a war-ravaged, devastated nation, the young ex-soldier's identity formation at an international airport requires a radical process that requires greater awareness. As such, it is difficult, at the novel's end that we are not informed of Bashir's final thoughts as his narrative abruptly ends.

The transnational migration of Africans to Europe—the novel's anxiogenic pulse—is a recalcitrant encounter with the process of othering. While Harbi's act of citizenship is "a radically democratic act," he is still a "deterritorialized, disconnected, and newly rootless figure" (*Dialectic* 205; Treacy 69). As such, the airport's hegemonic supremacy lies in its anticipatory power to delineate the right(s) of the non-status, which are often refutable and revocable in the metropolis (*Wretched* 53;

Gordon 57). Isin confirms that, for the immigrant Other to represent themselves, the right to becoming political occupies a space (Isin 276; 277). At Roissy, Harbi's struggle with Djibouti's future reaches a decisive climax. The epilogue begins like this: "Today, exile is making eyes at everybody: individuals young and old, entire families, and whole regions have thrown themselves on the roads with their pockets full of hope and fear spurring on" (Waberi 133). His subaltern voice emerges, critical of migration: "We've left our stories, our books of magic, and our ancestors behind. The danger awaiting us is this: if you live in the present, you're likely to be buried with the present" (135). Certainly, in the epilogue, from the mass exodus of displaced Africans, the emptiness of exilic life, and the paralysis felt in the body in the metropolis, provokes Harbi to say, "deaf-mutes now, we drag around our diminished silhouettes in silence, so lost in solitude that we cannot talk any more and no longer know how" (134). In contrast, Bashir is crude and clear: "the whole world saying: Somalians, Africans, all a bunch of savages make civil war all the time" (81). Both Bashir and Harbi reach a climatic agreement: Harbi sighs, "no one running after us and no sign of hospitality in sight," while Bashir's fervently states, "us, we don't got comfort, villa, car, pay vacation like French, English, an even Norwegians who're nice cause they give NGO money an keep their trap shut" (135; 81).

By constituting themselves as citizens before leaving the airport, Harbi's material condition in Djibouti, his flight to France, his temporary detention, and his exit interview at the holding area are forces which disrupt dominant discourses of citizenship. Indeed, Harbi concealing Bashir's (true) identity activates the space for the non-citizen Other. For in the face of deportation, Harbi sets into motion, without any political mobilization, Bashir's redemption. In other words, in order to cross the frontier, Harbi must resuscitate the dialectic—the uncovering of a new self through the painful process of reconstruction. In this unfolding, and critical of the absolute power of the global North, Harbi seeks no recognition from France—from Roissy—by refusing an idealized, romanticized acceptance of the metropolitan space: "Roissy-Charles de Gaulle Airport. Five am. Silky milky gray. Silence in the departure hall that has seen so many departments and returns, so many separations and reunions, so many absences and presences. Cargoes of exiles, theaters of cruelty and bitterness...And there are a few of us, hunching into the bottom of our seats to get away from the viscous flow of the waves of travellers" (140). Harbi's final act, from the self to collective consciousness, is to save Bashir: "The only courageous act I ever did was to save a poor devil pushed around by the herd of animals who killed my family and the whole country, too. Luckily for him, he was light enough to pass for my previous only child" (141).

Transit offers a restless concourse of experiences of its five characters, exploring how belonging is a process of agentic power that pushes the (im)migrant to act, and in turn, how that act exposes the arbitrariness of hegemonic power. By upholding the *sui generis* of the immigrant's past life in *Transit*, Waberi confronts the border as a place where the contours of a hyper-surveilled, crisis-prone geopolitics of enmity, war, and anti-terrorism creates new forms of segregation in our contemporary world. As such, I have argued that Roissy is a silent character that enacts the sovereign power of France, while the novel uncovers France's patterns of colonial domination that have necrotized Djibouti—beyond the economic and the political—into a carceral continuum. Indeed, the novel's overarching structure is realized at the end when Bashir reveals his existential mobility is made possible by Harbi's transcendental political act. In Roissy's confessional complex, Harbi also realizes his exilic reality is provisional to the material reality of his Otherness. But the novel is hopeful: it offers the individual's act of courage as transformative, while solidifying that migration is, and was always, a way of life: Abdo-Julien says, "all blood is mixed and all identities are nomadic" (26).

Works Cited

Adam, Hussein M. "Somali Civil Wars." *Civil Wars in Africa: Roots and Resolution*, edited by Tasier M. Ali and Robert O. Matthews, McGill-Queen's UP, 1999, pp. 169–192.

Auge, Marc. Non-*Places: Introduction to an Anthropology of Supermodernity*. Verso, 1995.

Ball, David, and Nicole Ball. Preface. *Transit*. Abdourahman Waberi, pp. xi–xv.

Black, Donald. "The Geometry of Terrorism." *Sociological Theory*, vol. 22, no. 1, 2004, pp. 14–25.

Bouchard, Jen Westmoreland. "Portrait of a Contemporary Griot: Orality in the films and novels of Ousmane Sembene." *Journal of African Literature and Culture*, vol. 6, 2009, pp. 49–67.

Daley, Suzanne. "Roissy Journal; 11 Years Caged in an Airport; Now He Fears to Fly." *New York Times*, 27 Sept. 1999, https://www.nytimes.com/1999/09/27/world/rois sy-journal-11-years-caged-in-an-airport-now-he-fears-to-fly.html.

Davidson, Robert A. "Introduction: Spaces of Immigration 'Prevention': Interdiction and the Nonplace." *Diacritics*, vol. 33, no. 3/4, 2003, pp. 2–18.

Fanon, Frantz. *Black Skins, White Masks*. Translated by Charles Lam Markman, Grove Press, 1967.

—. *Dying Colonialism*. Translated by Haakon Chevalier, Grove Press, 1965.

—. *The Wretched of the Earth*. Translated by Constance Farrington, Grove Press, 1963.

Foucault, Michel. *Discipline and Punish: The Birth of the Prison*. Translated by Alan Sheridan, Vintage Books, 1991 (1977).

—. "Of Other Spaces." *Diacritics*, vol. 16, no. 1, 1986, pp. 22–27.

—. "The Ethics of Care for the self as a Practice of Freedom." Translated by J. D. Gauthier. *Final Foucault*, by J. Bernauer and D. Rasmussen, MIT Press, 1988.

Gordon, Lewis R. *Fanon and the Crisis of European Man: As Essay on Philosophy and the Human Sciences*. Routledge, 1995.

Isin, Engin F. *Being Political: Genealogies of Citizenship*. U of Minnesota P, 2002.

Khalfa, Jean. "My Body, This Skin, This Fire: Fanon on Flesh." *Wasafiri* (Frantz Fanon Issue), no. 44, 2005, pp. 42–50.

Kristeva, Julia. *Strangers to Ourselves*. Translated by Leon S. Roudiez, Columbia UP, 1994.

Kumar, Amitava. *Passport Photos*. U of California P, 2000.

Lisle, Debbie. "Site Specific: Medi(t)ations at the Airport." *Rituals of Mediation: International Politics and Social Meaning*, edited by Francois Debrix and CynthiaWeber, U of Minnesota P, 2003, pp. 3–29.

Mbembe, Achille. *Out of the Dark Night: Essays in Decolonization*. Columbia UP, 2021.

—. *Necropolitics*. Translated by Steven Corcoran, Duke UP, 2019.

Moulier-Boutang, Y. and Grelet, S. "The Art of Flight: An Interview with Yann Moulier-Boutang." *Rethinking Marxism*, vol. 13, no. 3–4, 2001, pp. 227–235.

Nyers, Peter. "No One is Illegal Between City and Nation." *Acts of Citizenship*, edited by E. F. Isin and G. M. Nielson, Zed Books, 2008, pp 160–181.

Pallitto, Robert, and Josiah Heyman, "Theorizing Cross-Border Mobility: Surveillance, Security, and Identity." *Surveillance & Society*, vol. 5, no. 3, pp. 315–333.

Quayson, Ato. Introduction. *The Cambridge History of Postcolonial Literature*. Cambridge UP, 2012, pp. 1–29.

Roman, Leslie G. "States of Insecurity: Cold War Memory, Global Citizenship, and Its Discontents." *Race, Identity and Representation*, edited by Cameron McCarthy, Warren Crichlow, Greg Dimitriadis, and Nadine Dolby, Routledge, 2005, pp. 73–94.

Salter, Mark B. "Governmentalities of an Airport: Heterotopia and Confession." *International Political Sociology*, vol. 1, no. 1, 2007, pp. 49–66.

Sekyi-Otu, Ato. *Fanon's Dialectics of Experience*. Harvard UP, 1996.

—. *Left Universalism, Africa-centric Essays*. Routledge, 2019.

Serequerberhan, Tsenay. *The Hermeneutics of African Philosophy: Horizon and Discourse*. Routledge, 1994.

Soguk, Nezvat, and Geoffrey Whitehall. "Wandering Grounds: Transversality, Territoriality, Identity, and Movement." *Millennium: Journal of International Affairs*, vol. 28, no. 3, 1999, pp. 675–98.

Treacy, Corbin M. "Nomadic Elocution: Transnational Discourse in Abdourahman Waberi's *Transit*." *Research in African Literatures*, vol. 43, no. 2, 2012, pp. 63–76.

Waberi, Abdourahman. *Transit*. Translated by David Ball and Nicole Ball, Indiana UP, 2012.

West-Pavlov, Russell. *Eastern African Literatures: Towards an Aesthetics of Proximity*. Oxford UP, 2018.

"You've Heard It Now"
Storytelling and Acts of Citizenship in Cherie Dimaline's
The Marrow Thieves

Vanessa Evans

> Want a different ethic? Tell a different story.
> *Thomas King, The Truth About Stories: A Native Narrative*

Positioning Statement

As a white settler scholar working and living on the lands of the Cherokee and Catawba Peoples in what is currently North Carolina, I am directly implicated in the very networks of colonial power analyzed in this chapter. Even though I am committed to being a good reader and listener who lets the texts with which I engage speak for themselves, as an outsider to the stories and communities discussed here there are undoubtedly ways in which my understanding falls short. Working to mitigate these limitations, I employ a specific attentiveness to citation politics and theoretical traditions, ensuring that the voices I engage with are those of Indigenous and settler scholars working ethically—that is, scholars who center and sustain Indigenous knowledges—within Indigenous (literary) studies and citizenship studies.

Introduction

In the first chapter of Cherie Dimaline's (Métis) *The Marrow Thieves*, the protagonist French(ie) is lost, wandering and wounded, on the apocalyptic lands of what was once Canada. Frenchie's brother, Mitch, has just been taken by settler Recruiters: "truancy officers" modeled after the Indian agents who took Indigenous children from their families and placed them in residential schools (Dimaline 2).[1] Mitch will be taken to a facility where his body will be mined for its bone marrow—the antidote to an illness that has rendered the settler population unable to dream and resulted in "a plague of madness" (Dimaline 53). In this "new" world, Indigenous Peoples retain the ability to dream and are hunted by Recruiters working for neo-residential schools, propping up a settler state structure that is once again actively pursuing genocide.[2] When Frenchie is found by an Indigenous family of two Elders and eight youth, he collapses into sobs: "no one made a motion or mouthed a reproach. They just let me be broken, because soon I wouldn't be anymore. Eventually, I wouldn't be alone, either. And maybe tomorrow I'd wake up and find myself closer to *home*" (Dimaline 17; emphasis added). The early feeling of belonging implied by the word "home" introduces some of the novel's core questions: what does belonging look like for Indigenous Peoples after another apocalypse? What kind of belonging can be cultivated in such a space, and how does it differ from—or extend—what came before?

Offering one possible answer, *Marrow Thieves* imagines what Leanne Betasamosake Simpson (Michi Saagiig Nishnaabeg) believes to be all too rare in contemporary Canada: "alternatives to our present situation and relationship with colonial government and settler states" (114). Imagining one such alternative, *Marrow Thieves* centers the role that storytelling plays in creating and affirming belonging beyond the constraints of settler state membership. Here, belonging within a particular Indigenous community or nation comes with its own citizenship responsibilities. Because Indigenous nationhood is "based on the idea that the earth gives and sustains all life," people should give more to the land than they take (Simpson, *As We Have Always Done* 8–9). In this way, the integrity of Indigenous homelands is protected for future generations through an understanding of nationhood that is based on a "series of radiating responsibilities" (Simpson, *As We Have Always Done* 9). Speaking about Nishnaabeg citizenship, Simpson writes: "[w]hile our ways d[o] not require [newcomers] to give up their identity, the expression of that identity [i]s modulated" such that those wanting to be Nishnaabeg have to be "willing to live as Nishnaabeg" (*As We Have Always Done* 90). Nishnaabeg citizenship, then, is "based on a self-determination of individual families to decide who their family members are; it is an individual choice in terms of maintaining those responsibilities *and* local community acceptance" (Simpson, *As We Have Always Done* 90; emphasis original).

---

1   As representatives of the Canadian federal government, Indian Agents upheld governmental policies on reserves.

2   I use the noun *Indigenous Peoples* because of its breadth, spirit of inclusion, and international recognition following the United Nations Declaration on the Rights of Indigenous Peoples. The proper noun affirms "spiritual, political, territorial, linguistic, and cultural distinctions" while the plural *Peoples* reflects "cultural integrity and diversity" (Justice, *Why Indigenous Literatures Matter* 6; Younging 65). At the same time, I acknowledge the erasure such an umbrella term can cause, and I invoke specificity wherever possible.

This reciprocal recognition informs my continued use of the word "citizenship" in this chapter which I employ in the same spirit as Simpson—in rejection of settler state citizenship and its forms of recognition.

Alternatives to present relationships with the settler state are expressed throughout *Marrow Thieves*. In particular, these expressions manifest in what citizenship studies refers to as "acts of citizenship": the "collective or individual deeds" that produce subjects who belong within the wider ecology of their worlds (Isin and Nielsen 2). In the context of *Marrow Thieves*, however, these acts of citizenship are articulated as acts of *Indigenous resurgence*: the "set of practices through which the regeneration and reestablishment of Indigenous nations [can] be achieved" (*As We Have Always Done* 16). These practices are those that make someone Nishnaabeg: "story or theory, language learning, ceremony, hunting, fishing, ricing, sugar making, medicine making, politics, and governance" (*As We Have Always Done* 19). Importantly, this significant reinvestment in Indigenous ways of being is a form of "nation building, not nation-state building" (Simpson, "Indigenous Resurgence and Co-Resistance" 22; Simpson, *Dancing on Our Turtle's Back* 17).[3] In this context, acts of resurgence are acts of decolonial citizenship that rebuild Indigenous nations and communities.

My reading of *Marrow Thieves* focuses on one act of citizenship in particular: storytelling. Story, or storytelling, is central to the identities and worldviews of Indigenous Peoples and their nations. Story carries knowledge imparted by the land and theorized over millennia to form codes of ethics for living a balanced life full of accountability (Settee 436). Within Indigenous communities the relationship between story and knowing is often inseparable as stories are essential pedagogical tools that empower their audience to become informed about the world in which they live and how they should relate to that world (Iseke and Brennus 245; Kovach 94). In this way, storytelling is often used as a method of teaching that invites its listeners to search for meaning by engaging with the storyteller in reflection and analysis (Dumbrill and Green 492). These teachings are the foundation for Indigenous ways of knowing which impart guidance on how to understand and relate to the environment. Story, then, does more than entertain: it conjures "vessels for passing along teachings, medicines, and practices that can assist members of the collective" (Kovach 95). In the oral tradition, stories cannot be "decontextualised from the teller. They are active agents within a relational world ... and are thus recounted relationally"

---

3   *Marrow Thieves* deeply engages with Nishnaabeg worldviews and, as such, my analysis relies heavily on Anishinaabe teachings and scholarship. Although they are not the focus of my analysis, I recognize that Cree and Métis worldviews also play central roles in community resurgence within the novel. See Turner for a reading of the novel that engages both Cree and Métis knowledges.

(Kovach 94). Storytelling is therefore a relational and reciprocal process that necessitates the presence of more than one participant: the presence of a community. As Lawrence W. Gross (Anishinaabe) writes, "the Anishinaabe are storytellers" and their stories teach "the stock of knowledge and wisdom found in the culture" (155). For Anishinaabeg, understanding the stories imparted by community Elders means understanding yourself, your world, where you come from and where you are going (Gross 157). Nishnaabeg thought—present throughout *Marrow Thieves*—underscores the importance of thinking about belonging as a social phenomenon, what citizenship studies calls "the art of being with others" (Isin et al. 7). After all, "citizenship is social before it is civil or political" (Isin et al. 285). In this way, *Marrow Thieves* shows readers how an Indigenous understanding of belonging, of a citizenship taught by the land through story, can create sustainable communities. This citizenship centers a relational understanding of the wider kinship networks each citizen is responsible to by virtue of their presence on the land. Ultimately, I contend that by theorizing acts of resurgence—and storytelling in particular—as acts of citizenship, *Marrow Thieves* imagines more equitable futures for all relations.

Context(s)

The importance of this bond between resurgence and citizenship becomes even more urgent when readers consider how belonging is too often theorized in terms of state-sanctioned citizenship. Within the Eurowestern imaginary, citizenship is "a set of practices (cultural, symbolic and economic) and a bundle of rights and duties (civil, political and social) that define an individual's membership in a polity" (Isin and Wood 4). Who makes a good candidate for citizenship is frequently defined through opposition with the citizen's other, through what the citizen is not (Isin 4). Settler state belonging in what is currently Canada has historically and contemporarily relied upon a particular iteration of this other—the concept of the "savage"—to delineate and arbitrate boundaries of belonging, as well as the grounds upon which Indigenous Peoples can be granted differentiated citizenship.[4] Tracing the concept of the "savage" from ancient Greece to the European Enlightenment and colonization of the "new" world, Robert Williams Jr. (Lumbee) notes that "From its very beginnings in ancient Greece, Western civilization has sought to invent itself through the idea of the savage" (1). This form of otherness attempted to legitimate westward expansion in what became North America by constructing Indigenous

---

4   Differentiated citizenship refers to "the legal entitlement of particular groups to different rights in addition to the individual rights common to all citizens of a polity" (Blackburn 66). Indian Status in Canada, as determined by the Indian Act, is one example of differentiated citizenship.

Peoples as "uncivilized" and, consequently, unable to hold property.[5] These attempts at legitimation hinge upon the 1823 legal precedent establish in *Johnson v. M'Intosh* which gave ownership rights to the European sovereigns who "discovered" the land "empty" of anyone "civilized" (Robertson 3). Over time, the concept of the "savage" became the Indian simulation: the "uncivilized" other responsible for the definition of the civilized settler citizen who always already belongs.[6] As Pauline Wakeham writes in *Taxidermic Signs*, Indigenous Peoples are too often conceived of as existing outside of the present. In this way, they are disappeared to an "always already anterior realm" so a settler future can be guaranteed (Wakeham 16).

For Indigenous Peoples living within Canada, citizenship was equated with loss. Canadian citizenship was initially only achievable through enfranchised assimilation—specifically, the giving up of differentiated citizenship, Indian Status, bestowed by the 1876 Indian Act. In other words, Indigenous Peoples "had to become 'civilized' before they could take on the rights and responsibilities of citizenship, including the franchise and the ability to own property" (Blackburn 67). Such enfranchisement, as James (Sákéj) Youngblood Henderson (Chickasaw and Cheyenne) writes, "inverts rather than respects the constitutional relationship" (415). This inversion comes through a stripping of the rights that make possible any nation-to-nation relationship between Indigenous and settler people. To this day, Indian Status remains determined by a politics of recognition arbitrated by the Indian Act. It is through activism and amendments that political and civil rights have been made available to Indigenous Peoples without the condition that they give up their identity and separate status (King, *The Inconvenient Indian* 68; Blackburn 68). Despite these amendments, Indigenous Peoples in Canada continue to agitate for self-determination against a hegemonic criteria of belonging that is bound to a normative white identity (Blackburn 68).

The politics and realities of Indian Status in Canada ultimately reveal the settler state's disturbing reliance on Indigenous disappearance through enfranchisement. The state's explicit goal of erasure is symptomatic of the complications Indigenous

---

5   Property ownership is problematic not only within the context of citizenship where inequality is entrenched by, for example, birthright citizenship's role in inheritance (see Shachar 2009), but by its ability to perpetuate the invisibility of marginalized peoples via limits to their material participation in what Scott Obernesser's chapter rightly calls petro-capitalism. As Obernesser points out, this erasure is thinly veiled as nation-building. Additionally, it is worth noting that because of the reciprocal relationship between Indigenous Peoples and land, a Eurowestern understanding of land as property is irreconcilable with Indigenous worldviews.

6   See Gerald Vizenor's *Fugitive Poses: Native American Indian Scenes of Absence and Presence* for his theorization of the concept of the Indian/*indian*, an "occidental invention that became a bankable simulation," drawn from Jean Baudrillard's concepts of simulation and simulacrum (11).

identity brings to bear on settler citizenship, "challenging the basis of the very existence of the nation-state" (Wood 371). Indigenous presence, then, is a reminder of the lack of legitimacy at the core of settler belonging in North America and is a threat to settler state permanence. The settler anxiety stemming from this reality has initiated and sustained systems of surveillance such as reserves/reservations,[7] the Pass System,[8] the Sixties Scoop and Millennium Scoop,[9] boarding/residential schools,[10] and prisons.[11] These modes of surveillance aim to maintain settler supremacy by limiting Indigenous Peoples' access to land.[12]

In stark contrast with Euroamerican interpretations of belonging to or within a particular state, theorizations of belonging within the Indigenous nations of North America have historically been grounded in the belief that people belong to the land and the land does not and cannot belong to people. To live by this understanding is to offer a further threat to the settler way of life which relies of the faulty Doctrine of Discovery to legitimize claim to land (Whitt et al. 712). According to Vine Deloria Jr. (Standing Rock Sioux), Indigenous Peoples "hold their lands—*places*—as having the highest possible meaning, and all their statements are made with this reference

---

7   In Canada, the legal term is "reserve"; in the US, it is "reservation." In Canada, Indigenous children were taken from their families and placed in "Indian Residential Schools." In the US, these are referred to as "American Indian Boarding Schools" and occasionally "American Indian Residential Schools."

8   The Pass System (1885–1951) was a segregationist policy primarily practiced in the western prairie regions that made it impossible for Indigenous Peoples to leave reservations without a signed pass from an Indian Agent. While heavily enforced, the system was never made law in part because it disrespected existing treaty agreements.

9   The "Sixties Scoop" refers to a series of decades that, beginning in the 1960s, saw the removal of Indigenous children from their families and the adoption of those children into primarily non-Indigenous, middle-class families in both Canada, the US, and beyond. The "Millennium Scoop" recognizes that this process continues to happen today in Canada. In September, 2019, the Canadian Human Rights Tribunal (CHRT) found that "40 000 – 80 000 First Nations children were deprived of public services and wrongfully removed from their families between 2006 and 2017" (Hay et al.). The CHRT ordered the federal government to pay $40,000 to each victim of discrimination—a decision which Prime Minister Justin Trudeau is appealing at the time of this work's publication.

10   The residential school system aimed to completely detach students from their societies and kin by "killing the Indian in the child" (Young 65).

11   The relationship between the Sixties Scoop, residential school systems, and incarceration is receiving steadily greater attention. It has been argued that the Canadian prison system is an extension of not only the Indian Residential School system, but the child welfare system as well (Chartrand; Finaly; MacDonald; "'Child Welfare to Prison Pipeline'"). Indigenous Peoples are disproportionately represented in Canadian prisons, with Indigenous men and woman making up thirty percent of the federal prison population ("'Child Welfare to Prison Pipeline'").

12   For more on citizenship and surveillance, see Cho.

point in mind" (62; emphasis original). Land is therefore more than home, land is an "ontological framework for understanding relationships" (Coulthard, "Place Against Empire" 79); land imparts the very ways of knowing and being that comprise Indigenous worldviews (Blaeser 31). In this way, land is "everything: identity, the connection to our ancestors, the home of our nonhuman kinfolk, our pharmacy, our library, the source of all that sustained us. Our lands are where our responsibility to the world was enacted, sacred ground. It belonged to itself; it was a gift, not a commodity, so it could never be bought or sold" (Blaeser 29–30). Rather than land functioning as property, resource, or capital, land is the foundation of a holistic and reciprocal set of relations that impart ways of being and knowing. It is for this very reason that settler colonialism is so deeply invested in "undoing" Indigenous relationships to land so that extractive structures may be installed (Justice, "A Better World Becoming" 21–22). Understanding this disturbing reality illuminates the logic behind settler colonialism's obsession with the separation of Indigenous Peoples from land that goes far beyond access to resources. As Daniel Heath Justice (Cherokee) reminds readers, the goal of destroying Indigenous Peoples' "specific, constitutive relationships" to place pursues the goal of total Indigenous erasure ("A Better World Becoming" 33). According to Glen Sean Coulthard (Yellowknives Dene), "Indigenous struggles against capitalist imperialism are best understood as struggles oriented around the question of *land*—struggles not only *for* land, but also deeply *informed* by what the land as a mode of reciprocal *relationship* ... ought to teach us" (*Red Skin, White Masks* 60; emphasis original). Even in the face of such destruction, Indigenous nations and people have found ways to carry these relations with them, to survive, adapt, and thrive in contexts that consistently work to discredit and devalue their knowledges. In the next section, I situate my contribution within the relevant literature before turning to my close reading of storytelling in the novel.

Critical Reception of *Marrow Thieves*

Marrow Thieves is Dimaline's fifth novel and arguably the one that has conjured the most attention: it won the 2017 Governor General's Award for English-language children's literature; a 2017 Kirkus Prize, in the young adult category; the Burt Award for First Nations, Métis and Inuit Literature; and the 2018 Sunburst Award for young adult fiction. Since its publication, *Marrow Thieves* has continued to receive steady critical attention. Scholars have attended to the text's critical take on resource extraction, climate change, racism, and the impacts of the anthropocene (Amanolahi; Ingwersen; Xausa); its unique approaches to transgenerational and transnational concerns (Brydon; Cannella; Heise-von der Lippe); the connection between grounded normativity (connection to land and community) and coming of age (Rose); as well as its pedagogic functions (Ketcheson). More recently, scholars

110   Citizenship and (State) Violence

have considered how water can be interpreted through wahkohtowin, the Cree and Métis concept for kinship, family, or relation (Turner); or how Dimaline infuses the novel with Anishinaabemowin as a means to connect with literary predecessors and ancestors (Fachinger 128). Taken together, these interventions highlight the ways in which *Marrow Thieves* attends to contemporary issues with a story about the not-so-distant future.

Little work has been done, however, to specifically consider the role of storytelling in *Marrow Thieves*. Emily Childers and Hannah Menendez have considered how linear reality, under scientific progress, is challenged by collective memory and storytelling in both *Marrow Thieves* and Louise Erdrich's *Future Home of the Living God* (Childers and Menendez). Differently, Patrizia Zanella asserts that the novel's depiction of "coming-to stories" (narrated personal experiences) and "Story" (communal oral history) "revea[l] settler colonialism's co-constitutive attempts at self-supersession and Indigenous elimination" (177). Zanella sees these storytelling episodes as disruptions to the larger settler narrative that uncover "the tracks settler colonialism seeks to hide" as it pursues a linear understanding of reconciliation without truth (177). Anah-Jayne Samuelson and I focus on how both storytelling and language empower youth through reconnection to knowledge systems and ways of being while creating the conditions for a collective resurgence (Samuelson and Evans). By observing how story functions as a resurgent act of citizenship, scholars can see how *Marrow Thieves* invites readers to imagine a world away from settler colonialism where belonging is defined by a reciprocal relationship with the land, imparted by story. In this chapter's next section, I turn to my close reading of the novel.

History of the Land

The Story chapters in *Marrow Thieves*—"Story: Part One" and "Story: Part 2"—present a communal oral history of the land upon which the characters reside. Told by Miigwans, Story communicates "precolonial Anishinaabe history and stories of resistance, from the West Coast to nêhiyawaskiy and Northern communities" (Zanella 181).[13] I observe this act of storytelling, and its reciprocal act of listening, as an act of resurgence *and* citizenship that situates Frenchie's family within a wider ecological community of human and non-human kin. Receiving and telling Story thereby offers one means through which the youth characters come to understand their citizenship responsibilities to the land.

---

13   In the novel, it is important that characters are ready to hear Story. Their readiness is decided by their community rather than an arbitrary age that they reach regardless of personal development. I discuss one example of this in reference to RiRi in the next section.

Through Story, Miigwans connects his family members to what they call the "real old-timey": Indigenous ways of being and knowing built over millennia (Dimaline 21, 174).[14] Frenchie thinks to himself, "[u]s kids, we longed for the old-timey. We wore our hair in braids to show it. We made sweat lodges out of broken branches dug back into the earth, covered over with our shirts tied together at the buttonholes" (21–22). Hearing Story puts them in touch with the "old-timey" continuum of events and knowledge that Frenchie and his family carry forward through acts of resurgence. Frenchie reflects on the importance of Miig's Story sessions:

> We needed to remember Story. It was [Miig's] job to set the memory in perpetuity. He spoke to us every week. Sometimes Story was focused on one area, like the first residential schools ... Other times he told a hundred years in one long narrative ... sometimes we gathered for an hour so he could explain treaties, and others it was ten minutes to list the earthquakes in the sequence that they occurred ... But every week we spoke, because it was imperative that we know. He said it was the only way to make the kinds of changes that were necessary to really survive. (25)

Making "the kinds of changes that [are] necessary to survive" means living in communion with the land. Frenchie's statement clarifies one of Story's key imperatives: understanding how people belong to the land and what happens when this understanding is abused or obscured. In "Story: Part One," Miig details how the Anishinaabe People "lived on these lands for a thousand years" and "welcomed visitors, who renamed the land Canada" (23). At moments like this the "boys always puffed out their chests" and the women "straightened their spines and elongated their necks" demonstrating pride in their histories (23). Among the chronology of events Miig details are conflicts with settlers and the diseases they brought to North America, the residential school system, the ten years of "Water Wars" that occurred when America "reached up and started sipping on our lakes with a great metal straw" (24), the melting of the North and the rising seas, the "tectonic shifts" and the "disease that spread from too many corpses and not enough graves" (26). Here, history is not just stories

---

14   Although "old-timey" can appear to characterize Indigenous ways of being and knowing as part of the past, the use of the term in *Marrow Thieves* asserts the presence of these knowledges in rejection of such characterization. The characters are regenerating Indigenous ways and knowledges in the present that have been a sustained (if challenged) presence for millennia. In depicting this regeneration across generations and in pursuit of Indigenous futures, the "old-timey" comes to describes Indigenous presence across the past, present, and future in a reflection of a spiralic understanding of temporality. As Anah-Jayne Samuelson and I write in our article on *Marrow Thieves* for *Studies in the Novel*, "[o]ld-timey resurgence in *Marrow* is therefore not only speculative of the ways things could be for Indigenous Peoples, but representative of a sustained and ongoing way of being that is an alternative to the iterative, cyclical process of colonialism" (289).

of the people but stories of the land that situate humans in a holistic relationship with non-human kin.

In "Story: Part 2," Miig underscores the importance of a reciprocal relationship with the land whereby humans care for land so it will care for them. Miig picks up where he left off: when the earth was broken by human exploitation after "[t]oo much taking for too damn long" (87). He explains that when rising water levels came so too did changing weather: tsunamis, tornadoes, and earthquakes, that permanently altered the borders of various countries. The pipelines in the ground "snapped like icicles and spewed bile over forests, into lakes, drowning whole reserves and towns" (87). Living outside of reciprocal relations with land results in dangerous weather patterns and the land's rejection of extractive infrastructures. Eventually non-Indigenous people stopped dreaming and the "plague of madness" began (53). That is, until scientists found the cure for the missing dreams "in the honeycombs of slushy marrow buried in [Indigenous Peoples'] bones" (90). This discovery resulted in the removal of Indigenous Peoples from their lands for the (re)building of residential schools that "gro[w] up from the dirt like poisonous brick mushrooms" (89). Miig states plainly that if caught by the marrow thieves: "'we join our ancestors, hoping we left enough dreams behind for the next generation to stumble across'" (90). This grim reality echoes the fallout from yet another settler-induced apocalypse as non-Indigenous people seek to secure their future at the expense of Indigenous lives.

To practically apply what they learn about this history of the land and respecting their relationship with it, Miig and Minerva alternate teaching the young characters Hunting and Homesteading. In doing so, the Elders seek to impart what it means to belong to the land. Alternating every three months, Miig takes a group into the bush to learn how to track, trap, hunt, and build shelter, while Minerva teaches Anishinaabemowin (the language indigenous to the land they reside upon), how to care for the camp, and how to prepare and cook what is brought back from the hunt. Miig refers to his teachings as "Apocalyptic Boy Scouts," a reference that falls flat for the youth: "[w]e didn't know what in the hell he was talking about, but we liked fashioning bows and arrows and whooping to each other through the bush and feeling all Chiefy" (34). From Miig and Minerva's perspective, to belong is to live *with* the land by embodying a "terrestrial consciousness" that ethically engages with place (Henderson 432). Miig's commitment to telling and retelling the oral history of the land which informs and grounds Hunting and Homesteading is an act of citizenship that imparts a narrative of sustainable and sustained Indigenous presence. In continually retelling and returning to Story, Frenchie's family bolsters their terrestrial consciousness with a deeper understanding of what it means to belong to place.

On a solo hunting exercise, Frenchie applies what he has learned from Story and from his Elders. When a moose appears, Frenchie initially sees "food for a week. Hide and sinew to stitch together for tarps, blankets, ponchos. This was bone for pegs and chisels" (Dimaline 49). He sees the materials, the resources the moose could provide. As Frenchie stares into the moose's eyes, he realizes that there would be too much meat to carry, no time to smoke or dry it, that they would leave at least half of the moose behind to rot (49). Reducing the animal to its parts results in waste and does not align with the teachings he has received from Miig and Minerva. To kill this relation, this non-human community member, would be to take more than his family needs. In deciding not to kill the moose, Frenchie performs an act of citizenship that shows a deep understanding of what it means to ethically belong to place. Frenchie demonstrates the terrestrial consciousness that reciprocally engages with place and manifests resurgence in the return to "old-timey" ways of being. Next, I turn to the role of genealogy in *Marrow Thieves* as I extend this consideration of storytelling as an act of citizenship.

Coming-To Stories

With survival so precarious in *Marrow Thieves*, the characters must be cautious about who they engage with and who they permit to join their family and community. The disclosure, acknowledgement, and recognition of genealogy is one way in which a sense of trust and safety is cultivated between characters. Coming-to stories are genealogies that reflect the Indigenous practice of what Dimaline calls "Indian geography ... how we figure out who we're related to and where we're from" (Dimaline qtd. in Battiste). The importance of land to Indigenous storytelling is underscored in this process through the way genealogies "map affiliations spatially ... placing individuals and families in relation to one another, and locating them in—by connecting them to—*the earth*" (Whitt et. al. 706; emphasis added). Genealogies are "stories ... [that] relate how a person or a people belongs in a particular time and place, how the nonhuman things in that place have to belong there, and how all of these belong to one another" (Whitt et al. 706). Knowing where someone is from importantly situates them within a broader ecology of belonging. Offering one's genealogy thereby affirms a reciprocal belonging, a moral bond, that communicates safety through a shared set of values imparted by the land (Whitt et al. 716).

In *Marrow Thieves*, readers are privy to the full coming-to stories of just three members of Frenchie's family of ten. His family consists of Elders (Miigwans or Miig, and Minerva) and youths ranging in age from seven to eighteen (RiRi, Chi-Boy, Rose, the twins Tree and Zheegwon, Slopper, and Wab).[15] Individual chapters are dedicated to each of the three characters who share their coming-to stories: Frenchie, Wab, and Miig. While most of the novel is told from Frenchie's

---

15 None of the members of Frenchie's family are "related by blood" (Dimaline 20), a reality that further underscores the importance of ethical relations with land through resurgence as signifier of belonging.

perspective, these specific chapters are each narrated in first-person by the respective storyteller—a use of the first-person that highlights how each coming-to story belongs solely to its teller.

In the novel's first chapter, "Frenchie's Coming-to Story," readers learn how Frenchie found his new community after being separated from his father, mother, and brother. When existing societal structures collapsed, Frenchie's father made the decision to move the family up North. At "what was supposed to be my father's last Council meeting before he took his family north, it was decided they'd make one last-ditch effort to talk to the Governors in the capital. They never came back" (Dimaline 7). Frenchie's mother goes out in search of food but never returns having likely been taken by Recruiters. After Mitch's abduction, Frenchie decides to travel "north to the old lands" as his father had planned. It is on this journey that he is found by Miig after passing out from hunger and exhaustion (9). Upon waking, Frenchie observes the group: "they seemed to all be Native, like me" (16). Asking who they are, the oldest man speaks "'I'm Miigwans, and this is my family ... We seem to be heading in the same direction. Might as well trudge on together then, eh?'" (16). This invitation to be part of Miig's family, regardless of affiliation with a particular Indigenous nation, becomes an integral part of Frenchie's coming-to story.

While readers experience Frenchie's coming-to story as the novel's first chapter where he is separated from his brother, the story simultaneously reads as though Frenchie is telling it to his new family at a later time. The events are narrated through the first-person in the past tense, shifting between simple past and past continuous. Consequently, the story exists both as beginning of the linear narrative and as a coming-to story told by Frenchie to this new family in the space between when he joins them and the years that pass before the second chapter. Frenchie's disclosure is an act of citizenship that strengthens his sense of belonging by situating him in relation to kin, thereby enacting resurgence.

Years after Frenchie's genealogy is disclosed, Wab's coming-to story is also given its own chapter. Prior to this moment, Wab is described as distant, never having said more than a few words to Frenchie in the years they have been living together (76). Frenchie reflects, "[w]e were all a little uneasy around her, I think. She was hard to figure out ... Wab's [trauma] was less defined, messier somehow, and therefore more dangerous" (77). Wab's trauma is written on her face in a "a long red slash from her right cheekbone to the middle of her forehead over the other. The scar had knotted itself into a raw seam that closed the [eye] socket forever" (77). As Miig later tells Frenchie, Wab was alone for two years before joining their family and she followed them for six weeks before announcing her presence (98). Wab knew that her odds of survival were increased by joining a group, but her previous experiences led her to isolate herself and prevented her from sharing her genealogy with anyone beyond Miig. When the boys beg Miig for her story, he reminds them that "'everyone tells their own coming-to story. That's the rule. Everyone's creation story is their own'"

(79). This rule underscores story's role as an act of citizenship, of reciprocal belonging. Although it has taken years for Wab to arrive at this moment, her story functions as her own expression of consent and commitment to belonging more fully.

Wab narrates her coming-to story while the group is staying in an abandoned Four-Winds hotel. Her story begins years earlier, not long after societal structures fell apart but before the cities had emptied out. A long-distance runner, Wab had been transporting packages and messages across the city for anyone who would pay. After a year spent surviving off messenger work, she is tricked into a false delivery by a group who felt she was infringing upon their courier business. Held hostage by the men for two days, Wab is physically and sexually assaulted before eventually being released (80–85). Sharing her coming-to story, Wab performs an act of citizenship by establishing a reciprocal connection with her family members as they bear witness to her experiences and gain an understanding of where she is from and how she relates to the world.

Miig's coming-to story appears midway through the novel, but is situated as having been told at an earlier time—"a story he'd told us when RiRi had asked about the black outline of a buffalo on the back of his left hand" (99). While sheltering with his husband Isaac at Isaac's grandfather's cottage, Miig explains that their location was revealed to Recruiters by two women and a man who pretended to be Indigenous and in need of help. Miigwans and Isaac are taken to one of the new residential schools where they are separated (100–07). Miig's coming-to story ends abruptly here as the family comes across the remains of a recently inhabited camp and decide to follow its trail.

The following chapter, titled "The Other Indians," explores the limits of genealogy as a means by which story can ensure safety and belonging. After three days of tracking, the family close in on a group of two men. Miig tells his family that they have an obligation to see "who they are and if they need help. Or if maybe one of us knows one of them from before" (119). If they are true strangers, he warns, the family needs to keep moving, to take care of each other first. When one of the men hears them approaching and asks who is there, Miig cautiously initiates introductions:

"Ahneen?"
Silence.
"Aandi Wenjibaayan?" Miig asked where they were from. Playing Indian geography meant you could figure out who was who before you even saw them. And for Miig, I could see why it was doubly important to establish nationhood. Silence. Then the reply came from a second voice. "Boozhoo. Anishinaabe?" "Mmmm. Niin Miigwans nindizhinikaaz." Miig moved slowly forward, introducing himself and asking for a name in return. "Aaniin ezhinikaazoyan?" "Niin Travis nindizhinikaaz."

> Mumbling from their end and then another voice: "Lincoln, from Hobemma Nation, out west. Tansi." The second man, the one who had called out to us at first, answered in English and then greeted Miig in Cree. (120)

This exchange, particularly the use of Anishinaabemowin in establishing genealogy, creates a sense of security that results in the family cautiously trusting Lincoln and Travis enough to set up camp with them. This sense of security proves false when events take a violent turn during the night. The men reveal themselves to be Recruiters and Lincoln grabs Riri, running off with her. In a traumatic scene, Lincoln and RiRi fall to their deaths off one of the very "sharp hills," "craggy cliffs," and "shifting rocks" grafted from "[p]recambrian rock" that the family has worked so hard to avoid as they travelled (113). Discovering RiRi's "single pink boot" at the edge of the cliff, Frenchie runs back to the camp and kills Travis in retaliation for RiRi's death (135–37). In taking advantage of genealogy's ability to create a sense of security and shared community, this scene suggests the limitations of "Indian geography" and the importance of its use alongside other modes of observation to ensure community safety. Here, Frenchie's family is reminded of the necessary risk that comes with new people and that genealogy, while an important act of citizenship, is not always a guarantee of mutual safety and shared ethics.

Frenchie killing Travis prompts Miig to reveal the rest of his coming-to story, underscoring the diverse role of story as not only an act of citizenship, but a medicine too. Miig explains how he managed to escape the school but when he went back for Isaac, he learned all the Indigenous Peoples had been killed for their bone marrow and that there was no Isaac to rescue. Miig shoots the man who provides this information, a truck driver transporting the vials of bone marrow, leaving him to die (140–45). Miig concludes by situating his story as one that Frenchie *needs* to hear as he contends with the emotional fallout from taking another person's life: "'sometimes you do things you wouldn't do in another time and place. Sometimes the path in front of you alters. Sometimes it goes through some pretty dark territory. Just make sure it doesn't change the intent of the trip…As long as the intent is good, nothing else matters. Not in these days, son'" (145). This code of ethics is part of a wider commitment to Indigenous resurgence—nation building—that Frenchie needs to hear so he can understand his actions do not put him outside the group but, rather, make him all the more a part of it.

Ultimately, specific acts of citizenship, like storytelling, are effective tools that safeguard the community at particular moments. Coming-to stories are told to the appropriate audience at the appropriate time in service of resurgence and keeping the community safe. When Wab tells her origin story "the littlest kids [RiRi and Slopper] were safe on the back porch in rocking chairs with Minerva," not yet ready to carry the weight of what Wab has to say (79). Still, protocols are occasionally transgressed, and RiRi reveals herself to have been secretly listening to Wab's story. Wab is mortified by the event: "God, how long had she been there? What did she hear? And how could I take it back?" (86). Because this act of citizenship is a two-way street, the damage of a story told too soon is taken seriously by the group as they want RiRi to "form into a real human before she underst[ands] that some saw her as little more than a crop" (26). By walking back family history, narrating their personal oral histories, and agreeing to live under a shared ethics, the characters create a space of belonging that aids their survival. By reasserting an Indigenous understanding of what it means to belong, to be in relation to others, these coming-to stories perform acts of citizenship.

Conclusion

When Minerva is captured by recruiters, Frenchie's family embarks on a mission to rescue her by allying with the growing resistance movement outside Espanola in what was northern Ontario. It is here that Frenchie is reunited with his father who joined the resistance after being unable to find Frenchie, Mitch, and their mother. While staying with the resistance at their settlement, the characters are informed of what happened to Minerva by one of the Council's undercover spies. At School #47E, Minerva was hooked up to the machine that would drain her bone marrow but she begins to sing in the language: "[a]s it turns out, every dream Minerva had ever dreamed was in the language. It was her gift, her secret, her plan. She'd collected the dreams like bright beads on a strong of nights that wound around her each day, every day until this one" (172–73). Her song creates a force so strong it reduces the entire school to rubble: "[t]orn down by the words of a dreaming old lady" (173). Dreaming in the language proves incredibly powerful because it indicates a strong connection to Indigenous ways of being and knowing.

It is a devastating loss, then, when the "key" to their survival—Minerva—is killed by a recruiter during the group's attempt to rescue her. But dreaming in the language can be taught, and Frenchie's community does the "hard, desperate work" to "craft more keys, to give shape to the kind of Indians who could not be robbed" by beginning a youth council "to start passing on the teachings right away" (214). Still, they lack enough knowledge to enact the kind of destruction Minerva did, and they hope to find someone who can teach them.

In the novel's final chapter, when investigating strangers near their camp, the group meets a man who is fluent in a very "old Cree" and who can walk "his lineage back" in the language (227). When asked what language the man dreams in, he responds: "'Nehiyawok, big man…I dream in Cree" (228). Energized by the prospect of connection with the land through language and a way to destroy the schools, they walk back to camp. On the walk, Frenchie realizes the man is Isaac, Miigwans' husband. Watching the men reunite, Frenchie reflects: "I understood that as long as there are dreamers left, there will never be want for a dream. And I understood just what we would do for each other, just what we would do for the ebb and pull of the dream, the bigger dream that held us all. Anything. Everything" (231). This "bigger dream" is the very process of nation building Simpson talks about when she describes resurgence, where acts of citizenship connect Frenchie and his family with their ways of being and knowing.

In demonstrating how an Indigenous community continues to survive and cultivate resurgence after yet another apocalypse, *Marrow Thieves* reminds readers of an inconvenient truth: by binding itself to the concept of the "savage" and making it necessary to the construction of its own subjectivity, citizenship as settler society has come to know it is as fragile as it is unsustainable. The complicated future presented in *Marrow Thieves* pushes the contemporary Canadian moment to its end, actualizing settler colonialism's fear of its own erasure and offering an opportunity for imagining the world otherwise through a decolonial understanding of citizenship and belonging. The novel's conclusion is hopeful, but it does not shield its audience from the work to come both for Frenchie and for the reader. The members of Frenchie's new nation safeguard their futures by sharing their coming-to stories and learning the oral stories of their people and the land so they might enter more ethical, reciprocal relationships. The reader, warned of the future being conjured by the current settler state's disregard for a sustainable understanding of citizenship through relation to land, would do well to remember Thomas King's (Cherokee) words about the responsibility of hearing story: "Take [this] story ... It's yours. Do with it what you will ... But don't say in the years to come that you would have lived your life differently if only you had heard this story. You've heard it now" (*The Truth About Stories* 60).

Works Cited

Amanolahi, Anahita. "The Suffering of Indigenous Communities: Environmental Racism in Cherie Dimaline's *The Marrow Thieves*." *Satura*, vol. 4, 2022, pp. 32–34. *Uni-muenster*, doi:10.17879/satura-2022-4527.

Battiste, Marie Ann. *Reclaiming Indigenous Voice and Vision*. UBC Press, 2000.

Blackburn, Carole. "Differentiating Indigenous Citizenship: Seeking Multiplicity in Rights, Identity, and Sovereignty in Canada." *American Ethnologist*, vol. 36, no. 1, 2009, pp. 66–78. *Scholars Portal Journals*, doi:10.1111/j.1548-1425.2008.01103.x.

Blaeser, Kimberly. "A Cosmology of Nibi: Picto-Poetics and Palimpsest in Anishinaabeg Watery Geographies." *Geopoetics in Practice*, edited by Eric Magrane et al., Routledge, 2020, pp. 29–47. *Taylor & Francis*, https://doi.org/10.4324/978042903 2202.

Brydon, Diana. "Risk, Mortality, and Memory: The Global Imaginaries of Cherie Dimaline's *The Marrow Thieves*, M. G. Vassanji's *Nostalgia*, and André Alexis's *Fifteen*

Dogs." *Revista Canaria de Estudios Ingleses*, vol. 78, 2019, pp. 97–112. *ResearchGate*, 10.25145/j.recaesin.2019.78.007.

Cannella, Megan E. "Dreams in a Time of Dystopic Colonialism: Cherie Dimaline's *The Marrow Thieves* and Louise Erdrich's *Future Home of the Living God.*" *Displaced: Literature of Indigeneity, Migration, and Trauma*, edited by Kate Rose, Routledge, 2020, pp. 111–20.

Chartrand, Vicki. "Broken System: Why Is a Quarter of Canada's Prison Population Indigenous?" *The Conversation*, 18 Feb. 2018, theconversation.com/broken-system-whyis-%0Aa-quarter-of-canadas-prison-population-indigenous-91562.

"'Child Welfare to Prison Pipeline' Feeding Rising Indigenous Incarceration Rates." *Aboriginal Peoples Television Network*, 23 Jan. 2020, https://www.aptnnews.ca/nation-to-nation/child-welfare-to-prison-pipeline-feeding-rising-indigenous-incarceration-rates/.

Childers, Emily, and Hannah Menendez. "Apocalypse When? Storytelling and Spiralic Time in Cherie Dimaline's *The Marrow Thieves* and Louise Erdrich's *Future Home of the Living God.*" *Text Matters: A Journal of Literature, Theory and Culture*, no. 12, 2022, pp. 211–26. *Lodz UP*, https://doi.org/10.18778/2083-2931.12.13.

Cho, Lily. *Mass Capture: Chinese Head Tax and the Making of Non-Citizens.* McGill-Queen's UP, 2021.

Coulthard, Glen Sean. "Place Against Empire: Understanding Indigenous Anti-Colonialism." *Affinities: A Journal of Radical Theory, Culture, and Action*, vol. 4, no. 2, 2010, pp. 79–83.

—. *Red Skin, White Masks: Rejecting the Colonial Politics of Recognition.* U of Minnesota P, 2014.

Deloria Jr., Vine. *God is Red: A Native View of Religion.* Fulcrum Publishing, 1992.

Dimaline, Cherie. *The Marrow Thieves.* Cormorant Books, 2017.

Dumbrill, Gary C., and Jacquie Green. "Indigenous Knowledge in the Social Work Academy." *Social Work Education*, vol. 27, no. 5, 2008, pp. 489–503, *Taylor & Francis*, doi:10.1080/02615470701379891.

Fachinger, Petra. "Anishinaabemowin in *Indianland*, *The Marrow Thieves*, and *Crow Winter* as a Key to Cultural and Political Resurgence." *Studies in Canadian Literature*, vol. 46, no. 2, 2021, pp. 127–49.

Finaly, Carol. "For Indigenous Women, Prisons Are the Adult Version of Residential Schools." *The Globe and Mail*, 28 Mar. 2016, https://www.theglobeandmail.com/opinion/for-indigenous-women-prisons-are-the-adult-version-of-residential-schools/article29388499/.

Gross, Lawrence William. *Anishinaabe Ways of Knowing and Being.* Routledge, 2016.

Hay, Travis, et al. "Dr. Peter Bryce (1853-1932): Whistleblower on Residential Schools." *CMAJ*, vol. 192, no. 9, 2020, pp. 223–24. https://doi.org/10.1503/cmaj.190862.

Heise-von der Lippe, Anya. "'What Language Do You Dream in?' Re-Imagining the Future Of (Post-)Human Kinships." *Kinship and Collective Action: In Literature and*

Culture, edited by Gero Bauer et al., Narr Francke Attempto Verlag GmbH + Co. KG, 2020, pp. 83–102.

Henderson, James (Sákéj) Youngblood. "Sui Generis and Treaty Citizenship." *Citizenship Studies*, vol. 6, no. 4, 2002, pp. 415–40. *Scholars Portal Journals*, https://resolver-scholarsportal-info.ezproxy.library.yorku.ca/resolve/13621025/v06i0004/415_sgatc.xml.

Ingwersen, Moritz. "Reclaiming Fossil Ghosts: Indigenous Resistance to Resource Extraction In Works by Warren Cariou, Cherie Dimaline, and Nathan Adler." *Canadian Literature*, no. 240, 2020, pp. 59–76.

Iseke, Judy, and BMJK Brennus. "CHAPTER SIXTEEN: Learning Life Lessons fromIndigenous Storytelling with Tom McCallum." *Counterpoints*, vol. 379, 2011, pp. 245–61. *JSTOR*, https://www.jstor.org/stable/42980900.

Isin, Engin. *Being Political: Genealogies of Citizenship*. U of Minnesota P, 2002.

Isin, Engin, and Greg Nielsen. "Introduction: Acts of Citizenship." *Acts of Citizenship*, edited By Engin Isin and Greg Nielsen, Zed Books, 2013, pp. 1–12.

Isin, Engin, and Patricia K. Wood. *Citizenship and Identity*, Sage Publications Ltd., 1999.

Justice, Daniel Heath. "A Better World Becoming: Placing Critical Indigenous studies." *Critical Indigenous Studies: Engagements in First World Locations*, edited by Aileen Moreton-Robinson, U of Arizona P, 2016, pp. 19–32.

—. *Why Indigenous Literatures Matter*. Wilfred Laurier UP, 2018.

Ketcheson, Ann. "The Marrow Thieves." *Canadian Review of Materials*, vol. 24, no. 1, 2017. *ProQuest*, http://ezproxy.library.yorku.ca/login?url=https://www-proquest-com.ezproxy.library.yorku.ca/docview/1942191740?accountid=15182.

King, Thomas. *The Inconvenient Indian: A Curious Account of Native People in North America*. U of Minnesota P, 2012.

—. *The Truth About Stories: A Native Narrative*. House of Anansi Press, 2011.

Kovach, Margaret. *Indigenous Methodologies: Characteristics, Conversations, and Contexts*. U of Toronto P, 2009.

MacDonald, Nancy. "Canada's Prisons Are the 'New Residential Schools.'" *Maclean's*, 18 Feb. 2016, https://www.macleans.ca/news/canada/canadas-prisons-are-the-new-residential-schools/.

Robertson, Lindsay Gordon. *Conquest by Law: How the Discovery of America Dispossessed Indigenous Peoples of Their Lands*. Oxford UP, 2005.

Rose, Gwen. "Coming of Age in Indigenous Science Fiction: Cherie Dimaline's *The Marrow Thieves* and D'Arcy McNickle's *Runner in the Sun*." *Journal of Science Fiction*, vol. 5, no. 2, 2022, pp. 8–18. *MOSF Journal of Science Fiction*, https://publish.lib.umd.edu/?journal=scifi&page=article&op=view&path%5B%5D=585.

Samuelson, Anah-Jayne, and Vanessa Evans. "'Real Old-Timey': Storytelling and the Language of Resurgence in Cherie Dimaline's *The Marrow Thieves*." *Studies in the Novel*, vol. 54, no. 3, 2022, pp. 274–92. *Project MUSE*, doi:10.1353/sdn.2022.0023.

Settee, Priscilla. "Indigenous Knowledge: Multiple Approaches." *Counterpoints*, vol. 379, 2011, pp. 434–50. *JSTOR*, http://www.jstor.org/stable/42980913.

Simpson, Leanne Betasamosake. *As We Have Always Done: Indigenous Freedom Through Radical Resistance*. U of Minnesota P, 2017.

—. *Dancing on Our Turtle's Back: Stories of Nishnaabeg Re-Creation, Resurgence, and New Emergence*. ARP Books, 2011.

—. "Indigenous Resurgence and Co-Resistance." *Critical Ethnic Studies*, vol. 2, no. 2, 2016, pp. 19–34. *JSTOR*, https://www.jstor.org/stable/10.5749/jcritethnstud.2.2.0019.

Turner, Christina. "Water as Wahkohtowin in Cherie Dimaline's *The Marrow Thieves*." *Studies in American Indian Literatures*, vol. 33, no. 3–4, 2021, pp. 98–124. *Project MUSE*, https://doi.org/10.1353/ail.2021.0011.

Vizenor, Gerald. *Fugitive Poses: Native American Indian Scenes of Absence and Presence*. U Of Nebraska P, 2000.

Wakeham, Pauline. *Taxidermic Signs: Reconstructing Aboriginality*. U of Minnesota P, 2008.

Whitt, Laurie Anne, et al. "Belonging to Land: Indigenous Knowledge Systems and the Natural World." *Oklahoma City University Law Review*, vol. 26, no. 2, 2001, pp. 701–43. *HeinOnline*, https://heinonline-org.ezproxy.library.yorku.ca/HOL/Page?handle=hein.journals/okcu26&id=709&collection=journals&index=journals/okcu.

Williams Jr., Robert A. *Savage Anxieties: The Invention of Western Civilization*. Palgrave Macmillan, 2012.

Wood, Patricia K. "Aboriginal/Indigenous Citizenship: An Introduction." *Citizenship Studies*, vol. 7, no. 4, 2003, pp. 371–78. *Taylor & Francis*, https://doi.org/10.1080/1362102032000134930.

Xausa, Chiara. "Decolonizing the Anthropocene: 'Slow Violence' and Indigenous Resistance In Cherie Dimaline's *The Marrow Thieves*." *Il Tolomeo*, vol. 22, 2020, pp. 87–99. *Research Gate*, https://www.researchgate.net/publication/350902487_Decolonizing_the_Anthropocene_'Slow_Violence'_and_Indigenous_Resistance_in_Cherie_Dimaline's_The_Marrow_Thieves.

Young, Bryanne. "'Killing the Indian in the Child': Death, Cruelty, and Subject-Formation in The Canadian Indian Residential School System." *Mosaic: An Interdisciplinary Critical Journal*, vol. 48, no. 4, 2015, pp. 63–76. *JSTOR*, https://www.jstor.org/stable/44030407.

Younging, Gregory. *Elements of Indigenous Style: A Guide for Writing By and About Indigenous Peoples*. Brush Publishing, 2018.

Zanella, Patrizia. "Witnessing Story and Creating Kinship in a New Era of Residential Schools: Cherie Dimaline's *The Marrow Thieves*." *Studies in American Indian Literatures*, vol. 32, no. 3–4, 2020, pp. 176–200. *Project MUSE*, doi: 10.1353/ail.2020.0023.

"Clean Body, Clean Mind, Clean Job"
The Role of Penal Voluntary Sector Organizations
in Constructing "Good" Carceral Citizens

Kaitlyn Quinn and Erika Canossini[1]

Introduction

Punishment and society is a subfield of research at the intersection of criminology and law and society (Hannah-Moffat and Lynch 119). Scholars in this area are connected by their desire to interpret punishment as a social process and phenomenon (Garland). In the United States, this has dominantly meant reckoning with the realities of mass incarceration. Between 1972 and 2000, the number of people incarcerated in this country rose more than 600 percent (Pettit and Western 151). At 639 prisoners per 100,000 population, the United States has the world's highest incarceration rate (World Prison Brief). At its peak, this amounted to almost 2.3 million people behind bars, to say nothing of the nearly 4.3 million others serving community sentences (Phelps and Ruhland 2–3). Scholars often use the term *mass supervision* to refer to the latter forms of punishment (e.g., probation, parole, electronic monitoring) as well as the continued nature of penal supervision after incarceration (McNeill 11–14)—or as Gwen Robinson et al. put it, forms of "punishment *in* society" (334). The vast majority imprisoned or under other forms of correctional supervision are people of color (Wacquant 96). Consider that one in seventeen white men have a lifetime likelihood of imprisonment compared to one in three Black men and one in six Latinx men (The Sentencing Project). These disparities are similar for women, with one in 111 white women facing a lifetime likelihood of imprisonment compared to one in eighteen Black women and one in forty-five Latinx women (The Sentencing Project). Some scholars have linked these racial disparities to the War on Drugs which disproportionately targeted people of color (e.g., Davis; Nunn).[2] Other schol-

---

1   Both authors contributed equally to this manuscript.
2   See Pfaff for an account that complicates the primacy granted to the War on Drugs in explanations of mass incarceration.

ars have focused on the continuities between mass incarceration and other racial caste systems like slavery, Jim Crow, and urban ghettos (e.g., Alexander; Wacquant).[3]

Upon release from prison, criminalized individuals must also contend with what Reuben Miller called *the afterlife of mass incarceration*. This phrase highlights mass incarceration's tentacular reach, suggesting that we cannot understand its impacts by only looking at the prison. Instead, we must center the realities and perspectives of those who are "trying to find a place in society after incarceration" (Western xiii). Existing research has demonstrated the lingering challenges incarceration creates for individuals (e.g., Harding et al.; Quinn "Dispositions That Matter"), their families (e.g., Comfort), and communities (e.g., Wacquant). Given the harsh realities individuals experience upon exiting prison, scholars have written about criminalization as cultivating a kind of attenuated citizenship (e.g., Lerman and Weaver; Smiley). Some scholars have even proposed *carceral citizenship* as a unique form of social membership (e.g., Miller and Stuart; Phelps and Ruhland). This view of citizenship eschews strictly legal or political interpretations of belonging in favor of a wider appreciation of how punishment, governance, and exclusion animate the daily lives and experiences of so-called carceral citizens. Accordingly, research on carceral citizenship cannot merely account for the consequences of direct contact between individuals and the criminal justice system (i.e., through police, courts, and prisons). Instead, understanding the "full nature of citizenship in the carceral age" requires explorations of informal and alternative sites of its construction and careful attention to how carceral citizens are disciplined by a "diverse universe of social actors" in their everyday lives after imprisonment (Miller and Stuart 535).

This chapter offers a response to this challenge by exploring the role that the penal voluntary sector (PVS) plays in the construction of carceral citizens. The PVS consists of charitable and non-profit organizations that work with criminalized individuals through prison- and community-based programming (Corcoran 33). Examples include organizations offering employment counseling, spiritual guidance, prison visitation, letter writing, housing support, drug/alcohol treatment, and a variety of soft skills programming. Scholars interested in these organizations have highlighted the role of neoliberalism and welfare state retrenchment in accentuating the longstanding work of volunteers and voluntary organizations in criminal justice contexts (Quinn, "Inside the Penal Voluntary Sector" 162). In the United States, for instance, the number of PVS organizations has tripled in recent years, growing "in tandem with the rise of mass incarceration" (Miller and Purifoye 207). Despite their increasing importance, PVS organizations remain poorly understood (Tomczak and Buck; Quinn et al.), particularly from the vantage point of citizenship.

In this chapter we focus on the (re)integrative roles PVS organizations perform for individuals exiting prison in the United States. We examine how they make

---

3   See Gottschalk for some limitations of these vantage points.

assessments about what is "wrong" with criminalized individuals, the ideals they encourage criminalized individuals to aspire to, and the practical techniques they rely on to shape criminalized individuals in this image (McKim 3; Quinn and Goodman). Our central argument is that in providing certain kinds of support and advice (and not others), PVS organizations are offering criminalized individuals a pathway to social inclusion as *"good" carceral citizens*. In mobilizing this expression, we seek to highlight the inclusionary aspirations of PVS organizations and simultaneously problematize how they wield these aspirations to discipline and shape criminalized individuals into good carceral citizens.

The rest of this chapter is structured as follows. We summarize the existing research on carceral citizenship and detail our specific contribution to this literature. We introduce our data and methods, describing the PVS organizations we examined and the websites and documents we analyzed. Our analysis unfolds across four sections. The first positions PVS organizations as sites for the construction of good carceral citizenship by examining their widespread use of the term *returning citizens* and the priority they granted to personal transformation. The remaining analysis sections trace a politics of inclusion among these organizations that depended upon former prisoners' pursuit and performance of three *core conditions* of good carceral citizenship: (i) employment, (ii) prosocial emotion management, and (iii) sobriety. We close with a critique of this conceptualization and propose an agenda for future research that may extend this chapter's key findings.

Carceral Citizenship

Broadly speaking, citizenship is understood as membership to a particular political community and its associated responsibilities, rights, and privileges (Kymlicka and Norman). Aligning with this view of citizenship as a legal category, sociologists and criminologists have written about possessing a criminal record as a kind of attenuated citizenship (e.g., Lerman and Weaver) involving losses of freedom (Sykes), voting rights (Manza and Uggen), and access to public funds (Owens and Smith). In addition to these impairments to civil and political citizenship, scholars have argued that possessing a criminal record also affects what Marshall named economic and social citizenship (Sered).[4] For instance, in the American context, participating in the work force and having a home are key markers of citizenship (Sered). However, employment and housing are difficult to attain for individuals with a criminal record (Pager; Kropf). If individuals are without a job or if they are

---

4   According to T. H. Marshall, the core components of citizenship are civil, political, and economic/social citizenship.

only able to secure temporary occupations, they cannot access citizenship entitlements such as healthcare and retirement benefits. Their ability to purchase goods and services—another core element of citizenship in capitalistic societies—is also limited (Sered). Furthermore, people with criminal records encounter challenges in attaining independence, self-control, and sobriety, which are attributes generally associated with social citizenship in the United States (Glenn "Citizenship and Inequality").

Therefore, when individuals are punished by and processed through the criminal justice system, it is not only their rights that are affected, but also their ability to participate in the public sphere. Criminalized individuals' membership to the community is not fully reinstated once they are released from prison. While they do not become stateless in Arendt's terms (as they still formally belong to the nation's political community), criminalization does "strip and differentiate rights among citizens," even after they serve sentences (Loyd 5). Such denial and disparity of the full rights of citizenship to individuals with felony convictions also impacts their abilities to perform the duties associated with citizenship, that is their engagement with public life (Manza et al.). As rights generally guaranteed and afforded to members of society are disregarded or left unprotected by the state, criminalized individuals' participation in civic, economic, and social life is compromised—a condition referred to as second-class, diminished, or conditional citizenship (Sered; Weaver and Lerman).

However, scholars have recently started to differentiate carceral citizenship from these conceptualizations to emphasize the unique way in which criminalized individuals experience citizenship. For instance, Miller and Stuart defined *carceral citizenship* as "a distinct form of political membership experienced by and enacted upon people" that "begins at the moment of criminal conviction" (533). Unlike second-class or diminished citizenship, carceral citizens are not only subject to restrictions and duties, but they also acquire (perverse) benefits. In fact, besides social exclusion and the collateral consequences of a criminal record, this alternate legal standing provides some unique entitlements such as the rights to food, clothing, and shelter when incarcerated, and added assistance or privileges under "felon friendly" policies while reentering society (Miller and Stuart). It is this mix of restraints, obligations, and entitlements that makes carceral citizens a community with a distinctive social, political, and economic life.

More specifically, Miller and Stuart identified three defining features of carceral citizenship which convey the supposed "essence" of "offenders" to others and lead to their exclusion and vulnerability. First, carceral citizens have a novel relationship with "stabilizing institutions" such as the labor and housing market. Second, they take part in "practices of supervision, corrections and care" which are not open to conventional members of society (e.g., reentry programs, counseling, and probation) (Miller and Stuart 536). Finally, carceral citizens are managed, corrected, and sanctioned by third parties (such as PVS organizations) both in their private and public lives. Whereas these three features constitute a distinct community, the collective experiences of carceral citizens should not be understood as monolithic (Smith and Kinzel). Individuals' intersecting identities such as race and gender (Loyd; Miller and Stuart) and different types of convictions (Smith and Kinzel) also interact with this alternate legal status.

Over the last few decades, scholars have spent considerable time untangling how mass incarceration has worked as a "crucial mechanism for constructing, diminishing and enforcing citizenship in the United States" (Sered 1; Alexander; Bosworth et al.). However, the literature examining citizenship in relation to mass supervision is limited (Uggen et al.; Miller and Stuart). More research is necessary to fully grasp the relationship between carceral citizenship and mass supervision, including how and where this type of citizenship is constructed and with what consequences for criminalized people. To do so, we argue that it is necessary to follow recent sociological theorizations of citizenship that go beyond citizenship as a fixed legal status to emphasize its fluidity. In particular, it is important to explore how "citizenship is produced through everyday practices and struggles" (Glenn, "Constructing Citizenship" 1). While citizenship continues to describe the relationship between the state and citizens, it also encompasses the relationship between citizens and the community. In other words, recognition by other members of the community (or *translation* as Miller and Stuart called it) also matters as it is through this process that the boundaries of citizenship are established (Glenn "Constructing Citizenship"). By granting or denying recognition, community members mark who is entitled to receive civil, political, and social rights. Therefore, citizenship is also a matter of belonging (Glenn "Constructing Citizenship").

Since PVS organizations work with individuals reentering society, who are reacquiring their full membership to the nation state, they constitute ideal sites to explore carceral citizenship. By assisting individuals in this phase of their lives, these organizations take part in local practices that recognize or deny citizenship status and its attributes to this population. In doing so, they act as intermediaries between returning citizens and the state (and its institutions), but also between carceral citizens and the community. PVS organizations, therefore, are located in a unique position—in locales where citizenship is built in practice (substantive citizenship) and in theory (formal citizenship).

Data & Methods

In this chapter we examined the complete public websites of twenty PVS organizations in the United States, including their organizational missions, descriptions of programming, client testimonials, and any documents that were downloadable from their websites. The organizations included were purposively sampled to differ across key dimensions of organizational variability: size, funding, geographic location, services offered, population served, and religious affiliation. Website links for each organization are provided in the works cited.

We approached our analysis with the goal of understanding how terms such as *citizen* or *citizenship* were used by PVS organizations and what kinds of discourses they were most often coupled with. We conducted qualitative coding collaboratively, each analyzing a subset of websites from our sample and meeting multiple times to discuss our results and broader readings of the data set. We found that when citizenship was invoked, it was dominantly coupled with discourses of criminalized individuals' employment, prosocial emotion management, and sobriety. In the sections that follow, we frame these themes as different facets of an overarching transformation: the construction of good carceral citizens.

As our sample is not representative, our aim is not to offer a set of generalizable findings, but rather to initiate a dialogue about carceral citizenship within PVS research. We hope that our findings will act as a set of *orienting statements* that may encourage other scholars to consider PVS organizations as theoretically important and empirically rich sites for investigating carceral citizenship (Goldstone 50).

PVS Organizations as Sites for the Construction of Good Carceral Citizenship

For many PVS organizations, helping former prisoners attain and embody the ideals of good citizenship was the goal of their rehabilitative interventions. Consider that at LUCK the stated goal of a new transitional housing facility was to help criminalized individuals "to be actual citizens." Across organizations, criminalized individuals accessing services were commonly referred to as "returning citizens." Women at the Well-Broward explained the importance of this term:

> The terms "ex-convict" or "ex-offender" emphasizes what they've done and hangs it around their neck as a millstone ... On the other hand, the language of "returning citizen" provides hope and honors both their humanity and their capacity to contribute to a flourishing society ...Yet, on an even deeper level it honors their humanity by reminding them that they are not defined by past actions, rather we expect them to contribute as one citizen among many.

These organizations were aware that language mattered. By referring to their clients as citizens, PVS organizations challenged and reframed dominant justice discourses that sustained discriminatory practices towards the population they served. They deliberately chose to redefine their clients' identity as ordinary members of society. While the language of citizenship is more inclusive, it also brings a body of assumptions about human actions and social life. PVS organizations were aware of the expectations associated with the designation of citizen, and made clear that their clients needed to follow them to reacquire this status. Most notably, criminalized individuals must work to change their life trajectories and, by extension, themselves. Fortune Society, for instance, suggested that their goal was to create "individuals who fit the description [of] deeply changed." Resonance underscored the permanence of the required transformation, explaining "it is our goal to help troubled women change ... for good." Timelist even went so far as to call one of their programs "The Change Academy."

PVS organizations invoked a variety of metaphors to describe this transformation and their role as facilitators. For example, The Center for Women in Transition sought to help their clients "reimagine who they are." One Touch Ministry suggested that they helped criminalized individuals "make a u-turn" in their lives. Project Return underscored the contrast between criminalized individuals' lives before and after their organization's intervention: "We all know a 180 when we see one. Those transformations that literally mean going in the opposite direction, that figuratively mean you have turned your life around. From night to day, from a season of decline to a season of hope and opportunity." Project Return also made connections between criminalized individuals' transformation and the kinds of belonging and community recognition that are central to citizenship: "When we finally get it right, when we finally manage to overcome our own patterns of failure or misbehavior, we begin to build from the ground up our new-found credibility and standing in whatever community we're in. No longer errant (in whatever way we were previously errant), we bring our better selves to the world."

Criminalized people agreed that PVS intervention was central to their transformation. For instance, Barry Campbell of Fortune Society offered the following testimony: "I tell people all the time this [organization] is where I grew up, this is where I learned what being a man means, and what being a productive citizen means." Aaron Cobos explained of his time at Homeboy Industries, "when I came here, I was a raw piece of metal and through the process of working on myself and getting to know myself now I'm a shiny new part."

The benefits of personal transformation were also underscored at the community level. As One Touch Ministry explained, "making a difference in the life of one returning citizen will not only affect that individual but will have a ripple effect that resounds positively throughout our community." New Jersey Reentry Corporation agreed, claiming that "we need to think of the reentry population as an economic asset to their larger communities—helping them gain employment adds to their communities' economic growth and cultivates the pool of human talent." Fortune Society also noted that the change they seek to encourage "can enhance the lives of individuals and, at the same time, improve their families, the institutions with which they interact, and the communities in which they live."

Not any type of change was acceptable at PVS organizations. Instead, they sought to cultivate a specific type of transformation (Quinn and Goodman). For instance, Project Return explained that they "work with folks who *want to live right*." Across the next three sections we examine what this declaration means in practice. While there is tremendous variation in PVS organizations' visions of transformation, rehabilitation, and belonging (see: Kaufman; Tomczak and Buck), in this chapter we prioritize the *core conditions* of good carceral citizenship. By core conditions, we mean the characteristics that comprise the essence of this designation and without which we could make no claim to observe good carceral citizenship (Buck 144). Our findings show that PVS organizations were collectively committed to constructing good carceral citizens who satisfied the core conditions of: (i) employment, (ii) "prosocial" management of their emotions, and (iii) sobriety. Together, these characteristics comprised what One Touch Ministry called "the intangible responsibilities associated with being productive members of the community."

A Productive Responsible Citizen: Securing a Job 101

Among the many services offered to returning citizens by PVS organizations, assistance in securing employment was the most pervasive. This focus reflected the central role bestowed upon work in the successful return of criminalized individuals to society. As Project Return stated, "a job is the key that opens the door to a new life." Similarly, New Jersey Reentry Corporation maintained that "securing gainful employment as quickly as possible following release dramatically increases the odds of successful reentry" and, therefore, services offered in this area are considered "essential tools for effective reintegration." Prison Fellowship explained that "when returning citizens can't find work, they're unable to meet their parole and probation requirements and can end up returning to prison."

Whereas PVS organizations framed employment as a necessary condition to succeed at a second chance in life, returning citizens often exhibit difficulty in securing a job. In addition to limited education, work experience, and skills, their criminal past makes their search a hurdle. Criminal record checks are increasingly part of the hiring process and, as audit studies have demonstrated, employers often discriminate against people with criminal histories (Pager). Many states also impose statutory bans on people with convictions in fields such as nursing, childcare and home health care—service jobs where women, and particularly women of color, are concentrated (Restoration of Rights Project). Chances to secure employment are even lower for people of color who are also subject to racial discrimination. Together these features result in under or unemployment for returning citizens (Western et al.).

Aware of these difficulties in finding an occupation, PVS organizations offered two types of support: programs targeting specific careers and/or training in soft skills. Certifications for blue collar occupations in construction, hospitality, transportation, and mechanics were regularly offered, but newer fields such as solar technology were also targeted. In some cases, training was paired with partnerships or apprenticeships with businesses to allow individuals to acquire hands-on experience before seeking employment. Soft skills programs taught individuals how to succeed on the job market through workshops and instructional content in resume writing, job interviews, team building, email etiquette, and emotional intelligence.

While offering these important services, PVS organizations also sought to shape criminalized people into successful or model returning citizens. As part of their job readiness training, these organizations instructed their clients how to behave and present themselves as ideal job applicants—this is what Halushka referred to as "the curriculum of work wisdom" (76). For example, Fortune Society explained the "the art of handshaking" in 10 detailed steps "to make the right first impression'" in a handout called "Handshake and a Smile 101." Examples included advising their clients to "pump your hand only 2–3 times" and "avoid offering a fish hand." As these instructions illustrate, returning citizens were encouraged to perform a specific version of themselves to guard against negative stereotypes during the hiring process and to match employers' expectations of responsible workers (Halushka). The gendered dimensions of this performance were made plain when this handout instructed: "Forget lady fingers ... in business settings you are an equal, not a 'lady.'" For Fortune Society, the performance of a model citizen and worker was also a hegemonically masculine one.

PVS organizations also constructed the model returning citizen through their program descriptions and client success stories. Individuals were expected to become "productive" and "working members of society." Employment was positioned in contrast to criminal behaviors as it was believed to give structure to life and, in doing so, limit the time available to commit crimes. As a past client, Alexzander Calderon, narrated, "I've never held a job before. All I've ever done was criminal activity—that was my revenue. Moving forward, the experience I'm getting while working in Merchandise will be vital to put on a resume." Women at the Well-Broward advanced a similar view on employment: "Making a livable wage is critical to ensuring that temptations to resume unhealthy relationships for financial reasons or engaging in unhealthy or illegal behaviors to earn income are minimized."

Employment was not only framed as crucial to gain lawful income, but also as a key step towards independence. Through employment, individuals became able to address key needs such as housing and healthcare, as well as support their families. Narratives emphasized how, after years of relying on the prison system, welfare, substances, or abusive partners, successful clients were now "self-sufficient" and "self-sustaining." Encouraging individuals to be independent was among the primary goals of PVS organizations. For instance, the mission of Community Solutions was "to promote the independence, responsible citizenship and well-being of individuals and families." As one of its representatives stated, "we need to successfully transition offenders from the prison rolls to the tax rolls." Similarly, Resonance's object was "helping women become productive tax-paying citizens." PVS organizations, therefore, emphasized returning citizens' productivity, independence, and contribution to the economy through tax paying—all of which are central markers and duties of neoliberal subjects and citizens. These findings speak to Gurusami's concept of *rehabilitation labor* (434), which highlighted how the combination of carceral threat and welfare discipline works to govern and transform "criminals" into "workers." However, our chapter broadens Gurusami's focus, envisioning employment as just one of the core conditions of good carceral citizens.

Whereas employment was positioned as a necessary condition for a full and free life and an expectation for model returning citizens, not all PVS organizations considered any job an accomplishment. In a video, Project Return stated, "no work is insignificant. All labor that uplifts humanity has dignity and importance and should be undertaken with painstaking excellence." However, most testimonies and success stories across organizations suggested the opposite. Individuals were not praised for finding a job, but for securing full-time, stable, and meaningful employment that also allowed them to grow. Essentially, according to most PVS organizations, a regular entry level position was not the goal, a career was. Women at the Well-Broward affirmed that their clients should aim for "a higher paying job and do more than just get by day-to-day" because "it is impossible to support oneself and a family on a minimum-wage job." The ambition and goal of a career was also emphasized through a picture posted on their program offerings' webpage. Here, an image of women in prison jumpsuits faded into a picture of a business woman on the phone wearing a suit and pumps while carrying hand-luggage. Underlying these narratives, therefore, was a sense that returning citizens should aspire to and search for a specific type of employment.

PVS organizations' discourses of employment also revealed their gendered dynamics. The blue-collar occupations generally framed as attainable and valid occupations for male clients, were not so for women. Aware that the traditional labor market can be discriminatory and inaccessible to many women with a criminal record, PVS organizations had to become more creative in the types of jobs they encouraged women to aspire to. As Women at the Well-Broward explained, "necessity entrepreneurship" is a "form of self-employment where entrepreneurship is an essential option and often the most expedient way to earn a living" for returning citizens. As Joanna's story exemplified, her criminal past hindered her chances of a career in the traditional workforce:

After working for a few businesses, Joanna realized her background prevent[ed] her from advancing in the companies. She found talking about her criminal record or the previous incarceration was a taboo topic, so she decided to take the entrepreneur route...Her experience in prison and her transition back home led her to turn her crochet passion into a business—Divine Designz Crochet Shoppe! Two years later she owns 2 businesses and co-own[s] a 3rd business. Joanna is living on her own with her 2 sons and is a productive citizen. She has her eyes set on a very bright future. (Women at the Well-Broward)

PVS organizations often framed self-employment as a pathway to independence and empowerment for criminalized women, with the added benefit of not requiring them to disclose their criminal past to their employers. Some of the small businesses featured on PVS organizations' websites were even empowerment themed. For example, Ladies of Hope Ministries explained how one of their residents, Dee, was "in the process of creating her own T-shirt line called Wear How You Feel that designs and sells T-shirts with positive affirmations."

Across *therapunitive* settings (Carlen and Tombs 339), like PVS organizations, this kind of empowerment talk was often blended with critiques of criminalized women as weak, unstable, and "dependent on outside sources of fulfillment and validation which can include drugs, men, children, and even the street lifestyle" (McKim 53). Under this logic, by empowering women, PVS organizations were also offering them a way out of crime. Yet, possible barriers to self-employment were rarely mentioned. Self-employment requires tremendous assets, support, and effort that are not always readily available to returning citizens. Moreover, starting a business may not quickly (or ever) result in the kind of stable or livable income that was showcased in the "success stories" offered on PVS organizations' websites. Pollack offered a similar critique of empowerment talk, arguing that in its implicit diagnosis that a "lack of self-esteem lies behind social problems," it "decontextualizes women from the social and political parameters of their lives" (78–9).

Among the alternative career pathways proposed by PVS organizations were also becoming a reentry coach, a speaker, and a mentor (Timelist). For instance, Ladies of Hope Ministries developed a "first-of-its-kind training program to prepare women and girls to be professional public speakers." This training allocated resources to women to change the narrative about the systems of oppression impacting their lives, while also providing them with a "platform (and entrepreneurial pathway) to tell their stories and support themselves after incarceration." Scholars often refer to criminalized individuals who choose these career pathways as *peer mentors* (Buck), *wounded healers*, or *professional exes* (LeBel et al.). In contrast to the barriers criminal records often create for employment (Pager), lived experience of incarceration is seen as a valuable credential in these professions.[5]

PVS organizations' narratives also highlighted excellence. Testimonies and client stories emphasized returning citizens' ability to secure promotions and pay raises in short time frames, even though we know that this population often encounters difficulties securing employment and discrimination on the job. For instance, on their blog, Project Return featured Amanda's achievements: "Amanda has been the picture of post-prison success. Released from prison more than a year ago, she came straight to Project Return and put all of our programs and services to her best advantage, propelling herself into a manufacturing job, gaining a promotion with that employer, and then enrolling in community college." While it is expected that PVS organizations highlight their clients' success stories, other skills or qualities such as effort or perseverance could have also been underlined. Instead, these narratives of success upheld returning citizens to (often unattainably) high standards. Returning citizens were expected to go beyond securing a job, they needed to excel at it. As Jon Ponder, the President and CEO of Hope for Prisoners stated, "our goal is to make sure that they are soaring like superstars." The expectations placed upon returning citizens were incredibly high given that they were not only asked to excel for themselves, but also as good ambassadors of criminalized individuals more generally. As Ponder explained, "When you hire someone from Hope for Prisoners, you're not just hiring them ... their success within those businesses are gonna open up the doors for the next folks that are gonna be coming through." In the next section, we turn to how PVS organizations' discourses surrounding emotion management also work to craft the image of the good carceral citizen.

"Prosocial" Emotion Management: Correcting Feelings during Reentry

Discussions of prosocial behaviors, attitudes, and attachments originated in the life-course criminological tradition which has sought to understand why most people age out of crime. Pathways out of crime are often explained by what scholars call *turning points* (Laub and Sampson 301), like obtaining a well-paying job, getting married, having children, or going to university. These events discourage criminality, and thus are characterized as prosocial. We use scare quotes in this section's subtitle in recognition of how this term is used to enforce a particular standard of behavior that ignores structural inequalities and cultural differences. Behaviors deemed prosocial are not only those discouraging of criminality, but also those that align with white, ostensibly middle-class, heterosexual American

---

5   For problems and limitations of these employment opportunities see Buck.

culture. The norms associated with dominant culture also determine the forms of emotional expression deemed acceptable (Stearns and Stearns 813). The emotions of dominant groups are normalized whereas those of subordinate groups are viewed as aberrant, treated with suspicion, and in need of correction. In this section, we explore how PVS organizations encouraged criminalized individuals to manage their emotions in prosocial ways to align with the norms of dominant culture and fulfil the expectations associated with good carceral citizenship.

PVS organizations often framed criminalized individuals' emotions, especially their "inappropriate" management, as the root of their criminal justice involvement. Criminalized individuals were dominantly characterized by these organizations as suffering at the intersections of past traumas and hardships. As Reaching Out from Within explained:

> The cruelty we are subjected to throughout our lives shapes and molds us, creating adverse feelings such as loneliness, hatred, insecurity and anger. In order to deal with these feelings, we form defense mechanisms such as, fighting, using drugs/alcohol, becoming anti-social and even using humor; however, these defense mechanisms have consequences: incarceration, misery, lack of trust and unhealthy relationships.

LUCK advanced a similar perspective. In a video testimony, one of their co-founders explained his own incarceration as originating in the way he was managing his emotions: "Hurt people hurt people. I was never able to process or deal with the hurt I was receiving. I was trying to figure out how to survive and sometimes that survival comes by inappropriate means."

Emotions were not only seen as initial risk-factors for criminalization, but also as continual threats to individuals' successful inclusion in the community. For example, Fortune Society suggested that particular emotions can be a "barrier to reintegration." Prison Fellowship explained that different stages of the reentry transition are paired with unique emotional challenges. When individuals are first released, they experience "fear, anxiety, excitement, and expectation, all mixed together ... To put it simply, they're overwhelmed." As time goes on, a different set of emotions takes center stage—and with it a new set of potential risks: "In the first three months, as the newness of freedom wears off, loneliness will be your enemy. The isolation you feel will tempt you to form relationships with people who don't share your values—and that can signal trouble" (Prison Fellowship). Underlying these declarations was the sense that there was a "correct" way for good carceral citizens to manage their emotions. For example, at New Beginnings, programming was designed to help clients "express [their] feelings appropriately." Or, at Resonance, a past client praised this organization for teaching them "how to talk about [their] true feelings, how to express them in the right way."

PVS organizations often framed their programming as offering a plan or template for criminalized individuals to learn prosocial ways of managing their emotions. The Center for Women in Transition claimed that without their intervention, many women would "lack the necessary resources to cope with trauma in healthy ways—like seeking professional care—and instead might turn to drugs or alcohol." Community Solutions offered multiple programs "designed to change maladaptive emotional reactions." One program used cognitive behavioral therapy to "address the emotional element of aggression." Reaching Out from Within explained how they help clients manage their emotions down to the cellular level:

> Simply to experience powerful emotions in the presence of others...without acting out or triggering a crisis or collapsing into helplessness is powerful for re-patterning and rewiring the brain. Slowly, over time, it re-regulates the participants' brain patterns, their emotional responses, which in turn re-regulates behavior ... The inmates slowly become different on the inside ... They learn to "sit with," or be present with their painful powerful emotions without acting out, blowing up or imploding.

In helping criminalized individuals manage their emotions in prosocial ways, PVS organizations believed they were also offering them a pathway for success in other domains, such as obtaining gainful employment, securing safe housing, and furthering their education—all of which are markers of citizenship.

PVS organizations' understanding of emotion management was a gendered process.[6] For women, the "right" way of expressing their emotions was finding and expressing their voices—taking an active and empowered role as an advocate in their own lives. Homeboy Industries, for example, quoted a past client who explained: "One thing we need to learn as women is that being emotional is not a weakness, but a strength. We need to learn to use our voices and take care of ourselves." Resonance characterized one of their clients as positively transforming from "timid and shy" to "an empowered woman through [their] program." New Beginnings explained that "expressing one's inner voice can guide formerly incarcerated females to work comprehensively on their emotional instabilities." For men, by contrast, emotion management was often framed as a process of learning how "to control their responses during anger-provoking situations" (Man2Man). LUCK, for instance, worked to disrupt the notion that "violence and aggression are the tools to resolve conflict" and instead offered men advice on how "to resolve conflict

---

6   Emotion management is also racialized. The range of "acceptable" emotions is circumscribed for people of color, as the harmful trope of the Angry Black Woman illustrates (Jones and Norwood 2045–51). We do not have the data to explore this relationship, but future research may wish to examine how race and gender together inform the types of support and advice PVS organizations offer to criminalized individuals.

peacefully." Co-founder Mario Bueno explained that men's aggression and violence "must be diluted" through appropriate organizational programming. In another example, Fortune Society provided specific instructions on how men could avoid being perceived as aggressive when initiating a handshake: "Extending your hand without a voice greeting may make you appear nervous or overly aggressive ... Do not use a forceful grip. A handshake should be a friendly or respectful gesture, not a show of physical strength." In the next section, we turn to PVS organizations' discourses surrounding sobriety and the connections we noted between sobriety and citizenship.

Supporting and Monitoring Sobriety

Standing alongside PVS organizations' discussions of employment and emotion management was the expectation that criminalized individuals commit to sobriety. Addiction to drugs and alcohol (and sometimes gambling) were framed as poor coping mechanisms. Consider the following client story from Resonance:

> [Victoria] had trouble dealing with her mother's death, and her drug usage spiraled out of control. When her roommate sold drugs to an undercover police officer, both women were arrested and Victoria went to prison ... She has worked closely with her therapist and other program staff to cope with the past trauma of losing her mother, and to understand how some of these feelings led to her addiction.

Homeboy Industries similarly suggested that "substances are a way of coping with the pain of gang involvement, homelessness, and mental health issues." Though PVS organizations often recognized the structural nature of criminalized individuals' traumas (e.g., income inequality, racism, patriarchy) and the addictions that followed, the solutions they proposed were almost entirely individualized. As Timelist described, "we firmly believe that we have the will and power to beat addiction of all kinds." This organization envisioned themselves as "play[ing] a key role in helping individuals learn the true meaning of personal responsibility." At Ladies of Hope Ministries, Cass Severe explained, "you have to come home and help yourself." Hope for Prisoners put their philosophy simply: "Change is an inside job." This individualized focus was also reflected in this organization's core values: integrity, accountability, motivation, honor, optimism, perseverance, and excellence.

Addiction, or "the drugs lifestyle" as it is sometimes called (Kaye 210), was positioned by PVS organizations as the antithesis of good carceral citizenship. These organizations frequently invoked a binary opposition between addiction and being accountable, responsible, and living what Fortune Society called a "purposeful life."

For instance, Resonance claimed that "many women who have been challenged by the criminal justice system may find substance abuse getting in the way of them meeting their full potential as happy, responsible individuals." This organization saw their role as guiding criminalized women "to achieve and maintain total abstinence from drugs and/or alcohol as part of a more satisfying, productive, and law-abiding lifestyle." PVS organizations also drew connections between sobriety and employment. New Jersey Reentry Corporation, for example, offered the following mantra: "Clean Body, Clean Mind, Clean Job." This organization also suggested that a commitment to sobriety may help criminalized individuals overcome the stigma potential employers may associate with their criminal record: "Evidence that [drug] treatment is in place can be determinative for a tentative employer." These declarations map onto the discourses Kaye uncovered in American drug courts, wherein "the drug addict [was] constituted as an 'anti-citizen,' a person whose drug dependency [was] symbolically related to non-productive labor, a leaching of state resources, and criminality" (214). By contrast, "eliminating the drugs lifestyle [was] sometimes said to produce NORPs: Normal, Ordinary, Responsible Persons" (Kaye 214).

Though PVS organizations often highlighted their roles in helping, encouraging, or supporting criminalized individuals, when they spoke about sobriety their punitive or disciplinary roles were prominently on display. Some of the organizations we examined participated in criminal justice diversion programs wherein a rigorous program of addiction counselling was offered as an alternative to incarceration. This meant that participation was not voluntary but *coerced* (Maguire et al. 434–37). If clients' participation in these programs was deemed unsatisfactory, the courts may recommend imprisonment instead. Illustrating this threat, Resonance warned participants that if they did not choose to pursue "a productive, responsible life" they must reckon with the consequences of their substance abuse (incarceration): "For some, Resonance will be their first hope to make a permanent change to a life without drugs or alcohol. For others, Resonance will be their final opportunity to choose a productive, responsible life over substance abuse and its consequences."

Because participation in addiction counselling was often court-ordered, PVS organizations were held responsible for monitoring their clients' compliance. This was often through random, mandatory drug testing. Hope For Prisoners, for example, stated that "incoming clients must submit to a drug test as part of the enrollment process." Community Solutions noted that their staff made use of random breathalyzer or urinalysis tests. The results of these tests and other assessments of clients' progress could be shared with other criminal justice actors. For instance, Fortune Society explained that they provided "periodic updates to the court." These findings complement Salole's research on how PVS organizations work *in tandem* with the criminal justice system to trigger further punishment. If clients are not meeting expectations of their rehabilitation, PVS staff may, in self-professed "acts of care," report noncompliance to police, courts, and probation officers who can use these assessments to justify further sanctions (Salole 305). Flores observed a similar phenomenon in his research on youth rehabilitation. In coining the term *wraparound incarceration*, he demonstrated how the drug, alcohol, and academic support offered to criminalized girls multiplied and diversified opportunities for their criminalization because of constant monitoring by program staff. Following Salole and Flores' work, we see similar opportunities for PVS organizations to directly—rather than merely discursively—intervene in the domains of punishment and citizenship. By reporting clients' progress and program compliance to the courts, police, or probation officers, PVS organizations may trigger a process of formal criminal justice sanctioning (i.e., a criminal record) and in so doing, become part of the very apparatus that "stamps" individuals as carceral citizens.[7]

Conclusion

In this chapter, we explored PVS organizations as important sites for the construction of carceral citizenship. Our research broadened scholars' existing focus on what these organizations are and do to include what they are striving for—the ideals that animate their everyday work with criminalized individuals. Our analysis revealed that they collectively prized employment, prosocial emotion management, and sobriety. Together, these qualities were seen as prerequisites for social inclusion: the core conditions of good carceral citizenship. In offering particular kinds of support and advice (and not others), PVS organizations were actively intervening in how criminalized individuals approached their lives after incarceration (Quinn and Goodman). Aligning with this assertion, Mijs suggested that PVS organizations offer criminalized individuals a *road to reentry* as they navigate the complexities of exiting prison. Our chapter builds on Mijs' contribution by demonstrating how the particular road these organizations encourage criminalized individuals to take is informed by their understandings of, and aspirations for, good carceral citizenship. The road to reentry, then, is not only the support and advice PVS organizations offer returning citizens, but also their promise of a certain type of social inclusion (or at least its possibility).

By extending the language of citizenship to their clients, PVS organizations emphasized their formal membership to society. They purposefully expanded the boundaries of democratic inclusion to facilitate criminalized individuals' civic, economic, and social integration. In doing so, these organizations acted as a site

---

7   PVS organizations are required to report outcomes for programs that act as alternatives to incarceration. Though partnerships with the criminal justice system are contested, funding realities often make these relationships (and the punitive practices they entail) financial necessities (Maguire et al.).

of resistance to the exclusionary practices of the carceral state and offered tangible, sometimes life-altering, help to criminalized individuals in the process. Yet, they also governed, disciplined, and responsibilized their clients in the process of helping them (see also: Phelps and Ruhland). As scholars of citizenship have underscored, citizenship does not only have positive connotations, it also includes "disciplinary possibilities" and a "cultural process of subjectification" (Lister 4). We observed both in PVS organizations' narratives and practices. The road to social inclusion that PVS organizations advanced was narrow and the expectations of good carceral citizens were rigid. These organizations enforced a particular standard of behavior that was premised upon individual excellence in the private and public spheres, and often ignored the formidable barriers and structural inequalities criminalized individuals faced upon their release. As a result, we close this chapter with reservations about the end point of this road and, by extension, the limits of the type of personal transformation advocated for by PVS organizations. No matter how well criminalized individuals may satisfy the core conditions of good carceral citizenship, real barriers to their civic and political inclusion remain. Even good carceral citizens are not free of their criminal records and the legal restrictions, stigma, and disenfranchisement that follow. Full and unencumbered citizenship for criminalized individuals will ultimately require modifications to macro-level systems that PVS organizations and individualized practice can scarcely accomplish alone.

Future research may wish to explore points of connectivity and/or contestation between the individualized approach to social inclusion documented in this chapter and the work of actors and organizations who seek to restore citizenship through structural change (e.g., pursuing legal reform, criminal record suspensions, penal abolitionism). Other scholars may wish to determine how the discourses of good carceral citizenship documented in this chapter inform actual practice using ethnographic methods or interviews with PVS staff and clients. These methods may offer greater insight into how the types of belonging advocated for on PVS organizations' websites may be differentially applied to and experienced by criminalized individuals occupying various identity categories (e.g., race, gender, social class, ability, sexuality) and possessing different types of criminal records (e.g., misdemeanors, felonies, crimes for which public registration is required). As Smith and Kinzel explain, "some formerly incarcerated people face more stigma and resistance than others based on their overlapping identities" and as a result the efforts of PVS organizations "may liberate some but also maintain the repression of others" (99–100). Pursuing this line of research might also reveal how any attenuation of citizenship in one sphere could lead to or amplify citizenship diminishment processes in other spheres (both in terms of status and participation), affecting civil, political, economic, and social life.

Works Cited

Alexander, Michelle. *The New Jim Crow: Mass Incarceration in the Age of Colorblindness*. The New Press, 2010.

Arms Around You. https://www.armsaroundyou.org/. Accessed 10 May 2021.

Bosworth, Mary, et al. "Punishment, Citizenship and Identity: An Introduction." *Criminology & Criminal Justice*, vol. 16, no. 3, 2016, pp. 257–66.

Buck, Gillian. *Peer Mentoring in Criminal Justice*. Routledge, 2020.

Carlen, Pat, and Jacqueline Tombs. "Reconfigurations of Penality: The Ongoing Case of the Women's Imprisonment and Reintegration Industries." *Theoretical Criminology*, vol. 10, no. 3, 2006, pp. 337–60.

Comfort, Megan. *Doing Time Together: Love and Family in the Shadow of the Prison*. U of Chicago P, 2007.

Community Solutions. https://www.csi-online.org/. Accessed 10 May 2021

Corcoran, Mary. "Dilemmas of Institutionalization in the Penal Voluntary Sector." *Critical Social Policy*, vol. 31, no. 1, 2011, pp. 30–52.

Davis, LaJuana. "Rock, Powder, Sentencing—Making Disparate Impact Evidence Relevant in Crack Cocaine Sentencing." *Journal of Gender, Race and Justice*, vol. 14, no. 2, 2011, pp. 375–404.

Flores, Jerry. *Caught Up: Girls, Surveillance, and Wraparound Incarceration*. U of California P, 2016.

Fortune Society. fortunesociety.org/. Accessed 10 May 2021.

Freedom Project. freedomprojectwa.org/. Accessed 10 May 2021.

Garland, David. *Punishment and Modern Society: A Study in Social Theory*. U of Chicago P, 1990.

Glenn, Evelyn N. "Citizenship and Inequality: Historical and Global Perspectives." *Social Problems*, vol. 47, no. 1, 2000, pp. 1–20.

—. "Constructing Citizenship: Exclusion, Subordination, and Resistance." *American Sociological Review*, vol. 76, no. 1, 2011, pp. 1–24.

Goldstone, Jack A. "Response: Reasoning About History, Sociologically..." *Sociological Methodology*, vol. 34, no. 1, 2004, pp. 35–61.

Gottschalk, Marie. *The Prison and the Gallows: The Politics of Mass Incarceration in America*. Cambridge UP, 2006.

Gurusami, Susila. "Working for Redemption: Formerly Incarcerated Black Women and Punishment in the Labor Market." *Gender & Society*, vol. 31, no. 4, 2017, pp. 433–56.

Halushka, John. "Work Wisdom: Teaching Former Prisoners How to Negotiate Workplace Interactions and Perform a Rehabilitated Self." *Ethnography*, vol. 17, no. 1, 2016, pp. 72–91.

Hannah-Moffat, Kelly, and Mona Lynch. "Theorizing Punishment's Boundaries: An Introduction." *Theoretical Criminology*, vol. 16, no. 2, 2018, pp. 119–21.

Harding, David J., et al. *On the Outside: Prisoner Reentry and Reintegration*. U of Chicago P, 2019.

Homeboy Industries. homeboyindustries.org/. Accessed 10 May 2021

Hope for Prisoners. hopeforprisoners.org/our-blog/. Accessed 10 May 2021.

Jones, Trina, and Kimberly J. Norwood. "Aggressive Encounters & White Fragility: Deconstructing the Trope of the Angry Black Woman." *Iowa Law Review*, vol. 102, no. 5, 2017, pp. 2017–69.

Kaufman, Nicole. "Prisoner Incorporation: The Work of the State and Non-Governmental Organizations." *Theoretical Criminology*, vol. 19, no. 4, 2015, pp. 534–53.

Kaye, Kerwin. "Rehabilitating the 'Drugs Lifestyle': Criminal Justice, Social Control, and the Cultivation of Agency." *Ethnography*, vol. 14, no. 2, 2012, pp. 207–32.

Kymlicka, Will, and Wayne Norman. "Return of the Citizen: A Survey of Recent Work on Citizenship Theory." *Ethics*, vol. 104, no. 2, 1994, pp. 352–81.

Kropf, Jesse. "Keeping 'Them' Out: Criminal Record Screening, Public Housing, and the Fight Against Racial Caste." *Georgetown Journal of Law & Modern Critical Race Perspectives*, vol. 4, 2012, pp. 75–99.

Ladies of Hope Ministries (LOHM). thelohm.org/. Accessed 10 May 2021.

Laub, John H., and Robert J. Sampson. "Turning Points in the Life Course: Why Change Matters to the Study of Crime." *Criminology*, vol. 31, no. 3, 1993, pp. 301–25.

LeBel, Thomas P., et al. "Helping Others as a Response to Reconcile a Criminal Past: The Role of the Wounded Healer in Prisoner Reentry Programs." *Criminal Justice and Behavior*, vol. 42, no. 1, 2015, pp. 108–20.

Lerman, Amy E., and Vesla M. Weaver. *Arresting Citizenship: The Democratic Consequences of American Crime Control*. U of Chicago P, 2014.

Lister, Ruth. *Citizenship: Feminist Perspectives*. New York UP, 2003.

Loyd, Jenna M. "Carceral Citizenship in an Age of Apartheid." *Occasion*, vol. 8, 2015, pp. 1–15.

LUCK. mariobuenoreformexpert.com/about. Accessed 10 May 2021.

Maguire, Mike, et al. "'Penal Drift' and the Voluntary Sector." *Howard Journal of Crime and Justice*, vol. 58, no. 3, 2019, pp. 430–49.

Manza, Jeff, and Christopher Uggen. *Locked Out: Felon Disenfranchisement and American Democracy*. Oxford UP, 2008.

Manza, Jeff, et al. "Citizenship, Democracy, and the Civic Reintegration of Criminal Offenders." *The Annals of the American Academy of Political and Social Science*, vol. 605, no. 1, 2006, pp. 281–310.

Man2Man. https://www.man2man-uya.org/. Accessed 10 May 2021.

Marshall, Thomas H. *Citizenship and Social Class and Other Essays*. Cambridge UP, 1950.

McNeill, Fergus. *Pervasive Punishment: Making Sense of Mass Supervision*. Emerald Group Publishing, 2018.

McKim, Alison. *Addicted to Rehab: Race, Gender and Drugs in the Era of Mass Incarceration*. Rutgers UP, 2017.

Mijs, Jonathan J. B. "The Missing Organizational Dimension of Prisoner Reentry: An Ethnography of the Road to Reentry at a Nonprofit Service Provider." *Sociological Forum*, vol. 31, no. 2, 2016, pp. 291–309.

Miller, Reuben J. *Halfway Home: Race, Punishment, and the Afterlife of Mass Incarceration*. Little, Brown and Company, 2021.

Miller, Reuben J., and Gwendolyn Purifoye. "Carceral Devolution and the Transformation of Urban America." *The Voluntary Sector in Prisons: Encouraging Personal and Institutional Change*, edited by Laura Abrams, et al., Palgrave Macmillan, 2016, pp. 195–213.

Miller, Reuben J., and Forrest Stuart. "Carceral Citizenship: Race, Rights and Responsibility in the Age of Mass Supervision." *Theoretical Criminology*, vol. 21, no. 4, 2017, pp. 532–48.

New Beginnings Re-entry Services. https://www.newbeginningsreentryservices.org/. Accessed 10 May 2021.

New Jersey Reentry Corporation. https://www.njreentry.org/. Accessed 10 May 2021.

Nunn, Kenneth B. "Race, Crime and the Pool of Surplus Criminality: Or Why the 'War on Drugs' was a 'War on Blacks.'" *Journal of Gender, Race and Justice*, vol. 6, no. 2, 2002, pp. 381–445.

One Touch Ministry. https://www.1touchministry.org/. Accessed 10 May 2021.

Owens, Michael L., and Adrienne R. Smith. "'Deviants' and Democracy: Punitive Policy Designs and the Social Rights of Felons as Citizens." *American Politics Research*, vol. 40, no. 3, 2012, pp. 531–67.

Pager, Devah. "The Mark of a Criminal Record." *American Journal of Sociology*, vol. 108, no. 5, 2003, pp. 937–75.

Pettit, Becky, and Bruce Western. "Mass Imprisonment and the Life Course: Race and Class Inequality in U.S. Incarceration." *American Sociological Review*, vol. 69, no. 2, 2004, pp. 151–69.

Pfaff, John F. *Locked In: The True Causes of Mass Incarceration—and How to Achieve Real Reform*. Basic Books, 2017.

Phelps, Michelle S., and Ebony L. Ruhland. "Governing Marginality: Coercion and Care in Probation." *Social Problems*, 2021, 10.1093/socpro/spaa060.

Pollack, Shoshana. "Reconceptualizing Women's Agency and Empowerment: Challenges to Self-Esteem Discourse and Women's Lawbreaking." *Women & Criminal Justice*, vol. 12, no. 1, 2000, pp. 75–90.

Prison Fellowship. https://www.prisonfellowship.org/. Accessed 10 May 2021.

Project Return. https://www.projectreturninc.org/. Accessed 10 May 2021.

Quinn, Kaitlyn. "Dispositions That Matter: Investigating Criminalized Women's Resettlement Through Their (Trans)Carceral Habitus." *Criminology & Criminal Justice*, vol. 23, no. 1, 2023, pp. 20–38.

Quinn, Kaitlyn. "Inside the Penal Voluntary Sector: Divided Discourses of 'Helping' Criminalized Women." *Punishment & Society*, vol. 22, no. 2, 2020, pp. 161–80.

Quinn, Kaitlyn et al. "'How You Keep Going': Voluntary Sector Practitioners' Story-Lines as Emotion Work." *British Journal of Sociology*, vol. 73, no. 2, 2022, pp. 370–386.

Quinn, Kaitlyn., and Philip Goodman. "Shaping the Road to Reentry: Organizational Variation and Narrative Labor in the Penal Voluntary Sector." *Punishment & Society*, 2023, pp. 1–25.

Reaching Out from Within. rofw.org/. Accessed 10 May 2021.

Resonance. https://www.resonancetulsa.org/. Accessed 10 May 2021.

Restoration of Rights Project. https://ccresourcecenter.org/restoration-2/. Accessed 10 May 2021.

Robinson, Gwen, et al. "Punishment *in* Society: The Improbable Persistence of Probation and Other Community Sanctions and Measures." *The SAGE Handbook of Punishment and Society*, edited by Jonathan Simon and Richard Sparks, SAGE, 2013, pp. 321–40.

Salole, Abigail. 2019. "'It's Kinda Punishment': Tandem Logics and Penultimate Power in the Penal Voluntary Sector for Canadian Youth." *Howard Journal of Crime and Justice*, vol. 58, no. 3, 2019, pp. 298–312.

Sered, Susan S. "Diminished Citizenship in the Era of Mass Incarceration." *Punishment & Society*, vol. 23, no. 2, 2020, pp. 218–240.

Smiley, Calvin J. *Purgatory Citizenship: Reentry, Race, and Abolition*. U of California P, 2023.

Smith, Justin M., and Aaron Kinzel. "Carceral Citizenship as Strength: Formerly Incarcerated Activists, Civic Engagement and Criminal Justice Transformation." *Critical Criminology*, vol. 29, no. 1, 2021, pp. 93–110.

Stearns, Peter N., and Carol Z. Stearns. "Emotionology: Clarifying the History of Emotions and Emotional Standards." *The American Historical Review*, vol. 90, no. 4, 1985, pp. 813–36.

Sykes, Gresham M. *The Society of Captives: A Study of a Maximum Security Prison*. Princeton UP, 1958.

The Center for Women in Transition. https://www.cwitstl.org/. Accessed 10 May 2021.

The Reentry Initiative. https://www.reentryinitiative.org/. Accessed 10 May 2021.

The Sentencing Project. Racial Justice, https://www.sentencingproject.org/issues/racial-disparity/. Accessed 22 June 2021.

Timelist Group. https://timelistgroup.org/. Accessed 10 May 2021.

Tomczak, Philippa, and Gillian Buck. "The Penal Voluntary Sector: A Hybrid Sociology." *British Journal of Criminology*, vol. 59, no. 4, 2019, pp. 898–918.

Wacquant, Loïc. "Deadly Symbiosis: When Ghetto and Prison Meet and Mesh." *Punishment & Society*, vol. 3, no. 1, 2009, pp. 95–134.

Weaver, Vesla M., and Amy E. Lerman. "The Political Consequences of the Carceral State." *American Political Science Review*, vol. 104, no. 4, 2010, pp. 817–33.

Western, Bruce. *Homeward: Life in the Year after Prison*. Russell Sage Foundation, 2018.

Western, Bruce, et al. "A Longitudinal Survey of Newly-Released Prisoners: Methods and Design of the Boston Reentry Study." *Federal Probation* vol. 81, no. 1, 2017, pp. 32–40.

Women at the Well-Broward. watwbroward.org/. Accessed 10 May 2021.

World Prison Brief. Highest to Lowest Prison Population Rate, https://www.prisonst udies.org/highest-to-lowest/prison_population_rate?field_region_taxonomy_ tid=All. Accessed 22 June 2021.

Between Imprisonment and Citizenship
Jessica Kent's Navigation of Carceral Citizenship

Nina Heydt

Introduction

This chapter explores the ways in which citizenship and US corrections inform American legal and social identity building on social media. Specifically, it considers Jessica Kent's *YouTube* channel as an articulation of post-incarceration punishment in connection with the making of American citizenship in the twenty-first century.[1] Here, Kent problematizes spheres such as housing, employment, voting rights, and social life as a 'carceral citizen.' I argue that she employs prison survival guides on *YouTube* as a tool to reclaim her status in society socially, while access to political and economic avenues remain limited by the law.

Prison studies scholars agree that after imprisonment, one's punishment is not over but instead continues spatially, politically, and socially in that it ultimately limits full legal citizenship.[2] Michelle S. Phelps and Ebony L. Ruhland investigate the ways in which probation (originally declared as an alternative to prison) introduces close state mass supervision into communities—thereby expanding punishment's boundaries onto Americans outside of the prison. While Christopher Uggen et al. observe this marginalization and continued political punishment as a threat to democratic principles, they reason for the full re-instatement of rights and privileges as key to successful re-integration. They also assert that incarceration (as a form of corrections) and citizenship inform each other legally and socially, explaining how a criminal record has detrimental effects on a criminalized individual's status as an American citizen, both inside and outside of the prison's immediate reach. Researchers also agree on the changed public perception this status brings forth for these citizens, one that renders them most vulnerable and at the outer margins of society. In *The New Jim Crow: Mass Incarceration in the Age of Colorblindness*,

---

1   See Loic Wacquant's *Punishing the Poor* and *Deadly Symbiosis*, which considers the periods before and during incarceration.

2   See Julia Velten's chapter in this collection for perspectives on the intersections of aging and citizenship.

Michelle Alexander emphasizes that this form of legalized discrimination creates "an *undercaste*—a lower caste of individuals who are permanently barred by law and custom from mainstream society" (13); this label declares criminalized Americans 'unfit' for full citizenship. She further underscores this phase of citizenship as "a permanent second-class citizenship" (13). Consequently, the criminal justice system further distances citizens with full participation rights socially from criminalized citizens that ultimately make up the so-called undercaste—Americans who remain in the most marginalized legal and social spheres of their communities.

In "The Price of Carceral Citizenship: Punishment, Surveillance, and Social Welfare in an Age of Carceral Expansion," Reuben Miller and Amanda Alexander describe the social effects of punishment. They write:

> [t]he carceral citizen experiences social, political, and economic life in ways that are unique to members of his or her class, or not typically shared by even the most marginalized people who have traditionally been marked by their race, religion, ethnicity, or gender. Indeed, the 'carceral citizen' is a novel legal and social category that has emerged in the age of mass incarceration. Carceral citizens face constitutionally justified forms of exclusion based solely on the presumption of legal guilt at some point in their lifetimes. (297)

The significance of this quotation lies in the understanding that the carceral citizen's legal citizenship status is not diminished but instead reduced socially; it seems to lay outside of and run parallel to full citizenship as an alternative form, a legally valid version of social citizenship for Americans marked by a criminal record. Carceral citizenship also shows how the legal label directly informs the ways in which the social, political, and economic spheres of life are equally tarnished. Miller and Alexander's emphasis, of course, is on the fact that 'carceral citizenship' defies already established categorizations. Lastly, they infer that this new mode of citizenship is automatically introduced upon entering the criminal justice system and that the complex layers that create the legal label magnify the maltreatment of already socially disadvantaged Americans.

Consequently, it seems that carceral citizenship as a legal brand reveals a new form of social citizenship. I thus focus on the social component of carceral citizenship in light of Joshua Price's concept of 'social death' and Reuben Miller's theorization of 'afterlife.' Price explains that "[t]o be sentenced to prison is to be sentenced to social death. Social death is a permanent condition. While many people integrate themselves back into society after imprisonment, they often testify that they permanently bear a social mark, a stigma" (5). In *Prison and Social Death*, Price emphasizes that while the actual legal punishment offers an expiration date, the social consequences last a lifetime. He describes a type of social death that the physical bodies seem to have survived. There is little chance to overcome this status socially, and this leads to what Miller calls the prison's 'afterlife': "a supervised society—a hidden social world and an alternate legal reality. The prison lives on through the people who've been convicted long after they complete their sentences ... because they are never really allowed to pay their so-called debt to society" (8). These concepts suggest that once one is legally vulnerable to punishment and pushed to the outer rims of society, the social ramifications that emerge with or after the legal punishment seem invisible to the public eye.

(Social) Media

As a next step, this paper makes the case for including media—and specifically social media—representations in the discourse on carceral citizenship. The role of the media, I argue, is complex: it can both work *with* and *against* common narratives. Within the American cultural self-imaginary, the media narrativizes punishment as having a definitive start and an end date. TV series such as *The Simpsons* or *Sons of Anarchy* portray exiting prison with a re-introduction to former standards of living. Sideshow Bob reunites with Krusty the Clown during his show and receives a hearty welcome. Likewise, a group of motorists leaves prison to be welcomed by club members, the scenes prior revealing how the homes are prepared for their expected return. As attorney imposter Mike Ross leaves prison in *Suits*, he exits the gates wearing his own suit; his former boss greets and reassures him with a confident smile and a handshake that everything is fine. Additionally, Ross's girlfriend elegantly ascends from the Lexus they both arrived in to pick Mike up. In slow motion she walks up to him, the sun is shining and "Beneath the Surface" by Demons of Ruby Mae plays in the background. They hug and kiss, foreshadowing the fulfilled life ahead of Mike that appears very similar to life before entering the criminal justice system: with a well-paying job and his future wife by his side ("The Hand That Feeds You" 39:34–40:56). The above examples thus represent a seamless re-entry and in so doing, implicitly and explicitly justify the institution as it stands.[3]

At the same time, media can help condemn its compliance in reintroducing simplistic images of punishment and Americans involved in the criminal justice system. Producers such as Ava DuVernay, John Oliver, and Comrade Sinque criticize both the prison industrial complex and the media's upholding and restoration of problematic depictions of the system's reach. They instead offer alternative representations of punishment that are vital to the analysis of prison survival guides on *YouTube*. Originally aired on *Netflix*, DuVernay's documentary *13th* has recently been added to *YouTube*.[4] DuVernay's documentary notes that: "the Thirteenth Amendment to the

---

3   See John Oliver's "Prisoner re-entry" for a montage of Hollywood film examples.

4   Thereby adding the documentary to an open-access platform, free of charge.

Constitution makes it unconstitutional for someone to be held as a slave. In other words, it grants freedom to all Americans. There are exceptions, including criminals. There's a clause, a loophole. Except as a punishment for crime" (2:20–2:35). This statement reveals how mass imprisonment must even be viewed as a continuation and new form of slavery for Black Americans within the system's reach. In short, this particular amendment allows for the systemic exploitation of Black individuals within the criminal justice system.[5] DuVernay's portrayal of a dysfunctional American criminal justice system stands in direct opposition to how the US usually understands itself (inter)nationally; namely: a granter of freedoms.[6] HBO's *Last Week Tonight with John Oliver* demonstrates an idealistic notion of prisoner re-entry, only to immediately disrupt it. By juxtaposing popular cultural narratives with short clips of ex-prisoner interviews, Oliver paints a devastating picture of continued restrictions on and sanctions over criminalized Americans. The TV host uncovers struggles such as poverty and limited employment, housing, voting rights, and lastly, the social stigma attached to felony convictions in society (2:50–18:44). Oliver illuminates the discrepancy between state-perpetuated self-imagery and first-hand accounts, consequently disrupting the common media narrative of the system in place. Prison *Tik-Tok* is a recent phenomenon that centers first-hand experience online. Here, Comrade Sinque criticizes continued limitations on his social life post-incarceration in the form of his ban from the vacation home platform Airbnb. When a background check causes his criminal record to resurface, he implicitly testifies to a form of social death as he is excluded socially and spatially. First-hand representations of carceral citizenship are rarely disseminated by criminalized individuals themselves, thereby enhancing the importance of social media representation.

DuVernay, Oliver, and Sinque thus represent the role of the media in criticizing not only *what* kind of stories are told about social punishment and carceral citizenship and *how*, but also *who* tells them in the first place. Their (pop) cultural media interventions thus attempt to bridge the gap between current scholarly research and (pop) cultural representations of the criminal justice system and its citizens. While

---

5   Michelle Alexander's *The New Jim Crow* traces the historical and legal perspectives on mass imprisonment "as a stunningly comprehensive and well-disguised system of racialized social control that functions in a manner strikingly similar to Jim Crow" (4). Alexander outlines how crime and ideas on race and criminalization have been intertwined since slavery, and that since its abolition, new, supposed colorblind systems of control over Black Americans have been introduced. Since this discussion goes beyond the scope of this chapter, an analysis of prison survival guides by Black Americans, addressing their experiences, would be fruitful in a future project as they potentially testify to the ramifications that are particular to (Black) American history and the effects of incarceration on Black communities.

6   See *Human Rights, Narrated Lives*, in which Kay Schaffer and Sidonie Smith address the role US citizens play in calling out a discrepancy between the US's international and national self-image (157).

the above explorations draw from prison studies and American cultural studies, they also raise important issues for citizenship studies: they offer to shed a new light on in the liminal spaces of citizenship that punishment brings forth socially in prison's afterlife. At the intersection of these diverse fields of research, particularly prison narratives on social media can play a tremendous part in how the treatment of Americans in the system and forms of punishment are viewed in the United States.

Carceral Citizenship and/on *YouTube*

In analyzing narratives on *YouTube*, I contribute to existing scholarship by exporting prison studies into the field of citizenship studies to analyze narrative explorations of carceral citizenship (Miller and Alexander 292). The emphasis here, of course, is on the fact that carceral citizenship defies already established categorizations that are indeed protected under the Constitution. Due to the significant reach of the "carceral state," the chances of becoming a carceral citizen at some point in one's lifetime are higher in the US than in other countries (Mitchell). As such, it is crucial to focus on prison reform activism and its role in the shaping of American identities and citizenship. It is against this backdrop that I analyze first-hand accounts in the form of prison narratives on social media, as the steadily growing number of formerly incarcerated individuals of different racial and ethnic backgrounds telling their stories, convey troubled versions of reintegration. In particular, I consider the genre of so-called prison survival guides that has emerged most prominently in the past five decades. These first-hand accounts exist somewhere between autobiographical writing and self-help handbooks, further contributing to the disciplines of prison and citizenship studies that together might uncover new ways in which carceral citizens can re-insert themselves safely into American culture. Anthony Accurso explains the newly emerged phenomenon as: "[s]uch videos maybe at times controversial or voyeuristic ... but they draw attention to the stark realities of incarceration in America in a way that defies scripted stereotypes and sometimes misleading 'reality TV' shows" and hence "offer a window into the prison experience for many Americans" (24). In other words, the genre of recorded prison survival guides contributes to the umbrella genre of prison narratives and offers fresh perspectives on the criminal justice system to an audience detached from the actual experience at home.

Oral and written prison narratives play a crucial role in prison studies since the "out of sight, out of mind" expression no longer applies (Franklin). These narratives not only lend a stage to voices that are not to be heard, but in their mere existence force the fundamental gap between a state's treatment of Americans inside and outside of prisons back into sight. An analysis of *YouTube*, as an unrepresented platform that offers survival guides can address how carceral citizens navigate American cul-

160   Citizenship and (State) Violence

ture in new forms. As a contrast to the first-hand written accounts of the prison experience, videos on *YouTube* present new dimensions that no longer allow viewers to detach a person's face and name from a story of incarceration and continued punishment. They thus counter dominant and problematic media narratives about prison's afterlife and shape how we understand carceral citizenship at large. Seeing *and* hearing about the carceral experience from a carceral citizen on a platform that a world audience can access free of charge strengthens the content creator's own voice and understanding of the carceral experience.

Social media fosters virtual socializing and allows the display of content on any topic to a world audience. In this way, I argue, *YouTube* can support prison reform efforts.[7] *YouTube* as a platform promotes an easy access to American social and cultural life in video form; consumers engage with content creators (and vice versa) and find like-minded communities. In search of a place in society after re-entry, content creator, prison reform activist, and formerly incarcerated individual Jessica Kent[8] uses *YouTube* to share stories of her carceral experience with more than 700,000 subscribers. She explains how incarceration impacts her freedom today, eleven years post-incarceration, and thus broadcasts her story in a digital space. Sharing her experience on her own terms and quasi-facing an audience online allows Kent to engage with viewers of many backgrounds either through the comments section, or by reaction or Q&A videos, and live streams. In referring to her subscribers as a "ride or die crew," she stresses identification and belonging (Kent), and ultimately participates in culture virtually. Kent therefore joins a greater movement of prison activism that we can see unfolding on social media as former prisoners also begin using platforms such as *TikTok* to disseminate their first-hand experiences with the criminal justice system.[9] I am particularly interested in the new contributions the discussion of *YouTube* narratives and prison studies make toward our understanding of carceral citizenship. On her channel, Kent paints a more somber picture of prison's afterlife

---

7   See "American Civil Liberties Union," "The Equal Justice Initiative," or "The Sentencing Project," to only name a few important organizations that bring together prison reform activists on the local, national, and federal level.

8   I am unaware of Jessica Kent's self-identification, but from her videos one might read her as a white woman. The number of women with incarceration experience has "increased by more than 525%" since 1980 which hints at alarming rates of imprisonment. (Monazzam and Budd)

9   The movement has gained momentum in social media outlets with the Prison *TikTok*-hashtag (#PrisonTikTok) which would be important to scrutinize as a follow-up discussion to this analysis of articulations found on *YouTube*. There is an entirely separate development underway, e.g., and in addition to prison survival guides: prisoners' usage of "contraband" phones to film and post either entertaining *TikTok*-dances or shed light on housing and meal conditions while in prison, possibly facing extension of their sentence length or other forms of punishment if detected.

by primarily discussing the stigma she encounters daily, even though she officially "did her time" and thus supposedly exited state supervision. This is why I read these stories as counternarratives to common media narratives revealing that one's involvement in the US criminal justice system expires with either the end date of one's prison sentence or serving one's sentence in the community ("Prisoner Re-entry").

I read these *YouTube* representations as narrative explorations of the criticism against the persisting punishment under the criminal justice system and the way criminalized individuals' identities are constructed and commonly negotiated in American society. Within her marginalized status in society, Kent takes new paths of actively engaging in American cultural life by making her voice heard on *YouTube*. Therefore, I argue that her *YouTube* channel reclaims the social component to her status as a carceral citizen, a participation that had been denied to her on the path of employment and political participation under state supervision. She consequently withstands an "unlearning" of citizenship, as explained by Amy E. Lerman and Vesla M. Weaver and similarly reassesses Price's concept of social death through social media in prison's afterlife.[10] Her social media account hence reimagines carceral citizenship at the intersection of legal label (formerly convicted felon)[11], social stigma, and denial of a full political voice which continues to shape her reintegration. In reviving her carceral experience online, Kent joins a broader anti-discrimination movement on social media.

Methods

Within the scope of this chapter, I primarily explore video prison survival guides that I consider an addition to written prison survival narratives. Viewers get to see, hear, and watch Jessica Kent speak about the criminal justice system's impact on her life in a familiar and comfortable setting, filming herself in either her car, kitchen, or on the living room sofa and thus inviting her audience into her personal space. My aim here is to lay bare the ways in which prison studies and citizenship studies

---

10   This "unlearning" process signifies an ultimate withdrawal from political and civil public life as an individual response to post-incarceration life or other state sanctions and imposed supervision. The expanded scrutiny of groups of citizens by the state, in which every encounter with state officials is experienced as predominantly negative or even dangerous/life threatening then leads to what they then observe as a "custodial lifeworld," a group of individuals experiencing the role of the state and democracy different from Americans unaffected by the criminal justice system (Lerman, Amy E., and Vesla M. Weaver pp. 15, 110–38).

11   This term is frequently used in legal documents. As I am aware of the derogatory connotations this expression carries, I choose to use "formerly incarcerated individual/person" or "criminalized individual/person" in my paper to reflect the person-centered standards of the field.

intersect when it comes to social media articulations of American lives stained by criminal records. In other words, I ask: in what ways does Kent's social media presence impact her status as a carceral citizen? How does she experience prison survival guides as a tool to reinsert herself socially, when other avenues remain limited in prison's afterlife? Hence, I close-read the *YouTube* prison survival guide in light of Miller and Alexander's carceral citizenship, Miller's conceptualization of prison's afterlife, and Price's social death, and thus focus on videos that predominantly comment on Kent's carceral experience during the early stages of reentering society. Here, Kent addresses housing, employment, voter restrictions, and a limited social life as core aspects of her carceral experience. In doing so, Kent points to how carceral citizens navigate this liminal space differently. Kent subsequently uses social media as a way out of social death by primarily socializing virtually, exploring housing and employment options, and reassessing political agency to navigate carceral citizenship.

Literature Review

In *Caught: The Prison State and the Lockdown of American Politics*, Marie Gottschalk explores the misconception of redemption after legal punishment "ends." Here, Gottschalk sketches how the US criminal justice branch controls "more than 8 million" Americans and she alludes to the carceral state as an extension of mass incarceration (1). She adds that this control marks an entrance point into the system, but instead of offering an end date, she highlights other forms of state supervision that limit a restoration of full citizenship. But what then constitutes this liminal space between criminalization and full citizenship?

Citizenship studies scholars stress "a social process" to conceptualizing emerging articulations of carceral citizenship (Isin and Turner 4). Here, citizenship by birthright or naturalization granted by the fourteenth Amendment to the Constitution includes the category of "action" (Miller and Alexander 296). Egin Isin and Bryant Turner trace social lines on top of the legal framework of how citizenship is defined in the American understanding. They argue for the agency of individuals to actively shape and define what this assumed legal status of personhood means to them and how they express it on a social level (1–4). Miller and Alexander highlight that the social dimension becomes crucial as carceral citizenship, a social classification, is a direct legal consequence of the policies arising from mass imprisonment and extended state supervision (296). Consequently, not only are the same rights and protections no longer applicable under the law, they instead craft a new path that carceral citizens are left to explore on their own.

Individual social explorations can negotiate the negative legal connotations inherent to carceral citizenship. Given how citizenship shapes identity within the social realm, citizens themselves can actively reassess their personhood under the law. At first glance, however, this assumed ability to redefine social capacity seems to confirm neoliberal ideas of the penal state.[12] Yet, if we recall the discussed paradigms so far, we conclude that carceral citizens are ranked the lowest among the American legal and social hierarchies—even lingering outside constitutionally granted protections—, the mere idea of being in charge of one's status seems too far away to grasp. Additionally, Price's concept of social death seems too powerful a consequence to defy for carceral citizens. However, at precisely these intersections of citizen and carceral citizen, legal punishment and social ascension, the genre of so-called prison survival guides makes a valuable contribution. As I argue in this chapter, the growing genre of prison survival literatures offers to reclaim and thus reassess what carceral citizenship looks like when expressed not through criminal justice officials or the American government, but carceral citizens themselves. Carceral citizenship's liminal space blurs stark contrasts and binary oppositions and instead gives criminalized individuals a chance to express their carceral experiences on their own terms. H. Bruce Franklin describes this phenomenon, stating:

> By the late 1970s the river of prison literature was overflowing its banks, pouring out into public in books, journals, and major motion pictures. Then came sweeping repression. Most states enacted laws making it illegal for convict authors to receive money from the writings. Creative writing courses in prison were defunded … The repression of prison literature coincided with the phenomenal growth of the prison system.[13] (Franklin)

Besides alluding to the rise of mass incarceration and simultaneous mass appearance of prison narratives, Franklin asserts that the written and visual genres feed into the fascination with crime, criminalized individuals, and forms of punishment. At the same time, Franklin addresses a discrepancy between silencing prisoners living in the system, former prisoners that have re-entered society, and their audiences. While for outsiders to the system access is easy and demand for these stories high, inside prison facilities the producers of such narratives are struggling to compile and financially profit from their stories. We could hence draw the conclusion that the carceral citizen's legal status automatically denies them a voice to convey these narratives in the first place and finally a potential financial yield.

---

12   See Wacquant's *Punishing the Poor*.

13   Book bans in prisons around the country are worth perusing in a future paper. Denying prisoners access to literature is a common practice in today's prisons. For example, Alexander's *The New Jim Crow* falls under this ban in many regions in the US. For more on book bans, see Casey Bastian's "In Prisons, the Press also Yearns to be Free," Lee V. Gaines's "Illinois Prison Removes More Than 200 Books From Prison Library," or Jonah E. Bromwich's "Why are American Prisons so afraid of this book?"

It is at the stage of re-entry that many criminalized people regain the freedom to share their experiences without intervention from the American judicial branch. Their reclaiming of a voice is what I understand as individual expressions of their carceral experience, and a testimony to their understanding of carceral citizenship. Additionally, I read prison survival guides as a reaffirmation of Gottschalk's assertion that "[s]tate actors and state agencies are considered part of the problem rather than part of the solution" (18). With this, Gottschalk demonstrates that "these problems are regarded 'as either the product of chance or individual action'" (18), thereby pushing responsibility away from institutional state agents and into the laps of the citizens facing destructive consequences. What we witness here is the judicial branch making stark the contrast between being considered guilty (and thus "deserving" of punishment) and a victim (hence "deserving" of rights). To be more precise, Gottschalk notes that: "we live in an oxymoronic age of DIY that is, do-it-yourself social policies. Those individuals deemed unable or unwilling to change must be banished either to the prison or to the prison beyond the prison" (18–9). This quotation reflects a neoliberal approach to carceral citizenship in two ways: the first being that of self-responsibility, of the citizens involved in the criminal justice system; and the second being communities citizens return to as both the limit to restoring full citizenship and the chance of exploring carceral citizenship on an individual level. Gottschalk addresses the multiple paradigms the carceral state taps into, leaving seemingly no other option than to self-organize as carceral citizens on a local level. What at first resembles a bottomless pit, the DIY character here frames a nearly unattainable goal for carceral citizens to prove their "worthiness" and restore the capacities full citizenship entails.

At a second glance, however, a DIY character already reflects the core of grass roots rights activism. Prison rights activism takes up the notion of DIY not only in the form of documentaries, such as DuVernay's *13th*, but also as social media content. Thus, born out of public silencing, the need for self-reliance, and continued mass punishment and supervision, the rich history of prison literature has gained new narrative forms that are disseminated on social media. These prison survival guides are what I consider the newest addition to the DIY character of prison rights activism. Within convict criminology, "individuals use their first-hand experience of incarceration and apply it toward justice activism" (Smith and Kinzel). In doing so, Justin Smith and Aaron Kinzel emphasize the strength that lies within carceral citizenship: "to reshape boundaries around individual and collective identity" (Smith and Kinzel). This in turn "holds the capacity to transform discourse" and hence influences how we perceive criminalization and its institution (Smith and Kinzel). Prison rights activism and its activists then mirror these goals, oftentimes both implicitly and explicitly, voicing critique of the current criminal justice system. I contribute to this current discourse by demonstrating how Jessica Kent, as a content creator addressing punishment post-incarceration on *YouTube*, helps shape the representation of carceral citizenship.

The multidimensional genre of prison survival guides emerged in response to mass incarceration in the US (Mitchell). Interviewing the producers of *Survivors Guide to Prison*, Mitchell learns that the genre serves to "give you tips on what to do if you get arrested, since you have more of a chance of going to jail in America than anywhere else in the world" (Mitchell). The content of prison survival guides oftentimes runs along formerly "unwritten rules of prison life," now in written form, that generally describe *dos* and *donts* of behavior inside prison, out on parole or probation (Pisano 39–47).[14] They provide exemplary lists of possible future employers (133 ff.) and other guidelines to successful reintegration into society (109 ff.). Survival guides leave the reader with the impression that no one exits the system for good, but that one's chances are higher the more one actively does on the inside to improve life on the outside (101 ff.). Ultimately, the declared goal of these manuals is disrupting the vicious cycle of criminality, avoiding recidivism, and restoring a future that is "productive" and "successful" (Pisano). Authors seek to equip future prisoners with knowledge only former prisoners can testify to and prepare newcomers for a system that extends far beyond release from prison (Pisano). Consequently, if we are to take the guides at face value, they seek to address a DIY approach to understanding life as a carceral citizen in the US; only with the help of such guides will one be able to withstand what authors describe as a dangerous criminal justice system. Prison reformists label criminalized individuals as survivors of the US prison system, which is especially striking, since this self-identification blurs the guilty/innocent dichotomy and the realms of perpetrator and victim (Gottschalk).Therefore, in a DIY fashion, Americans themselves seek to prepare to survive a system that swallows them whole.

Jessica Kent's *YouTube* Prison Survival Guide

This section examines carceral citizenship in prison's afterlife by analyzing Jessica Kent's *YouTube* channel as a prison survival guide. In 2015, Kent established her *YouTube* channel which chronicles her experience inside and outside of prisons in what I consider five thematically interrelated chapters: addiction and recovery, motherhood, life in prison and after re-entry, and rehabilitation. In her nearly five hundred videos with eighty-four million views to this date, the content creator shows how her carceral experience works against attaining full American citizenship, long after she officially "paid her debt" to society. I study how Kent's portrayal

---

14 See also Cory Henderson's *It's Jail not Yale* andAbdullah Ibraheem's *The Black Peoples Prison Survival Guide: How to Survive Mentally, Physically, and Spiritually while Incarcerated.*

166 Citizenship and (State) Violence

of the above examples defies the assumed unworthiness of formerly incarcerated Americans and hence renegotiates carceral citizenship on *YouTube*. Kent implicitly challenges social death and a potential unlearning of citizenship through her own carceral experience. Her presence on *YouTube* reflects a reinsertion into social life by reinventing her place in the US as a carceral citizen and thus reinjects a social dynamic into her status that has been denied to her in other avenues of life.

In "My last Day in Prison / Walking out Homeless," Jessica Kent describes a very different exit from prison than we observe in *Suits*. As opposed to leaving the prison in her own clothing, she testifies: "they have nothing to dress me out in, because I have no clothes. I have my prison shirt with my number 711548, my prison sweatpants with 711548 and prison shower shoes" (11:51–12:10). With little to no personal belongings, she describes her exit:

> I'm just pacing in in-take, pacing and pacing, for one hour, two hours, three hours have gone by. I don't know if my ride is outside ... Lunch trays come. I'm like: (sighs) I cannot eat, I'm shaking, I'm nervous. I'm pacing. No one's telling me anything, I don't know what's gonna happen. Then finally, they say: 'Kent to Sally Port,' (her eyes looking beyond the camera now, she holds her breath). Sally Port is where you walk in (holding her breath again, now holding back tears) and it's where inmates leave (voice breaks) ... I hear it on the radio. And she pops the door for me, and I walk up to Sally Port and ... I'm just overcome with emotion ... I was terrified. (12:11–13:34)

Kent's behavior shows how the memories still seem to take her back into a difficult moment, many years later. Her out-processing experience is marked by nervousness, uncertainty about what is to come next, and a sense of being at the prison's mercy to the very last minute of her stay. This experience, and having to leave in prison clothing, reveals how her introduction to carceral citizenship is described more negatively than positively. To Kent, being unable to grasp what life will bring after this point, re-entry signifies foremostly an emotional challenge. When she is greeted by the friend that comes to pick her up, the stark reality sets in when she is met with the words "Girl, you look homeless" (14:27–14:32),[15] to which Kent replies "Bitch, I am! Like, I had nowhere to go," followed by insecure laughing (14:33–14:36). Kent's relief having left prison and her worries about the future thus shape her first experience of re-entry as a carceral citizen. These sequences expose a counter image to common media representations such as *Suits*, one that complicates the representation of carceral citizenship through social media. Here, Kent lays bare how she perceives that re-entry comes with a shift in identity and one's place in society.

---

15   Kent was incarcerated in Arkansas but her family lives in New York State. Hence, it is not possible for her family to be close to her upon release ("My first year out of prison").

Her feeling of metaphorical homelessness adds to the new space she explores spatially. Kent's survival guide thereby criticizes the nonexistent guidance for housing options as well as the space she inhabits socially post incarceration.

In "Leaving Prison / Halfway House," her audience learns that the halfway house she stayed at charged one-hundred dollars per week, which introduces the next re-entry challenge: finding employment. As a criminalized person on parole, Kent offers a window into what her first job interview was like after release in "Whats [sic] it like being a FELON." She explains that

> [one of] the first challenge[s] to anyone getting out of prison is to find a job ... the prison I went to did not give me a state-issued ID, so I didn't have like a driver's license or anything. I didn't have a prison ID, I didn't have a birth certificate or a social security card, so like literally, you guys, like I just sales-talked them into giving me a job. I just told them straight up: I am who I say I am; I'm saying: I need a job. I'm wearing prison shower shoes right now, like flip flops, to this interview, like, I'm sorry. (1:12–1:37)

Without any government-issued identification, Kent describes an exceptionally precarious state financially, emotionally, and legally. Her experience as a carceral citizen is thus defined by the absence of government identification; she rejoins society with only prison identification. Further, she emphasizes the desperation derived from this precarious state, nearly begging for the chance of employment against all odds. The primary issue here is that Kent is without official papers validating her personhood *in combination with* her criminal record. This example points to the limited chances of success in the job market as a carceral citizen on a legal level. To challenge the continued punishment on the economic level, Kent includes the above example of how to get a job in her survival guide.

Secondly, the absence of valid identification highlights the in-between status Kent suffers from: being legally somewhere within American citizenship and at the same time outside of its reach, setting the limit of her agency at the mercy of employers recognizing her "worthiness." Consequently, her "being on paper"—what Kent calls her criminal record—quite literally substitutes for her government ID ("Whats it like" 8:26). She also suggests that wages from companies that do employ formerly incarcerated people, such as McDonalds or Walmart, oftentimes are not high enough to survive ("Whats it like" 6:34–6:46), implying that the degradation of citizenship comes with economic hardships for carceral citizens. Consequently, these videos address the limited employment opportunities criminalized Americans struggle with by saying: "we just put all these offenders out into the world and we tell them to go get your life together ... and then they're pushed into a society that is not welcoming to them ... ("Whats it like" 7:55–8:06). Here, Kent directly refers to

168   Citizenship and (State) Violence

the marginalized status that emerges from the legal label and illustrates the stigma socially attached to a prison experience.

The above quotation also gestures at a neoliberal approach to punishment in American society, one which Kent openly criticizes but uses for her own benefit. It is precisely this subordinate status that Kent attempts to escape when she recalls that "because no one wanted to hire me I decided to get my bachelor's degree and eventually I started *YouTube*. So I took my own path" ("10 Things" 7:06–7:16). Here, we recognize the DIY character that Gottschalk alluded to earlier, as Kent transforms her precarious situation into a self-determined route of "strength" that sheds light on how economic challenges can be tackled differently (Smith and Kinzel). Further, Kent demonstrates how her self-redirection into social media parallels her ambitions to attain a university degree to then support the carceral community in the future. She promises that "next year I'll graduate with my Bachelor's degree and I wanna work in any prison or rehab it will take me but I started my *YouTube* channel to bring awareness to that life and to bring awareness to how difficult it is for felons outside of prison" ("Whats it like" 7:05–7:17). Kent's social media presence signifies a new option on the job market for carceral citizens: that of being a content creator on *YouTube* that specializes in prison survival guides. Ultimately, Kent's guide clarifies that the list of future employers might be short and pay might be low; further options for carceral citizens include working with other criminalized individuals as professional exes, pursuing higher education to later join the scholarly discourse, or becoming content creators on social media.[16]

Jessica Kent also uses her platform to address the political consequences of carceral citizenship. In 2018, she resided in the state of Arkansas and decided to register to vote after she had finished her parole in the same state.[17] As the content creator recalls:

> I applied to vote and they told me: NO. (chuckles, showing the undecipherable letter into the camera) So, I'm gonna read that to you guys. 'Your application has been cancelled.' Underlined—like no! 'Due to the following reasons: information was received from the department of community corrections per the Secretary of State office, indicating that you have been convicted of a felony' (or seven, she adds). 'Arkansas law requires that voter registers cancel their voter registration

---

16   Kent supports her family from her income on social media ("How Much $ Did I make on Youtube in 2021?").

17   Kent, originally from New York State, also briefly addresses the differences in states' laws on voter registration as a criminalized individual. Within US borders, regional/spatial varieties in rights reveal an ambiguous gray area of either granting or withholding entire clusters of voting rights granted to Americans without a criminal record. A discussion of the regional varieties to carceral citizenship would thus be interesting to dive into in a future paper.

of a convicted felon within 10 days ... So, basically, nooo! The felons cannot vote in the South ... or live or breathe (chuckles). ("Whats it like" 9:08–9:39)

The rejection letter confirms that due to her status as a criminalized person, Kent is denied voter registration. Even though her hesitant laughs and comments imply that she is taking the state's dismissal lightly, Kent also equates the embarrassment with suffocating under the voter restriction. This stark contrast reveals her confusion in being excluded from voting even though she is officially declared off state supervision. With state laws denying her a political voice, Kent feels yet again defined solely by her status as a carceral citizen, seemingly unable to overcome the political consequences of a label that renders her "unfit" to exert political action. Katherine Petus notes that "what is presented as a moral justification for franchisement between those 'worthy' and 'unworthy' of political rights as a result of crime is in fact a political justification ... Disadvantagement is a direct result of conviction for crime, not of the criminal act itself" (129). In other words, the mere fact that one has a felony conviction on record results in reduced political agency while emphasizing the moral culpability as an element that remains for life. The fact that Kent tries to register, however, signifies a discrepancy in how the state views her and her own identification as a carceral citizen. In addressing Arkansas voter restrictions in the video, she illustrates how continuous punishment takes place after prison and thus disrupts mainstream narratives. However, the fact that she is continuously impacted by the prison's afterlife makes her pursue a degree in criminal program support services, which is not only in line with the work that convict criminologists do, but simultaneously reveals how she plans to exert her political voice in the near future. For the time being, her work as a prison activist on *YouTube* already follows the same intentions but in a virtual space. Kent thus succeeds in contributing a political voice grown out of her social media work.

Lastly, Kent comments on her social experiences in "TOP 10 HABITS PR!SON N A LIFE OF CRIME CAUSED." She explains that she suffers from PTSD and anxiety from life in prison and as a former drug dealer who subsequently has to avoid crowds. For example, she recalls a visit to the aquarium with her children: "and people were just bumping into me ... and that was driving me so crazy. I don't know if that was the combination of the crowd or being touched constantly—it just triggered me. I felt so anxious. And I started to get really really hot, and I was not able to enjoy even being in the aquarium" (5:31–5:59). What Kent planned as a fun outing became a site of struggle. She experiences severe emotional and physical responses to everyday situations that she considers remainders of her carceral experience. Additionally, the radio at places such as Target, or the sound of keys "sends [her] straight back to prison. I don't like it, I get on edge" (6:37–6:45). The mental strain that Kent experiences continues to linger over her life even though she is no longer physically imprisoned; this strain thus shapes how she perceives herself as a carceral citizen in a "prison beyond the prison" (Gottschalk 18–9). She concludes by adding that she is an "introvert ... People always think *YouTubers* are extroverts because we make videos. But, I (stuttering) I'm alone in house" (8:40–8:49). This need for social (physical) distance also makes her career path as a content creator on *YouTube* so intriguing. Kent has found a way to experience social life online to make up for encounters in person that would further strain her mental health. It seems her work on *YouTube* and her interactions with subscribers signify a stand-in for interactions with the public sphere. Hence, through social media Kent has found a way to reintroduce a social component into her life that her experience as a carceral citizen denied her after imprisonment.

Kent self-identifies "as a mom, a student, and a *YouTuber* and I'm not breaking the law" but at the same time she cannot seem to shake the realities of prison's afterlife (11:25–11:27). What we observe in Kent's accounts about her social life after re-entry recalls what Reuben Miller describes as "a new form of prison. It's one that has no bars, and sometimes no formal connection to the police or criminal courts" (18). Miller refers to what carceral citizens experience, and the subsequent *vulnerability* that emerges is unique to the carceral experience in its afterlife. Kent is made socially vulnerable and hence balances out social distance with virtual presence. This socially precarious state also reflects what Lerman and Weaver describe as a "denaturalization" and a subsequent "unlearning" of citizenship for people affected by the criminal justice system. This unlearning stems from the anticipation of negative or traumatic encounters with state officials in public, deriving from former experience (94 ff.). Being legally within but affectively excluded from full citizenship causes carceral citizens to internalize their status as social, political, and legal outcasts. This phenomenon plays out in Kent adding the line "and I'm not breaking the law" and in the adjectives she uses to describe how she sees herself. Her statements allude to the liminal space she occupies as a carceral citizen that she considers formative to her social status. While in-person and close physical interactions continue to fall short for Kent, her work as a content creator making a prison survival guide on *YouTube* clearly marks a path for her to successfully and safely interact online. Because she presents and implicitly and explicitly criticizes commonly disseminated images of criminalized people, Kent manages to transform her social death into a powerful depiction of what carceral citizenship as a lived reality looks like on social media.

Ultimately, Kent's channel offers a DIY exploration of the social components to carceral citizenship, one that defies an unlearning of citizenship and instead introduces a re-learning, even re-inventing of the definitions of "how to show fitness" in carceral citizenship (Gottschalk). Her version of DIY primarily grows out of her involvement in social media, but her success—many followers, a source of income, connection with others through social media has led to a much wider range of possibilities for prison's afterlife. Kent presents a new version of what reintegration after prison might look like and offers a how-to guide for prison's afterlife on social media in which she redefines what a "new normal" can mean for carceral citizens.

Conclusion

This chapter explored (social) media narratives in which carceral citizenship is renegotiated and extended beyond the actual prison sentence and state supervision. I read Jessica Kent's *YouTube* channel in light of citizenship studies and prison studies to show how social media articulations transform the marginalized and muted voices of American carceral citizens into a site of strength within the cause of prison activism. A new category adjacent to constitutionally granted full citizenship, carceral citizenship economically, politically, and socially redefines what legally granted birthright citizenship looks like for millions of Americans today. Jessica Kent's *YouTube* prison survival guide is a local cultural and social example of a wider, even national social media phenomenon that is magnified in light of citizenship studies. The spheres in which legal labels inform our understanding of carceral experience should thus be broadened by analyzing social media articulations and this consequently can impact the ways in which we are given a window into *how* and *which* aspects of American life these groups want addressed: namely that punishment does not end with one's supposed exit from the system. Between formal citizenship and lived experiences, the primary goal lays in the visibility and recognition of carceral citizenship as a double status: blurring the victim/perpetrator dichotomy and thus humanizing the "villain," and painting a less heroic image of the criminal justice system. Here, legal, political, and social realities continue to mutually inform what carceral citizenship looks like, testifying to what survivors address as life-long parallel paths to full citizenship. By publicly addressing the issues of limited housing and job opportunities, restricted political action, and narrow social avenues, Kent sheds light on how carceral citizenship belongs differently in American society. Her take on carceral citizenship also reveals an active social membership, which illuminates the negotiation of the social and cultural components of a legal label. Kent shows how, within her marginalized status as a carceral citizen, she finds new ways of engaging in American life by speaking from her own experience on social media, denying the state's take on refusing her that voice. Ultimately, Kent's narrative explorations on *YouTube* challenge common media narratives that speak for carceral citizens but that lack the first-hand experience of this lived reality. By contributing to the genre of survival guides, she joins a collective effort for a renegotiation of "justice" and thus carceral citizenship in social media representations of carceral experience (Smith and Kinzel).

Works Cited

"10 THINGS I CAN NOT DO AS A FELON." YouTube, uploaded by Jessica Kent, 29 June 2020, https://www.youtube.com/watch?v=nFNOks5lx44.

"About." *The Sentencing Project*, 29 June 2023, https://www.sentencingproject.org/about/.

"About the Equal Justice Initiative." *Equal Justice Initiative*, 6 Sept. 2022, https://eji.org/about/.

Accurso, Anthony. "The Popularity of *YouTube* Prison Lifestyle Videos." *Prison Legal News*, 1 July 2020, https://www.prisonlegalnews.org/news/2020/jul/1/popularity-youtube-prison-lifestyle-videos/.

"Airbnb vs Felons." *TikTok*, uploaded by Comrade Sinque, 05 Oct. 2021, https://vm.tiktok.com/ZMLVh972H/.

Alexander, Michelle. *The New Jim Crow: Mass Incarceration in the Age of Colorblindness*. 2010. The New Press, 2012.

Bastian, Casey. "In Prisons, the Press Also Yearns to be Free," *Prison Legal News*, 01 Jan. 2021, https://www.prisonlegalnews.org/news/2021/jan/1/prisons-press-also-yearns-be-free/.

Bromwich, Jonah E. "Why are American Prisons so afraid of this book?" *The New York Times*, 18 Jan. 2018, https://www.nytimes.com/2018/01/18/us/new-jim-crow-book-ban-prison.html.

DuVernay, Ava. *13th*. Kandoo Films and Forward Movement, 2016.

Franklin, H. Bruce. "Prison Literature." *Encyclopedia of American Studies*, edited by Simon J. Broenner, Johns Hopkins UP, 2018, https://eas-ref.press.jhu.edu/view?aid=111&from=search&query=prison%20literature&link=search%3Freturn%3D1%26query%3Dprison%2520literature%26section%3Ddocument%26doctype%3Dall#biblio.

Gaines, Lee V. "Illinois Prison Removes More Than 200 Books From Prison Library." *Illinois Public Media*, 29 May 2019, https://will.illinois.edu/news/story/illinois-prison-removes-more-than-200-books-from-prison-library.

Gottschalk, Marie. *Caught: The Prison State and the Lockdown of American Politics*. Princeton UP, 2015.

Henderson, Cory. *It's Jail not Yale: How to Stay Out If You Can or Survive Prison If You Must Go*. OnDaNose Publishers, 2017.

"How Much $ Did I make on Youtube in 2021?" *YouTube*, uploaded by Jessica Kent, 19 Feb. 2022, https://www.youtube.com/watch?v=7B2pXVDLoB8.

Ibraheem, Abdullah. "The Black Peoples Prison Survival Guide: How to Survive Mentally, Physically, and Spiritually while Incarcerated." *The Talking Drum*, http://www.thetalkingdrum.com/prisonguide.htm.

Isin, Engin F. and Bryan S. Turner. "Citizenship Studies: An Introduction." *Handbook of Citizenship Studies*, edited by Engin F. Isin and Bryan Turner, Sage Publications, 2002, pp. 1–10.

"Leaving Prison | Halfway House." *YouTube*, uploaded by Jessica Kent, 31 May 2019, https://www.youtube.com/watch?v=5rp1lQEFB2M.

Lerman, Amy E., and Vesla M. Weaver. *Arresting Citizenship: The Democratic Consequences of American Crime Control*. U of Chicago P, 2014.

Miller, Reuben J. *Halfway Home: Race, Punishment, and the Afterlife of Mass Incarceration*. Little, Brown & Company, 2021.

Miller, Reuben Jonathan, and Amanda Alexander. "The Price of Carceral Citizenship: Punishment, Surveillance, and Social Welfare Policy in an Age of Carceral Expansion." *Michigan Journal of Race and Law*, vol. 21, no. 291, 2016, pp. 291–314.

Mitchell, Molly. "'Survivors Guide to Prison' tackles a broken criminal justice system: More movement than movie." *Prison Legal News*, 23 Aug. 2018, https://arktimes.com/news/cover-stories/2018/08/23/survivors-guide-to-prison-tackles-a-broken-criminal-justice-system.

Monazzam, Niki, and Kristen M. Budd. "Incarcerated Women and Girls." *The Sentencing Project*, 17 May 2023, https://www.sentencingproject.org/fact-sheet/incarcerated-women-and-girls/.

"My first year out of prison." *YouTube*, uploaded by Jessica Kent, 26 Nov. 2018, https://www.youtube.com/watch?v=qwkRxRIQbQc.

"My Last Day In Prison | Walking Out Homeless." *YouTube*, uploaded by Jessica Kent, 12 Sept. 2019, https://www.youtube.com/watch?v=3Z1VTzGoLjk.

"Out." *Sons of Anarchy*, season 4, episode 1, FX, 6 Sept. 2011. *Amazon Prime Video* App.

Petus, Katharine Irene. *Felony Disenfranchisement in America: Historical Origins, Institutional Racism, and Modern Consequences*. LFB Scholarly Publishing LLC, 2005.

Pisano, Angelo. *Prison Guide: Survival Secrets: Revealed*. Page Publishing, 2016.

Price, Joshua M. *Prison and Social Death*. Rutgers UP, 2015.

"Prisoner Re-entry: Last Week Tonight with John Oliver (HBO)." *YouTube*, uploaded by LastWeekTonight, 8 Nov. 2015, https://www.youtube.com/watch?v=gJtYRxH5G2k.

"Prisoners' Rights." *American Civil Liberties Union*, 15 Feb. 2022, https://www.aclu.org/issues/prisoners-rights.

Schaffer, Kay, and Sidonie Smith. "Life Sentences: Narrated Lives and Prisoner Rights in the United States." *Human Rights, Narrated Lives: The Ethics of Recognition*. Palgrave Macmillan, 2004. pp. 153–86.

Smith, Justin M., and Aaron Kinzel. "Carceral Citizenship as Strength: Formerly Incarcerated Activists, Civic Engagement and Criminal Justice Transformation." *Critical Criminology*, vol. 29, no. 1, 2021, pp. 93–110, https://doi.org/10.1007/s10612-020-09538-w.

"The Hand that Feeds You." *Suits*, season 6, episode 9, USA Network, 20 Jul., 2016. *Netflix*, www.netflix.com.

The Simpsons, created by Matt Groening, 20th Century Studios, Gracie Films, and Film Roman, 1989.

"TOP 10 HABITS PR!SON N A LIFE OF CRIME CAUSED." *YouTube*, uploaded by Jessica Kent, 28 Feb. 2020, https://www.youtube.com/watch?v=OrGZH2HuIiA.

Uggen, Christopher et al. "Citizenship, Democracy, and the Civic Reintegration of Criminal Offenders." *The ANNALS of the American Academy of Political and Social Science*, vol. 605, no. 1, May 2006, pp. 281–310, doi: 10.1177/0002716206286898.

Wacquant, Loïc. *Deadly Symbiosis: Race and the Rise of Neoliberal Penalty*. Polity Press, 2010.

—. *Punishing the Poor: The Neoliberal Government of Social Insecurity*. Duke UP, 2009.

"Whats it like being a FELON." *YouTube*, uploaded by Jessica Kent, 6 Dec. 2018, https://www.youtube.com/watch?v=4yoEoVooPIg.

Performing Citizenship

Paragon of Aging, Paragon of Voting
Centenarians and the Imaginary of a Model Citizen

Julia Velten

Introduction: Centenarians and the Struggle to Vote

Citizenship as a concept entails many different aspects that are all loosely connected with a sense of belonging to a certain place or "political entity" as well as a right and duty to participate within that entity (Cooper 4). This does not only incorporate the right to political participation or political citizenship, including the right to elect and be elected, but also what is called social citizenship. In his 1992 lecture "Citizenship and Social Class," T. H. Marshal speaks about this concept, claiming that full citizenship includes "a share in the social heritage, which in turn means a claim to be accepted as full members of the society" (6). Thus, in order to be a full citizen, not only political participation but also social and cultural inclusion are necessary. The notion of social participation that Marshall describes, however, is frequently denied to people within the US because of their class, gender, ethnicity, religion, ability, age, or many other factors that seem to draw an invisible line between what is considered a social "norm" versus a social minority. It is along this line, Judy Rohrer argues, that "citizenship in this country has long been (re)produced through the violences and exclusions that establish normalcy" (107), pointing towards the often-violent attempts of a powerful majority in the US to secure their political influence by establishing themselves as the "norm" and deeming everyone outside this "norm" as not eligible to political or social participation. Following this line of argument, social citizenship is not only a part of full citizenship but becomes a prerequisite for it, acting as a method to select who is close enough to a social "norm" to being granted participation.[1]

By looking at voting narratives of centenarians, I will deal with one deviation from what Rohrer calls normalcy, namely age. While centenarians, as part of an el-

---

[1] I am assuming throughout this paper that African Americans and other minority groups in the United States are still largely denied political and social citizenship to this day. Although legally they, of course, have the right to vote, mechanisms of voter disenfranchisement often prevent them from exercising that right.

derly demographic, are often seen as outside of society, they are frequently photographed and interviewed when engaging in acts of political participation. Centenarians are regarded as the "paragon[s] of positive aging" in a sense that they have managed to live an exceptionally long life which, in the general imaginary, has been exceptionally healthy (Robine and Vaupel x). Looking at centenarian (auto)biographies and media representations of centenarians voting in the 2020 US general election, I argue that centenarians are also idolized as role models of political participation.[2] This idolization is especially strong in narratives of African American centenarians, supporting discourses of the US as a post racial society in which every individual can achieve full citizenship, no matter their background. Consequently, these narratives cover up struggles for or problems with citizenship, implying that through self-improvement, hard work, and social assimilation, every individual can become a US citizen in a social and a political sense. This neoliberal narrative of centenarians as the model citizens, however, hides historical and current struggles and barriers that have denied and are denying voting rights to many people in the United States. Ultimately, then, the politics of centenarians' voting narratives are representative of more general structures of citizenship in the United States as it presents itself as inclusive to all, while excluding many.

Renegotiating Citizenship in Centenarian (Auto)Biographies

The oldest old are frequently questioned concerning their ability to participate socially and politically in a discourse that is closely linked to citizenship and disability. In public discourse, old age and disability—mental as well as physical—are inextricably linked. It is this link that makes it impossible to think about centenarians and participation without pondering the concept of biological citizenship. Biological citizenship is defined as "forms of belonging, rights claims, and demands for access to resources and care that are made on a biological basis such as an injury, shared genetic status, or disease state" (Mulligan). Besides making certain claims possible, however, the condition of the human body can also be used to deny access, as Douglass Baynton argues. According to him, "disability has functioned rhetorically to structure thought about social hierarchy in general" (562). Hence, discourses of disability have historically been used in order to deny individuals access to political participation. Biological citizenship then becomes another piece of the puzzle

---

2   I put the "auto" in parentheses throughout this paper because, although often advertised as autobiographies, all narratives discussed here are collaborations between centenarians and co-authors whose influence is more or less tracible. These collaborations pose their own set of questions concerning the centenarians' participation in terms of voice, agency, and autonomy, which will be discussed in more detail in a coming section.

when trying to understand access to political participation. If old age in the public imaginary is linked to a physical and mental narrative of decline—as suggested by leading scholars in the field of aging studies, including Margaret Morganroth Gullette who, in her monograph *Aged by Culture*, argues for the necessity to overcome this cultural imaginary—biological citizenship of the aged is up for debate. At the same time, the elderly are often imagined as disengaged from society, existing only in the figurative space of a "'waiting room' in which people bide their time until they die" (Hartung and Kunow 18). In this sense, then, being old and therefore confined within a 'waiting room' restricts access to social citizenship.

Narratives about centenarians often contradict these normative assumptions about old age. Centenarians are frequently portrayed as role models of aging and experts on diet, exercise, wisdom, and life in general. The *Guinness Book of World Records*, for instance, not only honors the oldest living people (all of them centenarians), it also elevates them into the role of teachers for the rest of the world by publishing articles such as "The World's Oldest People and Their Secrets to a Long Life" (Punt). This title not only suggests that it is desirable to live as long as possible but also that every individual can "learn" how to do so. The age of 100 seems to present a magic threshold into the realm of those who are done learning and get to teach their life lessons. In line with this connection, centenarian Waldo McBurney titled his own (auto)biography *My First 100 Years: A Look Back From the Finish Line*. As a runner, McBurney certainly imagined this title as a pun; yet, it also suggests that he has arrived at the finish line of life, having made it as far as anyone would need to. Generally, then, centenarians are not connected to a loss of citizenship. Rather, they are idolized as beacons of wisdom whose voice actually counts. Consequently, centenarian (auto)biographies (and media coverage of centenarians in general) seem to counter stereotypes of decline in old age. As Mita Banerjee and myself argue, "[a]s master narratives of aging, centenarians' autobiographies, with their emphasis on performance and a lack of dependency, serve to widen the gap between aging and disability" (2). While a discontinuation of the instant image of old age in connection with bodily decay may be desirable, these narratives gloss over the problems at hand, namely, that old age often does lead to a loss of social and/or biological citizenship. Moreover, in order to establish the role model figure of the centenarian, these narratives only function as long as the centenarian presented is imagined as a model citizen.

Agency, Autonomy, and the Right to Participation: The Genre of Centenarian (Auto)Biographies

The genre of centenarian (auto)biographies has been growing since the late 1990s. While there are a large variety of different narratives from centenarians of different backgrounds, in publication numbers, prestige of publishing houses, and general

180 Performing Citizenship

professionalism, almost all these narratives share the authorial structure of a centenarian author and a younger co-author. When looking at these collaborations from the angle of social citizenship this means that often a person who holds social citizenship helps, encourages, or writes for a person whose social citizenship may be contested due to old age. Interestingly, the most successful centenarian (auto)biographies are those of African Americans, a large number of which are women.[3] When looking at the respective co-authors for the narratives, it stands out that gender boundaries have been met, meaning that the gender of the centenarian matches that of their co-author. At the same time, age and race seem to not have been considered as African American centenarians usually work with white middle-aged co-authors. G. Thomas Couser argues in his monograph of the same title that collaborative life writing is prone to produce "vulnerable subjects" that is, subjects of the narrative who are "vulnerable to misrepresentation" by their co-authors (3). This vulnerability may well increase if the co-author does not share a common cultural and social background with the subject of their writing. Moreover, as Kay Schaffer and Sidonie Smith suggest in their book *Human Rights and Narrated Lives: The Ethics of Recognition*, other stake holders, such as publishing houses, can influence stories in order to make them more approachable for a mainstream audience, thereby tapping into normative ideologies of a given society (23). Both co-authors and publishers then have a significant influence on the work itself, calling into question the experience the audience is presented with. On the other hand, when considering the concept of "relational autonomy," it also becomes clear that co-authorship may be the only way to make centenarians' stories heard and thus a means to advocate for social citizenship of the elderly: "If centenarians become role models for autonomous lives lived into extreme old age, their stories might not have been made public had it not been for the support of a co-author. There are hence different degrees and forms of autonomy which have to be considered here" (Banerjee and Velten 2). While the question of co-authorship and autonomy thus remains complex, it is important to note that when reading autonomy, agency, and voice as aspects of social citizenship, the means of production of centenarian (auto)biographies seems to undermine this form of participation.

The readers of centenarian (auto)biographies have to trust in the writing process and assume that the co-authors managed to keep their own ideologies out while remaining aware of the power they are given. Speaking to this complexity, one co-author of a centenarian (auto)biography uttered the following in an unpublished interview:

---

3   Examples of these phenomena are *Having Our Say: The Dalany Sister's First 100 Years* by Annie Elizabeth Delany, Sarah Louise Dalany with Amy Hill Hearth; *Life is So Good!* by George Dawson and Richard Glaubman; *It is Well with My Soul: The Extraordinary Life of a 106-Year-Old Woman* by Ella Mae Cheeks Johnson with Patricia Mulcahy.

Oh, you mean, did [the centenarian] have concerns that I was white? ... Never! No. I was from [a good publishing house], they hired me. [They were] glad to have a contract! [They weren't] going to say "Give me an African-American [person]" in that contract! [They] said "Okay, if this [person] is who you want, I'm glad to work with her." ... I think [they're] one of the least racially concerned people I've ever met, frankly. I mean, [they were] thrilled with Obama, believe me, [they] understood the significance of all that ... [They] interacted well with everyone. I mean, it was a big deal to [them] because the society made it a big deal but in terms of her personal views ... I think, unfortunately, that whole topic what one would call "cultural appropriation" or whatever has become much more problematic in the last five years. It wasn't so much even when I interviewed [them], now it's become quite a talking point at universities and this whole political correctness thing with trigger warnings and people from different ethnic groups not wanting certain things said.[4] (unpublished interview)

The co-author here portrays themselves as a professional who justifies their right to tell the story at hand through the credentials of a prestigious publishing house. For the purposes of legitimacy, professionalism is thus more important than shared experience. In a way, this appears to be a valid point: a professional co-author should be trained to untangle their own ideologies from the person whose voice they are trying to capture. However, the patronizing tone of this statement counters any hope for an equal partnership between author and co-author. By emphasizing that the centenarian "understood the significance" of the Obama election, the co-author implies that this would be surprising to their audience. In fact, this statement questions the centenarians' maturity, and therefore their claim to citizenship. Speaking to this, Corinne T. Field argues that historically, citizenship as tied to adulthood, has been denied to women and African Americans because their maturity was questioned by a white, male "norm" (3). This claim to "equal adulthood" likewise appears to be denied to the centenarian by their co-author most likely because of their age and race (1). By belittling the centenarians' political and social awareness and therefore questioning their maturity, the co-author implicitly questions their claim to any citizenship rights.

Moreover, the co-author's elaboration on mechanisms such as cultural appropriation indicate that they may be ignorant of the subject. By arguing that identity in this instance does not matter, they suggest that differences in ideology are unimportant in collaborative life writing. This then indicates that they have not untangled

---

4   As part of a research project on centenarians' autobiographies within the research group "Un/Doing Differences: Practices of Human Differentiation" funded by the German Research Foundation (DFG Research Group FOR-1939/2), I conducted several interviews with co-authors of centenarian (auto)biographies. In order to ensure the anonymity of the interviewee, the quote here has been anonymized.

their own ideologies from those of the centenarian. Although this presents just one example of the relationship between a centenarian and their co-author, it strongly suggests that centenarians are used as pawns by the middle aged to satisfy their hope that growing old is not as negative as the media posits. Furthermore, in the case of African American centenarian (auto)biographies, there is always an implicit notion of a white savior—a white person who appears to support African Americans (or other minorities) but in the attempt to do good ends up patronizing them.[5] These mechanisms then suggest that the centenarian here is denied the right to their own story and therefore voice, agency, participation, and ultimately, social citizenship. The centenarian is dragged out of the "waiting room" of old age and is presented by a co-author in the way the co-author sees fit. The centenarian thereby becomes a pawn of the public perception rather than an active agent in society. Ironically, despite always being on the verge of being patronizing and of conveying the white middle-aged conception of what a centenarian should be like, centenarian (auto)biographies give a stage to narratives of empowerment and the struggle for social citizenship that would otherwise remain unheard. Yet, when looking at these narratives closer, we have to bear in mind the means of production and remember that the narrative may be a white middle-aged person's idea of what a centenarian should have to say. Because centenarians are regarded as "paragons of positive aging," it is in turn crucial for a performance of centenarianism to have the narratives emphasize how much the centenarians carry all forms of citizenship: social, political, and biological. In other words, narratives about centenarians seem to be produced in a manner that challenges claims to citizenship while the narratives themselves, as I will illustrate in the following sections, aim at painting a picture of centenarians as "paragons of citizenship."

Female African American Centenarian (Auto)Biographies and the Struggle for Political Participation

While the means of producing centenarian (auto)biographies appear to contradict social citizenship, the contents themselves reveal narratives of belonging, adaption, and ability, therefore offering a demand for social, biological, and political citizenship. In order to exemplify this, I will briefly discuss two different narratives: Ella Mae Cheeks Johnson's and Patricia Mulcahy's *It Is Well with My Soul: The Extraordinary Life of a 106-Year-Old Woman* and Ann Nixon Cooper's and Karen Grigsby Bates' *A Century and Some Change: My Life Before the President Called My Name*. Both texts tell

---

5   Similar mechanisms are also present in other centenarian (auto)biographies. For further discussion on this topic, see "The Elephant in the Living Room: Centenarians' Autobiographies, Co-Authorship and Narratives of Extreme Longevity" by Banerjee and Velten.

the life stories of African American female centenarians and therefore touch upon the struggle of civil rights for African Americans. By discussing these issues, both narratives portray a claim to participation and belonging and, ultimately, suggest that this claim has been heard.

Although social citizenship can be regarded as a prerequisite for political citizenship, many African American female centenarian (auto)biographies use the centenarian's peaceful endeavor to achieve political participation as a narrative tool to advocate for social citizenship. That is, the narratives emphasize a sense of belonging within mainstream society by stressing that the individuals presented are willing to play by rules deemed adequate. In that sense, the relationship between political and social citizenship presents itself as a chicken-egg scenario: it is by no means easy to entangle what comes first. This interconnectedness of social and political citizenship is echoed, as Frederick Cooper states in reference to Charles Taylor, in "[t]he question of who has voice in deciding how a state will act and who is entitled to assistance or protection" (17). Thus, with the right to vote there should come the power to alter who is accepted within the benefits—and therefore the social structures—of a nation. These struggles also become apparent within the two narratives that serve as examples for this chapter. What both narratives have in common is that they do mention the struggle for equal social and political rights leading up to and during the Civil Rights Movement, but they stress how little they were interested in causing disorder or harm to the political and social structures at hand. Thereby, they establish themselves as model protesters who would never fight for their citizenship rights in a way that would disrupt what was considered to be the "norm." The two narratives also touch upon inequalities but ultimately tell the story of their own success which was made possible through hard work and despite their minority status. In that sense, these stories are narratives of the myth of the American Dream, indicating that by working hard, Cheeks Johnson and Nixon Cooper have earned their citizenship socially, as well as politically. Moreover, they managed to live an exceptionally long and healthy life leaving them physically and mentally able to perform their citizenship rights.

In *It is Well With My Soul*, Ella Mae Cheeks Johnson and Patricia Mulcahy describe Cheeks Johnson as a "good Samaritan," whose purpose it is to help others more than anything else (3).[6] This philosophy establishes the centenarian as a do-gooder who is in no way threatening to strive for power. This image is intensified through her occupation as a social worker, giving back to the community. Framing Cheeks Johnson as a peaceful person whose purpose in life is to support others leads to an image

---

6   For more on the politics of help, see Kaitlyn Quinn and Erika Canossini's chapter in this volume, "'Clean Body, Clean Mind, Clean Job': The Role of Penal Voluntary Sector Organizations in Constructing 'Good' Carceral Citizens." Here, Quinn and Canossini focus on how non-profits seek to "help" criminalized individuals reenter society as carceral citizens.

184   Performing Citizenship

of a person who will not interfere with the status quo. Thus, despite being African American, she does not incite fear within those in power who may perceive her as wishing to undermine social structures as they are.

This reality is emphasized through Cheeks Johnson's and Mulcahy's portrayal of racial issues. Cheeks Johnson was enrolled at Fiske University during the student protests of 1924–25 in which she took part by boycotting her classes. While she did participate, her (auto)biography emphasizes that her personal approach to racial issues differed fundamentally from that of W. E. B. DuBois, who sparked the protests in the first place. She explains that "[DuBois] was the fighter" (28), "I didn't yell. I wasn't openly rebellious. I didn't fight" (33); she even describes DuBois' manner of protesting as "disturbing" (32), meaning too aggressive. By separating Cheeks Johnson from a more "aggressive" form of protest, the narrative claims that she is eager to adapt to what a mainstream society would deem appropriate, as long as she gets to be a part of this society in return. Hence, the narrative advocates for social and political citizenship of African Americans by promoting a discourse of assimilation. In this way, the (auto)biography shows how belonging in the United States still has to be achieved through adaptation.

Similar mechanisms are on display in Ann Nixon Cooper's and Karen Grigsby Bates's *A Century and Some Change: My Life Before the President Called My Name.* Nixon Cooper is described as a woman who stands up for her rights but always does so in a manner that would be deemed appropriate by mainstream society. Her acts of rebellion include getting out of a bus's front exit and staying in her seat on public transport when a white person wants her to leave (146–47).[7] Of course, this form of protest reminds the reader of Rosa Parks whose actions are now recognized as justifiable by mainstream US society. Both Ella Mae Cheeks Johnson and Ann Nixon Cooper thus engage in a discourse of respectability politics, asking for change in a way that is deemed appropriate by those in power. Their struggle for citizenship is portrayed as a politely phrased inquiry rather than a strong demand. This portrayal leads to their framing as model citizens as they emphasize their adaptability and focus on the wish to belong and participate rather than to fundamentally change social structures. The narratives thus emphasize the social belonging of Ann Nixon Cooper and Ella May Cheeks Johnson by elaborating on their efforts to assimilate to whatever is considered the norm in US society. Therefore, they are idolized as role models for people who may feel left on the outside of social citizenship. Read against the grain, this approach offers a pessimistic reading of the concept of citizenship and belonging in the United States: it appears that the national ideals of "life, liberty, and the pursuit of happiness" are solely granted to those who assimilate to the "norm." In turn, one

---

7   Nixon Cooper's protest, of course, would not have been regarded as appropriate at the time but would have been deemed acceptable when the story was told in 2009.

could then easily ask the question of how free or liberated a person can be when they have to make sure to assimilate to mainstream society.

The example of Ann Nixon Cooper's (auto)biography not only addresses issues of the struggle for African American citizenship and political participation, it also presents a positive outcome of these struggles. The narrative describes Nixon Cooper voting for Barack Obama, implicitly connecting this act to the past through the Civil Rights Movement: "After all we'd been through as a people, if there was a black man who was a good candidate and he needed my vote, I was going to be there. I have been a registered voter since 1940, but this time—sixty-eight year [sic] later—I wanted to walk into that little booth and pull the curtain around me and vote. In person. For Barack Obama" (2). Ultimately, Nixon Cooper regards the struggle for political citizenship as won, not only because she has been an eligible voter for more than sixty years but also because the United States had elected their first African American president. Indicating that the goal of equal citizenship has been reached, this narrative thus supports the myth of the US as a postracial nation. According to Judy Rohrer, this mechanism is a common one in the time after Obama's election. She argues that "dominant narratives regarding citizenship [wer]e being reinforced through colorblind notions of a postracial nation" (108). Hence, Ann Nixon Cooper's (auto)biography becomes part of a vicious cycle of discourses of equal citizenship being reinforced through the notion of a postracial society and vice versa. Looking closer reveals, however, that neither the tale of equal citizenship, nor the tale of a postracial society are prevalent in the United States.

Besides touching upon racial issues, Nixon Cooper's narrative also frames her as a paragon of voting. She emphasizes that, even at the age of 100, voting was not a challenge: "Casting my vote took only a minute, but it was an important one for me, my people, and my country" (3). She is described as a patriot, doing her duty for her country and, so the narrative suggests, if she can do this as an African American centenarian, there is no reason for anybody not to vote. This notion is echoed as Barack Obama mentions Nixon Cooper in his victory speech: "*But one that's on my mind tonight is about a woman who cast her ballot in Atlanta. She's a lot like the millions of others who stood in line to make their voice heard in this election except for one thing. Ann Nixon Cooper is one hundred six years old*" (5). Obama himself appears to be in awe about Ann Nixon Cooper's ability to vote at her age and puts her on a pedestal, for everyone to strive to be like her. In that sense, she becomes the "citty upon a hill" that puritan minister John Winthrop expected America to become in 1630 (121), namely, to be a role model for the world to look up and aspire to. Moreover, Rohrer argues that Obama's election led to a "revitalization of the myth of meritocracy" (110). This myth is intensified through the figures of centenarians managing to cast their ballots against all odds because they, like Barack Obama, managed to get to this point because they were determined and worked hard. Through the connection of Ann Nixon Cooper to inherently US American myths, the narrative imagines her as a model American. Of course, this portrayal then propagates a US American utopia of equality when it comes to age, race, and gender.

Conclusively, both Ann Nixon Cooper and Ella Mae Cheeks Johnson are portrayed through the lens of assimilation, suggesting that social and political citizenship is reachable to those who are willing to adapt to the so-called norm. The politics of co-authorship, the framing of the narratives, and the emphasis on assimilation turn these centenarian (auto)biographies into stories that feed a discourse of a postracial, as well as post-ableist, US society in which inequality is an unfortunate chapter of the past. As opposed to Faith Ringold's story quilts, discussed by Malaika Sutter in this volume, these centenarian (auto)biographies neither use an inherently African American medium, nor question the current citizenship status of African Americans in the United States. Rather, they seem to be white-washed narratives, justifying the exclusion of any individual that does not show the same efforts of assimilation.

Centenarians, Citizenship, and Voting in the 2020 Election

Frederick Cooper suggests that "[t]he discourse of elites and ordinary people is often laden with images of what the proper citizen looks like, what his or her religious beliefs should be, how he or she should behave" (15). Centenarian voting narratives present narratives of proper citizens in terms of determination and patriotism. As I have pointed out with regard to centenarian (auto)biographies, centenarians are often established as role models not only of aging but also of citizenship. The two examples discussed above, however, only describe centenarians' roles in citizenship discourse until 2008. With Obama's election, it seems, social and political citizenship is possible for everyone. Yet, accusations of voter disenfranchisement and general hurdles to take part in the political process in the US steadily increase. The US 2020 general election and a global pandemic add to the already strained situation of the political process in the United States. With these reports about the state of US democracy, there is an increasing need to advocate for the right to vote thereby not only encouraging people to make the effort but also indicating that the democratic system is working for everybody.

Thus, leading up to the 2020 US general election, there were numerous media reports of voting centenarians, either those who engaged in early voting or those who came out on election day. The stories, told by different media outlets, often follow the same formula: emphasizing the importance to vote, framing it as civic duty, and pointing out that there really cannot be any obstacle for anyone if a centenarian, being considered frail and immobile as well as at high risk to die from Covid-19, can overcome all of them. Yet, while in centenarian (auto)biographies concerns of citizenship are mostly found in the narratives of African Americans, the centenarians portrayed voting in the 2020 US presidential elections are more racially diverse. More than covering up social exclusion due to race, media outlets thus gloss over the exclusion often coming with old age—especially during a pandemic, where the role of the biological informs processes of belonging more than ever.[8] At the same time, by blurring the obstacles faced by the extremely old these narratives suggest that no obstacle is too high to overcome when it comes to voting.

There are countless examples of centenarians voting in the 2020 general election on the internet, most of them rather short social media posts, such as, for instance, Queen Latifah sharing an image of Roscoe Draper mailing his ballot on *Instagram*. She adds the caption "This is Mr. Roscoe Draper. He is 101 years old! If he can do it so can you! This is America! This is patriotism! I believe in us so let's do this! VOTE! VOTE! VOTE!," thereby indicating that in order to be a true American, one has to overcome all obstacles in order to vote, implicitly shaming those who cannot. In the following, I will focus on two longer news clips, following and interviewing Rosalind Rosner and Ana Belfield throughout their voting process, connecting these clips to the portrayal of biological, social, and political citizenship.

The news segment on Ruth Rosner aired on "CBS Sunday Morning" and includes typical characteristics of centenarian narratives. While essentially focusing on the topic of voting, the interviewer is also interested in how Rosner managed to live to an exceptionally old age, thereby implying that centenarianism is an achievement that everybody should strive for. Moreover, the clip provides a recap of Rosner's life, emphasizing that this is the twenty-second election she has voted in and that she was born before women had the right to vote. This information reminds the audience of the struggle for women's political citizenship. Of course, Rosner herself never had to fight for it—she was four when the nineteenth amendment was passed—but the fact that she lived during that time seems to suffice as a reminder that political citizenship cannot be taken for granted and that participating in the democratic process is a duty every citizen must perform. Pointing out the number of elections Rosner participated in underlines her consistent participation in this process, giving her a certain expertise on the topic as well as showing her qualities as a model citizen.

During the clip, the focus is on Rosner promoting the importance of voting as well as the obstacles that make it difficult for her to do so. While she states that voting "is the most important thing I can do" (00:36–00:40), she is depicted wearing a face mask and moving around with a walker. The images thus depict everything that would exclude her from social or biological citizenship: she is physically weak and needs help moving. During the Covid-19 pandemic, she is part of the high-risk

---

8   For a discussion of biological and medicalized citizenship in this collection, see Mita Baner-
     jee's "'What the Eyes Don't See': Medical Citizenship and Environmental Justice in Mona Han-
     na-Attisha's Medical Memoir" and Amina Touzos's "'You're My People Now': *The Last of Us* Se-
     ries on the Question of Belonging and Citizenship during the Age of Pandemics."

group of people who are especially vulnerable to the SARS-CoV II virus. Nonetheless, her statement suggests that all these obstacles cannot hinder her from performing the important act of voting. While emphasizing the importance of voting and conveying it as civic duty, this narrative also promotes the image that there is no obstacle too high, thus evoking the neoliberal narrative of a meritocratic United States where those who belong work hard to stick to a supposed "norm" and, in turn, that this "norm" is reachable for everybody.

This message becomes more nuanced when the video quotes a tweet by Hillary Clinton who mentions Rosner and explicitly says what the clip implicitly shows: "If Ruth can get out to vote, the rest of us don't have much excuse" (00:40–00:47). With her tweet, Clinton gives Rosner and her efforts, as well as the image that everyone should be able to vote, a world stage. She then not only urges United States citizens to vote but implies to the rest of the world that the democratic system of the US is intact and that, in fact, participation is open to everyone. The CBS clip sends the same message on a more local level, again emphasizing the struggle of voting during a pandemic: "And if this masked centenarian can do it, she wants you to do it, too" (02:39–02:43). Here, the video goes one step further, claiming that Rosner wants other people to go to the polls as well, despite the fact that she never utters such a request herself. While voting is important to her, she does not directly summon others to do the same. This reintroduces concerns around the centenarian's autonomy and raises the question of whether she is used to send a message that is stronger than what she intends to personally say.

What becomes certain, however, is that Rosner has no objections to being portrayed as a patriot and CBS seems to make use of this to bring their message across. At the end of the video, having her "I voted early" sticker attached to her jacket, Rosner sings "god bless America, my home sweet home" (02:43–02:50), closing the sequence with a certain sentiment that may be expected from a US morning show segment but also intensifies the image that Ruth Rosner is a model citizen in all regards.

Ana Belfield is portrayed in a similar fashion. She is featured in a segment on CBS New York where the anchor introduces her story as follows: "We should all have the positive energy and attitude of one Queens voter. Some people come up with excuses, why they shouldn't vote or don't need to. This woman gives us 101 reasons to vote" (00:01–00:12). This video then introduces Belfield's age as the main reason to encourage others to vote. Like Rosner, she is framed as a paragon of voting for participating in the election despite her age. In order to support this notion, the clip also features the imagery of Belfield needing the support of a walker to move around as well as the prominent face mask, signifying the pandemic this election is set in.

Besides these images that the two news segments have in common, Belfield's story also touches upon another topic: the digital divide. During the Covid-19 pandemic communication via digital resources became the main means of social interaction for many. At the same time, elderly populations are generally not as well versed in digital communications as younger ones. Speaking to this point, Garbriel Martins van Jaarsveld explains that

> [a]ccess to, and ability to proficiently use technology is much lower in older populations than in younger adults. This uneven distribution of technological access and skill is known as the digital divide, or the gray digital divide, and researchers have suggested it has continued to increase as the rate of technological innovation speeds up. This results in a paradoxical situation, in which the population most affected by the lockdown is also the population least helped by the digital tools aiming to mitigate the negative effects.

One could thus argue that older people are often excluded by means of digital citizenship. This exclusion intensified through the Covid-19 pandemic, forcing those "at risk" into isolation, which becomes more difficult without the means to use modern technology to communicate. The CBS segment on Ana Belfield briefly engages with the topic of the digital divide in imagery and voiceover as she is shown using a tablet to sign herself in at the polling station and the audience hears a surprised sounding commentator saying, "she verifies her identity on a smart pad" (00:56–01:13). While this does not imply anything about her online communication skills, it shows that she is not intimidated by technology and is willing to interact with it in order to participate in society. Ultimately, what this suggests then is that the digital divide is yet another factor that can be overcome if people are willing to work hard for it.

Within the segment, Belfield herself gets to speak about political participation and elaborates on why she thinks it is crucial to engage: "It's important to vote to help bring this nation as one" (00:17–00:21). Hence, Belfield has no selfish reasons to participate but thinks about the benefit of the community. This echoes the spirit of Ella Mae Cheeks Johnson's role as a good Samaritan. Furthermore, it shows that she is convinced that this democratic process is necessary for the country's unity and, at the same time, implies that only who votes can belong. As in Rosner's case, the makers of the segment go a step further and claim that Belfield "believes not voting is disrespecting those who made days like this happen" (01:21–01:28). As the audience does not hear Belfield herself utter this statement, we cannot know what she said on the matter and how much of it is a product of CBS's interpretation. However, it is crucial that the emphasis is on "days like this" in general, as it directs the audience's attention towards democracy as a whole. In that sense, Belfield would see not voting as an assault towards the founders of the US and those who fought in the revolutionary war to gain independence. Yet, Ana Belfield, as an African American woman, may not wish to thank the founding fathers, as they actively denied people like herself any kind of citizenship; rather, she may emphasize the struggles of abolitionists, suffragettes, and civil rights leaders who made her personal act of voting possible. By leaving this open, and having her refer to "days like this," the message is

190 Performing Citizenship

made more inclusive, in turn showing that this model citizen shares the same values as the county's "norm."

Like Ann Nixon Cooper, Rosner and Belfield are elevated to role model figures of voting and thus become the personification of Winthrop's "city upon a hill." Neither of the two centenarians discussed here is shown complaining about the system. Neither of them criticizes voting in person because mail-in voting is so difficult (and has been deprecated by members of the Republican Party). Neither of them recognizes that they could only vote because they have a supportive infrastructure behind them, for instance people driving them to the polls, etc. These narratives thus not only gloss over the fact that there are people who are not allowed to vote (for instance criminalized individuals, cf. Nina Heydt in this volume), but also that every individual who shows up at the polls has their own obstacles to overcome. There may be people, for example, who have to work during opening hours of polling stations and may lose their job if they go vote. In these cases, people must sacrifice their political citizenship in order to keep their social citizenship in the sense of remaining a contributing member of society. Others may need assistance in getting to the polls but lack the infrastructure that both Rosner and Belfield seem to have. If physical reasons keep people from voting, a lack of biological citizenship hinders political citizenship. By positioning centenarians as the paragons of citizenship and democracy and by deliberately leaving out those who struggle to participate in the process of voting, the narratives discussed here all suggest that the latter cases are non-existent. Thereby, these narratives contribute to an imaginary of the United States as a country with an exceptional democracy that holds true to the values of equality, liberty, and justice for all—or, in line with meritocratic practices, for those who are willing to work for them.

At the same time, however, representations of centenarians in this light only work because they derive from the underlying assumption that the elderly are generally less able or willing to participate. By presenting centenarians as paragons of citizenship, these narratives thus not only reinforce the myth of meritocracy but also uncover the structures of a deeply ageist society. While in these stories extreme old age is presented as a factor that does not inevitably lead to the loss of social, political, biological, or even digital citizenship, the implicit message remains that such a loss would generally be expected. Yet, as with all obstacles, according to the framing of centenarians, through hard work exclusion can be avoided.

Conclusion

According to Heike Paul, US national identity is based on a set of "myths," as she elaborates in her monograph *The Myths that Made America*. Prominent amongst these myths are the myths of puritan settlement, including Winthrop's "city upon a hill" metaphor; the myth of the founding fathers, including the celebration of the democracy they have established; and the myth of the American Dream, including meritocratic ideals of the self-made man. As this paper has shown, these myths are all to be found within narratives about centenarians, including them in the very fabric of US national identity. This myth-making elevates centenarians to the status of model US citizens while also mostly leaving out their own voices in the matter. Centenarians could thus be called "pawns of citizenship," used to promote belonging in any area of US society through a neoliberal, meritocratic myth. The narratives discussed in this paper portray all obstacles to citizenship and belonging as easy to overcome and therefore blame those who cannot participate. This then supports a myth of inclusion that can be used to silence all critics of the political system of the United States. The portrayal of centenarians' performances of citizenship rights paints an inclusive picture of US citizenship, propagating the lie that no groups are excluded, that there is no suppression of minorities, that there are no struggles for the simple right to vote. Images of centenarians—often female, often African American—aim to serve as proof that the struggles of the past have been successful. However, this imagery glosses over realities of voter disenfranchisement, upkeeping the myth of US American democracy.

Read against the grain, these narratives reveal traces of deeply rooted ageism and racism. In terms of age, the examples discussed here not only frame physical decline as a failure but also make the individual responsible for the way they age. In terms of race, they suggest that once a person assimilates to the norm, social and political citizenship will be granted. Both the discussion of age and race thus suggests that in order to belong, US society still requires its members to conform to a white, able-bodied, middle-aged ideal. Regarding this connection, the paper also touched upon the complexity of the concept of citizenship by looking at it from different angles. Social and political citizenship clearly influence each other and are influenced by other manifestations of belonging which may include but are not limited to biological and digital citizenship.

Similar to the glossing over of issues of aging and promoting neoliberal ideologies of the human body, centenarian narratives gloss over issues of inequality and disenfranchisement. As the centenarians discussed here did not necessarily have the right to their own voice—a problem of social citizenship that only reveals itself upon closer inspection—they act as mere mascots for the political system they live in. Reading these narratives through the lens of ageism then reveals how these supposedly inclusive narratives exclude many by implying that only those who age like the centenarians presented aged in the right way and are therefore rewarded. This can in turn be applied to the larger narrative of citizenship and democracy in the United States which implies a certain inclusiveness despite establishing more and more obstacles for those who are not considered part of the social "norm."

Works Cited

Banerjee, Mita, and Julia Velten. "The Elephant in the Living Room: Centenarians' Autobiographies, Co-Authorship and Narratives of Extreme Longevity." *Journal of Aging Studies*, vol. 52, 2020, pp. 1–8.

Baynton, Douglass. "Slaves, Immigrants, and Suffragists: The Uses of Disability in Citizenship Debates." *PMLA*, vol. 120 no. 3, 2005, pp. 562–567.

CBS New York. "101-Year-Old Anna Belfield Casts Her Ballot in Queens." *YouTube*, 29 Oct. 2020, https://www.youtube.com/watch?v=4cMjr1T4ITs.

CBS Sunday Morning. "104-Year-Old Ruth Rosner on Casting her Vote." *YouTube*, 1 Nov. 2020, https://www.youtube.com/watch?v=6brNsfY6Ba8.

Cheeks Johnson, Ella Mae, and Patricia Mulcahy. *It Is Well with My Soul: The Extraordinary Life of a 106-Year-Old Woman*. Penguin, 2010.

Cooper, Frederick. *Citizenship, Inequality, and Difference: Historical Perspectives*. Princeton UP, 2018.

Couser, G. Thomas. *Vulnerable Subjects: The Ethics of Life Writing*. Cornell UP, 2003.

Dawson, George and Richard Glaubman. *Life is So Good!* Penguin, 2000.

Delany, Annie Elizabeth, Sarah Louise Delany, and Amy Hill Hearth. *Having Our Say: The Delany Sisters' First 100 Years*. Dell, 1994.

Field, Corinne T. *The Struggle for Equal Adulthood: Gender, Race, Age, and the Fight for Citizenship in Antebellum America*. U of North Carolina P, 2014.

Gullette, Margaret Morganroth. *Aged by Culture*. U of Chicago P, 2004.

Hartung, Heike, and Rüdiger Kunow. "Introduction: Age Studies." *Amerikastudien / American Studies*, vol. 56, no. 1, 2011, pp. 15–22, https://www.ncbi.nlm.nih.gov/pmc/articles/PMC7693633/.

Latifah, Queen. "This is Mr. Roscoe Draper. He is 101 years old! If he can do it so can you! This is America! This is patriotism! I believe in us so let's do this! VOTE! VOTE! VOTE!" *Instagram*, 2 Nov. 2020, https://www.instagram.com/p/CHGPJP3jZ8u/?utm_source=ig_embed.

Lopez, Ian Haney. *White By Law: The Legal Construction of Race*. NYUP, 2006.

Marshall, Thomas H. "Citizenship and Social Class." *Citizenship and Social Class*, T. H. Marshall and Tom Bottomore, Pluto Press, 1992, pp. 3–51.

Martins van Jaarsveld, Gabriele. "The Effects of Covid-19 Among the Elderly: A Case for Closing the Digital Divide." *Fronties in Psychology*, vol. 11, 2020, pp. 1211.

McBurney, Waldo. *My First 100 Years: A Look Back From the Finish Line*. Leathers Publishing, 2004.

Mulligan, Jessica. "Biological Citizenship." *Oxford Bibliographies*. Feb. 2017. https://www.oxfordbibliographies.com/view/document/obo-9780199766567/obo-9780199766567-0164.xml.

Nixon Cooper, Ann, and Karen Grigsby Bates. *A Century and Some Change: My Life Before the President Called My Name*. Atria Books, 2010.

Paul, Heike. *The Myths that Made America: An Introduction to American Studies.* transcript, 2013.

Punt, Dominic. "The World's Oldest People and Their Secrets to a Long Life." *Guinness World Records*, 2020. https://www.guinnessworldrecords.com/news/2020/10/the-worlds-oldest-people-and-their-secrets-to-a-long-life-632895.

Robine, Jean-Marie, and James W. Vaupel. *Longevity: To the Limits and Beyond.* Springer, 1997.

Rohrer, Judy. "Black Presidents, Gay Marriages, and Hawaiian Sovereignty: Reimagining Citizenship in the Age of Obama." *American Studies*, vol. 50, no. 3/4, Fall/Winter 2009, pp. 107–130. https://doi.org/10.1353/ams.2009.0044.

Schaffer, Kay, and Sidonie Smith. *Human Rights and Narrated Lives: The Ethics of Recognition.* Palgrave Macmillan, 2004.

Winthrop, John. "A Model of Christian Charity." *Key Concepts in American Cultural History*, 2nd ed., edited by Bernd Engler and Oliver Scheiding, Wissenschaftlicher Verlag Trier, 2007, pp. 118–123.

Making Material Borders
Petro-Cultures and Modern Citizenship

Scott Obernesser

Introduction

The 2018 film *Green Book* loosely retells the story of Dr. Don Shirley's (Mahershala Ali) 1962 musical tour through the US South. Shirley is accompanied by Frank Vallelonga (Viggo Mortensen), a bouncer at the Copacabana Club. At the request of Shirley's record label, Vallelonga would act primarily as Shirley's driver, but also as a security guard, if needed. Early in the film, the label presents Vallelonga with a copy of Victor Hugo Green's Jim Crow-era travel book *The Negro Motorist Green-Book*, a travel guide that identified Black-friendly businesses throughout the United States. The *Green-Book* mimicked a rash of travel guides distributed throughout the US during the nation's first age of automobility, increasing domestic tourism and, in turn, stipulating the need for a more comprehensive national road network.[1] In *See America First: Tourism and National Identity, 1880–1940*, Marguerite Shaffer claims the growth of domestic tourism in the late-nineteenth and early-twentieth centuries was, "central to the shifting notions of citizenship shaped by the emergence of America as an urban-industrial nation state" (6).[2] Shaffer further explains "mobile citizenship," citizenship defined by one's ability to *see* the country and *experience* the nation, "redefined political rights in consumer terms, celebrating seeing over speaking, purchasing over voting, and traveling over participating" (6). Other scholars—such as

---

1 Most of these guides were created and published by oil companies, the target audience being largely middle-class white Americans. In a review of Green's *Green-Book*, William Smith explains the guide "is a book badly needed among our Race since the advance of the motor age. Realizing the only way we knew where and how to reach our pleasure resorts was in a way of speaking, by word of mouth, until the publication of 'The Negro Motorist Green-Book.' ... We earnestly believe 'The Negro Motorist Green-Book' will mean as much if not more to us as the A. A. A. means to the white race" (Green 2).

2 Shaffer recognizes increasingly complex renderings of citizenship throughout the twentieth century, where the boundaries of citizenship status are defined by any number of sub-divided identifiers that create and exclude membership according to social, cultural, or political distinctions.

Engin Isin and Patricia K. Wood, Leti Volpp, and Ayelet Shachar—have theorized similar conceptions of citizenship based around identity, immigration, or national belonging. What many of these studies identify is the increasingly paradoxical position of a global human mired in citizenship rights regulated by increasingly abstract and indiscriminately discriminatory nation states. In terms of the *Green-Book*: that white US citizens and Black US citizens required separate travel guide archetypes to shape, direct, and even participate in nationally evolving citizenship rituals at the mid-century conveys citizenship not as a solid state, but as a constantly shifting vector regulated within the boundaries of the state's fluctuating allowance.

In this project, I trace an arc of US citizenship bounded by oil, encompassing geographic, racial, generational, and ontological distinctions from the mid-century to the post-9/11 era. In particular, I focus on modern petro-infrastructures as a material criterion of citizenship, specifically infrastructure's exclusionary/inclusionary capacities that precondition citizenship with material obligations to petro-capitalism. This is to say that visibility is a central vector by which citizenship is measured and regulated by national material networks—in the twenty-first century, those material networks take the form of petro-infrastructures: roads, highways, and automobiles, but also cultural recognition, commerce, or energy production, as we see most notably in the modern dilemma over oil pipelines like the Dakota Access Pipeline (DAPL) and the Keystone XL pipeline. I will focus on two primary examples: first, the history and actuation of national highway planning and construction, emphasizing consciously manufactured consequences in minority communities. While this practice is most clearly exposed by Robert Moses' reconstruction of New York City beginning in the 1920s,[3] the consequences of infrastructure and access perpetuate racist practices that separate and bind minority communities from their surrounding region. Eddy Harris' 1993 memoir, *South of Haunted Dreams: A Ride Through Slavery's Old Backyard*, observes continuing discrimination for Black Americans through the example of Atlantic Beach, South Carolina. Second, I will examine oil pipelines, particularly the DAPL in North Dakota, as attempted sites of continued Western commitment to petro-capitalism, despite growing opposition to new construction. As Louise Erdrich makes clear in her short story "The Red Convertible," the reservation has long been a conflictual site between economic/cultural perceptions of citizenship, petro-culture, and the realities of mobility, access, and exclusion. Opposition to the DAPL, led primarily by the Standing Rock Sioux tribe and other Indigenous communities, represents citizens who benefit least from these material networks, yet experience disproportionate ecological impact and economic gain. Ultimately, what begins as material expectation transforms into ideological allegiance, leaving those on the outskirts of citizenship seeking inclusion through petro-infrastruc-

---

3   Though, Shaffer indicates these infrastructural inequities begin far earlier.

tures constructed expressly to filter out those who cannot effectuate a corresponding material compliance.

The Shifting Nature of Citizenship in the Twenty-First Century

Many scholars make clear that citizenship, both conceptually and in practice, is immensely complicated. Early in *Citizenship and Identity*, Isin and Wood broadly describe citizenship as, "*both* a set of practices (cultural, symbolic and economic) and a bundle of rights and duties (civil, political and social) that define an individual's membership in a polity" (4). Citizenship might, incorrectly, be perceived as a gateway: once achieved, the rights, privileges, protections, and conveniences of citizenship are fully granted to that citizen (Shachar, 3–10). However, Isin and Wood go on to explain that globalization undermines "personal attachment to membership in the state," even while a more contemporary digitality transforms political allegiances and agencies.[4] Shachar's *The Birthright Lottery: Citizenship and Global Inequality* claims that privileges guaranteed to affluent nations and corresponding citizens come, ultimately, at the expense of a larger global poor. Yet, this same inequity applies within nation-states as well. As the *Green-Book* legacy makes clear, "the sets of practices" and "bundles of rights and duties" afforded to a nation's citizens do not equitably define membership for all individuals. The 15th Constitutional Amendment, ratified in 1870, guaranteed citizens' voting rights—specifically voting rights for African Americans—but voter suppression tactics prevented widespread voting until the Voting Rights Act of 1965 and persists in new forms with each election cycle. This is not even considering the battle for women's suffrage, guaranteed in the 19th Constitutional Amendment ratified in 1920, or Native American struggles for citizenship, who, though naturally born, were not recognized citizens or voters until the 1924 Indian Citizenship Act. And again, nearly sixty years *after* the Voting Rights Act, the US is facing unprecedented conflicts concerning voter rights in the wake of the 2020 elections, where urban Black communities and other minority voting blocs essentially determined a Democratic Party victory.[5] While many attacks on voter freedoms manifest in silly declarations (usually procedural obstacles that are an inconvenience but are "not insurmountable objects"), the more serious limitations make use of existing material networks to limit access to polling, redistribute minority populations, or redraw voter precincts (Millhiser).

As many of my colleagues in this collection make clear, citizenship has only become more complicated in the twenty-first century: identity and belonging have be-

---

4   Also see Aytekin Isman and Ozlem Canan Gungoren's article "Being Digital Citizen."
5   Simply look at battles in Georgia and Texas over voting rights restrictions as evidence of this continued discrimination.

come increasingly important to citizenry, but this mirrors a global movement in mass communications and digitality that diffuses state boundaries previously regarded as firm geographical and, therein, embodied boundaries of citizenship. The end of Keystone XL, which I discuss later, is proof of such diffusion. While the legislation, expectations, and allowances that constitute citizenship in the US are in constant flux, late-capitalist petro-infrastructures obscurely maintain the very divisions at the heart of debates concerning citizenship. Rhetorical struggles to define citizenship—whether online or in the Capitol Building—are *not* reflected in, say, interstate highway construction, where discussions of rights and equality are superseded by the need to modernize, affirming much-needed national maintenance and vital structural upgrades. In the US, rebuilding domestic infrastructures is almost universally applauded.[6] But, improving and reinforcing modern petro-capitalism's existing infrastructures perpetuates structures of racial injustice and, further, spreads those injustices subtly beyond regional boundaries. In *South of Haunted Dreams*, Eddy Harris realizes the racist ideologies he initially associates with the South are actually national ideologies disseminated via roads and highways. Further, progressive communities attempting ideological change are, in essence, erased from the nation. Herein lies the paradox: "normalized" citizenship requires participation in the nation's economic and cultural material networks, but othered citizens are regulated or excluded by the same material networks. If citizens are no longer able to make use of the infrastructures that connect them to a larger regional and national consciousness, their citizenship status is threatened, or, even invalidated.

The "Old South" Is Just The South: Citizenship Obstructions in *South of Haunted Dreams*

Take, for instance, the story of Atlantic Beach, South Carolina, as remembered by Eleanor Tate. Tate is an artist and writer Harris meets while cruising the US East Coast. Tate's home, the *very* small Atlantic Beach, lies on the northern border of Myrtle Beach, a popular American beach destination since the late-nineteenth century. Domestic tourism surged in the early-twentieth century, particularly during World War I—however, segregation prevented Black southerners from vacationing at white beaches or white resorts. As tourism increased through the 1920s, a man named George Tyson realized the need for a Black resort. In the 1930s, Tyson bought some acreage north of Myrtle Beach and began constructing a resort that would

---

6   At least, infrastructure in the more traditional sense: roads, tunnels, and bridges (aka: the petro-sense).

cater to wealthy Black people along the coast.[7] Tyson was unable to keep hold of the land over the course of the Depression and the resort was purchased by a group of Black doctors, lawyers, and teachers. Between 1940 and 1970, Atlantic Beach, nicknamed "The Black Pearl," was a haven for Black families: a place of relative luxury where nationally known entertainers performed, but most importantly, where "blacks could relax and vacation without insult or racial harassment" (Harris 195). In the 1970s, Atlantic Beach started a slow decline. The town, Tate explains, was decimated by integration as Black businesses were not prepared to compete with white resorts in the area.[8] "As soon as it was all right to go to the white hotels," Tate asks, "who could be bothered with the black ones?" (196). Tourism declined over the 1970s and 1980s and the town fell into financial ruin. Tate's history ends there, though Harris notes she continues to work towards "something to uplift them [other residents] so they could be better off, spiritually and physically" (196). Residents facing financial crisis desperately sought new attractions that would bring in tourists but also preserve Atlantic Beach's Black history. This led to the Atlantic Beach Bikefest (sometimes referred to as Black Bike Week), an oft-disputed motorcycle rally that has come to define Atlantic Beach in the twenty-first century, despite the town's long, rich history. More importantly, Bikefest exhibits the efforts citizens must go through to reestablish visibility and recognition once their citizenship is imperiled through infrastructure exclusion.

Via road-building, petro-culture profoundly impacts citizenship through wealth and population distribution. What makes Atlantic Beach such an interesting case study comparatively is its specific placement within modern oil capitalism and the community's racial purposefulness. Simply look at a map of the South Carolina coast and you will see that Atlantic Beach bisects two predominantly white cities: Myrtle Beach and North Myrtle Beach. In 1968, North Myrtle Beach annexed coastline surrounding Atlantic Beach, but Atlantic Beach residents refused incorporation. Why, after years of exclusion and distrust, would Atlantic Beach suddenly accept invitation into the once-homogenous white beach community? After all, the town had developed in response to alternative conditions of citizenship oppressively forced upon African Americans during Jim Crow. Black citizens were denied access to the material networks that accompany citizenship privileges (such as a beach vacation or other versions of domestic tourism) and responded by acquiring and cultivating

---

7   Atlantic Beach is not listed in *The Negro Motorist Green-Book* because, from what I can tell, it did not need to be identified as Black-friendly. Atlantic Beach was well known for catering specifically to Black patrons. The date of publication could also be a factor: the first version of the *Green-Book* was published in 1936, but Atlantic Beach did not gain in popularity until after World War II. However, since the *Green-Book* was still used well into the 1960s, I find this the less likely speculation.

8   Similar phenomena occurred throughout the country, i.e., Farish Street in Jackson, Mississippi or Michigan Ave. in Detroit.

200 Performing Citizenship

spaces such as Atlantic Beach. Residents like Tate refuse to sacrifice a notable Black space to the white communities that had historically ostracized them, knowing that annexation would require a distinct "whitening" of their community (Harris 196).

As one might expect, rejecting annexation carried serious consequences, particularly regarding infrapolitics throughout the region. On that same map of the South Carolina coast, you can see that Atlantic Beach has been essentially hemmed in by roadways maintained by North Myrtle Beach *without* extending into Atlantic Beach itself. Harris immediately comments on Atlantic Beach's roads, which are "rutted" and difficult to navigate compared to the highways he is used to (194). Atlantic Beach's poorly maintained roads signal the community's absence from the material infrastructural and economic networks in the region. "It is not a very pretty place," Harris writes, "dusty streets with no sidewalks. The grass at the edge of the roads has been worn completely away. Broken bottles in the streets ... Too many broken down cars" (194). Vacation destinations thrive on aesthetic appeal—if Atlantic Beach is "not a very pretty place," that separation from the regional economy compounds an already discriminatory redistribution of wealth and population. Roads to the south and west of Atlantic Beach run primarily through Myrtle Beach, while roads north of Atlantic Beach redirect travelers back into North Myrtle Beach. Even S. Ocean Blvd, constructed directly adjacent from the ocean for the entirety of the North Myrtle Beach coast, detours *around* Atlantic Beach—the only section of Ocean Blvd that does not directly follow the coast. Apart from Highway 17, which bounds the northern edge of town, Atlantic Beach is completely cut off from coastal tourism.[9] The further Atlantic Beach is separated from surrounding infrastructures, the more the roads that actually do allow access into the town fall into increasing disrepair, and the town becomes what Tate recognizes as a space distinctly bounded from local and national economies. Rather than the blatant violence and spectacular racial discrimination Harris initially expects of the US South, petro-infrastructure exhibits how the racial politics of citizenship are renegotiated via subtle (less visible) regulations and insidious systems.

In an effort to gain stability amidst the economic turmoil brought on by exclusion, Atlantic Beach took on a new symbol: the motorcycle. The Atlantic Beach Bikefest was modeled after mid-century Harley Davidson rallies in neighboring Myrtle Beach that were exclusively white (as was much of biker subculture in the immediate postwar era). The festival was first imagined in 1980 as a collaborative effort between City Councilman John Skeeters and the Carolina Knight Riders Motorcycle Club (MC) to invigorate the economy and maintain cultural independence from surrounding white neighborhoods (King 150). The rally would generate much needed revenue but would also offer a distinctly Black alternative to discriminatory rallies

---

9   Highway 17 was constructed in the 1920s as part of the United States Highway System and *before* Atlantic Beach was established.

in surrounding townships. While there was some dispute as to the nature of the rally (residents wanted a wide "social event" while bikers imagined something more exclusive), Bikefest quickly gained in popularity, exceeding sixty thousand participants by 1997. P. Nicole King explains, the "festival offers hope for the town both because the event permits Atlantic Beach to act as a location for the growth and diversification of African American leisure culture, and because it brings back the lively, crowded streets, blasting music, and sidewalk vendors so fondly recollected by early inhabitants of the town" (150). The Black Pearl was known for lively recreation; what is livelier than a motorcycle rally?

Throughout the 1990s Bikefest became increasingly controversial within surrounding white communities. The festival drew criticism for reasons that were discriminatory, rooted in the region's segregated history. As the event grew, reports of "public nudity, drug activity, what appeared to be a stabbing and a near riot" earned Bikefest a reputation for being unruly and out of control (King 154). However, there had been no stabbing and no riot; King explains the number of incidents did not warrant the massive outcry from nearby Myrtle Beach (154). Many surrounding residents were particularly upset by the noise of the festival—young Black bikers had moved from the Harley (emblems of post-war white MCs) to louder, faster Japanese bikes (King 169). This was in part due to speed pleasures, but was certainly a commentary on class and race as well: imported Japanese bikes were cheaper than Harley's and were not associated with the largely white, racist Outlaw MCs. White residents complained this was proof that Black youth partied "differently" and made "more noise than their white counterparts" (153). The noise of the bike disrupts racist narratives, a "metaphor for the nation's descent from an imagined bygone era of race relations, when blacks knew their place and were deferential to whites" (King 153). King's distinction here is important: white US citizens enjoyed their version of citizenship and Black US citizens enjoyed a different/deferential citizenship, one regulated by white culture through the region's material infrastructural networks. Black bikers "roared through barriers in the *de facto* segregation of the region's leisure space," reclaiming Atlantic Beach amidst furious attempts at hostile takeover (153).

Yet, as we have established, citizenship is more complicated than we might initially imagine: even as Bikefest roars through discriminatory barriers, it is a site of resistance that can be regulated indirectly by petro-infrastructures, therein limiting activist impact. Bikefest helped Atlantic Beach continue independently into the twenty-first century. The festival shows one method for othered citizens to create space that allows opportunity to act out citizenship rights. At the same time those exact spaces identify chokepoints where infrastructure can regulate self-determination. King aptly explains Atlantic Beach and the town's new symbol—the motorcycle—as an example of how racist ideology "travels with new technologies" (154). Bikers were separated from the motorcycle itself. The machine, historically a symbol of cultural dissidence, became a new way of framing racial conflict: white motorcycle rallies were an essential part of Grand Strand culture while the singular Black motorcycle rally remained a target (169). The transversal nature of this conflict conveys the inadequacies of activism *using* material networks built by the oppressor. Atlantic Beach represents a collective effort to reclaim citizenship through oil; however, the material networks that connect citizens to the privileges of a polity become the very infrastructures that counter the town's attempts at reclamation. Notably, King identifies this as a strategy to consolidate power that goes beyond just racial modifiers. The controversies surrounding Bikefest are not simply issues of race, but rather a "larger trend in southern (and American) politics" that defines citizenry discriminately against "age, class, sexuality, and taste" (155).

Here, King presciently anticipates ongoing problems defining citizenship beyond reductive versions of identity politics, while acknowledging the vectors US cultures plot various citizens upon. Interestingly, in the case of Atlantic Beach, we witness how visibility via the region's material networks is central to the town's larger assertions within the community—conversely, we witness how petro-infrastructures are restructured to essentially conceal the town and its citizens from that community. Visibility becomes *the* central vector for establishing citizenship: the hope is visibility demands recognition, recognition implores representation, and representation finally awards the full rights and privileges of citizenship. Beginning with Western European notions of property rights, the reality is visibility has long been countered by aggressive erasure disguised in material production—or erasure, thinly veiled as "nation-building," has preconditioned visibility in ways that constantly anticipate and limit othered peoples from full citizenship rights. This practice has deep historical reach: Isin and Wood note that Australia, the US, and Canada all became nation-states "at the expense of, not with the cooperation of, Native Nations already inhabiting those territories" (68). Thus, visibility has been one of the more confrontational conditions of Native and European relations in the Americas for centuries. Despite the few spectacular examples like King Philip's War or Custer's Last Stand, "face-to-face encounters were often unnecessary" because European powers who had laid claim to lands traded territory they had no physical connection to (68). "This political practice," Isin and Wood explain, "in its oblivion, was the beginning of a long history of silencing and rendering invisible Native peoples" (68). Unlike Atlantic Beach, whose citizens "needed" to be erased, European and, eventually, US colonizers had been working to erase Native tribes for centuries despite varying adaptive resistances.

This is not to say tribes did not make efforts to regain National recognition. As Cristina Stanciu makes clear, the history of Native American citizenship has been contested throughout the entirety of continental colonialism. Each era of US westward expansion resulted in forms of erasure: Native American Removal in the mid-nineteenth century displaced southeastern tribes west of the Mississippi

River, followed by the Dawes Act in 1887 which divided Native lands into individual parcels in an effort to both assimilate Native peoples and destroy tribal unities. By the early-twentieth century, Stanciu claims Native Americans were able to author forms of their own citizenship through organized activism vis-à-vis the Society of American Indians (SAI) and the Red Progressives, therein navigating the tenuous relationship between "two competing nationalisms—American and Indian" (112–113). Stanciu further notes, "the most politically active and savvy members of the SAI argued for political integration rather than an erasure of Native identities and sovereignty through a blind replication of the imagined model of immigrant Americanization," evoking models of welcomed early-twentieth century European immigration while acknowledging the immensely complicated history between US Federal governance and tribal sovereignty (112). House Resolution 108 in 1953 effectively abolished tribal sovereignty until the mid-1990s, when congress passed legislation aimed towards tribal self-governance and economic development. Though the 1924 Indian Citizenship Act stated all Native Americans born in the US were officially granted citizenship, abrupt and self-serving transitions between guiding Federal policies worked to destabilize Native American identity.[10] Offering citizenship might seem like a proverbial olive branch, when in fact it serves as another form of erasure.[11]

Indigenous Literatures as Activisms in Louise Erdrich's "The Red Convertible"

Erasure has evolving contemporary consequences. I see these consequences clearly represented in two examples: first, in Native peoples' struggles with identity, National obligation, and material economies, expertly conveyed in Louise Erdrich's short story "The Red Convertible"; and second, in ongoing protests against the DAPL—bourgeoning positive activisms *not* focused on citizenship through petro-infrastructures. Stanciu explains that Native Americans have long imagined progressive forms of citizenship that end wardship without vanishing,[12] where *representation* is affected as a function of US jurisprudence while tribal identity remains tribal (114). Still, pursuing belonging is a consistent theme in late-twentieth and twenty-first century Native American literatures, a conflict complicated by what

---

10 See Vanessa Evans's chapter in this volume, "'You've Heard it Now': Storytelling and Acts of Citizenship in Cherie Dimaline's *The Marrow Thieves*", for a discussion of how citizenship is reimagined by Indigenous characters after the settler apocalypse comes to what is currently known as Canada.

11 Stanciu gestures at the Six Nations Iroquois Confederacy as one example.

12 Here, Stanciu refers to the common critical trope of the Vanishing Indian.

204   Performing Citizenship

citizenship (in its more reductive Western European imagining) offers, what it requires, and what it ultimately rejects. In its most contemporary form, this conflict is the struggle for *human* visibility defined by or projected through visible/invisible material infrastructures—particularly petro-infrastructures—that link or separate tribes from national trends beyond reservation boundaries. This doubly imposes Federal regulations in tribal self-determination and self-governance: it encourages Native peoples to assimilate through road building or automobility—positive, visible extensions of citizenship—while simultaneously marking geographies for modernization—infrastructural "necessities" forged through invisible spaces so as to remain invisible from "normalized" citizens. Erasure fabricates the prospect of national belonging while unduly coopting land and resource that does not—cannot—create the more progressive synergistic citizen Stanciu explores.

Erdrich's "The Red Convertible," from her 1984 collection *Love Medicine*, illustrates a version of citizenship in which US petro-cultures dictate Native American identity—a citizen missing Stanciu's proposed synergy. The story is narrated in 1974 from the perspective of Lyman Lamartine, a recurring Chippewa in Erdrich's works who recounts the history of "a red Olds" convertible purchased early in 1969, co-owned with his brother Henry, "until his boots filled with water" and "bought out my [Lyman's] share" (177). The Chippewa are part of the larger Ojibwe Peoples stretching from "Bands" (tribes) in the northern-US Midwest into Eastern Canada. Lyman and Henry are part of the Turtle Mountain Band of Chippewa Indians based in North Dakota parallel to the contemporary Canadian border.[13] Already we see a number of ways Nativity and geography complicate citizenship in traditional Western-European terms. First, as American Indians born after 1924, Henry and Lyman are US citizens. Second, both are members of the Turtle Mountain Band of Chippewa Indians, a federally-recognized tribe, meaning the Turtle Mountain Band is in a government-to-government relationship with the US Federal government—essentially, this allows the tribe some semblance of self-governance and entitles them to minor support from the US Federal Government through the Bureau of Indian Affairs (BIA).[14]

Third, and perhaps most importantly: as part of the Ojibwe Peoples, the Turtle Mountain Band of Chippewa Indians are linked to innumerable migratory Bands that traveled seasonally throughout the Great Lakes Region's significant waterways for millennia. This is to say that Henry and Lyman are part of a pre-colonial tribal conscious that moved freely across the contemporary Canadian-US border. When Henry and Lyman take the Olds on a long summer road trip across the western United States and Canadian provinces, they implicitly acknowledge an ancestral history that mirrors that pre-colonial mobility, but that we would now consider

---

13   The Turtle Mountain Band of Chippewa Indians is Erdrich's own Band.

14   For more information, see: https://www.bia.gov/frequently-asked-questions?page=6.

"transnational." By Western-European definitions of citizenship, Henry and Lyman present a mire of complexities that imprint upon the brothers in significant ways. By Native standards, the brothers contribute to what N. Scott Momaday prefaces the entirety of *The Way To Rainy Mountain* upon: the generational journey, a Native journey—for Momaday, the journey is specific to the Kiowa but the practice extends to many intracontinental American tribes (3). In 1983, Kenneth Lincoln termed the same ancestral compulsions as a regenerate "sense of relatedness" (8–11). And the same forces press Victor to return his father's body to the Spokane Reservation in Sherman Alexie's "What It Means to Say Phoenix, Arizona" despite his father's long geographical absence from the region and Victor's own spiritual cynicism—skepticism outweighed by a "sudden need for tradition" (62). This kind of impulse—a sort of mycelial humanitarian/ancestral/environmental compulsion—is much closer to Stanciu's synergistic optimism.

This far more complex "citizenship" is powered by ancestry, revitalization, spiritual guidance, and adaptation—*not* the material networks of petro-capitalism or social recognitions of petro-culture. What Erdrich makes clear is how difficult this placement on the vector is. With economic, social, governmental, and infrastructural forces all complicating individual representations, reaching a productive vector for a larger populace is even more difficult. The brothers symbolize the central citizenship conflict vis-à-vis the red Olds: Lyman emblematizes a form of citizenship marked by successful assimilation through capitalism, while Henry represents the consequences of citizenship for those incorporated into and rejected by Western-European materiality. The red Olds functions as a material emblem of the brothers' citizenship status, but also as entry into the larger material networks that both sustain and implicate the modern petro-citizen. In essence, the convertible becomes the vehicle for a deeper discussion of belonging and community, as imagined by Isin in "Citizens without Nations."

Lyman is proud of the red convertible for a number of reasons. First, the convertible sets him apart from other Chippewa on the reservation. "I was the first one to drive a convertible on my reservation," Lyman states, implying his own acumen as an earner and the material benefits that follow (177). Lyman has a unique talent for making money, "unusual in a Chippewa" (177). He claims to have "good luck with numbers," but he also recounts various capitalist ventures, beginning at a very young age, that ultimately reveal the secret of Western capitalism: "the more money I made," Lyman explains, "the easier the money came" (178). These successes foreshadow a recurring identity conflict throughout Erdrich's larger oeuvre, but the convertible is Lyman's first tangible material pleasure acquired *because* of his difference. The car is flashy and fun, which is what first attracts Lyman's attention, and it suggests his "difference" might be capitalized on for his own benefit. For instance: Lyman acquires his money for the Olds through a (perhaps embellished) confluence of hard work and luck that lands him with a significant check from a US insurance company.

Henry, however, only has enough because of two checks: "a week's extra pay after being laid off, and his regular check from the Jewel Bearing Plant" (178).[15] Lyman takes advantage of a system that has historically denied his people success, while Henry is subject to more common US labor narratives: downsizing and exploitation.

A second reason Lyman is proud of the Olds is it allows him to participate in the domestic tourism Shaffer identifies as a ritual of US citizenship—here, I would extend Shaffer's argument, noting the move towards a highway-citizenship at the mid-century is only further reinforced by US oil investments throughout the 1950s, 60s, and 70s.[16] "We went places in that car, me and Henry," Lyman reminisces (179). They head south along the Little Knife River towards Fort Berthold, west into Montana, and even north into Alaska. They travel roads built by the Federal government and consume fuel refined by global and US-based corporations. In this way, Lyman and Henry are very much consumed by petro-modernity's material networks. Lyman even subscribes to automobility's romantic cultural ethos when he remembers the Olds. The car, he says, seemed more than just a machine: it seemed to be alive, not "simply stopped, parked, or whatever" but "reposed, calm and gleaming" as if it had been patiently waiting for Lyman and Henry to find it (178). The car, a machine, is imbued with life because it emblematizes possibilities beyond the boundaries of the reservation—beyond centuries of erasure. This is the same trap we see at Atlantic Beach: working to achieve citizenship through petro-infrastructures. It is this conflict that ultimately defines the brothers' divergent paths: Lyman, who had "good luck with numbers," and Henry, who was "never lucky in the same way" (182).

When Lyman and Henry begin to explore their US citizenship via petro-infrastructures outside the reservation, they implicitly accept the consequences that come with those citizenship rights. In late-1969, Henry is drafted into the Army and sent to Vietnam. After World War II, Frederick Buell explains how oil binds together National triumphs over fascism and celebrations of emerging US global power: "the allies floated to victory on a sea of oil," after which wartime petrochemicals become part of daily American life as "agent[s] of chemical *and* social metamorphosis" (81). But where oil is the surreptitiously celebrated material champion of WWII, during Vietnam oil is conversely *the* emblem of destruction (human and environmental *vis-a-via* petrochemicals) and wanton violence. Large oil reserves allowed the US to deploy and sustain massive military operations overseas for more than a decade.

---

15   Like Henry, much of the tribe worked at the Turtle Mountain Jewel Bearing Plant in Rolla, North Dakota, making parts for extremely accurate watches, something many WWII veterans recognized as a national security need after watching the Axis powers use time accurately against them. Ironically, when Henry goes to Vietnam, he's made much of the destruction that occurs in the jungle (and his mind) possible by building those discrete mechanical pieces.

16   Buell explains, "postwar [oil] exuberance" reinvents the "oil-electric energy system" (81).

More notable was the widespread use of petrochemical herbicides, defoliants, and incendiaries—the most famous being Agent Orange and napalm.[17] Henry comes home from the war three years later, "very different" (182). Baptized into US Cold War geopolitics through napalm and Rainbow Herbicides, Henry is the one who pays for the brothers' forays into citizenship rights. He clings to the emblems that supposedly mark his place within US culture, like his "field jacket and the worn-in clothes he'd come back in and kept wearing ever since" (186). He suffers from PTSD: once contemplative, quiet, and meditative, Henry is now restless, "jumpy and mean" (182). In their youthful optimism, the brothers gravitate to the rights of national fraternity promised to them through the mythos of US citizenship, pursuing citizenship through ritualistic observation on the highway. What they find are moments of pleasure followed by a much larger commitment: a demand to sacrifice both mind and body to the machinations of petro-capitalism that sustain US material networks. "The change was no good," Lyman says (182).

Lyman does not understand what is happening to Henry. He first considers the hospital, but his mother claims "they don't fix them in those places ... they just give them drugs," another reference to the infusion of petrochemicals in US culture through pharmaceuticals (Buell 81). Lyman even acknowledges, "we wouldn't get him there in the first place," noting that Henry is denied community access despite suffering for institutional citizenship (183). In fact, Henry seems a fulcrum of Isin's Derridean application of "friendship" that avoids the "risks associated with naturalization, genre, race, gens, family, and the nation" imbued in the image of community (465). In "Citizens Without Nations," Isin discusses "how community has been mobilized as a strategic concept invoking certain images against others in political struggles" (450). In a very material way, Henry is rejected. At the same time, there are "no Indian doctors on the reservation," no Chippewa doctors who might treat Henry in the old ways, reminiscent of the troubles Tayo faces in Leslie Marmon Silko's *Ceremony* (1977) when he returns home from war. Where can Henry go if he is rejected by the encompassing phallogocentric community that has, over generations, erased his ancestral community? Henry embodies "the vexed relationship between citizenship and nationality," part of the genealogy Isin critiques

---

17 Agent Orange is one of the Rainbow Herbicides deployed as a part of Operation Ranch Hand (*Blue Water*). A study by the Institute of Medicine published in 1994 states "herbicide operations in Vietnam had two primary military objectives: (1) defoliation of trees and plants to improve observation, and (2) destruction of enemy crops" (Institute of Medicine 3). Essentially, planes and helicopters would spray jungles with defoliants, napalm would burn the dying plant life, and the herbicides would prevent any new growth. Ecological warfare dramatically changed Vietnamese ecology and agriculture, the extent of which the National Academy of Sciences has been unable to accurately measure (9). According to *Blue Water Navy Vietnam Veterans and Agent Orange Exposure*, similar exposures to toxic petrochemicals occurred during ship maintenance, which had great—though varied—impacts on sailors (8).

208   Performing Citizenship

concerning "how citizenship became membership that binds an individual to the community of birth" (450). Desperate for some healing, Lyman thinks back to the last time he and Henry seemed happy: driving the West in the red convertible.

Lyman and Henry's complication comes in their recognized citizenship as both US citizens and Turtle Mountain Band of Chippewa Indian members *and* purposeful exclusion from either "community"—hence Derrida and Isin's warnings concerning the term. I would expand to note the brothers are denied access—denied recognition, belonging, health, or political voice—through material exclusion: as US material networks proliferate, they further strand those othered peoples by reinforcing material boundaries. It leaves individuals like Henry with no support and individuals like Lyman with no way to help. It is no wonder, then, that Lyman's attempt to heal Henry is channeled through US petro-citizenship, the very symbol that initiated their earliest negotiations. Hoping to focus Henry's anxiety, Lyman takes a hammer and busts the red Olds to shit, despite keeping it in pristine condition the three years Henry was in Vietnam. "By the time I was done with the car," he says, "it looked worse than any typical Indian car that has been driven all its life on reservation roads, which they say are like government promises—full of holes" (184). He destroys the Olds as a machine—as a vehicle that allows access to the material networks that sustain US citizenship outside the reservation—and in so doing destroys what Olds symbolizes: the brothers' difference from the rest of the Chippewa within the reservation. Derrida and Isin warn against community conceptually, but Lyman inadvertently recognizes that Henry's sickness, signs of post-traumatic stress, are in part due to his abrupt transition from the cultural personages of US life—the paved highway, oil-petrochemical commerce, and of course the Vietnam War itself—to the cultural personages of Turtle Mountain Reservation life. What Lyman views as task-based medicine—a sense of purpose fixed upon repairing the convertible—is inadvertently a warrant to retune Henry with his more immediate surroundings.

What Lyman cannot predict is the mechanical work places Henry, again, at least partially within the petro-modern framework he experienced before, during, and now after the war. Like Atlantic Beach attempting to restore its place within their regional material network, Henry is reincorporated into the very infrastructural system that rejected him time and time over. When the convertible can finally run again, Lyman and Henry go for a drive, east this time "toward Pembina and the Red River" (186). "'The top was down and the car hummed like a top,' Lyman says. 'It was beautiful. When everything starts changing, drying up, and clearing off, you feel like your whole life is starting. Henry felt it, too'" (186–187). Here, Lyman finds refuge in seasonal progression, spring as rebirth where Lyman and Henry feel like nature: shedding the old and starting anew. At the same time, Lyman refers to the convertible itself and the roads it allows them access to. Just as when they first purchased the Olds, the car seems to offer up a whole new chain of possibilities. However, this is not

1969 and the brothers are more cautious. When they reach the river, Lyman claims he is, "feeling what Henry was going through at that moment," a "squeezing inside of me and tightening and trying to let it go at the same time" (187). Lyman realizes Henry's attempts to mend, but not the obstacles that prevent his healing.

Here is, perhaps, a place where we encounter a different version of citizenship—an ecological citizenship akin to the "friendship" Derrida and Isin explore—rooted in a seemingly paradoxical, global mycelial humanitarianism recognized *in* environmental networks *rather* than the material networks of petro-capitalism. The brothers' proximity to the river heightens their environmental awareness. The convertible tethers them to a deceptive "American" route they recognize does not represent their Native American roots: both recognize nature, *not* the Olds, is restorative. For Henry, the recognition is deep and indescribable because it conflicts with the trauma he has encountered through petro-culture. He tries to give Lyman the convertible, but Lyman does not want it. The urge towards nature, away from the material networks of petro-capitalism, is so strong that Henry leaps into the Red River, overwhelmed by the high water. Lyman remembers Henry's last words: "My boots are filling" (189). "He says this in a normal voice," Lyman recalls, "like he just noticed and he doesn't know what to think of it. Then he's gone" (189). Lyman does not mourn Henry's death. He does not drive home, or to the police to begin search and rescue. Instead, he turns on the convertible's high beams, puts it in first gear, and watches as the Olds "plow[s] softly into the water" (189). The car disappears. Lyman, specifically, recognizes the Olds as a poison, that his truest moments of belonging occur in "this one place with willows," where one could lie under the branches and feel comfortable, "feel good" (179). Most importantly, he recognizes these moments do not require the Olds—in rejecting the Olds, Lyman admits the car bounds the brothers within a reductive, Western model of citizenship that cannot account for the far more complex—and far more productive—eco-ancestral kinship. The reductive form of US citizenship that Stanciu critiques drowns Henry in petro-culture's burdens and expectations. Erdrich, however, suggests an alternative citizenship informed by ecological networks, rooted in the willow and the river, yet experientially aware of the petro-modern nation-state's material networks. These experiences give birth to a new generation of American Indians who do not simply accept that reservation roads are "like government promises—full of holes" (184). They recognize that their citizenship bears inequitable burdens for a larger population that has shut them out culturally, geographically, and materially. They now work towards a more balanced, rooted recognition, a version of citizenship that reflects Erdrich's alternative imagining.

Non-Violent Agitants as Adaptive Contemporary Citizenship

Facing the complex nature of citizenry in the twenty-first century, rather than reverting to reductive rhetorics that dominated the nineteenth and twentieth centuries, is essential to recognizing a new form of global citizenship that tangibly matches the inclusive, imaginative potentials Erdrich and others propose. This is the form of citizenship, I argue, agitants in North Dakota explore opposing the DAPL. I use the term "agitants" specifically to reference both how "water protectors" have been referred to in media but also to emphasize their dissent. Meredith Privott describes the DAPL protesters, led by the Standing Rock Sioux women "water protectors," resistance as protection, not protest (75). Privott interviewed Misty Perkins regarding the difference—Perkins explains protest implies a land dispute, whereas protection safeguards "the land and waters against its very destruction for ALL OF US, for ALL life" (75).[18] Perkins' emphasis on "ALL life" is one way "water protectors" have begun to agitate the shifting limitations that embody an older, less inclusive citizenship, leading towards a more contemporary vision that can account for twenty-first century citizenships. A Guest Editorial by Shawn McCoy in *Pipeline and Gas Journal* conveys an oppositional narrative: that the Sioux were uncooperative with the US Army Corps of Engineers, unresponsive to meetings conducted by corporate and government officials, and have falsely woven "an emotionally charged tale of greed, racism, and misbehavior by corporate and government officials" (2). But, as Danielle Delaney states in "Under Coyote's Mask: Environmental Law, Indigenous Identity, and #NODAPL": "To be recognized by the law, one must use the law's language as a character within the larger national story. This requires that one fit inside the legal narrative, the history of jurisprudence, and the juridical decisions about the stories judges find compelling" (303). McCoy's claims that the Sioux did not adhere to federal law ignores the Federal government's history regarding Native Americans—as Delaney clarifies: "Finding space within the story that the law tells about federal power has been a challenge for American Indians and Alaska Natives since the Cherokee Cases" (303). What the "water protectors" have done in their activism is agitate their role within that story, working towards recognition *not* through the material networks of petro-capitalism, but rather through mycelial humanitarian and environmental networks. They do not repeat Henry's mistakes in "The Red Convertible" or the mistakes we see at Atlantic Beach. This generates a new point-of-entry recognizing *agency*.

The DAPL represents two larger symbolic problems. First, investing in long-term petro-infrastructures perpetuates global commitments to late-capitalism, the very

---

18   See Anah-Jayne Samuelson's chapter in this volume, "We had to control the narrative": The Innovations and Limitations of Youth Citizenship, for a discussion of how protest can function as an act of citizenship.

systems that bound and reduce citizenship to nineteenth and twentieth-century nation-state models. Second, re-routing the DAPL through the Standing Rock Indian Reservation, despite vehement opposition from the Standing Rock Sioux tribe and other allies, shows the double-nature of what a material citizenship requires from many peoples. The DAPL was initially routed north of Bismarck, North Dakota, but was redirected per EPA guidelines because the pipeline threatened Bismarck's city water supply. Redirecting the pipeline south of Bismarck, through the Standing Rock Indian Reservation, threatened the "confluence of the Missouri and Cannonball Rivers, the tribe's central source of drinking water and a sacred site" (Privott 75). Additionally, the pipeline would "pass under Lake Oahe, a large reservoir created by the Oahe Dam on the Missouri River and used by the Standing Rock Sioux and Cheyenne River Reservations as their primary source of water" (Dorau 3). In other words: threatening Bismarck's water supply was untenable, whereas threatening Native peoples' water was acceptable.[19] Though all US citizens, the material needs of one citizenry outweigh expected citizenship rights for a different vector of that citizenry—material infrastructures manipulate pockets of citizens, undermining the very nature of the protective obligation citizenship supposedly embodies.

For the former citizenry, the pipeline was a necessity: not only did it sustain US petro-capitalism into the future, but by the time the Standing Rock Sioux began formal opposition in 2016, the company overseeing the DAPL, Energy Transfer Partners, had already acquired (with great expense) lands in North Dakota, South Dakota, Iowa, and Illinois. As McCoy points out, "water protesters" impeded a project that was eighty-five percent complete and had already cost over three billion dollars (2). The pipeline, which is now active (and still contested) transports shale oil from northwest North Dakota to a terminus near Patoka, Illinois—from there, "the oil is transported around the world" with a significant volume shipped south to refineries in Louisiana (Dorau 1).[20] But what remains noteworthy throughout the years of conflict is the inequitable burden the Standing Rock Sioux shoulder for the material well-being of other US citizens who actively and violently refuse to recognize the Sioux. The Standing Rock Tribe saw little to no material gains from the DAPL on their land, especially as the resource (the oil itself) that justified the material infrastructure was "transported around the world" while reservation roads remain as Erdrich describes them.

---

19   For more on how infrastructure, health, and citizenship intersect (with a particular focus on the Flint water crisis), see Mita Banerjee's chapter in this volume: "'What the Eyes Don't See': Medical Citizenship and Environmental Justice in Mona Hanna-Attisha's Medical Memoir".

20   The Standing Rock Sioux have a long history of federal mistreatment—despite the binding 1868 Fort Laramie Treaty, congressional actions in 1873, 1875, 1877, and 1889 (the infamous Dawes Act) all "greatly reduced" the Standing Rock Sioux Reservation (Faith).

Ultimately, the protests and legal battles could not be framed through petro-capitalist rhetorics. For the latter citizenry, the Standing Rock Sioux and allies, the focus became a mixture of Indigenous violations and environmental protection—that the pipeline was eighty-five percent completed was of no consequence when the last fifteen percent posed the largest threats to both Native rights and ecological health. "Water protectors," "agitants" solidified in obstructionist, non-violent activism, focused their confrontation on water and, in so doing, what citizenship means for twenty-first century peoples. As Delaney states, "the more indigenous activists dressed their resistance in Western legal language and used theories unrelated to the tiny corner of legal accommodation the tribes have carved out for themselves within US federal law, the more they sought to ground their political protests and direct actions within indigenous language and values" (304). The DAPL protestors worked towards innovative activism focused on humanitarianism, recognition and sustainable ecologies for "ALL." Perhaps most importantly, these same "agitants" moved beyond the treaties that governed Native policy in the US for centuries, creating new images alongside invective jurisprudence.

Conclusion

Facing the complex nature of citizenry in the twenty-first century realizes citizenship that tangibly matches the active, imaginative potentials exampled by the DAPL protestors—particularly when the alternative is fixed within reductive rhetorics that dominated the nineteenth and twentieth centuries, *literally* trapped by the material infrastructures that substantiate reductive citizenship. I can identify two correspondingly positive futures as global peoples refine the nature of citizenship in the twenty-first century. The first—and least productive—comes in more recent progressive conceptualizations of "infrastructure" within impending US legislation. Rather than the typical "roads, bridges, and tunnels" that define infrastructure in terms of petro-capitalism, recognizing "infrastructure" as a much larger collection of labors, relationships, support, and connections does begin to address material limitations that restrict citizenship rights. This future presents new and recurring obstacles. Though well-intended, the dangers of reconceptualizing infrastructure conflict with the first symbolic problem the DAPL protesters worked to agitate and disrupt: reconceptualizing still requires we recognize these infrastructures through rhetorics that fundamentally bound citizenship. Even if childcare and leisure become part of infrastructure legislation, it is still legislation focused on definition, boundaries, and—ultimately—limitation.

The second—and more hopeful—future comes in a singular example of long-term activism successfully converging with shifting material desires. As of June 10, 2021, the Keystone XL Pipeline project has been officially cancelled.

The multi-nation pipeline funded by TC Energy required construction across Canada and the US, accompanied by trade deals between Canada, the US, and Mexico, effectively committing all *three* nations to petro-capitalist futures while reinforcing economic, material, and geographic ideologies. Keystone XL—material infrastructure—would again be the insidious foundation reinstituting policies that limited citizenship to political boundaries and constructed margins. And though the protests have been lauded as successful transnational activism, I would go as far as to say Keystone XL's termination is No-Nation activism: activism that recognizes life in the twenty-first century transcends bounded versions of citizenship, thus necessitating a vision of citizenship that reflects a porous global cohabitation of things. Afterall, as Joye Braun, "a member of the Cheyenne River Sioux and an organizer with Indigenous Environmental Network" states: "This pipeline would have come with such tremendous costs and expenses to health, to land, to water, which of course would be costs ... to everyday people" (Noor). As with the DAPL, the costs of Keystone XL would be inequitably shouldered by citizens who are continuously denied citizenship rights: they would act as Atlas for peoples that refuse citizenship rights and dare not look to see who shoulders their luxury. Similar to the plights in Atlantic Beach, a visible community refused citizenship recognition, and in "The Red Convertible" where Henry's citizenship is repeatedly rejected despite his many attempts towards recognition through assimilation. Under those circumstances, the only real solution is in systemic agitation, disrupting the material infrastructures that ultimately determine what or who is recognized and the degree to which their contributions are received.

Works Cited

Alexie, Sherman. *The Lone Ranger And Tonto Fistfight In Heaven*. Grove Press, 1993.

Aytekin Isman, Ozlem Canan Gungoren. "Being Digital Citizen." *Procedia - Social and Behavioral Sciences*, vol. 106, 2013, pp. 551–556.

Buell, Frederick. "A Short History of Oil Cultures; Or, The Marriage of Catastrophe and Exuberance." *Oil Culture*, edited by Ross Barrett and Daniel Worden, Minnesota UP, 2014, pp. 69–90.

Dorau, Bethany Groff. "Dakota Access Pipeline: Overview." *Points of View: Dakota Access Pipeline*, Jan. 2021, pp. 1–3. *EBSCOED*, https://alabama.ebscoed.com/eds/detail?db=pwh&an=148703580.

Delaney, Danielle. "Under Coyote's Mask: Environmental Law, Indigenous Identity, and #Nodapl." *Michigan Journal of Race & Law*, vol. 24, no. 2, 2019, pp. 299–333. https://repository.law.umich.edu/cgi/viewcontent.cgi?article=1292&context=mjrl.

Erdrich, Louise. *Love Medicine: A Novel*. Harper Perennial, 1984.

Faith, Mike. "History." *Standing Rock Sioux Tribe*, https://www.standingrock.org/History/.

"Frequently Asked Questions." *Frequently Asked Questions | Indian Affairs*, https://www.bia.gov/frequently-asked-questions?page=6.

Green Book. Directed by Peter Farrelly, performances by Viggo Mortensen, Mahershala Ali, Universal Pictures, 2018.

Green, Victor Hugo. *The Negro Motorist Green-Book*. Victor H. Green, 1941.

Harris, Eddy. *South of Haunted Dreams: A Ride Through Slavery's Old Backyard*. Simon and Schuster, 1993.

Isin, Engin. "Citizens Without Nations." *Environment and Planning D: Society and Space*, vol. 30, no. 3, 2012, pp. 450–67.

Isin, Engin F., and Patricia K Wood. *Citizenship and Identity*. SAGE Publications, 1999.

Institute of Medicine (US) Committee to Review the Health Effects in Vietnam Veterans of Exposure to Herbicides. "3 The U.S. Military and the Herbicide Program in Vietnam." *Veterans and Agent Orange: Health Effects of Herbicides Used in Vietnam*. National Academies Press (US), 1994. https://www.ncbi.nlm.nih.gov/books/NBK236347/.

Institute of Medicine. *Blue Water Navy Vietnam Veterans and Agent Orange Exposure*. The National Academies Press, 2011. https://doi.org/10.17226/13026.

King, P. Nicole. *Sombreros and Motorcycles in a Newer South: The Politics of Aesthetics in South Carolina's Tourism Industry*. UP of Mississippi, 2012.

Lincoln, Kenneth. *Native American Renaissance*. UP of California, 1985.

Millhiser, Ian. "There are two kinds of GOP attacks on democracy—and one is much worse." *Vox*, 3 Jun. 2021, https://www.vox.com/22463490/voting-rights-democracy-texas-georgia-suppression-jim-crow-supreme-court-sb7.

Momaday, N. S., and Al Momaday. *The Way To Rainy Mountain*. U of New Mexico P, 1998.

McCoy, Shawn. "What the Dakota Access Pipeline Protesters Aren't Telling You." *Pipeline & Gas Journal*, vol. 244, no. 1, Jan. 2017, pp. 2. *ProQuest*, https://www.proquest.com/docview/1861758313.

Noor, Dharna. "Keystone XL Pipeline Developer Wants $15 Billion in Taxpayer Dollars." *Gizmodo*, Gizmodo, 6 Jul. 2021, https://gizmodo.com/keystone-xl-pipeline-developer-wants-15-billion-in-tax-1847239237.

Privott, Meredith. "An Ethos of Responsibility and Indigenous Women Water Protectors in the #NoDAPL Movement." *American Indian Quarterly*, vol. 43, no. 1, 2019, pp. 74–100. *EBSCOhost*, doi:10.5250/amerindiquar.43.1.0074.

Shachar, Ayelet. *The Birthright Lottery: Citizenship and Global Inequality*. Harvard UP, 2009.

Shaffer, Marguerite S. *See America First: Tourism and National Identity, 1880–1940*. Smithsonian Institution Press, 2001.

Stanciu, Cristina. "Americanization on Native Terms: The Society of American Indians, Citizenship Debates, and Tropes of 'Racial Difference.'" *NAIS: Journal of the Native American and Indigenous Studies Association*, vol. 6, no. 1, 2019, pp. 111–48. *Project MUSE*, https://muse.jhu.edu/article/725908. Accessed 6 Jul. 2021.

Volpp, Leti. "The Indigenous as Alien." *UC Irvine Law Review*, vol. 5, 2015, pp. 289–326. https://lawcat.berkeley.edu/record/1126973

Citizenship of the Dead
Antigone and Beyond

Marcus Llanque and Katja Sarkowsky

Introduction

The dead and their deeds—particularly those in connection with their death—carry a particular weight for the deliberations of the living. Since Pericles (at the latest!), funeral oratory has been a central component of democratic governance's repertoire, public mourning a crucial occasion to renegotiate who one is, what one did, and what remains to be done. Thus, interpreting the dead and their deeds is a decisive opportunity to interpret and determine the actions of those who remain. To understand the dead as co-citizens is a different matter, however: here, the dead might impact life beyond their death and appeal to the living to act in specific ways that might contribute to such ends. Such an understanding presupposes a particular bond between the dead and the living, and citizenship is one central possibility to address such a bond.

Citizenship tends to be regarded as a prerogative of the living, entailing the possibility of active political and civic participation, the enactment of voting rights, the bearing of civil and legal rights, and thus the recognition as part of a political community. Yet, the dead play a central role in the conceptualization of citizenship and the citizen. They are reminders of the past with symbolic significance for the present: the struggle over cemeteries and who might be buried where; rituals of public mourning and whose death is considered legitimately "grievable," to use Judith Butler's term here;[1] or the remembrance of citizens' death at the hand of the state or state officials. These seemingly random examples reveal how a political community

---

1   Butler uses the term to highlight that not all lives are framed equally as a 'life' and that central to this consideration is that a life's loss might be grieved in the future: "The future anterior, 'a life has been lived', is presupposed at the beginning of a life that has only begun to be lived. In other words, 'this will be a life that will have been lived' is the presupposition of a grievable life, which means that this will be a life that can be regarded as a life, and be sustained by that regard. Without grievability, there is no life, or rather, there is something living that is other than life" (*Frames*, 15).

deals with its dead and the question of who belongs to that community and on what grounds.

Such questions have been addressed extensively in and through political debates and cultural practices, but also in literature and political theory. In this context, Sophocles' tragedy *Antigone*, first performed in 442 BCE, has generated significant interest in both fields; it has served as a crucial text extensively analyzed by political theorists regarding the relationship between citizenship and mourning as well as the role of tragedy for citizenship (e.g., Honig; Euben; Stow), and as a text reworked and rewritten in different literary contexts around the world to negotiate membership and belonging, the rights of the dead, and questions of democratic citizenship (e.g. Głowacki; Shamsie; Köck; or in film, e.g., Deraspe).[2]

The connection between Sophocles' *Antigone* and the modern topic of citizenship first emerged as part of a feminist theoretical debate in the 1980s that asked which conclusions political feminism might draw from the figure of Antigone regarding the political role of women: Is there a specific bond that binds women to the (male dominated) political order, and which role can women play in it? *Antigone* centers on the conflict between the princess Antigone and her ruling uncle Creon over the burial of her treacherous brother Polyneices. Because Polyneices was killed attacking his own city, Creon orders his body to be left to rot, an edict Antigone does not accept and instead insists on her family duty to bury him, even if it means breaking the law—an insistence that has her sentenced to death. This conflict lends itself well to address the political conflict line between women and men. Might Antigone be regarded as the symbolic embodiment of women excluded from the political world of men, and does her defense of the familial sphere mark the political function of women?

This particular view is taken by the self-declared "social feminist" Jean Bethe Elshtain (1982).[3] It was a view shared by few, and criticized by proponents of other understandings of feminism (Dietz; Hartouni; Holland). These critics emphasize that the separation of public and private spheres has always been a politically motivated juxtaposition and instead shift the debate to the question of whether Antigone's decision for her family indeed constituted a stand against politics, or if by doing so, she rather practiced a more comprehensive and appropriate understanding of a citizen's role. In this understanding, Antigone's resistance against masculine hubris rests on the assumption that the bond of citizenship not only entails actual laws (such as those ordered by Creon), but also includes the conventions of how to appropriately deal with the dead (Dietz 28–29). Thus understood,

---

2   We discuss this aspect in detail in our monograph *Der Antigonistische Konflikt. 'Antigone' heute und das demokratische Selbstverständnis* (2023).

3   As a modern example of the position that Elshtain uses to connect with Antigone, she names Las Madres de Plaza de Mayo, the Argentinian mothers in the struggle for their children killed and thrown into the sea by the Junta (Elshtain 1989).

Antigone defends a specific understanding of the citizen—she does not represent the 'Other' of politics, but a different understanding of politics. The assumption made in this essay is that this understanding does not only include the relation between the living, but also that between the living and the dead.

More recently, Charles Wells has brought together different strands of the play's theoretical reception regarding citizenship—Bonnie Honig's and Nicole Loraux's in particular—when he looks at the four possibilities of Antigone's claim for her dead brother's citizenship: her assertion of her brother's status as a citizen of Thebes, despite his betrayal; as a 'citizen' in the body of the family, in modern reception usually juxtaposed to the state; as a citizen in a polis-transcending body, namely what is now usually referred to as humanity; or her refusal of the logics of citizenship altogether (79). While Wells asks also about Antigone's own acts of citizenship when claiming the rights to burial on behalf of her brother—and her right, even obligation, to bury him—, in either case, it is Antigone who claims (or disavows) 'citizenship'—her own as well as that of the dead. This claim of belonging, if not always explicitly cast as 'citizenship,' has become the centerpiece of literary reworkings of the tragedy as well: In Kamila Shamsie's novel *Home Fire* (2018), the British citizenship of the Polynices-figure Parvaiz is posthumously revoked by the Home Secretary for Parvaiz's joining of ISIS; to the end, the Antigone-figure Aneeka insists on her brother's British citizenship, the only one he ever held. Other rewritings combine death with social marginalization but shift the conflict by taking out the aspect of Polynices' betrayal: Janusz Głowacki's play *Antigone in New York* (1993) focuses on a fragile community of homeless people and replaces Creon with the democratic state and the theatrical public; Sophie Deraspe's film *Antigone* (2019) has Étéocle killed by the police, Polynice jailed, and their sister Antigone fighting Polynice's impending deportation—here too, Creon is replaced by the democratic state, split into a benevolent lawyer and a female-dominated judiciary; Thomas Köck's play *antigone. ein requiem* (2019) holds on to the figure of Creon but replaces Polynices with nameless refugees drowned in the Mediterranean. In all of these examples, the dead are important, crucial even, but they are acted *upon*, recognized, revered, dismissed, or instrumentalized; the time of their own agency as citizens or potential citizens is over.

But what if this view on the role of the dead as being for the living is expanded to understand them also as agents? This might be understood metaphorically, when for instance Antigone declares herself to not be among the living anymore (Sophocles v. 559–560), and is interned alive in her tomb-to-be, neither fully alive anymore in a social sense nor dead in a physical one, but a powerful actor nevertheless. Agency of the dead might also be understood more literally, with citizens acting beyond their death. Three recent examples that illustrate what this might mean: A young woman, Amber Pflughoeft, cast her early vote in the 2020 American presidential election; she died briefly after, before Election Day, and the state refuses to count her vote.

On her deathbed, Supreme Court Justice Ruth Bader Ginsburg wished for her replacement to be nominated by the next president (in vain). The late Congressman and civil rights icon John Lewis arranged for his call to the American nation to be published by the *New York Times* after his death in the midst of the contentious 2020 presidential election. Such expressions of will can, of course, be seen in terms of the dead's legacy to the living; yet, they can also be understood as acts that function as obligations to the living, as acts beyond death with the dead as citizen-actors, and, what is more, as an assertion of community that includes both the living and the dead.

It is this latter understanding that this essay seeks to explore. In political theory as well as in literature, Greek tragedy has served as a lens to focus on the connection of citizenship, the rights of the dead, and their role in a society's conception of community. This recourse, this essay argues, is not accidental, for it allows refocusing the understanding of citizenship to ask what role the dead play for the community of the living. In the following, we thus set out to explore examples from our respective fields—political theory and literary studies—to understand how such an extended notion of membership and belonging and the practices that potentially follow from it may question and challenge the self-conception of contemporary liberal democracies as a community of the living only.

Citizenship, Tragedy, and the Dead: Agency and Transgenerational Community-Building

The idea that the dead have agency is not per se new. In *The Work of the Dead*, Thomas Laqueur argues that the dead "make social worlds" (1) and continues to insist that they "remain active agents in [cultural] history even if we are convinced, they are nothing and nowhere. [...] Living bodies do not have the same powers as dead ones" (18); the dead, in Laqueur's understanding, have an immense impact on the living *because* they are dead, because of the significance that the living assign to them and their care (or lack thereof). Along different lines and focusing on the representation of the dead in popular culture, Ruth Penfold-Mounce argues that "the concept of the dead possessing agency provides a vital arena for safely exploring cultural fears, norms, traditions, and perceptions about mortality" (5); 'agency' here is understood as the lasting effect the dead have on the living, e.g., as celebrities, organ donors, etc.. And in forensic sciences, the 'speaking corpse' (cf. Crossland; M'charek & Carsatelli) is not just a metaphor; it speaks by different means, 'telling' its story to be recorded, witnessed, and, ideally, to be avenged. As such, it also serves an important function in literature, from the generic conventions of detective fiction to questions of human rights violations (such as in Michael Ondaatje's 2000 novel about a forensic anthropologist in the Sri Lankan civil war, *Anil's Ghost*).

In these examples, the dead remind the living of their own inevitable death, but they also confront them with obligations; by doing so, they point to a sense of continuation of the bond between the living and the dead that exceeds death. Yet, the ample scholarly literature on burial rituals, on human rights excavations, or on the importance of the dead for cultural memory does not take up the question if and how the dead can act after death (with the exception of the figuration of the undead, of course). This, we suggest, has to do with a liberal perspective—hegemonic in modern democratic societies—that focuses on the living and neglects the dead. The examples referenced in the introductory section of this essay—the cast vote that is not counted because the voter dies before election day, Justice Ginsburg's wish to be replaced by the next president, the publication of Representative Lewis's opinion piece after his death—are difficult to reconcile with a liberal understanding of citizenship participation that regards only the living as potential citizen-actors and agents.

This difficulty motivates much current work on the role of the dead, mourning, and of notions of tragedy with regard to the Greek tragic tradition. The relevance of Greek tragedy and political philosophy for contemporary contexts has both been questioned and defended (cf. Euben). But the initially mentioned extensive reception of Sophocles' *Antigone* reflects the broad engagement with Greek tragedy not only in literature, but also in contemporary political theory, which, in turn, attests to the productivity of the lens for framing the role of the dead and mourning for contemporary polities beyond liberalism. In *American Mourning*, Simon Stow argues that "the dead will *always* participate in democratic politics"; crucial for democracy, he argues is "*how* they do so" (19), or rather, how the living make them do so, for "it is only through the living that the dead can participate in politics: either by being made to speak—in a process that the Greeks called *prosopopeia*—or by being invoked as an example of sacrifice and suffering" (19). Stow, like other critics, does not regard the dead as actors or agents, but as acted upon by the living in the context of public mourning and cultural memory. He juxtaposes what he calls romantic to tragic modes of (public) mourning; while he sees the former invested in the reconstruction and celebration of democratic unity, he suggests that the latter be seen as a productive lens of critical democratic self-reflection (21).

This is an instructive perspective for revisiting both the role of public mourning in democratic politics and polities (for Stow, the United States and more specifically, the United States after the attacks of 9/11) and the productivity of Greek tragedy as an angle from which to approach public mourning and democratic self-reflection. Stow's perspective builds on the function of Greek tragedy as a public ceremony of democratic assurance, as discussed for instance by Bonnie Honig and Nicole Loraux, on the power of tragedy to affirm democratic unity as well as to offer a space of mourning.

Productive as these approaches clearly are, this essay proposes a different take on the relation between tragedy and democratic politics. It sets out by focusing less on the function of tragedy but on its underlying sense of a community that incorporates the living and the dead, a sense clearly taken into account in approaches that focus on public mourning, but that sideline the question of how the dead can be understood as agents other than in metaphor or through the actions of the living. Remembering, commemoration is, of course, crucial. "Whether they are acts of remembering or acts of forgetting, rituals of commemoration are among the most important instances of the enactment of citizenship," writes Ian Morrison (289). And J. Peter Euben has highlighted the dual meaning of remembering as "recalling to mind or recollecting and becoming a member again" (157); membership, he continues, "makes us who we are. It sustains and empowers us, connecting us with a place and *with a community of the dead, living, and unborn*" (158; emphasis added). In theories of citizenship, membership and belonging have been central notions of this embeddedness in a community, but Euben's off-hand notion of community as encompassing not only the living, but also the dead and the unborn, implies a sense of the political community as transgenerational, directed not only towards the present by remembering the past, but also directed towards the future.

This perspective requires a sense of action that expands beyond the agency of the living and their lifespan. With regard to the examples referenced in the first section of this text, we thus propose refocusing the question: What if we do not understand those actions taken by the living that will come to fruition only after death as a mere expression of will but as a form of action beyond death, as community-oriented beyond the lifespan of the individual? Such 'action' is more obvious in the context of family, in which the action of the deceased are/can be understood as binding (even if their will is not adhered to). But what does that mean for the more abstract, even anonymous relation between citizens? How can the bonds that are necessary to keep the dead present, to have their actions understood as effective also beyond their death, be conceptualized? In short, how does an understanding of community as one consisting of the dead, the living, and the unborn impact our thinking about the agency and membership, that is, citizenship of the dead?

Citizenship of the dead can, of course, be and has been understood with regard to the individual's right to dignity, a proper burial, compliance with their final will, and so forth, and much of the discussion has focused on such an understanding. If understood as conceptualizing the agency of the dead, however, the focus shifts from an individual whose rights are to be protected even after death to an individual who continues to be part of a community—and whose actions potentially continue to impact this community. Such a shift is not so much a move toward a communitarian understanding of citizenship and its focus on group membership, as this requires an understanding of action and agency that is not limited to the living, but an understanding of the dead in continued interaction with the living. As such, this shift in focus presents a challenge to liberal notions of citizenship as it does not restrict the notion of community to those simultaneously present and alive, but includes both the dead and the not-yet-born. The current debate about intergenerational justice and the importance of immediate action regarding climate change and its effect on future generations displays such an understanding of community, obligation, and responsibility; earlier manifestations of such an understanding in terms of citizenship emerged in the 1990s, framed as ecological or environmental citizenship (Dobson; Isin and Wood). And while the understanding of community in Greek tragedy as a community that exceeds the living is not unique to tragedy, the recourse to it provides a productive lens to capture a more expansive understanding of the link between individual agency, community, membership, and citizenship.

The Time(s) of Citizenship: Agency Beyond Death?

In contemporary debates of citizenship, 'space' appears to be the central category that circumscribes the individual citizen's belonging. The "territorial principle," that is, the "proposition that control over a defined territory is a constitutive feature of political community" has been preeminent (Walker 553). This applies most obviously to the notion of national citizenship, but in terms of its focus on space also to the numerous expansions and revisions that this territorial understanding has undergone as transnational or diasporic citizenships, in the debates about refugeehood and statelessness, or as subnational categorizations such as urban citizenship. In contrast, 'time' has received less attention as a potentially relevant category to the understanding of citizenship;[4] while citizenship has been discussed with regard to both the historicity of the concept and its relation to the past citizenship of a political entity, it tends to be self-evidently understood in terms of the present as the relevant time of action and participation, a present, that is—at best—productively informed by the past and results—again, at best—in equally productive changes in the future. In short, debates about citizenship tend to focus on the present and the resulting narratives of citizenship tend to imply a linear, at times even teleological understanding of time. Yet, the directedness of citizenship towards the future, beyond the lifetime of the present members of a political community, discussed in the

---

4   Within this collection, Mitchell Gauvin's chapter addresses this gap by considering the intersection between citizenship, time, and temporal variability in Jamaica Kincaid's *A Small Place*. Gauvin reads citizenship as a neo-imperialistic and neo-capitalist weapon against transgressive identities, thereby illuminating the ways *A Small Place* implicitly confronts temporal spaces were the local and global meet and reveal how citizenship is also a type of temporal valuation.

previous section, can be seen as a more complex approach in terms of its temporal organization. Here we find one of the reasons for the interest of contemporary citizenship studies in the genre of tragedy.

"If citizenship could be said to have a genre," writes Carrie Hyde, "that genre would be tragedy" (181). Unlike the link drawn between citizenship and tragedy by the previously discussed critics, Hyde reads citizenship's 'tragedy' primarily in terms of the continuing processes of exclusion that characterize its history as well as its present. Regarding the future, then, "tragedy offers an agonic confrontation that holds out no necessary promise of rescue or reconciliation or redemption" (Scott 201). Directing acts of citizenship towards the future, in other words, is based precisely in the knowledge that there is no promise of progress, that the meanings of citizenship and democracy remain contested, and that citizens' visions for the future require explicit affirmation, even mobilization beyond the individual's lifetime.

One example of such a future-directed act of citizenship is the op-ed by the late Congressman and civil rights icon John Lewis published by *The New York Times* on July 30, 2020. Lewis died on July 17; he had written the article several days before his death, to be published on the day of his funeral. Lewis was the author of uncounted previous articles, but with regard to the questions we consider here, this last, posthumous publication bears crucial significance for a revised understanding of citizenship of the dead and a notion of action that ascribes agency to citizens beyond their death. The fact that the letter was meant to be read on the day of the funeral—a day of commemoration of his life's achievements as well as an acknowledgement of what his death meant not only to his family but also to the nation—added additional weight to his posthumous words, and are a good example of how the dead can be considered acting citizens.

Heike Paul has argued with regard to Senator John McCain's meticulous preparation of his own funeral, that he activated a sense of what she calls "civic sentimentalism"—an appeal to emotion and empathy as culturally specific mode of crisis management in the United States (8)—beyond his death, and that this activation served as a counter-point to then-president Trump's blatant disregard for established codes of democratic civility (85). John Lewis' op-ed, effectively a letter to the nation, can be understood along similar lines—like McCain, he wrote from a position imbued with symbolic capital and even more so than McCain, was read as a voice with undisputed moral authority. His letter also activated central codes of American political rhetoric; rhetoric steeped in, to speak with Paul, civic sentimentalism. The op-ed's title "Together, You Can Redeem the Soul of Our Nation" already draws on a central trope, redemption. The text itself begins thus:

> While my time here has now come to an end, I want you to know that in the last days and hours of my life you inspired me. You filled me with *hope* about the next chapter of the great American story when you used your power to make a

difference in our society. Millions of people motivated simply by *human compassion* laid down the *burdens* of division. (emphases added)

The text makes suffering and the alleviation of suffering central to its agenda. 'Compassion' is the crucial term that links it to the rhetoric of sentimentality, and 'hope' to a (secularized) Christian promise of a better future for the nation. But hope is not certainty; what is hoped for is but one possibility. "Democracy is not a state," Lewis writes, "*It is an act and each generation must do its part* to help build what we called the Beloved Community, a nation and world at peace with itself" (emphasis added).

There is "no necessary promise of rescue or reconciliation or redemption," to reference Scott once more (201); progress is not assured, it has to be fought for. Lewis' letter—addressed to a 'you' that is the nation's youth and future—has to be read in the context of Black Lives Matter activism which intensified in the wake of George Floyd's death at the hand of a police officer, and the impending election campaign in which the 45th president did not tire to announce that he could lose the election only by massive fraud on part of his opponents. Lewis' letter works by creating a direct analogy between his own experiences growing up as a Black man in the segregated South in the 1950s, the murder of Emmett Till, the struggle for Civil Rights, and the contemporary young generation's witnessing of an unabashed presidential support for white supremacists, the murder of unarmed Black men and women by the police, and the rise of Black Lives Matter. Lewis creates continuity between his generation and contemporary youth, with Martin Luther King Jr.'s teachings as a guideline—non-violence, the centrality of the democratic vote, and the insistence on the ideal of an inclusive United States as both a promise and an obligation. And Lewis expands this obligation beyond the borders of the nation when, towards the end; he writes:

People on every continent have stood in your shoes, through decades and centuries before you. The truth does not change, and that is why the answers worked out long ago can help you find solutions to the challenges of our time. Continue to build union between movements stretching across the globe because we must put away our willingness to profit from the exploitation of others.

What is of interest here, then, is how this passionate appeal to the nation and particularly the nation's youth can be considered not merely as a prominent citizen's political testament but as a citizen's act beyond death. Lewis' understanding of the political community encompasses the dead—whose sacrifices present a reminder to the living that indeed "democracy is not a state" that can be reached once and for all—as well as present generations and those not yet born. His self-positioning in this regard is relevant: He begins by acknowledging that his "time here has now come to

226 Performing Citizenship

an end," speaking, literally, from his deathbed, and he arranges for his words being read *after* his death. His act of citizenship is thus deliberately placed at the threshold between life and death, thereby calling into question the definite nature of this boundary for his agency as a citizen; if anything, his speaking across that boundary makes his intervention all the more powerful. What his text and the circumstances of its publication and circulation manifest is a notion of community in which the dead still speak and act, in which 'the future' is no abstract notion beyond the individual lifespan, but a concrete realm of responsibility not only for the living. The linear time of modernity that underlies liberal notions of the political community, that is, time as a neat succession of past, present, and future in which the past may be remembered but in which those who act always have to be present, is complicated by a sense of simultaneity of the living and the dead as citizen-coactors.

Citizenship of the Dead and the Limits of Liberal Self-Understanding

Liberalism has its issues with the dead. Liberal citizenship, as Iseult Honohan summarizes, "is primarily a formal, and in principle universal, legal status protecting individuals" (84), particularly against infringements by the state. It is a notion centered on individual rights and freedoms which "does not prioritize shared goods or a broader common good among citizens. Nor does it emphasize the commitment or civic virtue of citizens" or consider active participation essential to the understanding of citizenship (87). This model of the liberal individual allows the dead to have some power beyond the grave, which is mostly the power of testament. But such power of the dead is limited to the distribution of private assets. In terms of politics, liberalism's is the citizenship of the living and not of the dead. There are political reasons for this. Upholding the concept of negative liberty—'liberty from interference'—as the core principle of liberalism, Isaiah Berlin, critically described its opposite, the concept of positive freedom—'liberty to'—as "the great society of the living and the dead and the yet unborn" and denounces any inclusion of the dead as indicative of "organic" or "collective" political thought (179).

Berlin's attitude reflects liberalism's limitation in thinking beyond the living and focusing on rights rather than agency. What he had in mind was Edmund Burke's famous critique of the French Revolution and its destruction of feudal society. Not that Burke had been a staunch defender of the feudal order, on the contrary, to some extent he even supported the American colonies' struggle for political independence. But whereas the American revolutionaries seemed to uphold political principals very much in line with British traditions, the French seemed to ignore traditions of political thought entirely. Burke rejected the idea of a social contract that did not include the dead as well as the living. Modeling the state in terms of a "partnership,"

Burke explains in his "Reflections on the Revolution in France," published in November 1790:

> As the ends of such a partnership cannot be obtained in many generations, it becomes a partnership not only between those who are living, but between those who are living, those who are dead, and those who are to be born. Each contract of each particular state is but a clause in the great primæval contract of eternal society, linking the lower with the higher natures, connecting the visible and invisible world, according to a fixed compact sanctioned by the inviolable oath which holds all physical and all moral natures, each in their appointed place. (101)

Bringing the dead into play—as Burke did in the cited passage—seemed to Berlin to confuse politics with metaphysics, an instrument of ideologists to determine what the living might be forced to do, even against their expressed will. For liberalism, the only refuge was to uphold the freedom of the individual against all claims by those who claimed to speak for or in the name of the dead. Indeed, it is the core of conservatism to keep a check on the political will of the living by reminding them of tradition's obligations, and tradition often implies honoring the dead—and their will. When the conservative Gilbert Chesterton spoke of the democracy of the dead, this is precisely what he meant. In *Orthodoxy*, published in 1909, we find him stating:

> Those who urge against tradition that men in the past were ignorant may go and urge it at the Carlton Club, along with the statement that voters in the slums are ignorant. It will not do for us. If we attach great importance to the opinion of ordinary men in great unanimity when we are dealing with daily matters, there is no reason why we should disregard it when we are dealing with history or fable. Tradition may be defined as an extension of the franchise. Tradition means giving votes to the most obscure of all classes, our ancestors. It is the democracy of the dead. Tradition refuses to submit to the small and arrogant oligarchy of those who merely happen to be walking about. All democrats object to men being disqualified by the accident of birth; tradition objects to their being disqualified by the accident of death. (83)

It is no surprise that democrats protested against such arguments that connect Chesterton in a direct line to Burke. Thomas Paine immediately rejected Burke's critique in his book on *Rights of Man* (its first part published in March 1791) and formulated the democratic credo that the dead shall not bind the living:

> Every age and generation must be as free to act for itself, in all cases, as the ages and generations which preceded it. The vanity and presumption of governing beyond the grave, is the most ridiculous and insolent of all tyrannies. Man has

228   Performing Citizenship

> no property in man; neither has any generation a property in the generations which are to follow … Every generation is, and must be, competent to all the purposes which its occasions require. It is the living, and not the dead, that are to be accommodated. When man ceases to be, his power and his wants cease with him; and having no longer any participation in the concerns of this world, he has no longer any authority in directing who shall be its governors, or how its government shall be organized, or how administered. (63-64)

Thomas Jefferson took the same line at several occasions (although without giving Paine due credit) to argue about the potential role of the dead for the living: "The dead? But the dead have no rights. They are nothing; and nothing cannot own something" (216). The dead are nothing and therefore they cannot bind the living:

> Can one generation bind another, and all others, in succession forever? I think not. The Creator has made the earth for the living, not the dead. Rights and powers can only belong to persons, not to things, not to mere matter, unendowed with will. The dead are not even things. The particles of matter which composed their bodies, make part now of the bodies of other animals, vegetables, or minerals, of a thousand forms. To what then are attached the rights and powers they held while in the form of men? (386)

Given conservative attempts to restrict the political will of the majority of the living in recourse to the dead, liberal as well as democratic critiques of any potential claim by the dead for having a say in what the living ought to do is therefore reasonable. But even if one concedes that in a democratic context the dead may have no "right" to bind the living, it is still within the bounds of the democratic polity that the dead might nevertheless try to persuade the living to continue what they started, to appeal to them to learn from their failures and achievements. There is a difference between the interpretation of the deceased's deeds and intentions by some of the living for political manipulation on the one hand, and the articulation of will for the future by the dead themselves in full knowledge that they have no right to bind the hands of the living, on the other.

Conclusion

In his posthumous *New York Times* op-ed, John Lewis does not refer to tradition or seek to bind the living by invoking the heritage of the dead and their deeds. But neither does he express a merely private wish for what should happen after his death. As a dead co-citizen with an authority established by his life's work and further deepened by this speaking beyond his own lifespan, he gives advice; he does not demand but reflect upon where both—the dead and the living—stand, and which path the living should follow. His words and their publication stand in a tradition of posthumous 'death-bed letters' by public figures. Understanding such a letter as we do here, as a citizen's future- and community-directed action beyond death, as enacted 'citizenship of the dead,' not only shifts the attention from citizenship as status and a set of rights to citizenship as obligatory participation. Our interpretation also expands the understanding of the community towards which such participation is directed: a community in which the obligation of citizens does not end with their death, and in which they still have a voice—not the decisive voice, not the only voice, but a voice, or rather, voices—that should be heard, weighted, and considered. Consequently, this supposes an understanding of politics that includes not only the living, but also the dead.

While this understanding can be found in a number of non-liberal and also non-western notions of community and politics, it is prominent in tragedy, and tragedy provides one central mode of making such a notion narratable. Sophocles' particular rendering of conflict lines in his tragedy *Antigone*—elsewhere we have called this the "Antigonistic conflict" (Llanque/Sarkowsky)—lends itself well to the exploration of such a notion and its actualization in our political present. The ongoing reworkings of *Antigone* in political theory and literature may, of course, be a result of the perpetuation of a canonical dynamic; but they clearly attest to the productivity of such reinterpretation in trying to expand the horizon of the living.

Works Cited

Antigone. Directed by Sophie Deraspe, Maison 4:3, 2019.

Berlin, Isaiah. "Two Concepts of Liberty." *Liberty*, Oxford UP, 2002, pp. 166–217.

Burke, Edmund, "Reflections on the Revolution in France." *Revolutionary Writings: Reflections on the Revolution in France and the First Letter on a Regicide Peace*, edited by Iain Hampsher-Monk, Cambridge UP, 2014, pp. 1–250.

Butler, Judith. *Frames of War. When is Life Grievable?* Verso, 2016.

Chesterton, Gilbert K. *Orthodoxy*. John Lane, 1909.

Crossland, Zoe. "Forensic Afterlives." *Signs and Society*, vol. 6, no. 3, 2018, pp. 622–647.

Deraspe, Sophie. *Antigone*. ACPAV, 2019.

Dietz, Mary G. "Citizenship with a Feminist Face: The Problem with Maternal Thinking." *Political Theory*, vol. 13, no. 1, 1985, pp. 19–37.

Dobson, Andrew. *Citizenship and the Environment*. Oxford UP, 2003.

Elshtain, Jean Bethe. "Antigone's Daughters." *Democracy Journal*, vol. 2, no. 2, 1982, pp. 46–59; reprinted in *Feminism and Politics*, edited by Anne Phillips, Oxford UP, 1998, pp. 363–377.

—. "Antigone's Daughters Reconsidered: Continuing Reflections on Women, Politics, and Power." *Life-World and Politics: Between Modernity and Postmodernity*, edited by Fred R. Dalmayr and Stephen K. White, University of Notre Dame Press, 1989, pp. 222–235.

Euben, J. Peter. *The Tragedy of Political Theory: The Road Not Taken*. Princeton UP, 1990.

Głowacki, Janusz. *Antigone in New York*. Translated by Janusz Glowacki and Joan Torres, Samuel French, 1997.

Honohan, Iseult. "Liberal and Republican Conceptions of Citizenship." *The Oxford Handbook of Citizenship*, edited by Ayelet Shachar et al., Oxford UP, 2017, pp. 83–106.

Hartouni, Valerie A. "Antigone's Dilemma: A Problem in Political Membership." *Hypatia*, vol. 1, no. 1, 1986, pp. 3–20.

Holland, Catherine A. "After Antigone: Women, the Past, and the Future of Feminist Political Thought." *American Journal of Political Science*, vol. 42, no. 4, 1998, pp. 1108–1132.

Honig, Bonnie. *Antigone Interrupted*. Cambridge UP, 2013.

Hyde, Carrie. *Civic Longings: The Speculative Origins of U.S. Citizenship*. Harvard UP, 2018.

Isin, Engin F., and Patricia K. Wood. *Citizenship and Identity*. Sage, 1999.

Jefferson, Thomas. "Letter to Samuel Kercheval, July 12, 1816." *Thomas Jefferson, Political Writings*, edited by Joyce Appleby and Terence Ball, Cambridge UP, 2004, pp. 210–217.

Köck, Thomas. *antigone. ein requiem. eine rekomposition nach sophokles*. SuhrkampTheatertext, 2019.

Laqueur, Thomas W. *The Work of the Dead: A Cultural History of Mortal Remains*. Princeton UP, 2015.

Llanque, Marcus, Katja Sarkowsky. *Der Antigonistische Konflikt. 'Antigone' heute und das demokratische Selbstverständnis*. transcript, 2023.

Loraux, Nicole. *The Mourning Voice: An Essay on Greek Tragedy*. Cornell UP, 2002.

Lewis, John. "Together, You Can Redeem the Soul of Our Nation." *The New York Times*, 30 July 2020, https://www.nytimes.com/2020/07/30/opinion/john-lewis-civil-rights-america.html.

M'charek, Amade, Sarah Casartelli. "Identifying Dead Migrants: Forensic Care Work and Relational Citizenship." *Citizenship Studies*, vol. 23, no. 7, 2019, pp. 738–757.

Morrison, Ian. "Acts of Commemoration. "*Acts of Citizenship*, edited by Engin F. Isin and Greg M. Nielsen, Zed Books 2008, pp. 289–291.

Ondaatje, Michael. *Anil's Ghost*. McClelland & Stewart, 2000.

Paine, Thomas. *Political Writings*, edited by Thomas Kuklick, Cambridge UP, 2000.

Paul, Heike. *Amerikanischer Staatsbürgersentimentalismus: Zur Lage der Politischen Kultur der USA*. Wallstein, 2021.

Penfold-Mounce, Ruth. Death, the Dead and Popular Culture. Emerald Publishing, 2018.

Scott, David. "Tragedy's Time. Postemancipation Futures Past and Present." *Rethinking Tragedy*, edited by Rita Felski, Johns Hopkins UP, 2008, pp. 199–217.

Shamsie, Kamila. *Home Fire*. Bloomsbury, 2017.

Sophocles. *Oedipus the King / Oedipus at Colonos / Antigone I.* Translated by F. Storr, Harvard UP, 1981.

Stow, Simon. *American Mourning: Tragedy, Democracy, Resilience*. Cambridge UP, 2017.

Walker, Neil, "The Place of Territory in Citizenship." *The Oxford Handbook of Citizenship*, edited by Ayelet Shachar et al., Oxford UP, 2017, pp. 554–575.

"We had to control the narrative"
The Innovations and Limitations of Youth Citizenship

Anah-Jayne Samuelson

On 14 February 2018 the deadliest school shooting in American history took place at Marjory Stoneman Douglas High School (herein referred to as MSD) in Parkland, Florida. The rampage shooting, enacted by a former student of MSD, injured and killed seventeen staff and students, which sparked national debates over gun control policies.[1] In the macabre reality of gun violence in the United States, MSD is not an exceptional occurrence: there have been an estimated 108 school shootings in the US between 2009 and 2019 (Walker). However, the response to the MSD rampage shooting was unique in that youth survivors directly and purposefully intervened in the news media's coverage of the event and debates on gun control. Within hours of the shooting, MSD students quickly mobilized and "stepped directly into the political arena to not only declare 'enough is enough,' but to demand common sense gun reform" (Bent 56), and the March for Our Lives Movement (herein referred to as MFOL) was born. The MFOL's mission is to "harness the power of young people across the country to fight for sensible gun violence prevention policies that save lives" ("Mission"). MFOL organized the largest single-day protest against gun violence, and of the MFOL's activities, it was this protest that gathered the most media attention. However, MFOL also utilized several strategies to communicate their demands to policy makers, and it is through these varied strategies that the MFOL youth activists claimed and enacted the rights and responsibilities of citizenship before they were legally able to vote.

The MFOL youth activists deliberately intervened with their voices into the "thoughts and prayers" rhetoric spouted by the media and politicians, taking control of their narratives to challenge those in power to meet their demands. These young people offer an example of youth citizenship that greatly challenges standard citizenship models that traditionally exclude young people from participation in

---

1 Rampage shootings are defined as attacks on multiple parties selected mostly at random (Newman et al. 15). Katherine S. Newman et al. were the first to do a systematic study on school shootings in *Rampage* (2004) and scholars have continued to use the term "rampage" to describe mass casualty lethal school violence.

234 Performing Citizenship

the political mechanisms that structure and govern their lives. Through an analysis of *Glimmer of Hope* (2018), an account of the MFOL movement written by the core founding members, this chapter explores the models of youth citizenship exhibited by the MFOL members. In their account, the young activists simultaneously assert themselves as subjects and citizens with the right to voice their concerns and have them heard and addressed, and undercut the power they have as citizens in emphasizing that voting is the strongest way to bring about change—a process they could not yet take part in. This dichotomy unveils some of the arbitrary boundaries of citizenship, in this case the legal voting age, and demonstrates the difficulty and limitations of asserting and claiming one's rights as a citizen before these rights have been legally granted and recognized. This chapter focuses on the methods with which the MFOL youth amplified their voices in order to put meaningful pressure on elected officials, and I argue that this is a method of citizenship available to those not yet legally able to vote. However, this chapter also investigates the limits that arise when youth make demands of elected officials when being unable to threaten the incumbency of these officials through the electoral process.

Defining Citizenship and Youth Citizenship

T. H. Marshall's definition of citizenship has long been considered the standard and encompasses three levels of rights to be granted to citizens: the rights to freedom of speech, to justice, to own property; the political rights to vote and to run for political office; and social rights that include social security, health care, and education. According to this seminal definition, citizenship provides members of a society civil, social, and political rights that Marshall believes would create equality: this form of citizenship would "become a form of equalization in which individuals gained a common identity" (303). However, rather than being an equalizing force, in practice this definition does not offer citizenship rights to every subject within a society, as the rights of citizenship have traditionally been consigned to adults (most relevant to this chapter) of a particular class and ethnicity.

Building from Marshall, Richard Bellamy defines citizenship as having "an intrinsic link to democratic politics," and he argues that voting is the most crucial component as it colours all other rights and responsibilities traditionally associated with citizenship (Bellamy 12). For Bellamy, voting is the most essential method to communicate with elected officials regarding concerns: "[t]he logic is simple ... if politicians consistently ignore citizens and prove incompetent, they will eventually lose office" (7). Bellamy unpacks the difficulties and complications in assigning this amount of power to voting in that the right to vote has been historically monopolized by property-owning white men, and he traces several suffrage movements relating to gender, class, and race.

One social group that is perpetually unable to vote, and that is not significantly discussed by Bellamy, is children and youth. Bellamy does mention that children are traditionally excluded from the full citizenship rights of voting because they "have yet to develop the capacity of independent reasoning or living on their own and are necessarily dependent on the views and support of their parents" (59). Bellamy notes the arbitrary nature of determining at what age children and youth become "capable of intellectual and economic independence" (59), and that because of this arbitrariness some nations, like the United Kingdom, have proposed the voting age be lowered. What Bellamy does not address is the false assumption that the legal age of majority automatically equates independent reasoning, when in reality many adults are also dependent (in varying degrees) on the opinions, views, and support of others. As well, using economic independence as a measure of who is granted the right to vote would exclude many individuals over the age of eighteen. In these standards that determine who should be granted the right to vote, it is seldom considered that children, youth, and adults can all embody similar characteristics, and this exposes the indiscriminate nature of these measures that exclude some from citizenship rights.

The authors of *Glimmer of Hope* largely agree with Bellamy that voting is the cornerstone of citizenship. Delaney Tarr argues "the best way to really make a difference is to get people to vote for the right leaders" (*Glimmer* 99), and David Hogg reflects that "unless every single one of those people [protesters who attended MFOL] votes, it doesn't matter ... you have to get out and fucking vote" (*Glimmer* 183). While imbuing the right to vote with such power, a right many of the MFOL organizers did not possess in 2018, they nonetheless demonstrate that children and youth can directly influence the polls without casting a vote themselves: in 2018, MFOL registered over 50,000 new voters during their Road to Change education campaign and they registered another 800,000 people on National Voter Registration Day during the Mayors for Our Lives campaign events ("Mission"); possibly as a result of these voter registrations, in the 2018 midterm elections there "was a 47% increase over the last midterm election and the highest percentage of youth voter turnout ever" ("Mission"). Yet, many (including the MFOL activists) still view children and youth as being restricted as democratic citizens because they cannot cast their own ballots.

In the model of democratic citizenship, in which one becomes a citizen when they can legally vote, children and youth are viewed as future citizens or citizens-in-the-making. Robert Lawy and Gert Biesta argue that models of citizenship like Marshall's and Bellamy's create a "citizenship as achievement mindset," and essential to this is the "assumption that young people should act and behave in a particular way in order to achieve their citizenship status" (38). In this model, children and youth are future voting citizens with little to no power in their current life stage. In addition, Hava Rachel Gordon argues that one consequence in positioning children and youth as citizens-in-the-making is that they are "socially constructed as citizen participants only in future tense: ill-equipped to participate in the social and political decision making as youth, only capable of this participation as adults" (9). Inherent in the citizens-in-the-making theory is the assumption that youth will transition synchronously and smoothly into active citizenship when they reach legal voting age; in practice this model breeds apathy, and this is demonstrated across many nations in the low youth voting numbers as compared to other age demographics. For example, a study of the 2013 Canadian Federal election found that sixty-one percent of youth aged twenty to twenty-four indicated they would be likely to vote in the next Federal election compared to eighty-four percent of seniors aged sixty-five to seventy-four (Turcotte). As well, the Canadian 2015 National Youth Survey found the two barriers that prevented youth from voting were motivation (lack of interest and the belief that their votes do not matter) and access (less likely to receive a voting card and less aware of how to register and vote) (Nielsen). Lack of motivation and difficulty accessing where and when to vote are directly related to a citizenship-as-achievement mindset: children and youth have been excluded from citizenship rights and responsibilities which breeds the assumption that their concerns do not matter, and they lack direct experiences with voting systems that make many ill-prepepared to be active voting citizens when they do join the legal majority. Lawy and Biesta suggest that rather than viewing citizenship as "a status or possession," or as "an outcome of developmental and/or educational trajectory that can be socially engineered," we should view citizenship as a "practice, embedded within the day-to-day reality of (young) people's lives, interwoven and transformed over time in all the distinctive and different dimensions of their lives" (47). As will be examined in the next section, the MFOL activists demonstrate a model of citizenship-as-practice in their acts of voicing discontent to lawmakers.

It is also a question of power and control in determining which subjects are allowed to exercise the rights and responsibilities of citizenship. Jessica Taft notes that "democracy means that those affected by a decision should have significant voice in the making of such decisions" (*Kids* 51), and in excluding youth from the rights and responsibilities of citizenship there is the assumption that children and youth cannot make a difference that is "rooted in conceptions of the inherent inequality of young people" (53). Children and youths' exclusion from many of the rights of citizenship, as defined by Marshall and Bellamy, results in their unfiltered perspectives and concerns being considered in a limited nature, if at all, in decision making. When adults run for office at any level, a large portion of a nation's population does not need to be directly addressed or engaged with. Rather, adults speak for children and youth which filters and potentially distorts children and youths' concerns. However, many youths, like the MFOL organizers, "refuse the suggestion that their politics is only relevant in a deferred future. In this view of the discourse of preparation is, in the end, incompatible with their efforts to claim authority because it makes no space for the democratic participation of youth as youth" (Taft, *Kids* 52).

This chapter uses an expanded definition of citizenship from that of Marshall and Bellamy that considers citizenship not as something that is achieved, but as a lifelong "cradle to grave" practice (Lawy and Biesta 43). It is through citizenship-as-practice, as Lawy and Biesta argue, that "young people learn to be citizens as a consequence of their participation in the actual practices that make up their lives" (45). Yet, how can youth fully participate in democratic citizenship when they cannot vote, which is heralded even by the MFOL youth as the corner stone of participating in a democracy? Besides voting, Bellamy notes that "speaking out" is also a crucial task in being involved in the democratic process, and thus another means to exercise one's citizenship (3). This chapter analyzes the methods utilized by the MFOL youths to "speak out" in order to regain control of how their narratives are being represented, address the issues entrenched in their narratives, and speak directly to policymakers. The methods (social media, face-to-face dialogue in legislation, and protests) which the MFOL youth harness to amplify their voices offer a model for children and youth to participate as citizens in the present and are a means to influence the voting process before being legally able to vote themselves.

"This is not your story": Intervening Through Social Media

School shootings have garnered much media attention throughout their history, but the repeated national outrage has not resulted in substantial gun reform policies. The Columbine Massacre in 1999, "was the deadliest school shooting in history at the time and the second-most-covered news event of the 1990s, second only to O. J. Simpson's car chase with police and televised murder trial" (Markland). Columbine's media focus was centered on adults interpreting the rampage shooting and its causes, and not on the youths' perspectives who had lived through the experience. As with many issues that directly affect children and youth, adults spoke on behalf of students and this resulted in attention being misdirected from the wider social factors (such as gun regulations) towards the individual (such as the violent media the shooters consumed and their mental health).

In the hours following the MSD shooting, MFOL activist Cameron Kasky witnessed the same trend unfold with the immediate media coverage, and this compelled him (and subsequently his peers) to interject with his voice to gain control over his own narrative:

This is not the media's narrative. This is not your story. This is nobody's tragedy to interpret but our own. The students of Stoneman Douglas know exactly what happened at Stoneman Douglas, and under no circumstances will you tell our story for us. (Glimmer 5).

238 Performing Citizenship

In writing that the MSD rampage shooting is for the youth survivors to interpret, Kasky disrupts the usual hierarchy of adults speaking on behalf of youth. Furthermore, Kasky situates the MSD youth survivors as those best suited to interpret this event because their direct experience makes them authorities on the subject. Kasky's statement that youths are the experts of their own experiences additionally unsettles the power imbalance between adults and youth in giving control to youth. The use of "interpret" in understanding the MSD shooting is also significant—Kasky argues that the youth survivors, as the authorities on this subject, will be the ones to "to make meaning of" this event ("interpret" v.1.b). In this section, Kasky demands that he and his peers be put in control of their narratives, and he asserts they will be the ones to understand and make meaning out of their experiences. Both rhetorical moves imbue youth survivors with power in declaring that they will directly voice their narrative and demands, rather than have this filtered through adult advocates to adult policymakers.

Kasky's above assertion transposes youth as authorities over their experiences, and this repositioning is a form of self-making. Self-making is, as Aihwa Ong argues, a form of citizenship: "citizenship [is a] process of self-making and being-made in relation to nation-states and transitional processes" (737). Ong sees citizenship as a "cultural process of 'subject-ifcation,' in the Foucauldian sense of self-making and being-made by power relations" (737). Kasky notes that in order for himself and his peers' concerns and demands to be heard, they must be in control of their narratives. In doing so, Kasky and others take an active role in their self-making as a process of citizenship that controls how they are presented and reframes how they are constituted as youth subjects: no longer silent figures in video clips who only speak when an adult journalist decides who a microphone is given to, Kasky and other MSD survivors share their voices through various means in order to reposition themselves as citizen-subjects needing to be heard. Furthermore, Kasky states it is essential he and other youth control their narratives to directly make demands: "I had to change the narrative as quickly as possible and let the country know that our generation—the school shooting generation—wasn't going to stand for this anymore" (*Glimmer* 7). Kasky's arguments reflect Ong's description of self-making citizenship as "the demand of disadvantaged subjects for full citizenship in spite of their cultural difference from mainstream society" (738). In this case, children and youth are disadvantaged citizens as their age precludes them from several rights and responsibilities of traditional citizenship, as defined by Marshall and Bellamy. Voicing their concerns repositions youth as subjects who will actively make meaning from the shooting, which, in this case, is gun policies needing to be significantly reformed.

A specific instrument the MFOL activists utilized to narrate their experiences and amplify their voices was social media, especially *Twitter*. Emily Bent explains that the "MFOL student-activists utilized social media not only to expose adult hypocrisy but to claim public voice and political agency in the gun control debate by intentionally violating youth citizenship scripts and codes of behaviour" (64). One such example of this comes from MSD survivor Sarah Chadwick who was frustrated by the "thoughts and prayers" unaccompanied with action being offered to victims by media and policymakers, many of which were communicated over social media. In one tweet, American President Donald Trump "offered his condolences and his thoughts and prayers," and these empty words from the highest governing power in the United States made Chadwick "so angry" that she spoke back to President Trump by retweeting, "we didn't want thoughts and prayers, we wanted policy and action" (*Glimmer* 43). Chadwick's tweet went viral: 300,000 likes and 100,000 retweets within hours (43). In this instance, social media offered the unique ability for Chadwick, a high school student, to respond directly to her president and voice her discontent regarding his muted response to the rampage shooting. Bellamy argues that alongside voting, speaking out is foundational to democratic citizenship. Chadwick, unimpressed with the hollow response by the White House, demonstrates her subjectivity as a citizen by voicing her discontent and expressing what she, as a citizen, demands (policy and action) in place of the meaningless and vague rhetoric.

Likewise, Jaclyn Corin, a founding member of MFOL, used "rhetoric that resembled no one else's" on several social media platforms (*Glimmer* 71). In emphasizing that she used distinctive language, Corin notes that youth narrating their experiences sounds different than when these experiences are filtered through adults. Corin's direct language and clear demands of policymakers regarding how the shooting should be addressed is what she credits as making several of her posts go viral. In one such instance, Corin posted "a picture that read 'MAKE IT STOP' above a drawing of a semi-automatic rifle. My caption read '... contact your state and local representatives, as we must have stricter gun laws immediately" (71). In both examples from Chadwick and Corin, their social media posts intervened directly with the adult-curated narratives surrounding the MSD shooting by exposing the empty nature of condolences without action. Both Chadwick and Corin refute the adult responses to the MSD shooting by demanding what should take the place of thoughts and prayers: gun reform. Corin's post goes a step further than Chadwick's in not only broadly expressing that policy change is required, but by also including a roadmap for other youth (and adults) in how this change could be achieved: speaking with representatives. Corin emphasizes the sustained need and value of citizens using their voices to apply pressure onto those in power when reform is needed. Neither Corin or Chadwick could legally vote at the time of their social media posts, but in voicing their discontent and providing demands, they potentially influence those who can legally vote to support a representative who would meet these demands. As well, in exercising their right and responsibility as citizens to speak out, Corin and Chadwick are taking part in the citizenship-as-practice model that fosters political interest and involvement before they are able to formally take part in the electoral process.

Yet, both Corin and Chadwick's examples have limitations and showcase how these young citizens have internalized the belief that active youth citizenship is extraordinary. Chadwick explains that she eventually was made to delete her viral retweet to President Trump because "my dad wasn't too fond of my language," and she "tweeted out an apology that basically said 'I'm apologizing for my language I used but not my anger" (*Glimmer* 43). Here, a parent/adult dominates, polices, and revises a young citizen's "speaking out," and this betrays the difficulty for some youth in being active citizens while under parental control. Her tweet was an instance in which Chadwick had control over how she presented herself as a subject, and this instance was deemed unacceptable by an adult authority figure because it violated the accepted passive script, rhetoric, and codes of behaviour reserved for young people. Chadwick was made to apologize for her language and behaviour violation—in other words, for being a youth citizen. As Lawy and Biesta argue, in many "situations young people are not seen as legitimate participants, their voices are ignored, and they have limited opportunity for shaping and changing the situations they are in" (45). Chadwick's example demonstrates the heightened level of difficulty for youth citizens in being fully able to control their narratives, voice their discontent, and influence or shape their circumstances when under parental/adult control.

Corin, in writing about her social media posts and her travels to legislature to meet with Florida senators, explains that "[n]ever in my life did I think I would involve myself in the world of politics" (*Glimmer* 73), nor did she think she *should* be involved in this political arena: "no kid should have to" (74). While it is of course true that no child, youth, or adult should have to be inspired to become an active citizen because of surviving a tragedy like a rampage shooting, Corin also discloses that she has internalized the assumption that children and youth are not *meant* to be involved in politics, and that it is only extraordinary measures that push them to do so.

This belief that children and youth should be "spared" having to be active citizens until they reach legal age is what Jessica Taft calls the "Exclusion Assumption," which is "an ideal of childhood innocence that suggests that children should not be concerned with social and political problems" (*Kids* 7). Taft furthers that this assumption and belief in childhood innocence "ignores the fact that many children are living these problems on a daily basis and do not have the option to ignore them" (*Kids* 7). As in the case of MFOL, the activists were often criticized for voicing their opinions concerning gun control as many conservatives argued "they are too young to know what they are talking about and that they have been manipulated by liberals" (Cummings), and that liberal-lensed adults were puppeteering the student survivors "to push their [adult liberal] agendas to the rest of us" (Carlson qtd. in Sanchez). These critics rarely acknowledged that the MSD students' lived experience with gun violence had made it impossible for them to ignore this issue—their peers have died as a direct result of lax gun legislation.

Even when immersed in "social and political problems," often when children and youth become involved in politics they are labelled as being "special" and "extraordinary," which the youth in Taft's study found to be damaging labels. In her interviews with female youth activists, Taft found that these young women "adamantly and actively refute the idea that they are special" (*Rebel* 44). Comments that position youth who are active citizens as being extraordinary assumes that "most youth are not capable of such involvement" and that in proclaiming youth activism and citizenship as

> extraordinary, adults perpetuate an association of youthfulness with political inaction or inability. Normal youth, in this narrative, are apathetic and politically disengaged. It is only the talented and committed few who are seen as capable of becoming politically active. (44)

Corin meaningfully used her voice to apply pressure to policymakers to meet her and her peers' demands for substantial gun reforms. However, in her writing, Corin demonstrates that she has internalized the belief that she should not have to be political, nor be a youth citizen—she is functioning in a citizenship-as-achievement model. Corin's assertion that "no kid should have to" be involved in politics communicates that she, as a youth, should not be taking an active role in democratic citizenship, and the fact that she has is only because of extraordinary circumstances.

In contrast, many of Corin's peers in the MFOL movement see their citizenship as a practice and that the MSD rampage shooting was a wake-up call that they needed to be actively involved in the procedures and structures that makes up their lives. For example, MSD survivor Jammal Lemy describes that "after previous school shootings happened, the last thing on my mind was to take action and fight the people who … have constantly dropped the ball … this is why young people needed their voices to be heard" (*Glimmer* 93, 97). In being directly involved in a school shooting, Lemy's perspective changed: "I know it's our duty as the youth of America to never stay quiet" (198). Regardless, Corin's internalization of the exclusion assumption demonstrates how difficult it is for children and youth to become more politically engaged when they have been socialized to believe they are "passive objects of socialization" rather than active citizens-in-practice (Taft *Kids*, 6).

"You work for the people": Talking to Legislators

The MFOL activists did not only engage with community and elected officials over social media, but also voiced their concerns and demands face-to-face with legislators, embodying the right of citizens to bring their concerns to elected officials. While the activists took part in events that average citizens (youth and adult alike) would not be afforded, like the CNN televised townhall where MSD students asked questions of Florida representatives, they also attended state and federal open sessions in legislature to share concerns and make demands: a practice available to any citizen.

Early in the MFOL organization's genesis, Corin, because of her viral social media posts, was encouraged by a Congresswoman to attend a session in the Florida Legislature. Corin knew that for her demands of policy change to be met she needed to speak directly to those with the power to make these policy changes: "I felt as though it was all up to me to urge the House to bring a bill to the floor regarding stricter gun laws" (*Glimmer* 72–3). Corin organized a group of MSD students to accompany her in order to meet with as many representatives as possible. During their visit, the group met with Democrat and Republican representatives, the attorney general, lieutenant governor, and governor to advocate for stricter gun laws (76).

Following this state legislature trip, MFOL member Delaney Tarr writes of the group's visit to Washington, D.C. to "have an open conversation with the people who can make real legislative change" at the federal level (*Glimmer* 93). For Tarr, the ability to speak directly with federal leaders made her and others feel like "more than just teenagers" (93). Tarr, like Corin, has internalized the belief that this sort of active citizenship should not be normally enacted by teenagers, and thus speaking directly with federal lawmakers is diametrically opposed to her "naturalized" subject position as a youth who has no real power or value in the present. Tarr remembers feeling "powerful" when standing inside the Capitol building because she was "there with a voice … to make real change" (94–5). Tarr initially felt empowered simply by physically inhabiting the Capitol building—empowered that she, as a teenager, was actively present in an adult-regulated space, and thus a subject with opinions and beliefs worthy of being heard.

However, these visits were also disheartening and revealed the difficulties of youth citizenship. The initial trip to the Florida Legislature was a lesson to Corin and her peers regarding the language games played by politicians: they offered their sympathy, but "avoid[ed] any real conversations about guns" (*Glimmer* 76). Sitting in a Senate meeting, the MSD students witnessed politicians send "thoughts and prayers to Parkland, but promised no action" (76)—direct and clear demands from the students from MSD were met with vague and slick language. Even though the students were disappointed that their presence did not immediately result in dramatic policy changes—indeed, after they asked for more psychologists to be placed in schools, mental health funding was instead cut shortly after their visit—and the politicians evaded genuine dialogue, Corin insists that their physical presence and their voices "made a difference" as they (the politicians), "surely did not expect immediate action, specifically one hundred teenagers swarming their building like bees"

(77). Put another way, Corin expresses that lawmakers did not expect to be answerable to, and to be applied pressure from, youth who were enacting their rights as citizens to express their discontent and demand change. Though it was of course disheartening that this visit did not end in substantial policy changes, it did show elected representatives how the MSD students were re-subjecting themselves as citizens who would not be passive.

Like Corin, Tarr also learned about the power dynamics and language games that take place at the Capitol: "[u]nsurprisingly, they would try and manipulate the conversation so they would get to say their piece, and often left us without any time to get a word in" (*Glimmer* 96). The Capitol politicians monopolized the room for speech to keep youth voiceless, and thus powerless: if youth citizens are not given space to express their concerns, then politicians do not have to directly address these concerns. Tarr's initial empowerment from taking up space in the Capitol was quickly extinguished: the first person she approached questioned why she and her peers were there and "treat[ed] us like kids and was rude to us" (95). However, among those who monopolized conversation or dismissed the group, there were some that listened and this "was very powerful" for the students (95). While Tarr is unsure if these figures took them seriously because "nothing has really happened yet," her meeting with Representative John Lewis bolstered her resolve to continue using her voice: "[t]o hear a civil rights activist say, 'We support you guys. We stand with you. We marched, now you do your marching'" (96–7). Representative Lewis did not marginalize the students, but he drew meaningful parallels to his own citizenship as a youth to encourage the groups' sustained political actions—a wonderful example of adult-allyship.

Cameron Kasky shares similar frustrations to Corin and Tarr over the elusive conversations that he experienced during the CNN townhall. Kasky describes that Senator Mark Rubio gave "political answers" and "sidestepped" a yes-or-no question: "[w]ould he stop accepting money from the NRA?" (*Glimmer* 83). Kasky argues that representatives like Senator Rubio have the obligation to answer questions directly and frankly: "[i]f you are a politician, you work for the people, and it is your responsibility to answer the questions that the people rightfully raise" (83). Kasky notes that Senator Rubio most likely hoped he would "make it out with zero consequences" from the town hall in having to field questions from youth, but Kasky was not going to "let him get away that easy" (83), further stating not only his status as a citizen who has the right to express discontent and have questions answered, but as having the responsibility of holding those in power accountable.

Just as youth citizenship is complicated as it crosses arbitrary boundaries to demand rights and responsibilities not yet bestowed, the outcomes of the MFOL visits with lawmakers is complex. There is no fairy-tale ending with gun laws being substantially and meaningfully reformed. Rather, like most institutional change, these visits moved the needle on gun reform. Even these small changes are significant

244   Performing Citizenship

because of the role that the pressure from MFOL played in making these changes. A week after the MFOL's visit to the Florida Legislature, the governor, Rick Scott, signed into law the Marjory Stoneman Douglas High School Public Safety Act. This law calls for a ban on bump stocks and raised the minimum age to purchase firearms from eighteen to twenty-one. While this law is "progressive," Corin argues "it wasn't enough" (78). Regardless of this small victory, Corin left the Florida Legislature with the resolve to "never stop fighting," and that "it might take years, but we must continue to move forward as a united front to bring about the change this country desperately needs" (78). Though many of the conversations with lawmakers were disappointing, it taught Corin that citizenship is an ongoing practice, not a single-event achievement.

For Tarr, after her visit to the Capitol, she views the MFOL's impact as a successful threat the incumbency of many politicians through the education of those who can vote on gun reform: "the best way to make [a] difference is to get people to vote for the right leaders" (*Glimmer* 99). While the MFOL youth are limited in their citizenship in that they demand action from representatives who do not technically represent them (as they are not voting citizens), Tarr demonstrates the potential for youth to be part of the electoral process in educating those who can vote.

"Politicians: either represent the people or get out": The March for Our Lives

It is estimated that between 200,000 (aerial estimates) and 800,000 (estimate of the MFOL organizers) people participated in the March for Our Lives protest in Washington, D.C., and approximately 800 "sibling marches" simultaneously took place across the globe (Lopez). Because of the momentum behind organizing the protest and the extensive media coverage leading up to it, it would be easy to position the protest as the pinnacle of the MFOL movement. In reality, though it may have been the most visible, the march was just one of several vehicles used by the MFOL's youth citizens to reframe themselves as subjects with the right to make demands of policy makers. Kasky describes protesting as "patriotic" and situates it as an act of citizenship: "getting out there and demanding more from our country is one of the best things you can do for yourself" (*Glimmer* 183). MFOL organizers John Barnitt, Sarah Chadwick, and Sophie Whitney compared their march to those of the Civil Rights movement and protests against the Vietnam war, and they align themselves with an American history "of the greatest changes ... [being] brought up by young Americans who were sick of not having their voices heard" (47). In situating the march as being American, patriotic, and part of a noble history, the youth organizers further reframe themselves as American subjects in that they are actively participating in patriotic methods of citizenship. The above statements not only imbue the youth activists with the right to protest as American citizens, but also with the right to have their concerns heard and seriously considered.

In addition to the physical act of marching in Washington, there were dozens of speeches given by the organizers of MFOL during the march, and *Glimmer of Hope* includes excerpts from several of the organizers' speeches. One such excerpt from David Hogg's speech makes significant and complicated rhetorical moves that both limits his political power as a youth, and re-subjects himself and other youth as American citizens who have the right to have their demands heard and met, and if not, a reckoning will follow:

> The winter is over. Change is here. The sun shines on a new day, and the day is ours … If you listen real close, you can hear the people in power shaking. They've gotten used to being protective of their position, the safety of inaction. Inaction is no longer safe … get your résumés ready. (150–1)

Hogg maintains the standard definition of democratic citizenship that Bellamy purports in that voting is the most essential act, but Hogg also expresses that youth have the power to remove policy makers right now. In the present, those that can legally vote are listening and being educated by youth like the MFOL activists, and their votes have the power to remove policymakers who do not support reform. Additionally, the youth citizens making these demands will soon be of legal voting age, and their concerns cannot be forever ignored. But this type of argument is the embodiment of the assumption that children and youth are citizens-in-the-making and only hold tangible political power in the future. Emily Bent explains that the complicated language that is used by Hogg "claims political voice and authority as a future voter … [but] by threatening politicians to fall in line with young people's demands and visions of the future, he paradoxically solidified age as a political threat and signifier of political innocence" (68). Although Hogg and others actively "reject … their status as only future citizens," they continue to position themselves as "future voters, future policy makers, and future citizens who will change the world" (68). However, as Bent argues, the MFOL activists' current engagement as "leaders and participants in the gun control movement" demonstrates the "necessity of seeing young people's politics as more than merely practice for the future" (69). In making demands before reaching legal majority, Hogg embodies citizenship-as-practice by learning how to be a citizen because of his current political participation.

Like Hogg, Cameron Kasky, in his march speech, addresses policymakers directly and warns that if youth citizens' voices are not engaged with, these same youth citizens have the power to remove them from their positions: "[p]oliticans: either represent the people or get out" (160). Kasky makes a strong demand here in positioning himself, and other youth, as "the people"—a direct reference to the preamble of the Constitution of the United States that opens with: "We the People of the

United States" ("Constitution: Preamble"). Erwin Chemerinsky and Michael Stokes Paulsen explain the significance of the preamble's first line in that it "proclaim[s] who is enacting this Constitution—the people of 'the United States,'" making this document "the collective enactment of all U.S. citizens" ("The Preamble"). In positioning "The People" as those who enact the Constitution, it is then "The People" who own the Constitution, and not the Government. In owning the Constitution, citizens of the United States "are the stewards of the U.S. Constitution and remain ultimately responsible for its continued existence and its faithful interpretation" (Chemerinsky and Paulsen). Kasky claims guardian-membership of the Constitution for himself, the survivors of school shootings, and other youth generally. In claiming this membership, Kasky simultaneously positions youth as citizens and as being stewards of upholding the Constitution alongside their adult counterparts, and thus makes porous the boundaries that "socially indenti[fy] [young people] as distinct from and 'other' to adult citizens" (Smith 429). Kasky's rhetoric places responsibility on youth, adults, and lawmakers to faithfully institute the Constitution: if youth are citizens and part of the collective "we the people," then they have the responsibility to uphold the Constitution and apply pressure to those in power to ensure it is enacted and enacted faithfully. For elected officials, it is the role of politicians to represent "The People," which Kasky has defined as encompassing youth, and thus it is their responsibility to hear and address the concerns of these citizens. Though these are clever rhetorical moves, Kasky's argument is undercut by his inability to vote. With children and youth not being directly involved in electing these officials, are they truly part of "The People," and are policymakers obligated to hear and meet the concerns of subjects outside of their constituency?

Kasky enveloping youth into the Constitutional umbrella of "The People" grants youth the rights and responsibilities of citizenship before they are legally recognized by the state and nation as having these rights and responsibilities. Therefore, Kasky is asking for elected officials to represent a body of subjects that do not directly participate (i.e., casting a vote) in the election process. Kasky is, as Judith Butler explains, "asserting a right they did not have in order to make the case, publicly that they should have that very right" (iv). Butler analyzes an instance in May 2006 in which illegal immigrants took to the streets of Los Angeles and sang the American National Anthem in English and Spanish, and Butler finds that "singing is a way of articulating a right to freedom of expression, to freedom of assembly, and the broader rights of citizenship by those who do not have that right, but exercised it anyway" (v-vi). The example Butler gives, and that of the march organized by MFOL, "raises the question of how a right can be exercised when it is not already conferred" (vi). In other words, how can the MFOL activists position themselves as "The People" when they have not legally been conferred the rights and responsibilities that go along with being the custodians of the American Constitution? For Butler, laying claims to the rights one does not yet have "means to translate into the dominant language, not to ratify its power, but to expose and resist its daily violence, and to find the language through which to lay claim to rights to which one is not yet entitled," and that "sometimes it is not a question of first having power and then being able to act; sometimes it is a question of acting, and in the acting laying claim to the power one requires" (x). Using the language of the U.S. Constitution, Kasky lays claim to the rights and responsibilities of citizenship. In doing so, he exposes how youth are actively excluded from participating in the structures that govern their lives and (in this case) deaths. Kasky resists this exclusion through using the language of the Constitution to lay claim to the power that he and other youth require.

Conclusion

Bellamy argues that speaking out is essential in democratic citizenship, and the MFOL activists have modelled various means of "speaking out" to policymakers. The MFOL youth embody a citizenship-as-practice model that affords them participation in the present, not just in the future as adult-citizens. Lawy and Biesta argue that citizenship should not be a rite of passage or an achievement that is granted when one is able to suitably reproduce a certain set of practices, but rather citizenship "is a practice, embedded within the day-to-day reality of (young) people's lives, interwoven and transformed over time in all the distinctive and different dimensions of their lives" (47). However, as this chapter has explored, there are limitations to youths' citizenship-as-practice: they must navigate adult/guardianship control and surveillance as they demand action from policymakers that are in principle unbeholden to them. This analysis has shown the difficulty of claiming democratic citizenship rights before one is legally able to formally take place in voting processes. The MFOL activists have demonstrated means of transgressing these boundaries, most significantly in educating those who can legally vote and laying the groundwork for their own future democratic practice. However, the orientation of future citizenship continues to leave children and youth disenfranchised in the present. In claiming and enacting rights they do not yet have, MFOL prepare for future amendments that address some of the constrictive arbitrary boundaries that enclose democratic citizenship. If continued and adopted by other youths, the MFOL youths' collective dissent may have the potential to push a reconsideration of the arbitrary boundaries of democratic citizenship and stop the marginalization of children and youths' political engagement.

Works Cited

Bellamy, Richard. *Citizenship: A Very Short Introduction*. Oxford UP, 2008.

Bent, Emily. "Unfiltered and Unapologetic: March for Our Lives and the Political Boundaries of Age." *Jeunesse*, vol. 11, no. 2, winter 2019, pp. 55–73. *Project Muse*, doi.org/10.1353/jeu.2019.0017.

Butler, Judith. "Performativity, Precarity and Sexual Politics." *Revista de antropología iberoamericana*, vol. 4., no. 3, 2009, pp. I–XIII. *AIRB*, https://aibr.org/antropolog ia/04v03/criticos/040301b.pdf.

Chemerinsky, Erwin, and Michael Stokes Paulsen. "The Preamble." *Interactive Constitution*, https://constitutioncenter.org/interactive-constitution/interpre tation/preamble-ic/interps/37.

"The Constitution of the United States: Preamble." *Interactive Constitution*, https://co nstitutioncenter.org/interactive-constitution/full-text.

Cummings, William. "The Bubble: March for Our Lives Protesters Dismissed by Con servatives." *USA Today*, 26 Mar. 2018, https://www.usatoday.com/story/news/p olitics/onpolitics/2018/03/26/media-reactions-march-our-lives/460029002/.

Gordon, Hava Rachel. *We Fight to Win: Inequality and the Politics of Youth Activism*. Rut gers, 2009.

Glimmer of Hope: How Tragedy Sparked a Movement. Razorbill and Dutton, 2018.

"interpret, v. 1. b." *The Oxford English Dictionary*, 2021, Oxford UP.

Lawy, Robert, and Gert Biesta. "Citizenship-as-Practice: The Educational Implica tions of an Inclusive and Relational Understanding of Citizenship." *British Jour nal of Sociology of Education*, vol. 54, no. 1, Mar. 2006, pp. 34–50, *Jstor*, https://ww w.jstor.org/stable/3699294.

Lopez, German. "It's Official: March for Our Lives Was One of the Biggest Youth Protests Since the Vietnam War." *Vox*, 26 Mar. 2018, https://www.vox.com/pol icy-and-politics/2018/3/26/17160646/march-for-our-lives-crowd-size-count.

Markland, Anah-Jayne. "Columbine (High School) Massacre." *SAGE Encyclopaedia of Children and Childhood Studies*, edited by Daniel Thomas Cook, Sage, 2020.

Marshall, T. H. *Citizenship and Social Class and Other Essays*. Cambridge UP, 1950.

"Mission & Story." *March For Our Lives*, 17 Sept. 2020, https://marchforourlives.com /mission-story/.

Newman, Katherine S, et al. *Rampage: The Social Roots of School Shootings*. Basic Books, 2004.

Nielsen Consumer Insights. "2015 National Youth Survey." *Elections Canada*, 6 May 2016, https://www.elections.ca/content.aspx?section=res&dir=rec/eval/pes201 5/nys&document=index&lang=e.

Ong, Aihwa. "Cultural Citizenship as Subject-Making: Immigrants Negotiate Racial and Cultural Boundaries in the United States." *Current Anthropology*, vol. 37, no. 5, 1996, pp. 737–62, *Jstor*, jstor.org/stable/2744412.

Turcotte, Martin. "Political Participation and Civic Engagement of Youth." *Statistics Canada*, 7 Oct. 2015, https://www150.statcan.gc.ca/n1/pub/75-006-x/2015001/article/14232-eng.htm.

Sanchez, Luis. "Tucker Carlson Criticizes 'Extremist' Parkland Students Calling for Gun Control." *The Hill*, 24 Mar. 2018, https://thehill.com/homenews/media/380071-tucker-carlson-pushes-back-on-extremist-parkland-students-calling-for-gun.

Smith, Noel, et al. "Young People as Real Citizens: Towards an Inclusionary Understanding of Citizenship." *Journal of Youth Studies*, vol. 8, no. 4, Dec. 2005, pp. 425–443, doi:10.1080/13676260500431743.

Taft, Jessica K. *Rebel Girls: Youth Activism and Social Change Across the Americas.* New York UP, 2011.

—. *The Kids Are in Charge: Activism and Power in Peru's Movement of Working Children.* New York UP, 2019.

Walker, Christina. "10 Years. 180 School Shootings. 365 Victims." *CNN*, 2019, https://www.cnn.com/interactive/2019/07/us/ten-years-of-school-shootings-trnd/.

"To Couple the Beauty of the Place and the Harsh Realities of Its Racist History"
Piecing Together African American Citizenship in Faith Ringgold's *Flag Story Quilt* and *Coming to Jones Road*[1]

Malaika Sutter

The pieced quilt has been a quintessential American object of heritage for more than two centuries. Focusing on a particularly African American inflection of this heritage, this chapter takes a closer look at Faith Ringgold's *Flag Story Quilt* (1985)[2] and her story quilt series *Coming to Jones Road* (1999–2000, 2009–2010).[3] As one of the most successful and prominent African American artists of the last quarter of the twentieth century, whose works of art are exhibited in many major art museums all around the world, Ringgold combines text, image, and textile—what I will call 'text(ile)-image constellations'—in order to trace the fragmented notion of as well as to craft uncomfortable yet empowering perspectives on African American citizenship.

For this, Ringgold's artworks use the American flag as an object that represents a seemingly fixed conception of citizenship and present in their reworking of the flag a notion of citizenship that is very much in flux. The intermedial and material aspects of the story quilt convey fragmentation yet they also illustrate the healing effect of piecing together past events, connecting past and present, and crafting alternative

---

1 Faith Ringgold (b. 1930) strongly emphasizes her African American heritage. She uses both Black and African American to describe her art. In line with scholarship on African American citizenship, this chapter relies heavily on this term, especially because of its historical dimension and Ringgold's substantial use of African American history in her art. The paper will also use the term Black in order to include Black people in the US who do not identify themselves with the term African American. The word will be capitalized in line with Black Feminists such as Brittney Cooper, using "Black" as a political and activist term (cf. Cooper).

2 The *Flag Story Quilt* is illustrated in Faith Ringgold's memoirs *We Flew Over the Bridge: The Memoirs of Faith Ringgold* (1995) on page 99.

3 The first part of the series is available as a booklet in *Feminist Studies*, vol. 33, no. 2, 2007, pp. 350–360. The second part was not published as a booklet and thus has to be "pieced together." Most artworks are available on Artstor and individual pieces are shown on Ringgold's official website: www.faithringgold.com.

American (hi)stories, historiography, identities, and citizenship. In this sense, the story quilt, like literary writing, "has the power to imagine alternative forms of citizenship" (Banerjee 86).

"History Is Not the Past": The Fragmented and Incomplete African American Citizenship

In the US, one is born an American citizen (*jus soli*) or one can obtain citizenship through naturalization after having met certain requirements ("Citizenship and Naturalization").[4] Citizenship grants rights such as the "right to vote in elections for public officials"[5] or, more abstractly, the "freedom to pursue 'life, liberty, and the pursuit of happiness.'" It also comes with responsibilities like to "respect and obey federal, state, and local laws" or to "defend the country if the need should arise" ("Should I Consider").

Apart from functioning as a factual status comprising certain benefits and duties, citizenship also serves as a concept, "a way of thinking about political and social membership" (Brubaker 3). This conceptual approach to citizenship also entails a communal aspect of being (and feeling as) part of what Benedict Anderson terms an "imagined community" (cf. Anderson). Citizenship is not only a legal status; it involves rights and obligations, it procures an identity and sense of belonging, and functions as an ideal to a community (Shachar et al. 5). Apart from rights and obligations, citizenship entails "a set of practices (cultural, symbolic and economic)" (Isin and Wood 4) and as such, cannot be analyzed through a legal framework alone; it is equally important to analyze it through a cultural lens (cf. Buikema et al.).

This cultural lens applies all the more since the possession of factual citizenship often does not mean equal access to rights in practice. As Lawrence D. Bobo's and other scholars' research has shown, despite being factual citizens, African American people are not granted "full citizenship" in the US. Bobo defines such "full" citizenship as the "complete and unmarked enjoyment of the full range of economic and material opportunities and resources, political and legal rights, and broader civil and social recognition and moral esteem that individuals in a society have available to them" (22). Bobo points to both "practices" and "status" as constituting "full citizenship." He argues that, despite the significant political, social, and cultural

---

4   In an attempt to restrict "birth tourism" to the US, the Trump administration issued a new policy January 24, 2020, to "deny any B visa application from an applicant whom the consular officer has reason to believe is traveling for the primary purpose of giving birth in the United States to obtain U.S. citizenship for their child" ("Birth Tourism Update").

5   A right that many people lose after incarceration as pointed out in Nina Heydt's chapter and Kaitlyn Quinn and Erika Canossini's chapter.

achievements by African Americans, this "unmarked" citizenship still stays out of reach as "basic racialized categories and identities remain alive and well in the United States" and African Americans "remain disadvantaged across most of the major domains of social life in the United States" (24).

American history demonstrates the vast number of, as Bobo terms them, "blockages and detours" that continue to obstruct full citizenship for African Americans (22), despite the duties and responsibilities fulfilled by them (for instance military service). Examining American history shows quickly that the incomplete citizenship of African Americans is rooted in a long tradition of exclusion. From a philosophical point of view, Charles W. Mills argues that nonwhite and non-European persons were never intended to be part of the "social contract" in the first place.[6] Using the term "racial contract" instead, Mills stresses that "we live in a world which has been *foundationally shaped for the past five hundred years by the realities of European domination and the gradual consolidation of global white supremacy*" (20; emphasis in the original).[7]

The effects of chattel slavery, the Jim Crow era, the long tradition of legal and social discriminatory practices within areas such as housing, employment, education, and health care can still be felt by Black Americans today. For instance, the massive wealth gap between Black and white people in the US can be traced back to "centuries of a compromised claim on citizenship" since wealth is chiefly inherited (Bobo 51). Mass incarceration or as Michelle Alexander terms it "The New Jim Crow," felony disenfranchisement, voter suppression, the continued violence against and the killing of Black people also but not only by police officers,[8] the four-year term of a racist (and misogynistic) president from 2017–2021, and the storming of the Capitol by white supremacists on January 6, 2021, after an election in which African American

---

6   The "social contract," an idea originating in the Age of Enlightenment, was shaped by philosophers such as Jean-Jacques Rousseau, Thomas Hobbes, John Locke, and Immanuel Kant and involves the idea that humanity began in a "state of nature" and then agreed to live in a civil society, submitting to an authority (e.g., a ruler, the majority of votes). Mills exposes the white, patriarchal philosophical tradition and demonstrates that the "social contract" "is not a contract between everybody ('we the people'), but between just the people who count, the people who really are the people ('we the white people')" (3).

7   In addition, Carole Pateman's *The Sexual Contract* (1997) makes clear that this contract is also gendered.

8   Consequently, #BlackLivesMatter was founded in 2013 after the acquittal of the police officer who killed Trayvon Martin in Florida. It was after the murder of Michael Brown in Missouri in 2014 that the slogan became more visible in mainstream media. It started as a hashtag on social media and evolved into worldwide protests, a global organization and a vast number of local organizations all over the world (cf. "About BLM"; Ransby). The movement has been active since 2013 and strongly reignited after the murder of George Floyd by a police officer in Minnesota on May 25, 2020.

254   Performing Citizenship

voters were instrumental—to name just a few—clearly illustrates the endurance of the "racial contract."[9]

It is this long tradition of and present day violent discriminatory practices and systemic racism that do not allow Black Americans to have equal freedom and equal access to rights and privileges that, on paper, are afforded to American citizens.[10] As such, the concept of citizenship and its practices are historically contingent. An engagement with history and its effects in our present day becomes inevitable when we want to discuss Black citizenship within the US. As James Baldwin explains in *I am not Your Negro*: "History is not the past. It is the present. We carry our history with us. We *are* our history" (107). As we will later see, Ringgold's story quilts emphasize the importance of history. They make use of it, connecting it to the present in order to exhibit "the as yet incomplete journey to full citizenship for African Americans" (Bobo 24). At the same time, they explore alternative conceptions of community and citizenship.

Text(ile)-Image Constellations: Quilting Identity, History, and Citizenship

Historian, quilter, and curator Carolyn L. Mazloomi argues that "[n]o artistic form is more closely associated with African-Americans than quilt making, representing skill, aesthetic beauty, and utilitarian need" (7). People from the African continent who were forced to the Americas brought with them long established sewing skills and although the pieced bed quilt was a particular European object that was unknown in Africa, patchwork techniques and quilted objects were produced on the African continent (Mazloomi 7).

Taken to another continent as enslaved people, they used these skills to make needlework objects such as quilts for the enslavers' houses but also for themselves (Mazloomi 7–11). Houston A. Baker, Jr. and Charlotte Pierce-Baker call these products "a double patch" (156) in which not only two cultures but also two experiences were woven together: "The quilts of Afro-America offer a *sui generis* context (a weaving together) of experiences and a storied, vernacular representation of lives conducted in the margins, ever beyond an easy and acceptable wholeness" (156). The patchwork signals fragments and at the same time wholeness, thereby creating "a patterned wholeness in the African diaspora" (156).

---

9   It should be noted here that people within other systems of oppression, such as gender, sexuality or disability, are even more exposed to racial discrimination and violence. This "intersectionality" should be kept in mind, particularly because Ringgold's artworks often depict women and are, evidently, made by a Black woman artist.

10   The racism that other ethnic minorities, such as Native American communities or Asian Americans, have to endure should lead to similar conclusions.

This "piecemeal" aspect of the quilt lends itself to discussing and materializing the fragmentary nature of memory, identity, and storytelling. However, what the quilt materializes is not only the fragmentation of experience, but also the different and creative piecing together of the blocks of history; filling gaps, offering alternative readings, and inscribing them with new political and cultural meanings. Carrying such charged messages, the quilt could and still can stimulate political activism ("craftivism").[11] As quilt tops pieced by individuals are often layered and stitched communally (e.g., "Quilting Bees" or "Quilting Frolics," cf. Berlo, "Chronicles" 215), they further enable people to bond and, in the process, to craft not only individual but also communal identities.

Art historian Janet Berlo argues that quilts are a quintessential American object of heritage "precisely because they represent so many things to so many people" and that the tales connected to the quilt are just as important in creating a particular image of American identity: "As symbolic objects, quilts give shape to an idealized story about American ingenuity and self-sufficiency in general, and female frugality, secrecy, originality, and artistry in particular" ("Acts of Pride" 9). Compelling myths and tales, such as the "scrap bag myth" (11) or the myth of an "Underground Railroad Quilt Code" (12), have a tight grip on an imagined American culture and genesis. The quilt's status within American culture "makes it thus an excellent medium to discuss and negotiate differently conceptualized notions of identities, histories, and forms of citizenship in the US" (Sutter 179–180).

In addition, the quilt as a woman connoted object enables the discussion of gendered issues as well as the use of this gendered history.[12] Throughout history, patriarchal culture connected needlework to a certain notion of "femininity" which has been linked to concepts of obedience, piety, chastity, fertility, and the domestic (Parker). This connection to femininity can be subverted but also used, for instance to mediate a traumatic history: "The quilts, as visual media, pose an alternative and non-threatening approach to topics ... labeled ... as the 'tough stuff of American history'" (Mazloomi 6). Through the quilt's associations with warmth, comfort, and the home, uncomfortable but crucial topics can be addressed.[13] Furthermore, the stark contrast between the cozy material and the traumatic and violent content can emphasize the discrepancies of what "home" can mean for different people.

---

11 The term "craftivism" was coined by writer Betsy Greer in 2003 "to designate work that combines craft and activism" (Parker xvii).

12 Men have always also engaged in needlework but while men were perceived as creators (weavers, tailors etc.), women were mostly linked to the acts of cleaning and patching things up (Goggin 40–41). Moreover, needlework was construed as inconsequential by the dominant patriarchal culture (cf. Parker). Yet and perhaps even because needlework was perceived as trivial, it has provided women with an opportunity to express themselves within this restrictive environment for centuries.

13 This is also visible in the NAMES Project AIDS Memorial Quilt.

256   Performing Citizenship

Ringgold's quilts have been extensively analyzed by scholars; however, the concept of intermediality has never been used to study her work. The term "intermediality" entails "a broad variety of exchanges and border crossings between media" (Rippl 210). Ringgold started to use text in addition to images and textiles in the 1980s "out of [her] need to tell stories not with pictures or symbols alone, but with words" (Ringgold in Gouma-Peterson 23). She points to a medium's limits and that using an additional, different medium can offer new ways of creating meanings. The interaction between these different media and their "meaning-making" process opens "a space of semiotic and material in-between-ness" which allows readers to perceive "the world differently" (Neumann 513):

> Intermediality is charged with specific values, often taking up and taken on existing medial representations and subjecting them to the transformative dynamics of ... translation. Accordingly, intermediality may intervene in the social fabric of existing medial configurations, reworking them in a way that allows readers to experience, see and imagine the world differently. (Neumann 513)

This aspect of reworking medial constellations in order for the reader to "imagine the world differently," I argue, is visible in Ringgold's *Flag Story Quilt* and her series *Coming to Jones Road*. Text, image, and textile each add a different dimension to the discussion of history, identity, and citizenship. Ringgold's text(ile)-image constellations allow the reader to reflect on the incomplete nature of African American citizenship. They function as means to expose the white violence implicated in this fragmentary citizenship and at the same time they re-imagine African American identities and histories, thereby giving "'colored folk' and women a taste of the American dream" (Ringgold in Roth 60).

Piecing Together the Flag: Fragmented Citizenship in the *Flag Story Quilt*

Faith Ringgold's artworks explore African Americans' incomplete citizenship and its history in many different ways but when we think of her story quilts, it is undoubtedly her *Flag Story Quilt* (1985) that comes to mind first. The 57x78-inch work of art combines text, image, and textile into a unique American flag. The border is a beige or off-white fabric which is the same fabric she uses for the stripes upon which she has painted her text. The binding is of an orange or ochre color. At the upper left, fifty off-white heads in profile are appliqued upon a pieced blue ground, mimicking the fifty stars of the flag that represent the fifty states of the US. The hovering skulls, in connection with the text and American history in general, allude to the many victims of lynching carried out by American mob violence over the last 150 years.

Ringgold's flag is composed of nine stripes. The stripes that can be read as the red stripes of the American flag are composed of rectangles of brightly colored tie-dyed fabric. The tie-dye creates the effect of splotches and drizzles which, with the strong use of the color red, evokes an uncanny resemblance to blood drips. However, the tie-dye effect, with its many different colors and swirls, simultaneously evokes creativity and excitement. Associating the tie-dye also with the hippie generations' tie-dyed t-shirts brings up images of peace and non-violent revolution. These tie-dyed stripes alternate with off-white stripes onto which the quilt's story is written in black. The color of "pure" white is excluded from this American flag, thus questioning notions of American "purity" and "innocence."

The fictional story told in the text concerns Memphis Cooly, a disabled Black man who was severely injured during the Vietnam War. He is imprisoned and faces the death sentence because he is accused of raping and killing a nineteen-year-old white girl. The story is told from the perspective of an omniscient, nameless narrator who knows the Cooly family. The narrator tells the reader bit by bit about Memphis' fate and reveals piece by piece the suspicion that his wife—a publisher from a big Madison Avenue company who acts as the "author" of Memphis' novels—framed him.

From the beginning, the story makes clear that the judicial system wants Memphis to be the perpetrator at all costs: "How he gonna slash some girl's throat and throw her in the Harlem River, and he ain' got no arms? How he gonna rape her sitting in a wheel chair paralyzed from the waist down? You reckon [they gonna say] Memphis scared that girl into slashing her own throat, and raping herself?" (Ringgold, We Flew 99, 255).[14] Using rhetorical questions, the narrator emphasizes the absurdity of the allegations and tells the reader later that Memphis is imprisoned and will be executed "for a crime he ain' commit" (99, 255). In addition, the narrator suggests that there was not even a murder: "They been draggin' that river for one year now and ain' come up with no dead white girl yet – cause ain' none" (99, 256). Despite ample evidence that Memphis Cooly is not the perpetrator of the crimes, and despite the fact that there may not even be a case in the first place, he is imprisoned and sentenced to death.

In her memoirs, Ringgold comments that the "story is based on the premise that the black man's guilt, whether likely or unlikely, is almost always taken for granted long before it is actually proven" (255). She thereby points to the myth of the "Black male rapist" which early activist and journalist Ida B. Wells unveiled

---

14   I use the illustration on page ninety-nine and the transcript on page 255 and 256 provided by Faith Ringgold in her We Flew Over the Bridge: The Memoirs of Faith Ringgold (1995). I use square brackets when significant text passages on the flag deviate from her transcript. I use the text from the flag, marked with square brackets, when I think it is relevant for the close reading.

258 Performing Citizenship

and challenged.[15] In Ringgold's story, the tenacity of this myth is heightened to the point that not even clear evidence stands a chance. The myth stands above the law. Ringgold's story shows just how powerful such myths are, even to the point of infiltrating the American judicial system.

The last line of the story reads: "If it hadn't been for that scheming wife of his, he wouldn't been jetting round in that fancy wheel chair bar-hoppin' till all hours of the night, when the police [they] be out there lookin' for a n[...] to pin some dirt on" (99, 256).[16] Instead of a police force's duty to protect citizens, it is in fact the police who are endangering Black people—a statement that resonates with the police violence Black people have faced in the past and still have to endure today. The word "they" in the quilt also has an air of mob mentality, reminding the reader of the long history of lynching in the US.

Memphis' lack of full rights is then contrasted with the fulfilment of his duties when he was drafted for the Vietnam War. It was in this war that Memphis lost his arms and was paralyzed; quite literally fragmenting him: "Uncle Sam took [they fine boy, sent him off to Vietnam, and ship] him back all messed up and now this" (99, 255). This depiction is striking as the words "took," "sent off," and "ship" remind one rather of an object than a person, alluding to the Transatlantic slave trade and equating it with the drafting of Black Americans into war. When we take Memphis' fragmentation further and draw a connection to fragmentation grenades used in the Vietnam War which were also used for "fragging"—an act in which American soldiers attempted to kill their own superiors during the Vietnam War—the point of killing one's own fellow citizen is even further underlined (cf. "frag, v.")

According to the narrator, Memphis won "[ribbons and] medals of honor" (99, 256). He did not simply fulfill a citizen's obligation by going to war for his country, he also carried out extraordinary acts of valor which earned him a medal of honor but cost him his body. In contrast to the narratives by African American centenarians analyzed in Julia Velten's chapter, which emphasize how through hard work and assimilation you can belong, Ringgold's story quilt shows a more pessimistic picture. On the one hand, Memphis is asked to fight for his country and then rewarded for his service; on the other, he is imprisoned and killed for a crime he did not commit by the very country he was serving. A sentiment that goes hand in hand with civil rights activists' questioning the duty to fight for the US on the premise of "freeing"

---

15   In the 1890s, journalist and civil rights activist Ida B. Wells (b. 1862) reported on lynching in the US and exposed it and its myth of the Black male rapist as a way to oppress and intimidate Black people but especially successful Black business owners. She also called out white women's complicity in this white terror (cf. Cooper 177–178).

16   Ellipsis mine.

the people of Vietnam, when the US actually refuses freedom to a large number of its own citizens.[17]

Ringgold's story quilt is an alternative American flag. In American culture the national flag is treated as a kind of "holy" object, as suggested by the detailed directions as to its handling as well as the Flag Protection Acts of 1968 and 1989.[18] Knowing that Ringgold was arrested for co-organizing and co-curating "The People's Flag Show" (1970), where the American flag served artists as means to protest social injustices and the Vietnam War, adds a revolutionary and certainly a political element to the artwork (Farrington 141). Her *Flag Story Quilt* was also not her first artwork in which she made use of the flag. Her famous paintings *The Flag is Bleeding* (1967) and *Flag for the Moon: Die N[...]* (1967–1969)[19] very explicitly use the icon to expose and resist white violence. Patrick Hill argues that Ringgold was aware that such acts of appropriation were "especially threatening because access to it by a woman artist of color was perceived as an assault on citizenship entitlements defined as the singular province of whites" (29). Ringgold's acts of deconstruction and construction shed new light on a seemingly fixed object, making us aware of its materiality and its potential of attaining new meanings.

Ringgold's flag makes use of a cozy domestic object—a quilt—to mediate the same critique as in her flag paintings but adding another (gendered) layer of critique: "juxtaposing the American flag with signifiers of a distinctively feminist consciousness ..., Ringgold extends the doubleness already contained in the flag ..., effectively reclaiming it as a ground for both race- and gender-based critiques" (Hill 36). Furthermore, the story of Memphis massively clashes with the flag as symbol of American pride as well as with the quilt as a domestic object, exposing different notions of home and of citizenship in the US. Ringgold literally inscribes the story of a Black disabled Veteran and his entrepreneurial family onto an American flag,

---

17 An excerpt from Martin Luther King's speech "Beyond Vietnam" encapsulates this stance very well: "It was sending their sons and their brothers and their husbands to fight and to die in extraordinarily high proportions relative to the rest of the population. We were taking the black young men who had been crippled by our society and sending them eight thousand miles away to guarantee liberties in Southeast Asia which they had not found in southwest Georgia and East Harlem. And so we have been repeatedly faced with the cruel irony of watching Negro and white boys on TV screens as they kill and die together for a nation that has been unable to seat them together in the same schools. And so we watch them in brutal solidarity burning the huts of a poor village, but we realize that they would hardly live on the same block in Chicago. I could not be silent in the face of such cruel manipulation of the poor" (King).

18 Although the Flag Protection Acts criminalize a person for burning or defiling the American flag, it was ruled in *Texas v. Johnson* (1989) that the act of burning the flag is in fact protected by the First Amendment (Brennan and Supreme Court of The United States).

19 Ellipsis mine.

260   Performing Citizenship

thereby reinserting stories neither unfamiliar nor prominently featured in American history.[20]

Ringgold's text(ile)-image constellation mediates Memphis' fragmentation textually, visually, and materially. The visual medium celebrates diversity and creativity, while at the same time pointing to the long history of white violence against Black people. The textile medium adds to this tension through its association with home as well as through the American flag as an object of honor and pride. The text reinserts an African American experience into American history and further exposes the fragmentation and incompletion of African American citizenship in the US. In this sense, Ringgold's text(ile)-image constellation gives new meaning to mediation in that the fragmentation is mediated via multiple media all at once, virtually keeping the fragmentation intact, a fragmentation that can be read, seen, and felt.

"Turn[ing] all the Ugliness of Spirit, Past and Present, Into Something Livable": Constituting the "Free Citizen" in the Series *Coming to Jones Road*

Whereas Ringgold's *Flag Story Quilt* discusses a fragmented notion of African American citizenship in one single artwork, Ringgold's story quilt series *Coming to Jones Road* takes a different approach. The series consists of two story quilt parts and the second part also entails a tanka part.[21] Each story quilt is composed of a large central canvas onto which Ringgold painted her subjects with acrylic and which is framed by pieces of fabric sewn together. Some of the story quilts use up to four different pieced frames and the text of the story is written onto the innermost textile frame using one line that circles the painted subject, thus creating an additional textual framework. Quilt stitches on the fabric surface create the effect of fragmentation.

Eight quilts produced between 1999 and 2000 comprise Part I of the series. Ringgold published a booklet containing an introductory text, images of the quilts, and a transcript for each quilt (cf. "Coming to Jones Road"). The narrative follows Barn Door and his wife Precious, her baby—born *en route* and named Freedom—and twenty-six other African Americans escaping slavery through the Underground Railroad. Their journey starts when Aunt Emmy appears as a vision before Barn Door, instructing him to come to Jones Road, Englewood, New Jersey and to look for her house which he will find by his own mother's star quilt on the roof.

---

20   In this context it is interesting to note that it was an African American girl who helped sew an American flag that would inspire Francis Scott Key to write lyrics that would later become the national anthem: "Black girls and women like Grace have literally stitched themselves into our nation's history in places of prominence and behind the scenes" (Berry and Gross 6).

21   *Tankas* or *thankas* are Tibetan paintings on fabric (Farrington 154).

In the introduction of her booklet, Ringgold explains that upon moving to Jones Road in 1992, she faced "hostile neighbors" and struggled with the town board "for more than six years" in order to receive permits to build her studio ("Coming to Jones Road" 352). This experience was "extremely traumatic" and inspired her to concentrate on African Americans who came to New Jersey before her. Ringgold explains in her introduction to the series that she "tried to couple the beauty of the place and the harsh realities of its racist history" in a series which "turns all the ugliness of spirit, past and present, into something livable" ("Coming to Jones Road" 351).

The first two quilts do not contain text. In the booklet, the artist explains that she started, in the first quilt, with the image of "a trail of shadowy figures under a moonlit sky stealing through the landscape in pursuit of freedom at Aunt Emmy's little white house on Jones Road" (353). The second quilt shows the same landscape in daylight, again depicting the shadowy figures and Emmy's white house in the background. Ringgold explains that she "needed to see the shadowy figures in a more positive view early on" and "envisioned them coming from church on a Sunday afternoon" (354). Thus, the first two works of art are set in the future when the group has already made it to Aunt Emmy's house. The series refers to the present (Ringgold's present), the past, and the future of the past.

These layers of time emphasize the role of history in understanding Ringgold's present experience of racism. Telling the story of enslaved people who came to Jones Road in the centuries before Ringgold in order to find freedom highlights the long history of incomplete citizenship for African Americans. Ringgold's experience of not being accepted in a white neighborhood in twentieth/twenty-first-century New Jersey furthermore illustrates the restrictions she still faces within a white space. Ringgold demonstrates, along the lines of Sara Ahmed's "A Phenomenology of Whiteness," that some spaces are "inhabitable for some bodies and not others" determining "who gets to be at home" and who does not (162). The quilt as a cozy bed comforter we associate with the home can emphasize this paradox of not "getting to be at home" and at the same time can be read as an alternative home constructed through the fictional fabric of a story, a home for the African American citizen.

Ringgold's third quilt depicts the character "Aunt Emmy" inspired by a photograph of Ringgold's "great grandmother, Betsy Bingham" ("Coming to Jones Road" 353). The rest of the quilts (number four to eight) all depict the "shadowy figures"—black silhouettes with a kind of glow outlining their bodies—amidst the woods. Rather small in comparison to the large trees surrounding them, these figures are always at the center of the paintings. The story ends with them arriving at Aunt Emmy's house with the Star Quilt on its roof, mentioned in the third quilt when Aunt Emmy appears in Barn Door's dream: "Look for an old white farmhouse with your dead Mama's star quilt on the roof" (355). The quilt is the last piece to look for on their journey, guiding them like the North Star. Because it is the quilt of Barn Door's mother, it is also a family heirloom passed on to other family members, illustrating its importance as an object of African American heritage. The quilts from the first part use rather dark and heavy colors as they depict the characters walking through the woods at night. The paintings are framed with colorful fabric stripes which often also show different and multiple shapes. The painted trees' outmost leaves always overlap with and partly escape the frame.

Like the trees escaping their framing, the characters emphasize their quest for freedom. The words "free" and "freedom" appear in almost all the quilt texts and are especially frequently used in the last quilt when the children sing or cheer: "'We free! We free! Aunt Emmy got us now! We free! We free now! ...'" (360). Precious' baby is named "Freedom" because "'this here baby is a freedom chile'" (358) and is furthermore declared a communal baby: "'she our baby too,' cause we all know she was born to be free" (358). The text mentions the struggles the characters face, but they are not shown in detail, rather it is Freedom's birth, a dinner in the woods, and the children playing at the end which are at the center of the story. The text gives the quilt an optimistic and joyous note; this perspective makes the dark color appear rather as calm and soothing.

Knowing from the first two quilts that they will make it to Aunt Emmy's house further adds to this calm atmosphere and emphasizes Ringgold's control over the narrative. Unlike many other stories from the eighteenth and nineteenth century, the story quilt's fictional tale ends happily. Ringgold's fictional historiography makes us wonder about the many other tales of escape that remain unrecorded. Her story quilts not only offer an alternative viewpoint on (hi)story and (hi)story-telling but they further point to the quilt as an alternative object onto which stories of African Americans have been recorded for centuries. The act of piecing together this (hi)story is further embodied in the series consisting of multiple artworks that may not always be exhibited together.

This fragmentation of (hi)story-telling is illustrated by a second part created ten years later, in 2009 and 2010. The series starts with a quilt depicting Ringgold's husband Burdette "Birdie" Ringgold and dedicating the series to Birdie with a statement of love and gratitude. Thus, Ringgold maintains the temporal fragmentation in this part of the series. The second quilt connects to the first part of the series, reiterating some of the text from the last quilt of the first part. The rest feature the same characters, depicting them in couples or groups, giving more information on the characters. This time, the fictional narrative is not as linear as in the first part, but rather sketches the characters' feelings and experiences. Whereas the quilts from the first part depict black silhouettes, the ones from the second part show all the figures in great detail. While still surrounded by nature, they occupy a larger part of the painting. Thus, the characters are now free to take shape as individuals with distinctive appearances and experiences within the group.

The second quilt of this part reiterates some of the text from the last quilt in the first part of the series but the image is different. The group who made it to freedom—including Baby Freedom swaddled in a quilt-like blanket—stands behind another quilt, a "welcome quilt" made by Aunt Emmy for the group (Ringgold *Part 2 #2*). This flag-shaped quilt features red and white alternating stripes onto which a large blue rectangle is sewn at the center with a white star with the year 1792 imprinted in red. In the story, 1792 is the year when the group made it to Aunt Emmy, achieving freedom. The artist's daughter, Michele Wallace, explains that Ringgold "chose this date, after the American Revolution and before the Civil War, to assign them *their* freedom" (27; emphasis mine). Ringgold creates a historical date for the fictional group of African Americans that is unconnected to any white historiography (especially because "New Jersey was one of the last states in the Union to free the slaves" [27]), for she is intent upon crafting a personal historiography.

Looking at this intradiegetic flag quilt, one immediately thinks of her *Flag Story Quilt*. Using the colors of the American flag but changing the design in order to highlight the personal history of the group illustrates the need for an alternative flag, an alternative conception of community, of belonging and thus also of citizenship. Together with the story, a story equally of hardship and joy and a story at the center of which freedom rests, Ringgold's quilt series pieces together the notion of the free citizen. Ringgold's personal story, which is interwoven in the first part of the series but also alluded to in the first quilt featuring Birdie, points to an "unequal freedom" she experiences in the twentieth/twenty-first century. Ringgold explains in an artist statement: "our white neighbors (unsuccessfully) sought to deny us the freedom to live there. Freedom, you know, is not free – It took me six years to realize my dream of a beautiful studio surrounded by a beautiful garden" ("Artist Statement").

This emphasis on both hardship and joy remains a focus in the last part. Each of the tankas illustrates an African American activist. One depicts Martin Luther King and an excerpt from his iconic "I Have a Dream" speech delivered at the March on Washington in 1963. Another depicts Sojourner Truth and some passages from her "Ain't I a Woman" speech from 1851. And another depicts Harriet Tubman and a description of some of her achievements. All three works feature the portrait framed in a rectangle with text in the background. Framing each portrait and text is a flowering bush and a pieced fabric border. These three famous activists emphasize both the hardship and the successes of African American communities. They embody the long tradition of African American activism and their fight for full citizenship.

Harriet Tubman, who used the North Star to guide her towards freedom, is mirrored in the story when the characters look for the Star Quilt placed on Aunt Emmy's roof in the first part of the series. The star, which can also symbolize a dream, is further visible in Martin Luther King's speech: "I have a dream that one day on the red hills of Georgia the sons of former slaves and the sons of slave owners will be able to sit down together at the table of brotherhood. I have a dream that one day even the state of Mississippi ... will be transformed into an oasis of freedom and justice" (Ringgold *Part 2 Tanka #3*). Drawing on history and looking into the future, Martin

Luther King's dream has yet to fully come true; the ability to hold onto this dream of complete freedom is encapsulated in the quilts' frequent use of the word "freedom" as well as in Ringgold's need to look back in order to envision a future. Sojourner Truth adds a gendered dimension, reminding us that not only the sons of formerly enslaved people and enslavers but also their daughters must be included in this dream.

In this impressive series, the text(ile)-image constellations highlight fragmentation on different levels: through the quilt as a "piecemeal" object, the temporal fragmentation in the text, and the serial aspect visible in the different aesthetics Ringgold used. The series pieces together the past through a fictional yet familiar story and connects it with the present, reminding us that the fight for freedom is still ongoing. Ringgold constructs a story and a sense of identity by interweaving it with her own story.[22] As cultural critic Stuart Hall reminds us, "the self is always, in a sense, a fiction" (45). The text(ile)-image constellations elucidate that identity has always been fragmented and such fragmentation offers new ways of piecing together a self, a (hi)story, a different world.

Epilogue

In 2020, when Ringgold turned ninety, she crafted yet another flag. The Rockefeller Center in Manhattan asked designers and artists to create flag designs which celebrate the city of New York which were then installed around The Rink. Ringgold's flag uses as a background a red, a white, and a blue horizontal stripe. The words "We are the world" are imprinted onto the red top stripe in white and in the same color and font the words "the life & Breath of Freedom" are written on the lower blue stripe. In the middle, detailed images of people are drawn on a circle. They are diverse in age, gender, and ethnicity. All wear brightly colored and patterned clothing giving the impression of variety and joy. Around the circle in a black font are the words Native Americans, Africans, Asians, Caribbeans, South Americans, Europeans. To the right of the circle is written "love, Faith Ringgold" (Chan).

The use of the word "Breath" in 2020 is striking, immediately bringing to mind the murder of George Floyd—as well as other Black people before him—who uttered the words "I can't breathe" before being murdered by police officer Derek Chauvin on May 25, 2020 (Baker et al.). These words became a rallying cry for the many national and international Black Lives Matter protests, events that touched activist and artist Ringgold: "His breath was stolen by a system that threatens our freedom" (Ringgold

---

22   In fact, Ringgold's use of textiles in her art making is very much connected to telling her own story. Ringgold explains in an interview that when she had issues getting her autobiography published, she decided to write her story onto the quilts instead (Serpentine Galleries).

in Morris). Ringgold's flag once more points to white supremacist violence while at the same time reminding us what to fight for: a diverse and free community, a kind of citizenship that includes, protects, and belongs to all.

Works Cited

"About BLM." *Black Lives Matter*, 16 Oct. 2020, blacklivesmatter.com/about/.

Ahmed, Sara. "A Phenomenology of Whiteness." *Feminist Theory*, vol. 8, no. 2, 2007, pp. 149–168.

Alexander, Michelle. *The New Jim Crow: Mass Incarceration in the Age of Colorblindness.* Tenth anniversary edition, The New Press, 2020.

Anderson, Benedict. *Imagined Communities: Reflections on the Origin and Spread of Nationalism.* Revised edition, Verso, 2016.

Baker, Houston A., Jr., and Charlotte Pierce-Baker. "Patches: Quilts and Communities in Alice Walker's 'Everday Use.'" *Alice Walker*, edited by Barbara T. Christian, Rutgers UP, 1994, pp. 149–165.

Baker, Mike, et al. "Three Words. 70 Cases. The Tragic History of 'I Can't Breathe.'" *The New York Times*, 29 Jun. 2020, https://www.nytimes.com/interactive/2020/0 6/28/us/i-cant-breathe-policearrest.html.

Baldwin, James. *I am not Your Negro*, compiled and edited by Raoul Peck, Vintage International, 2017.

Banerjee, Mita. "Race and Citizenship." *Handbook of the American Novel of the Nineteenth Century*, edited by Christine Gerhardt, De Gruyter, 2018, pp. 74–90.

Berlo, Janet Catherine. "'Acts of Pride, Desperation, and Necessity': Aesthetics, Social History, and American Quilts." *Wild by Design: Two Hundred Years of Innovation and Artistry in American Quilts*, edited by Janet Catherine Berlo and Patricia Cox Crews, International Quilt Study Center at the University of Nebraska in association with U of Washington P, 2003, pp. 5–31.

—. "Chronicles in Cloth: Quilt-Making and Female Artistry in Nineteenth-Century America." *Local/Global: Women Artists in the Nineteenth Century*, edited by Deborah Cherry and Janice Helland, Ashgate, 2006, pp. 201–222.

Berry, Daina Ramey and Kali Nicole Gross. *A Black Women's History of the United States.* Beacon P, 2020.

"Birth Tourism Update." *U.S. Department of State*, 23 Jan. 2020, travel.state.gov/content/travel/en/News/visas-news/20200123_birth-tourism-update.html.

Bobo, Lawrence D. "An American Conundrum: Race, Sociology, and the African American Road to Citizenship." *The Oxford Handbook of African American Citizenship, 1865–Present*, edited by Henry Louis Gates, Jr. et al., Oxford UP, 2012, pp. 19–70.

266   Performing Citizenship

Brennan, William J., Jr, and Supreme Court of The United States. *U.S. Reports: Texas v. Johnson, 491 U.S. 397*. 1989. Periodical. Retrieved from the Library of Congress, https://www.loc.gov/item/usrep491397/.

Brubaker, William Rogers. "Introduction." *Immigration and the Politics of Citizenship in Europe and North America*, edited by William Rogers Brubaker, UP of America, 1989, pp. 1–27.

Buikema, Rosemarie, et al. "Introduction." *Cultures, Citizenship and Human Rights*, edited by Rosemarie Buikema et al., Routledge, 2020, pp. 1–8.

Chan, TF. "'The Flag Project' at Rockefeller Center shares messages of hope, unity and love."*Wallpaper**, 10 Aug. 2020, https://www.wallpaper.com/art/the-flag-projec t-rockefeller-center-new-york.

"Citizenship and Naturalization." *USCIS*, 5 Jul. 2020, https://www.uscis.gov/citize nship/learn-about-citizenship/citizenship-and-naturalization.

Cooper, Brittney. *Eloquent Rage: A Black Feminist Discovers Her Superpower*.Picador, 2018.

Farrington, Lisa E. *Creating Their Own Image: The History of African-American Women Artists*. Oxford UP, 2005.

"frag, v." *OED Online*, Oxford UP, March 2021, https://www.oed.com/view/Entry/74 111. Accessed 21 Apr. 2021.

Goggin, Maureen Daly. "Stitching a Life in 'Pen of Steele and Silken Inke': Elizabeth Parker's *circa* 1830 Sampler." *Women and the Material Culture of Needlework and Textiles, 1750–1950*, edited by Maureen Daly Goggin and Beth Fowkes Tobin, Ashgate, 2009, pp. 31–49.

Gouma-Peterson, Thalia. "Modern Dilemma Tales: Faith Ringgold's Story Quilts." *Faith Ringgold: A Twenty-five Year Survey*, edited by Eleanor Flomenhaft et al., Fine Arts Museum of Long Island, 1990, pp. 23–48.

Greer, Betsy. *Craftivism: The Art of Craft and Activism*. Arsenal Pulp Press, 2014.

Hall, Stuart. "Minimal Selves." *The Real Me: Post-Modernism and the Question of Identity*, edited by Lisa Appignanesi, The Institute of Contemporary Arts, 1987, pp. 44–46.

Hill, Patrick. "The Castration of Memphis Cooly: Race, Gender, and Nationalist Iconography in the Flag Art of Faith Ringgold." *Dancing at the Louvre: Faith Ringgold's French Collection and Other Story Quilts*, edited by Dan Cameron et al., U of California P, 1998, pp. 26–38.

Isin, Engin F. and Patricia K. Wood. *Citizenship and Identity*. SAGE Publications, 1999.

King, Martin Luther, Jr. "Beyond Vietnam: A Time to Break Silence." *Thirteen*, 4 Apr. 1967, https://www.thirteen.org/blog-post/martin-luther-kings-most-con troversial-speech-beyond-vietnam/.

Mazloomi, Carolyn L. "And Still We Rise: Race, Culture, and Visual Conversations." *And Still We Rise: Race, Culture, and Visual Conversations*, edited by Carolyn L. Mazloomi. Schiffer Publishing, 2015, pp. 6–11.

Mills, Charles W. *The Racial Contract*. Cornell UP, 1997.

Morris, Bob. "Faith Ringgold Will Keep Fighting Back." *The New York Times*, 11 Jun. 2020, https://www.nytimes.com/2020/06/11/arts/design/faith-ringgold-art.html.

Neumann, Birgit. "Intermedial Negotiations: Postcolonial Literatures." *Handbook of Intermediality: Literature – Image – Sound – Music*, edited by Gabriele Rippl, De Gruyter, 2015, pp. 512–529.

Parker, Rozsika. *The Subversive Stitch: Embroidery and the Making of the Feminine*. I. B. Tauris & Co Ltd, 2010.

Pateman, Carole. *The Sexual Contract*. Stanford UP, 2018.

Ransby, Barbara. *Making All Black Lives Matter: Reimagining Freedom in the Twenty-First Century*. U of California P, 2018.

Ringgold, Faith. "Coming to Jones Road." *Feminist Studies*, vol. 33, no. 2, 2007, pp. 350–360.

—. *Coming to Jones Road Part 2: Martin Luther King Jr. Tanka #3: I Have a Dream*. 2010, Serpentine Galleries, London. *Faith Ringgold*, edited by Melissa Blanchflower et al., Serpentine Galleries, 2019, pp. 145.

—. *Coming to Jones Road Part 2 #2: We Here Aunt Emmy Got US Now*. 2010, Serpentine Galleries, London. *Faith Ringgold*, edited by Melissa Blanchflower et al., Serpentine Galleries, 2019, pp. 141.

—. "Faith Ringgold's Artist Statement." *faithringgold.blogspot*, 21 Sep. 2007, http://faithringgold.blogspot.com/2007/03/bio-chronology.html.

—. *We Flew Over the Bridge: The Memoirs of Faith Ringgold*. Bulfinch Press, 1995.

Rippl, Gabriele. "Intermediality and Remediation." *Handbook of Anglophone World Literatures*, edited by Gabriele Rippl et al., De Gruyter, 2020, pp. 209–225.

Sutter, Malaika. "Hate Speech in Threads: Stitching and Posting a Resistance in the *Tiny Pricks Project. Discourse*, vol. 45, no. 1–2, 170–198.

Roth, Moira. "Of Cotton and Sunflower Fields: The Making of *The French* and *The American Collection*." *Dancing at the Louvre: Faith Ringgold's French Collection and Other Story Quilts*, edited by Dan Cameron et al., U of California P, 1998, pp. 49–63.

Serpentine Galleries. "An Evening with Faith Ringgold." *YouTube*, 15 Jul. 2019, https://www.youtube.com/watch?v=EcUPrr9nNJg.

Shachar, Ayelet, et al. "Introduction: Citizenship – *Quo Vadis?*" *The Oxford Handbook of Citizenship*, edited by Ayelet Shachar et al., Oxford UP, 2017, pp. 3–11.

"Should I Consider U.S. Citizenship?" *USCIS*, 5 Jul. 2020, https://www.uscis.gov/citizenship/learn-about-citizenship/should-i-consider-us-citizenship.

Wallace, Michele. "Black Power." *Faith Ringgold*, edited by Melissa Blanchflower et al., Serpentine Galleries, 2019, pp. 10–29.

Citizenship, Science, and Medicine

"What the Eyes Don't See"
Medical Citizenship and Environmental Justice in Mona Hanna-Attisha's Medical Memoir

Mita Banerjee

Is there a connection between medicine and citizenship? At first sight, these two realms would seem to have nothing in common: medicine is the domain of health and healing, while citizenship is rooted in the sphere of the law. Where both domains can be said to converge, however, is in the idea of access. Citizenship regulates both the rights and the responsibilities of a nation's subjects. These rights include the right to medical care. This is nowhere as pronounced than in heated public debates surrounding the right of undocumented migrants to health care. In recent US history, a number of initiatives tried to exclude migrants from health care. In 1994, California passed Proposition 187, which banned undocumented migrants from access to public health care, schools, and social services ("California Proposition 187"). Opponents of such initiatives, on the other hand, claimed that these measures would constitute a breach of human rights.

At the same time, the question of access to medical care is by no means limited to undocumented migration. Rather, what is at stake here is the idea that within a given nation state, the right to adequate health care may not be equally extended to all. These questions have loomed large in the debates surrounding "Obamacare." Under his presidency, Barack Obama proposed a bill to ensure that all citizens would be covered by health care; an initiative that his successor, Donald Trump, immediately set out to counter. Obama writes about his plan for universal health care in his most recent autobiography, *A Promised Land*. He notes how during his presidency, he was supported by his friend Teddy Kennedy:

> Through seven Presidents, Teddy had fought the good fight. But, for all his power and legislative skill, the dream of establishing universal health care—a system that delivered good-quality medical care to all people, regardless of their ability to pay—continued to elude him…. My interest in health care went beyond policy or politics; it was personal, just as it was for Teddy. Each time I met a parent struggling to come up with the money to get treatment for a sick child, I thought back to the night Michelle and I had to take three-month-old Sasha to

> the emergency room for what turned out to be viral meningitis. I remembered the terror and the helplessness we felt as the nurses whisked her away for a spinal tap, and the realization that we might never have caught the infection in time had the girls not had a regular pediatrician we felt comfortable calling in the middle of the night. Most of all, I thought about my mom, who had died in 1995, of uterine cancer. (368)

It is characteristic of Obama's autobiography that he personalizes the abstract issue of health care: he acknowledges his own privileged access to health care, and wonders what might have been if this had not been the case. What this passage does not quite say, however, is that access to health care may be determined not only by class, but also by race lines, since people of color work in lower-paying jobs to a disproportionate extent. At the same time, there is a sense in which Obama's description of the need for universal health care in the US is akin to the practice of narrative medicine. As a father, Obama speaks of his daughter's sickness and imagines what it might have been like had he not been able to pay for her doctor's bill. In Obama's account, illness is conveyed on the level of experience: Obama writes of himself as an anguished father trying to care for his baby daughter, and as a son who has had to watch his mother pass away. Narrative medicine teaches us that we should honor the stories of illness (Charon). Inaugurated by Rita Charon, narrative medicine seeks to bring the tools of literary analysis to the practice of medicine, urging physicians to engage in the close listening of their patients' narratives. Charon's expression that we should honor the stories of illness implies that patient narratives need to be considered in all their complexity: the complexity of the illness experience, its interwovenness with the patient's identity, as well as the social circumstances in which the patient is embedded. Ultimately, Barack Obama reminds us that we honor stories of illness if we empathize with those who have to watch their loved ones suffer and are unable to afford the medical care which would be needed to cure or alleviate this suffering. Under Obama's presidency, part of what he is trying to accomplish for US citizenry, then, is universal access to health care.

The intersection between medicine and citizenship, however, may not only be limited to an adequate access to medical care. It may also include the right to live in a non-toxic environment. At this juncture, medical rights—in the sense of an individual or communal access to health care—are closely linked to the right to well-being. This right, in turn, is tied up with the issue of housing. Whether one lives in a middle-class suburb or the inner city may have substantial consequences for one's health and life expectancy. To the extent that people live in environments that are unsafe for human health, they will run a much higher risk of illness. This environmental health risk, in turn, may be tied back to the question of citizenship. To what extent does a nation have to ensure not only the right to health care, but also the right to live in a non-toxic environment?

As my paper argues, this is a question which links medicine, citizenship, and social justice. Democracy may fail, I suggest, when the state not only fails to protect all its citizens from harm to their health and physical integrity, but when it looks on even after such health hazards have been uncovered. Mapping the question of civic failure onto the concept of health equity, this paper examines a particular case in recent US history: the Flint water scandal of 2016. In this incident, the state of Michigan devised a specific business venture. In order to attract new forms of investment, it proposed to entrepreneurs a scheme that focused on building new water pipes for the city of Flint, Michigan. While the new pipes were being built, however, the water supply would have to be switched from Lake Huron to the Flint River. As a CNN report describes it:

> In 2011, the state of Michigan took over Flint's finances after an audit projected a $25 million deficit. In order to reduce the water fund shortfall, the city announced that a new pipeline would be built to deliver water from Lake Huron to Flint. In 2014, while the pipeline was under construction, the city turned to the Flint River as a water source. ("Flint Water Crisis")

This switch, it would turn out, had disastrous consequences for the population of Flint, which was predominantly comprised of African Americans and poor white people. Due to corroded pipes in combination with the poor water quality of the Flint River, the inhabitants of Flint were exposed to massive doses of lead. The children in particular suffered acute cases of lead poisoning. The CNN report goes on to note:

> Tests in 2015 by the Environmental Protection Agency (EPA) and Virginia Tech indicated dangerous levels of lead in the water at residents' homes. Lead consumption can affect the heart, kidneys and nerves. Health effects of lead exposure in children include impaired cognition, behavioral disorders, hearing problems and delayed puberty. ("Flint Water Crisis")

This paper considers how we can interrogate the Flint water scandal, and it explores the discursive frames within which such an interrogation might take place. I argue that the concept of "medical citizenship" may be key in examining the nexus between citizenship, racial and economic difference, and health equity.[1] As Jenny Munro and Gerhard Hoffstaedter suggest,

> [m]edical citizenship refers to acts, claims, and expressions of political belonging that revolve around health, healthcare, and responses to illness. The idea

---

1   For a discussion of how medical status can arbitrate the border between citizen and non-citizen, see Amina Touzos's chapter in this collection: "'You're My People Now': *The Last of Us* Series on the Question of Human Belonging and Citizenship during the Age of Pandemics".

is that actions and decisions in relation to health and disease are political acts that demonstrate, and generate, belonging or exclusion. This includes decisions about who has the right to health care and broader social protections, and what it symbolises when people follow health advice or contribute to the health of the broader community. (Munro and Hoffstaedter)

Looking back at the Flint water scandal, we may ask a simple question: would such a massive case of lead poisoning have happened, and would it have been allowed to continue for such a long time, if the inhabitants of Flint had not been predominantly African Americans and poor white folks? What, in other words, is the relationship between race and class, on the one hand, and the right to civic protection as medical protection, on the other hand?

On a methodological level, I employ two frameworks through which the Flint water scandal might be viewed. First, I will refer to the idea of environmental racism, and second, I will explore the methodology of narrative medicine. Environmental racism argues that the right to live in a toxin-free environment is substantially inflected by racial difference; people of color may be affected by environmental damage to a disproportionate extent. Narrative medicine, on the other hand, explores how "stories of illness" can be told from an individual perspective (Charon). Because illness is hence "told" through the perspective of lived experience, this telling can also highlight breaches of social justice which may have led to illness in the first place. Narrative medicine and social justice can thus be said to be intricately interconnected. As Sayantani Dasgupta puts it,

[n]arrative medicine, its practice and scholarship, is necessarily concerned with issues of trauma, body, memory, voice, and inter-subjectivity. However, to grapple with these issues, we must locate them in their social, cultural, political, and historical contexts. Narrative understanding helps unpack the complex power relations between North and South, state and worker, disabled body and able body, bread-earner and child-bearer, as well as self and the other (or, even, selves and others). If disease, violence, terror, war, poverty, and oppression manifest themselves narratively, then resistance, justice, healing, activism, and collectivity can equally be products of a narrative-based approach to ourselves and the world.

While all of these concepts and methodologies—environmental justice and environmental racism, narrative medicine, and social justice—have been discussed both separately and in connection to each other, their relevance to concepts of citizenship is only beginning to be explored. As this paper will try to illustrate, these questions may actually be at the forefront of what citizenship may mean in the twenty-first century. Medical citizenship, I suggest, may not be tangential to the notion of the citizen, but central to it.

Environmental Racism and the City of Flint

The concept of citizenship, it can be argued, includes the right to health and well-being. The state must protect all its citizens from harm in terms of life and liberty. While these concepts are at the core of modern constitutions, going all the way back to the Habeas Corpus Act of 1679,[2] they may need to be revised in order to keep pace with the complexity of the social and political context of the new millennium. What, in other words, would the protection of life mean in the twenty-first century? I would argue that the very notion of "life itself" has become increasingly complex (Rose 3), particularly due to the expansion of industrial production and the proliferation of toxins polluting the environment as a side effect of this industrial production.

In light of these developments, the right to "life" may hence assume an entirely new dimension: It may include the right to live in a non-toxic environment. As Carl Zimring insightfully argues in his study *Clean and White: A History of Environmental Racism in the United States*, there is an intricate and troubling connection between waste and whiteness. He notes,

> [w]aste is a social process. We usually consider waste as material we discard, relying on public and private systems to remove unwanted materials from our homes, neighborhoods, and workplaces. These practices are consequences of our decisions to classify particular materials as waste, employ people to handle those materials, and develop systems to dispose of them. Waste informs the construction of our social and cultural values.... The social dimensions of waste are visible in recent American history. The Environmental Justice Movement emerged in the 1980s as a response to hazardous waste sitting in or near communities of color across the United States. (1)

Zimring's argument has profound consequences for the discourse of rights. Seen from his perspective, the right to a clean environment is inextricably tied to whiteness. While Zimring discusses the practices of waste dumping in the history of the US, I would suggest that his argument also has key implications for analyzing the Flint water scandal. Applying Zimring's line of thought to the events of Flint, Michigan, we may argue that the nexus between cleanness and whiteness also pertains to the right to clean water flowing from non-corroded water pipes. In other words, whiteness may ensure not only the right to dump one's waste elsewhere, but also the privilege of living in houses with safe plumbing. This right, on the other hand, was

---

2   The Habeas Corpus Act is commonly seen as the beginning of the juridical premises of modern states. Ratified as an act of parliament in England in 1679, "habeas corpus" meant that no-one could be detained by state authorities without reason, and that the lawfulness of such detention had to be examined immediately by a court. The act thus protects citizens from an arbitrary use of power by the state (Fallon and Meltzer).

denied to the inhabitants of Flint once the business venture was under way. As the CNN report observes, "Soon after the switch [of the water pipes], residents reported changes to the water's color, smell and taste" ("Flint Water Crisis").

Following Zimring's argumentative trajectory, we may thus inquire not only into the history of waste, but also into the history of whiteness. Where Zimring's interlinking of whiteness and cleanness is so intriguing is that he does not only refer to class to explain questions of what may be termed "medical disparity," but he suggests instead that such disparity arises from differences in both race and class. Whiteness, it can be proposed on the basis of Zimring's argument, is closely aligned with both medical rights and the concept of citizenship.

At this juncture, it may be interesting to briefly revisit the history of citizenship and its relationship to whiteness. Historically, citizenship was closely tied to whiteness in the US. As Matthew Frye Jacobson has argued, the right to naturalization was granted only to "free white persons" (13). Jacobson notes, "Citizenship was a racially inscribed concept at the outset of the new nation: by an act of Congress, only 'free white' immigrants could be naturalized" (13). In US legal history, this premise led to a series of remarkable court cases, the so-called "racial prerequisite cases." In these cases, immigrants had to prove before a court of law that they were in fact white and hence eligible for naturalization. What was unclear, however, is just what feature of their identity claimants had to refer to in order to "prove" their whiteness. As Jacobson goes on to say, referring to Tom Ellis, a petitioner from Syria, "in identifying Ellis as [white], the judge … could have been referring to any of a number of things … —Ellis's social bearing, his proficiency in English, his dress, his manner, his style, his demeanour" (Jacobson 239). As the racial prerequisite cases illustrate, then, citizenship was the prerogative of white citizens.[3]

At first sight, the racial prerequisite cases seem to have nothing to do with the Flint water scandal. While these cases concern the discourse of nineteenth-century naturalization law, the Flint water crisis does not concern immigrant communities but rather those of African Americans and poor whites in small town Michigan. I would argue, however, that both scenarios can be said to hinge on the connection between citizenship and whiteness. In nineteenth-century naturalization law, citizenship was itself based on the prerequisite of whiteness. In the twenty-first century, as I will illustrate below, citizenship continues to be tied to whiteness. In its current incarnation, this connection concerns the right to live in a non-toxic environment, as Zimring notes in his investigation of whiteness and cleanness.

These considerations also have methodological implications. If we follow Zimring's argument, an investigation of toxins in inner-city neighborhoods not only falls

---

3   For further discussion on the intersection of race and citizenship, particularly regarding Indigeneity, see Vanessa Evans's chapter in this collection: "'You've Heard it Now': Storytelling and Acts of Citizenship in Cherie Dimaline's *The Marrow Thieves*".

into the domain of medicine, but also that of cultural analysis. "Waste," Zimring suggests, "is a social process" (1). As I will argue in more detail as this paper progresses, waste, whiteness, citizenship and medicine are intricately connected. As the Flint water scandal sadly illustrates, the connection between citizenship and whiteness, which was so bluntly evident in the nineteenth-century racial prerequisite cases, continues into the twenty-first century. Here, communities of color may be said to bear the burden of pollution and the dumping of toxic waste. It is here that medicine comes into play. Medical citizenship, seen from this angle, implies the right to live in a non-toxic environment.

As Joni Adamson et al. have suggested, this right to live in an uncontaminated environment has been unevenly distributed, with sixty percent of African Americans currently living in neighborhoods that constitute health hazards. According to Adamson et al.,

> [studies] found race to be a leading factor in the location of commercial hazardous waste facilities and determined that poor and people of color communities suffer a disproportionate health risk: 60 percent of African American and Latino communities and over 50 percent of Asian/Pacific Islanders and Native Americans live in areas with one or more uncontrolled toxic waste sites. (4)

This implies that social and economic status may have an impact on the extent to which the right to health and well-being is actually put into practice. Moreover, Adamson et al. have introduced the concept of race to further problematize this uneven access to non-toxic environments. They refer to the idea of "environmental racism" in this context. According to Adamson et al., environmental racism can be defined as "racial discrimination in environmental policy making and the enforcement of regulation and laws, the deliberate targeting of people of color communities for toxic waste facilities, [and] the official sanctioning of the life-threatening presence of poisons and pollutants in our communities ..." (4). To put it differently, racial difference may thus in fact entail a health risk. Racial disparity, in combination with economic disenfranchisement, may result in a lack of access to housing in non-toxic environments.

Yet, how would the concept of citizenship be relevant in this context? I propose that the role of citizenship rights lies not only in guaranteeing specific rights on paper, but also in enforcing these rights in concrete social practice. What happens, in other words, once a breach of rights has been detected? This paper examines the role of spectatorship as well as of representation in this context. It looks at how the Governor of Michigan and other elected officials "looked on" as the Flint water scandal came to light. Moreover, it investigates the specific media and genres through which the Flint water crisis was eventually "leaked" to public discourse. In the latter context, it focuses on one author in particular: Dr. Mona Hanna-Attisha, a local pediatrician in the city of Flint, who eventually became the whistleblower exposing the extent to which the state and the nation had failed to protect its own citizens. What happens, Hanna-Attisha asks in her book *What the Eyes Don't See*, when the state poisons its own citizens? She writes,

> [t]he crisis manifested itself in water—and in the bodies of the most vulnerable among us, children who drank that water and ate meals cooked with that water, and babies who guzzled bottles of formula mixed with that water.... But this is also a story about the deeper crises we're facing right now in our country: a breakdown in democracy; the disintegration of critical infrastructure due to inequality and austerity; environmental injustice that disproportionately affects the poor and black; the abandonment of civic responsibility and our deep obligations as human beings to care and provide for one another. (13)

This passage may well be said to refer to the concept of medical citizenship. Hanna-Attisha explicitly links the Flint water crisis to a breakdown of democracy. For her, the exposure of the inhabitants of Flint to lead-contaminated water constitutes a failure of "civic responsibility" (13). It is this failure of the state to protect its citizens from what might be called medical harm that Hanna-Attisha goes on to expose. For her, this uncovering and exposure of the Flint water scandal is her duty both as a physician and a citizen.

"What the Eyes Don't See": Environment, Health, and Social Justice

At the core of the Flint water scandal, there is an intersection between medical justice and environmental justice. As Hanna-Attisha writes in her memoir, written about the events of Flint in retrospect, the longer the inhabitants of Flint were exposed to the lead in the corroded water pipes, the more symptoms of sickness they began to show. It is this disparity—a disparity which is both social and medical—that Hanna-Attisha set out to bring to light as she became the whistleblower on what she saw as a blatant breach in the civic responsibility of both the state of Michigan and the nation.

One of the questions at the heart of the Flint water incident, then, is through what channels the whistle may be blown. It is crucial to note in this context that Hanna-Attisha emphasized the scandal of the Flint water switch not only in the media, through interviews and features, and by writing letters to politicians and health officials. She also proceeded to write a book. *What the Eyes Don't See*, as I will argue below, is both case report and the autobiography of a pediatrician who has to witness her young patients getting sick due to tap water that is no longer safe for drinking.

The question of genre, in turn, is closely linked to the field of the so-called environmental humanities. One of the issues at the heart of the environmental humanities is the question of how the practice of sustainability might be enforced. What texts, what forms of representation might we use to convey to the public, but also to politicians on local, national and transnational levels the necessity of protecting the environment and of reducing the level of toxicity in our life worlds? As Adamson et al. have argued, there is a certain didacticism inherent in both the environmental humanities and in the literary texts which it examines. How might a literary text, a memoir, or a poem be especially suited to change readers' minds when it comes to matters of environmental sustainability? As studies have shown, reading literature can enhance empathy in the reader. Danielle Spencer and Maura Spiegel have referred to

> the clinical applications of literary knowledge. A recent study published in *Science* found that subjects performed better on tests measuring theory of mind, social perception, and emotional intelligence after reading literary fiction. Notably, those who read nonfiction or popular fiction did not perform as well. (16)

Such empathy, in turn, may be especially powerful when it comes to witnessing the effects of environmental pollution on human health. While an autobiography is not a work of fiction, it may similarly seem to enhance readers' awareness of a breach of social (and medical) justice. Autobiography, as Alfred Hornung has argued, verges on fiction in a number of ways. It selects certain events and dismisses others for the sake of constructing a "storyline"; it enables the reader to delve into a world of characters who are fictionalized even as they are rooted in the "real" (Hornung).

It is in this context of creating empathy through narrative that I now discuss Mona Hanna-Attisha's *What the Eyes Don't See*. Where the text is so powerful is in its defiance of categorization, participating in a number of genres at once. First, *What the Eyes Don't See* is an unsparing account of the Flint water scandal and hence partly non-fiction. Second, however, it is also the life narrative of its author, Mona Hanna-Attisha, who came to the US as a refugee from Iraq when she was still a child (Hanna-Attisha 7). Third, it is also a book which could be called a biography of the inhabitants of Flint, Michigan: a biography which, fourth, might also be read as a medical case report. It is these multiple registers, I claim in this paper, which make Hanna-Attisha's narrative a powerful vehicle through which the right to medical citizenship might be enforced.

As a medical case report, *What the Eyes Don't See* can also be seen as a detective story. As Hanna-Attisha writes at the outset of her narrative, she was initially confronted with symptoms that she could not quite explain. Parents were reporting itches on their children's skin. Crucially, Hanna-Attisha writes in her medical memoir that while parents suggested that the switch of the water pipes might have some-

280   Citizenship, Science, and Medicine

thing to do with their children's symptoms, she herself ruled out this possibility. Her certainty, in turn, was ultimately rooted in a belief in the system which ensures the safety of drinking water for all citizens.

> [Grace] planned to switch to powdered formula mixed with water but had some concerns. "Is the water all right?" she asked, looking skeptical. "*I heard things.*" The water. I'd been asked about it before.
> "Don't waste your money on bottled water," I said, nodding at Grace with calm reassurance, the way doctors are taught. "They say it is fine to drink." (18)

One of the aspects that looms especially large in Hanna-Attisha's narrative is the pediatrician's relationship to both the children and the parents. The passage quoted above can be read from a number of perspectives, all of which are mutually complementary. First, there is at the heart of Hanna-Attisha's relationship to her young patients and their parents the idea of the pediatrician immersing herself into her patients' life worlds. Medical practice, for Hanna-Attisha, is social practice. This idea of linking medicine to patients' lived realities, in turn, is also at the core of narrative medicine. As Hanna-Attisha observes,

> Years ago we talked about these environmental factors as "social determinants of health." Today we call them "adverse childhood experiences" (ACEs) or "toxic stress." ... This new understanding of the health consequences of adverse experiences has changed how we practice medicine by broadening our field of vision—forcing us to see a child's total environment as *medical*. (24–25)

Moreover, the passage quoted above could also be read through the concept of "citizen science." As Vohland et al. describe, "Citizen science broadly refers to the active engagement of the general public in scientific research tasks. Citizen science is a growing practice in which scientists and citizens collaborate to produce new knowledge for science and society" (1). As it will later turn out, Grace's suspicion about the quality of the water was not at all unfounded. What emerges in this passage is the idea that by word of mouth, the citizens of Flint form an alliance. They communicate their suspicion to each other: "*I heard things*," Grace tells her pediatrician (18; italics original). It is a testimony to Hanna-Attisha's form of medical practice, which is strongly inflected with elements from narrative medicine, that she begins to trust in the parents' intuition. Ultimately, she enters a coalition with her young patients and their parents. In keeping with the paradigm of citizen science, the community collects evidence which proves the quality of Flint water to be harmful. It is this evidence which will eventually lead to the full disclosure of the Flint water scandal. As Hanna-Attisha emphasizes, "For all the villains in this story, there are also everyday heroes: the people of Flint. Each one has a story to tell—100,000 stories in all—about months of pain, anger, betrayal, and trauma, along with incredible perseverance and bravery" (14). Hanna-Attisha's narrative can be said to fuse the elements from citizen science with those of narrative medicine. What she emphasizes in *What the Eyes Don't See* is that the citizens of Flint gather evidence to counteract the assurance by city officials that Flint water is safe to drink. Yet, this evidence is not only provided on the cognitive level, but it has an emotional content as well: it is also evidence of "pain, anger, betrayal, and trauma" (14). The concept of citizen science, it could be suggested, takes on particular resonance in the context of the Flint water scandal. This scandal arguably took place only because the inhabitants of Flint were denied their full citizenship rights. In a form of what may be called citizen science, then, they proceeded to reclaim those rights by getting the university to test the quality of their drinking water.[4] As Brian Palmer notes,

> Citizens groups partnered with scientists from Virginia Tech in the summer of 2015 to show the city how the testing should have been done. In their first sample of 252 homes, the Virginia Tech researchers found that 10 percent of samples exceeded 25 parts per billion—40 percent higher than the federal action level. One of the samples exceeded 1, 000 parts per billion. (Palmer)

The initiative taken by Flint residents strongly corresponds to the model of citizen science. Flint residents thus distrust the evidence provided by health officials that their drinking water is safe; they go on to provide their own evidence. Through the collaboration between Flint inhabitants and scientists from Virginia Tech, the Flint water switch is eventually revealed as a blatant case of systemic racism and a denial of medical citizenship.

At the intersection between citizenship and medical practice, however, it is at first important to note that initially, Hanna-Attisha assuages the parents' doubts about the quality of the Flint water. She does so, she notes in retrospect, because of her trust in the system of American democracy and the system of public health. It is here that citizenship and medicine are intricately connected: for Hanna-Attisha, the principle of American democracy ensures that the state protects its citizens from harm, personal as well as medical harm. As Hanna-Attisha bluntly asks, "If we stop believing that government can protect our public welfare and keep all children safe, not just the privileged ones, what do we have left? Who are we as a people, a society, a country, and a civilization?" (14).

Where the narrative is so powerful, then, is that it focuses not only on the riddle that needs to be solved but also on the medical detective herself. This reference to the

---

4   A discussion of citizen science and scientific citizenship is traced through the origin of modern science from its roots in the so-called "Scientific Revolution" by Jessica Gray in her chapter: "Foreign Relations: Utopian Fictions and the Birth of Scientific Citizenship."

282   Citizenship, Science, and Medicine

pediatrician-detective's own identity is closely connected to her own understanding of her civic duty. She owes it to the children and to her civic responsibility as an ordinary citizen, Hanna-Attisha notes, to solve the riddle of why the children are getting sick. In this context, the narrative speaks in great detail about Hanna-Attisha's medical role and her vision of being a pediatrician. She notes,

> A crying baby gives me a sense of mission. Deep inside I have a powerful, almost primal drive to make them feel better, to help them thrive. Most pediatricians do. For some of us, that sense of protectiveness becomes much more powerful when the baby in our care is born into a world that's stacked against her and her needs aren't being met—a world where she can't get a nutritious meal, play outside, or go to a well-functioning school, all of which will diminish her health. (20)

What is so remarkable about Hanna-Attisha's particular understanding of her role as a pediatrician, however, is that for her, this medical care includes an attention to her young patients' social and economic environment. In order to truly care for the children, Hanna-Attisha writes, she has to immerse herself into their world, to step into their shoes. What emerges from this scenario could not be more central to the practice of medicine. Medicine, in Hanna-Attisha's narrative, is both a scientific and a social practice. At this point in her narrative, her account is deeply in line with the concept of narrative medicine. As a practitioner of a form of narrative medicine, Hanna-Attisha listens not only to the medical stories, but also to the social narratives that the children and their parents tell. It is this notion of care that she also stresses in the program she runs at Hurley Medical Center:

> [s]o at the beginning of the Community Pediatrics block, residents go on a tour of the city and learn the history of Flint.... They record the number of blighted neighborhoods, liquor stores, neglected playgrounds, and boarded-up schools.... Residents also meet with community leaders and activists, and they visit non-profits and schools and daycare centers. They are sent to home visits, to court hearings and trials, to state protective services and community events.... My objective ... is to get the residents out of the hospital and into the city, into the lived experience and environment of our kids. (26–27)

What emerges from the act of listening could not be more central. In fact, if she had not listened to their social stories, Hanna-Attisha might not have been able to uncover the scandal of Flint, Michigan.

What is central to Hanna-Attisha's narrative, however, is not only the fact of her work as a medical detective, but also her reasons for becoming a medical detective in the first place. Why, she asks herself in the narrative, did she go to such great lengths to uncover why the children of Flint kept getting sick? Her motivation, Hanna-Attisha stresses, was not only her role as a physician dedicated to the local community, but also the story of herself as an immigrant from Iraq. As Hanna-Attisha notes in an interview with filmmaker Michael Moore in the film *Fahrenheit 9/11*,

> Hanna-Attisha: I wasn't born here, and we came to this country very much for that American Dream. Uhm, and, you know, with nothing besides educa-tion—my Dad was a GM employee, my Mom was a teacher, benefitted from Union contracts, send their kids to two, you know, to Michigan's public schools. The American Dream worked for us, it worked for me and my family the way that it does not work for the kids that I take care of in my clinic every day. They are literally waking up to a nightmare. A nightmare of injustice, poverty, lost democracy. And that is another lesson that we learn from Flint.
> Moore: Maybe that's why it's called a dream, because it's not a reality for everybody.
> Hanna-Attisha: No, it's not.
> Moore: Right?
> Hanna-Attisha: No, there are multiple Americas. (*Fahrenheit 9/11*)

Similarly, at the core of *What the Eyes Don't See*, there is the medical narrative of the American Dream (Paul 367). In Hanna-Attisha's rewriting of the myth of the Ameri-can dream, the right to life, liberty and the pursuit of happiness include the concept of health justice and environmental justice, and the right to live in an uncontami-nated environment.

Hanna-Attisha describes not only the lengths that she goes in order to finally solve the riddle of the children's sickness, but also the cost of acting as a medical detective in the first place. She recalls watching her two daughters play:

> Nina and Layla were playing together when I got home, arranging stuffed ani-mals in a make-believe zoo.... One day, a month or so back, the stuffed animals were all over the floor, in groups of two and four, multiplied.
> "What's going on, my little squid monkeys?" I asked.
> "Parent-teacher conferences."
> "Okay," I said, sitting on the floor, grabbing a stuffed animal, and joining in the playacting.
> But not this weekend. When I saw them playing, my heart tugged to join them, but I was soon distracted by more thoughts of lead-tainted water. (108–109)

In many different senses, *What the Eyes Don't See* is a quest narrative. It is a quest nar-rative which is both a personal memoir of migration and a medical detective story.

At the same time, *What the Eyes Don't See* is also a scathing critique of the state of American citizenship at the turn of the twenty-first century. As Hanna-Attisha writes, "This is the story of the most important and emblematic environmental and

284 Citizenship, Science, and Medicine

public health disaster of this young century. More bluntly, it is the story of a government poisoning its own citizens, and then lying about it" (12–13). This critique in turn is framed in terms of spectatorship. How can the state, Hanna-Attisha asks her readers, simply look on as the children are being poisoned by massive doses of lead? Hanna-Attisha observes,

> [b]ut even when lead exposure is demonstrated across a population, it is almost impossible to *prove* causation. Did lead in the water cause Brandon's ADHD? We will never know for sure. Did water cause Jasmine's rash? Maybe. Exposure to environmental toxins usually doesn't come with glaring symptoms, like purple spots or even a rash. The symptoms are things like learning disabilities that have a time lag. Sometimes they don't show themselves for years or even decades. For a pediatrician on the front lines, often the most you can hope for is establishing a correlation. The more I thought about it, the angrier I got. (98; emphasis original)

This is where the title of Hanna-Attisha's memoir, *What the Eyes Don't See*, hits home: if indeed the Flint water scandal constitutes a public health scandal, this, Hanna-Attisha knows, will be hard to prove. The point is not only that lead in the water is invisible to the human eye, but also that evidence of the causal effects of lead poisoning is hard to attain. This may be even more devastating in a community like Flint, which is predominantly African American and poor white. Both these groups have historically been stigmatized as being unwilling to work and as being intellectually inferior (Wray; Taylor). This is where lead poisoning seems all the more devastating: how will Brandon be able to prove that his ADHD was caused by the water? The situation, as Hanna-Attisha emphasizes, is all the more devastating because she had alerted health officials from the very beginning that there seemed to be something wrong with the Flint water. She remembers, "in an effort to be persistent but pleasant, I added: I never heard back from anyone. 'I would love to discuss this further to see what we can do to protect and prevent lead poisoning in our kids.' But the county health department was silent" (106). Eventually, it would take another year for the officials to finally take action. In this context, the role of racial and economic difference and disenfranchisement looms particularly large. When, Hanna-Attisha's narrative asks, do we condone a breach of citizenship rights in terms of health justice, and when do we sanction it?

Ultimately, the riddle to be solved is not only a medical riddle, but also a social one. It is here that we seem to have come all the way back to the concept of environmental racism. Would the Flint water scandal have continued to happen, we may ask with Hanna-Attisha, if the inhabitants of Flint had not been African American and poor white? In other words, in what particular contexts may the state fail to protect the rights of some of its citizens, and enforce the rights of others?

What is so crucial in Hanna-Attisha's account, is that it refuses to understand the scandal of Flint, Michigan, as an isolated incident. Rather, what the narrative uncovers is a systemic failure. *What the Eyes Don't See* is thus clearly connected to what has been called "systemic racism" (Feagin). As Melissa Denchak notes,

> [a] story of environmental injustice and bad decision making, the water crisis in Flint, Michigan, began in 2014, when the city switched its drinking water supply from Detroit's system to the Flint River in a cost-saving move. Inadequate treatment and testing of the water resulted in a series of major water quality and health issues for Flint residents—issues that were chronically ignored, overlooked, and discounted by government officials even as complaints mounted that the foul-smelling, discolored, and off-tasting water piped into Flint homes for 18 months was causing skin rashes, hair loss, and itchy skin. The Michigan Civil Rights Commission, a state-established body, concluded that the poor governmental response to the Flint crisis was a "result of systemic racism." (Denchak)

Ultimately, the situation in which contaminated water severely affected the health of Flint residents was allowed to continue for two years. Nearly 9,000 children were exposed to lead-infected water. Moreover, due to an insufficient supply of chlorine in the water, Flint experienced a severe outbreak of Legionnaires' disease. As Denchak goes on to observe, "The third-largest outbreak of Legionnaires' disease recorded in U.S. history—as well as the discovery in 2014 of fecal coliform bacteria in city water—was likely a result of the city's failure to maintain sufficient chlorine in its water mains to disinfect the water." In the end, the dramatic situation ended only after the inhabitants of Flint filed a petition to the US Environmental Protection Agency (EPA), which failed; they then went on to sue the city and state officials, and in 2016, they finally won. As Denchak concludes:

> A more momentous win came the following March with a major settlement requiring the city to replace the city's thousands of lead pipes with funding from the state, and guaranteeing further funding for comprehensive tap water testing, a faucet filter installation and education program, free bottled water through the following summer, and continued health programs to help residents deal with the residual effects of Flint's tainted water. Even after this settlement, however, Flint residents continue to struggle for the measures to be enforced (Denchak).

The very nature of systemic racism is that it is deeply embedded into different social and institutional structures, including the medical system. In order to uncover such systemic racism, Hanna-Attisha reminds us, it needs a physician who takes their patients' place. As a whistleblower, Hanna-Attisha becomes a spokesperson

286 Citizenship, Science, and Medicine

for the children of Flint, who have become "vulnerable subjects." As Thomas Couser has noted, "Conditions that render subjects vulnerable range from the age-related (extreme youth or age), and the physiological (illnesses or impairments, physical or mental) to membership in social or culturally disenfranchised minorities" (xii). According to Couser, "vulnerable subjects" are authors who are as yet unable to write their own life narratives (ix). It is here that other "surrogate" authors may need to step in (Couser xi): it is this surrogate authorship that Hanna-Attisha assumes. She writes a medical case report on the children of Flint which she then turns into a social justice narrative.

The idea of systemic racism can also be found in the title of Hanna-Attisha's medical memoir. As scholars from the field of Critical Race Theory have argued, privilege is often transparent in that it remains unseen. Privilege is so deeply embedded into the social and institutional structures that we are unable to see it (Crenshaw et al.; Gotanda). Ian Haney López speaks of the "transparency syndrome" in this context (111). This concept of "transparency syndrome" takes on multiple meanings Hanna-Attisha's narrative: social privilege is also the right to living in a non-toxic environment. Thus, as Zimerling also argues, whiteness, citizenship and the right to live in a "clean" environment may all be juxtaposed. In keeping with López's idea of transparency, then, white privilege as the right to live in a non-toxic environment remains unseen. What is visible to the eye, in other words, is only the location of whiteness in a certain neighborhood. What remains unseen, on the other hand, is the *health privilege* that such a neighborhood may carry.

At the same time, in Hanna-Attisha's memoir, the dichotomy between visibility and invisibility takes on yet another dimension. The most blatant breach of social and medical justice, she argues, is the politicians' deliberate un-seeing of the Flint water scandal even after the whistle had long been blown, both by Hanna-Attisha and others. The "eyes" of local politicians refused to see that the children of Flint were getting sick: even as the effects of lead poisoning on the children were already becoming visible, they continued to "look on." As Hanna-Attisha emphasizes, "A disaster of this scale does not happen completely by accident. Many people stopped caring about Flint and Flint's kids. Many people looked the other way" (13). Hanna-Attisha's narrative is thus also a form of witnessing: she bears witness to the state's crime of looking on, of letting medical injustice continue to happen. The failure of the state, as the guarantor of full citizenship rights, is hence also a medical failure.

Conclusion: Shared Authorship, Resilience, and the Future of Citizenship

What does this context mean for the notion of medical citizenship? Crucially, it could be argued that the concept of citizenship is in need of adjectives which describe and qualify it only when it has been shown to *fail* in certain contexts. There is a need for further qualification only where citizenship as a universal concept has already broken down. Medical citizenship, seen from this perspective, is already a diagnosis of failure.

However, it is interesting to note in this context that Hanna-Attisha's groundbreaking medical memoir also has a subtitle: *A Story of Crisis, Resistance, and Hope in an American City*. In writing the biography and the medical case report of the citizens of Flint, Hanna-Attisha also testifies to their resilience. As she notes at the end of her memoir,

> I will share with you a few stories of my Flint kids. They are my inspiration. To protect their privacy and dignity, I have changed or modified their names and identities…. They are strong, smart, beautiful and brave—and so resilient…. Resilience isn't something you are born with. It isn't a trait that you have or don't have. It's learned. This means that for every child in a toxic environment or unraveling community—both of which take a terrible toll on childhood development and can have lasting effects—there is hope. (14)

It is here that the pediatrician shares her authorship and speaks not about or for, but *with* the people of Flint. In this collective authorship, the inhabitants of Flint blow the whistle not only on the medical system, but also on a nation who has failed to protect all its citizens. The people of Flint de-individualize their illness by emphasizing that what is at stake here is a systemic failure born of environmental racism. The people of Flint blow the whistle not only on the politicians and the corporate interest that caused the Flint water scandal in the first place, but also on the concept of failed citizenship itself. The future resilience of the concept of citizenship, Hanna-Attisha implies, will lie in its ability to heed the sound of this whistle.

Works Cited

Adamson, Joni, et al. "Introduction: Environmental Justice Politics, Poetics, and Pedagogy." *The Environmental Justice Reader*, edited by Joni Adamson et al., U of Arizona P, 2002, pp. 3–14.

"California Proposition 187, Prohibit Undocumented Immigrants from Using Public Healthcare, Schools, and Social Services Initiative (1994)." *Ballotpedia* https://ballotpedia.org/California_Proposition_187,_Prohibit_Undocumented_Immigrants_from_Using_Public_Healthcare,_Schools,_and_Social_Services_Initiative_ (1994).

Charon, Rita. *Narrative Medicine: Honoring the Stories of Illness*. Oxford UP, 2008.

Couser, G. Thomas. *Vulnerable Subjects: Ethics and Life Writing*. Cornell UP, 2004.

Crenshaw, Kimberlé, et al. *Critical Race Theory: The Writings that Formed the Movement*. New York: New Press, 1995.

Dasgupta, Sayantani. "Narrative, Health, and Social Justice." *Institute for the Study of Human Rights*. http://www.humanrightscolumbia.org/courses/narrative-health-and-social-justice.

Denchak, Melissa. "Flint Water Crisis: Everything You Need to Know." *NRDC*, 8 Nov. 2018, https://www.nrdc.org/stories/flint-water-crisis-everything-you-need-know.

Fahrenheit 9/11. Directed by Michael Moore, Lionsgate Films, 2004.

Fallon, Richard, and Daniel Meltzer. "Habeas Corpus Jurisdiction, Substantive Rights, and the War on Terror." *Harvard Law Review*, vol. 120, no. 8, 2007, pp 2029–2112.

Feagin, Joe. *Systemic Racism: A Theory of Oppression*. New York: Routledge, 2006.

"Flint Water Crisis Fast Facts." *CNN online*. https://edition.cnn.com/2016/03/04/us/flint-water-crisis-fast-facts/index.html. Accessed 4 Aug. 2021.

Gotanda, Neil. "Race, Citizenship, and the Search for Political Community among 'We the People.'" *Immigration and Nationality Law Review*, vol. 607, 1997, pp. 233–60.

Haney López, Ian. *White by Law: The Legal Construction of Race*. New York: New York UP, 1996.

Hanna-Attisha, Mona. *What the Eyes Don't See: A Story of Crisis, Resistance, and Hope in An American City*. London: One World, 2018.

Hornung, Alfred, editor. *Autobiography and Mediation*. Heidelberg: Winter, 2009.

Jacobson, Matthew Frye. *Whiteness of a Different Color: European Immigrants and the Alchemy of Race*. Harvard UP, 1999.

Munro, Jenny, and Gerhard Hoffstaedter. "COVID-19 and "medical citizenship": How the pandemic is generating new forms of belonging and exclusion." *ABC Religion and Ethics*, 22 Jun. 2020, https://www.abc.net.au/religion/coronavirus-and-medical-citizenship/12379794.

Obama, Barack. *A Promised Land*. Penguin Random House, 2020.

Palmer, Brian. "Why Is it So Easy for Officials to Cover Up Drinking Water Scandals?" https://www.nrdc.org/onearth/why-it-so-easy-officials-cover-drinking-water-scandals. Accessed 14 Apr. 2022.

Paul, Heike. *The Myths that Made America*. transcript, 2014.

Rose, Nikolas. *The Politics of Life Itself: Biomedicine, Power, and Subjectivity in the Twenty-First Century*. Princeton UP, 2007.

Spiegel, Maura, and Danielle Spencer. "This is what we do, and these things happen: Literature, Experience, Emotion, and Relationality in the Classroom." *The Principles and Practice of Narrative Medicine*, by Rita Charon et al., Oxford UP, 2017, pp. 37–59.

Taylor, Evi, et al. "The Historical Perspective of Stereotypes of the African-American Male." *Journal of Human Rights and Social Work*, vol. 4, 2019, pp. 213–25.

Vohland, K., et al. "The Science of Citizen Science Evolves." *The Science of Citizen Science*, edited by K. Vohland et al., Springer, 2021. https://doi.org/10.1007/978-3-030-58278-4_1.

Wray, Matt. *Not Quite White: White Trash and the Boundaries of Whiteness*. Duke UP, 2006.

Zimring, Carl. *Clean and White: A History of Environmental Racism in the United States*. New York UP, 2015.

Foreign Relations
Utopian Fictions and the Birth of Scientific Citizenship

Jessica Hanselman Gray

The circulation of terms like "citizen science" and "scientific citizenship" underscore the political logic by which both academics and the general public conceive of regimes of knowledge. These terms imply rights and responsibilities associated with access to certain forms of knowledge about the natural world.[1] "Scientific community" generally refers in a limited sense to researchers, practitioners, and other professionals involved with the institutional production and application of a narrow array of sciences; the phrase posits and defends a friendly but distinct border between those credentialed professionals and the general public. "Scientific citizenship," on the other hand, is a plastic term that sometimes extends rights and responsibilities of the scientist to the public—rhetorically, if not practically, democratizing science—and sometimes figures the scientist as a sort of supercitizen of the larger society, encouraging responsible application of their inherently powerful position. It most often refers to communications and exchanges (of knowledge, trust, and credit) at the border between the scientific community and the general public, often troubling that boundary as it attempts to invoke it—a logic that also obtains in political rhetoric.[2] Appropriating the political category of citizenship to imagine a separation between science and the rest of society serves to justify the institutional priority of defending that border from erasure even while it narrates its intention to reach across it.

The implications of this metaphor and its intimate connection with authority, truth value, and political power can be better understood by tracing the origin of modern science's culture of citizenship to its roots in the so-called "Scientific Revolution." The seventeenth century's milieu of political and social contexts gave rise

---

1   See Mita Banerjee's chapter in this volume, "'What the Eyes Don't See': Medical Citizenship and Environmental Justice in Mona Hanna-Attisha's Medical Memoir," for an investigation into how citizen science and narrative medicine converge during the water crisis in Flint, Michigan.

2   For more on the implications of social exchanges that happen at the disciplinary boundary imagined between "science" and "non-science," see Thomas F. Gieran.

292 Citizenship, Science, and Medicine

to both our modern understanding of citizenship and the institutional reorganization of authority over natural knowledge. At that time, the emerging discipline of experimental science was writing itself into being as the exclusive arbiter of truth about the natural world—grounded, ostensibly, in its method, which relied explicitly on observation and experimentation and implicitly on self-selecting investment of credit and authority.[3] This method, modeled upon Francis Bacon's vision of scientific orthopraxy, gave rise to a modern notion of authority over nature that would end up being crucial for modernity and its increasingly secularized claims about states, sovereignty, and citizenship. Both rely on invoking an imagined separation between the public and private spheres, producing and reproducing a narrative that valorizes objectivity while investing real authority and power in specific bodies.

This essay considers two works of seventeenth-century fiction, written by authors of scientific treatises, that focus on voyagers' discoveries of hidden societies and their engagement with the scientific knowledge production happening in each. Both Bacon's *The New Atlantis* (1627) and Margaret Cavendish's *The Description of a New World, Called the Blazing World* (1666) narrate border-crossing adventures in which travelers enmesh themselves ritually, tediously, and imperfectly into new worlds. Both present models of organized, methodical inquiry into the natural world; both assign high importance to border control, connecting it intimately with conditions of knowledge production. While Bacon generates an austere and straightforward vision of masculine authority, later so pivotal for science's self-conception, Cavendish raises troubling questions about which bodies can be included in the production of authoritative knowledge and why. These two fictions reveal a tension between disciplinary gatekeeping and the very language of authority that writes this emerging discipline into being. In considering Bacon and Cavendish's tales alongside their antipodal relationships to the Royal Society of London, I focus on the implications of the figuratively reproductive body (and its strategic rhetorical erasure) on the early negotiation of what will come to be called "scientific citizenship." Our contemporary scientific community still struggles to overcome these implications as we wrestle with an array of life-or-death challenges that occupy the intersection of scientific knowledge, authority, and global politics.

Public and Private

Hannah Arendt posits a theory of citizenship that relies upon producing and maintaining the spatial and functional separation of the public sphere from the private.

---

3   For continuity and brevity, I am using the terms "science" and "scientific" somewhat anachronistically throughout this essay as a shorthand for activities and products that would have, in the seventeenth century, more properly been called "natural philosophy."

In the public sphere,[4] like the idealized conception of the Athenian *polis*, citizens interact and exchange ideas; the public represents a conceptual and literal space for discourse, a constructed "space of appearance" where people come together, recognize each other, and through reason make responsible joint decisions (198). The public sphere permits and encourages plurality, because it functions as a space where people can represent themselves to each other as individuals, irrespective of the social categories of identity that they inhabit by virtue of their bodies. This spatial distinction structures Arendt's concept of citizenship as being bound to a public-facing context, and political metaphors like "scientific citizenship" rhetorically extend this conception to disciplines of science. Distinct from other categories of political identification and belonging, "citizenship" generally implies reciprocity of duty that infuses rights with responsibilities—expectations as well as privileges, often viewed as mutually constitutive. In the Global Citizenship Observatory's definition, citizenship confers "rights and duties" and is both "a legal status and relation"—sometimes idealized as a way of being, an attitude, and a relation, while at the same time it is policed as a received/assigned condition ("citizenship"). Citizens are distinct from subjects in this way, and the status benefits from the term's connotation of merit, which is to say that citizenship is imagined as a set of ideal behaviors as well as an assigned or otherwise passive condition. The status requires relational duties.

For all of these reasons, citizenship is implicitly bound up with policing borders and with categorizing bodies. The category of citizenship relies on imagining the body as a repository of the essential quality of belonging, as is evident in policies surrounding citizenship through descent, or *jus sanguinis* ("right of blood"), and birthright citizenship, *jus soli* ("right of soil"). The notion of "naturalized citizens" reveals the extent to which both forms of citizenship are imagined as organic states of being rather than artificial, rhetorically authorized conditions; implying that the body holds a "natural" citizenship obscures the agency involved in establishing this condition. And yet citizenship clearly also denotes a *relation* between the private body and some external public which can determine its membership. Some boundary, in other words, must precede the authority required to adjudicate a person's relationship to it. Since authority to define inside/outside must come from inside, this rationale often requires an origin story—a history that establishes the founding condition or event from which the governing body derives authority to delimit citizenship. However arbitrary geographic political boundaries may be, an origin myth provides

---

4   Jürgen Habermas introduced this term into scholarly discourse with *The Structural Transformation of the Public Sphere*. His work generated substantial debates, especially among critics informed by feminist theory, such as Nancy Fraser; see, for example, Craig Calhoun, *Habermas and the Public Sphere*; Seyla Benhabib, "The Embattled Public Sphere."

a guiding rationale, [5] a narrative of how and why the current conditions are right and natural. Heritage, heroism, or divine prerogative: there is always an Excalibur. Scholars agree that narrative fiction was often invested in naturalizing the illusion of a clear and stable boundary between the public and private spheres. Elizabeth Maddock Dillon, for example, has shown how eighteenth-century fiction served as public reasoning documents, which circulated within an ostensibly disembodied "public" space while depicting the "private" realm on the page, discursively reproducing and naturalizing the split between public and private. This same naturalization of public and private, I argue, structured even earlier fictional explorations of scientific praxis, shaping the form of knowledge production that we will come to call "science."

Disciplines of knowledge production must also be constituted by imagined boundaries, which require policing much as state borders do. Geopolitical metaphors are commonplace in intellectual histories, especially science studies; Michel Foucault and Bruno Latour, for example, organize their critiques around figuring disciplines as "regimes" and "fiefdoms" and other political power centers, stressing the extent to which scientific discourse relies on narrative to justify (often-concealed) practices of inclusion and exclusion (Foucault 133; Latour 8). But while the body has long served as a physical space and as an imagined entity that posits a boundary between private and public in political and scientific discourses, feminist critics have revealed this boundary to be constructed and unstable,[6] a division historically and conceptually reinforcing a gendered hierarchy of power that served to reconcile Enlightenment ideals of individual liberty with the reality of social difference and patriarchy. The "scientific community" depends on practices rooted in the "Scientific Revolution," a sea change in practices of knowledge production that culminated in the calving of science from philosophy in the seventeenth century. Yet modern science's origin myth takes an overtly gendered view of the mind and its products, one that is predicated on the public/private divide, and it relies on the naturalized hierarchy of gender to elevate some perspectives above

---

5   I am applying the idea of origin myths as Mircea Eliade conceives of them in *Myth and Reality*, in terms of their social function as primarily a way to account for, naturalize, and make sense of present conditions.

6   There is a wealth of scholarship that participates in this conversation: see, for example, Nancy Fraser, "Rethinking the Public Sphere"; Joan Wallach Scott's landmark *Gender and the Politics of History*, which argues that the relegation of women to a feminized domestic sphere, separate from the political, is a tool of subordination; Catharine McKinnon, *Feminism Unmodified*, which explores gender, the body, civil rights, and the law; *Feminism, the Public and the Private*, edited by Joan Landes, which offers feminist critiques from multiple disciplines; *Languages and Publics*, edited by Susan Gal and Kathryn Ann Woolard, which examines "the public" as a "language-based form of political legitimation" that is connected to the construction of authority (4).

others. Although exclusion is usually naturalized with an official rationale, the history of the academy includes countless examples of how the body often forecloses belonging. Juxtaposing fictional narratives by Bacon and Cavendish foregrounds this naturalization and its fault lines: Bacon, the imputed "father" of empiricism, imagines the abstraction of pure unmediated reasoning, while the marginalized Cavendish, as we will see later, engages with the myriad ways in which some bodies must be excluded in order to sustain that fantasy.

The Royal Society: Citizens of a Public Science

In seventeenth-century England, The Royal Society of London, modeled on Bacon's prescriptions, sought to claim for a self-selecting group of wealthy, well-connected men authority over natural knowledge.[7] In what Eve Keller calls their institutional "myth of origins," Thomas Sprat, a Fellow of the Society, writes a fawning history, apology, and virtual hagiography in language that vigorously and sometimes defensively argues for both the indispensability of the Society's founding and the natural fitness of its members to serve as arbiters of such authority ("Producing Petty Gods" 447). The urgent need to mark this line by establishing an organization, and to promote it in this way, suggests that the boundary and the authority it conferred were not otherwise extant. In fact, there was considerable skepticism, even among their learned peers, about the Society's program. Proponents of experimental science strove to present it as a new discipline that was distinguished from others specifically by virtue of its methodological difference. Bacon's experimental model promised to correct the perverting influences of bodies and minds on the study of nature. They promoted these methods as a way to produce knowledge uncorrupted by subjectivity: in this vision, the person was not the source of knowledge but rather a witness to the experiment's trial of nature. The knowledge was disembodied, separate from the subject—public reason operating operating independently of the private body that offers, as Steven Shapin puts it, a "disengaged and nonproprietary presentation of authorial self" (179).

Claiming authority as a purportedly objective witness, however, requires creditability, some pre-existing belonging. The Royal Society grew out of an "invisible college" of natural philosophers who were already gathering before the official establishment of the Society ("History of the Royal Society"). The term suggests an implied, "invisible" culture of citizenship that eventually became formalized—not only visible but sanctioned by the King and populated entirely through election, creating

---

7   For a thorough analysis of the connection between the institutional aims of the Royal Society and the historically specific priorities of the English upper class in connection with the Restoration, see P. B. Wood.

a closed pipeline controlled by current members. Envisioning the early Royal Society as a culture of citizenship reveals that its explicit and implicit conditions of inclusion center the body in determining belonging. In his *History of the Royal Society*, Sprat makes an argument for the qualifications of Society members based on what he lauds as a kind of diversity—that they admit "Men of all religions" and "Of all countries" and "Of all professions (64–65).[8] However, other parts of the *History* offer qualifications to these categories: he had earlier called for "all civil nations" to join arms against the "common enemy of Christendom"; other context confirms that by "all religions" he means only sects of Christianity and by "all countries" he means only those nations that he deems "civil" (57).[9] He follows this section with one entitled, "It consists chiefly of gentlemen," which argues, essentially, that wealth inoculates against corruption. According to Sprat, the Society ought to include only "such men, who, by ... the plenty of their estates, and the usual generosity of noble blood, may be well supposed to be most averse from such sordid considerations" (67). Sprat argues here that containing authority within a group made up primarily of men with inherited wealth solves the otherwise insurmountable problem of corruption in knowledge production.[10] He explains that wealthy men are "free, and unconfined," which he says protects against "corruptions" such as profit motive and institutional hierarchies (67). Exemplifying the logic of Engin Isin's theorization of *acts of citizenship*, the Society's founders were determined to "call established forms of responsibilization into question" and replace scholastic authority with their own form of gatekeeping (37). It was important to tether the logic of this gatekeeping to characteristics of the individual rather than to method, because, as Deborah Harkness and Pamela Smith have shown, the work of science largely developed out of practices of observation and craft already commonplace in the domestic lives of everyday folk. Inclusion and authority did not follow naturally from that labor and expertise: the Society's exclusion of women as Fellows was a given, and Sprat takes no pains to offer an explanation or apology for it.[11] By the time Margaret Cavendish—a prolific natural philosopher in her own right—became the first woman to attend a meeting in 1667, she was crossing a well-defended border as an acknowledged outsider. Her

---

8   Note on spelling: I have silently modernized spelling and punctuation in the seventeenth-century texts for ease of reading.

9   For further discussion on how citizenship has been deployed as an arbiter of the false boundary between the civilized and the uncivilized with regard to Indigenous Peoples, see Vanessa Evans's chapter in this volume: "'You've Heard it Now': Storytelling and Acts of Citizenship in Cherie Dimaline's *The Marrow Thieves*."

10 For a treatment of how the Royal Society evaluated reports from outsiders, including travel narratives and cases where only a secondhand report was available, see Barbara J. Shapiro, *A Culture of Fact: England 1550-1720*, especially Ch. 3, "Discourses of Fact," and Ch. 5–6, "The Facts of Nature [I and II]."

11 The Royal Society did not admit any women Fellows until 1945.

body rendered her alien even to an emerging field being defined by its attempt to separate authority over knowledge production from the body of the practitioner.

The rationale for exclusion centers qualities connected to one's imagined fitness for participating in the public sphere, underscoring the importance of that division to the Society's gatekeeping. Sprat pits private against public explicitly in describing the impact of the Reformation on textual archives:

> The first thing that was undertaken, was to rescue the excellent works of former writers from obscurity. To the better performing of this, many things contributed about that time. Amongst which ... the dissolution of abbeys: whereby their libraries came forth into the light, and fell into industrious men's hands, who understood how to make more use of them, then their slothful possessors had done. (23)

This characterizes the takeover of knowledge from scholastics not in terms of a democratization of that knowledge but rather as a process by which self-described "industrious" men claimed control over resources in order to "make more use" of them than their animal-like former stewards. Sprat's language obscures agency: he begins with passive voice, then has an unnamed entity "rescue" texts, before shifting agency to the knowledge itself and finally to nature—the libraries "came forth" and then "fell" into the right hands. Both the texts and nature itself seem to be choosing sides rather than being acted upon. This romantic fable positions scholastics as private hoarders of knowledge and the Society as a well-lit public square—but, given that the Society's membership was also closed and maintained a secrecy code, this "rescue" of archives seems more a colonizing move than a democratizing one.

The priorities for this new method of inquiry, and its implied restriction to an aristocratic, masculine authority, were given their iconic articulation by Bacon. In *Novum Organum*, Bacon sets forth his plan for a reworking of the methods of natural philosophy, which he characterizes as aiming to extract truth from matter in order to reclaim mankind's domination over nature. Sprat's *History* celebrates the experimental method as a corrective for specific defects of thought, the "idols" that Bacon enumerates in *Novum Organum*. But Bacon's program of experimental philosophy was an explicitly masculinist one, and one project of the Royal Society was to make that gendered separation key to what its members saw as a productive and socially beneficial hegemony over the production of natural knowledge. Sprat's introductory material makes explicit the Society's investments in masculinizing philosophy; its dedicatory poem even muses that the personified Philosophy, gendered "she" in the classical tradition, ought to be "he," and it defines its intellectual products as "masculine" in opposition to the "feminine" mode of poetry: "[A]s the feminine arts of pleasure, and gallantry have spread some of our neighbouring languages ... so the English tongue may also in time be more enlarged, by being the instrument

298   Citizenship, Science, and Medicine

of conveying to the world, the masculine arts of knowledge" (129). Unlike feminine language that invents or creates, their masculine language simply "conveys." The implicit claim of experimental science, then, is that Nature is telling its own story and that these "masculine" methods convey that narrative unmodified; in this way, their role in its construction is rendered invisible.

In his utopian fable *The New Atlantis*, Bacon makes this rhetorical erasure of subjectivity into one of the defining characteristics of Bensalem, where he will imagine a society built around his principles and practices of knowledge production. Bensalem, explains the narrator, is "known to few, and yet knew most of the nations of the world," situated in a "secret conclave of a vast sea," where it is hidden from the sight and knowledge of other nations (272). The islanders strictly enforce their entry policies with the narrator's company of travelers, first keeping them cloistered indoors and thereafter giving them freedom to roam only within a tightly controlled distance from the Strangers' House where they are lodged. The islanders explain that they prioritize "preserving the good which cometh by communicating with strangers, and avoiding the hurt" (280). They maintain strict secrecy when interacting with foreigners abroad or on their own shores, even obscuring their national identity when traveling, and they employ an armed patrol to guard their borders and control entry. They also tell of their own regular explorations overseas, through which they maintain the power advantage gained by the island's hiddenness: "we have twelve that sail into foreign countries, under the names of other nations, (for our own we conceal); who bring us the books, and abstracts, and patterns of experiments of all other parts" (297). They send out explorers to report back "knowledge of the affairs and state of those countries ... and especially of the sciences, arts, manufactures, and inventions of all the world" (288). The narrator wonders at this asymmetrical invisibility, which does not seem humanly possible: "[I]t seemed to us a conditioner and propriety of divine powers and beings, to be hidden and unseen to others, and yet to have others open and as in a light to them" (275). This aspect of Bensalem's project—no less than "finding out of the true Nature of all things"—is essential to understanding Bacon's vision of an intellectually responsible praxis for producing natural knowledge; it also underscores the extent to which the story tacitly acknowledges the intimate connection between knowledge and political power.

In the apparent climax of the tale, the group elects the narrator to receive a private audience with one of the "Fathers" of Salomon's House, the pride of Bensalem, a learned (patriarchal) Society that would directly inspire the founders of the Royal Society. One Father regales the narrator with a "relation of the true state of Salomon's House": structured like a scientific paper, it includes "the end of our foundation," the "preparations and instruments we have for our works," the "several employments and functions whereto our fellows are assigned," and finally the "ordinances and rites which we observe" (290). The Father enumerates these elements—introduction, materials, methods, references—at length; over 100 sentences begin "we have" or "we make," detailing the resources, instruments, and labor that Salomon's House employs. Interestingly, the narrator witnesses none of this himself; all of the knowledge of Salomon's House derives from the relation he hears in private after his group elects him to serve as witness.

Reproducing Knowledge

Bensalem's careful attention to controlling narratives and dissemination of knowledge echoes the commitments to the masculinized system that Bacon sets forth in *Novum Organum*. He admonishes scientists to avoid false "idols" of thought which arise in part from the "mode of impression" (40). His aphorisms on the idols betray a deep mistrust of the role of language in knowledge production: "it is by discourse that men associate, [but] ill and unfit choice of words wonderfully obstructs the understanding" (41). In Bacon's view, language is a means by which a subject imposes form upon the matter of thought, and the violence that he perceives in this imposition is reflected both in his choice of metaphors and in his expressions of concern over the use of metaphors. He bemoans that words are unstable vessels of meaning, and especially the way they leave potentially contagious marks of subjectivity upon ideas. These concerns about "impression" are deeply connected with early modern ideas about gender and the body: in seventeenth-century England, there was widespread belief in "maternal impression," the idea that a pregnant woman's mind could physically mark the body of her fetus as a result of something she imagined, saw, or desired. This idea circulated among physicians and in print materials that purported to educate readers about the mysterious mechanisms of human reproduction. The pseudonymous *Aristotle's Compleat Master Piece*, for example, advises: "[T]he imagination of the mother works forcibly upon the conception of the child. Women therefore ought to take great care that their imaginations be pure and clear, that their children may be well formed" (46). Such warnings reveal anxieties not only about the power of a mother to physiologically shape another body but also about the possibility that what happens in the hidden, secret interior space of one body can have a lasting and material influence on future generations. Maternal impression is figured as an act of inscription, a form of authorship, and because authorship is a generative act that neatly aligns with the process and function of biological reproduction—giving form to what is "inside" the body and then putting it "outside" into the public sphere—they are effortlessly analogous, and reproductive metaphors of authorship are ubiquitous.

In discourses about the "new science" in seventeenth-century England, experimental philosophers were invested in making their subjectivity invisible to the receiving public; they claimed authority in part by purporting to transmit Nature's own

300   Citizenship, Science, and Medicine

narrative unmodified, uncorrupted by the private, embodied individual. Anxieties about authoritative knowledge often surface in metaphors of reproduction not only because both deal with bringing what is "inside" the body "out," but also because both threaten to pass on undesirable traits—errors or defects—by impressing them into new bodies or minds, thus carrying patterns of deformity forward through time. It is not surprising, then, that prescriptions for preventing monstrosity by controlling "impression" pervade the discourses surrounding both the production of knowledge and the production of bodies. Such metaphors alternately structure and challenge both Bacon's practical advice to natural philosophers and his work of fiction: echoing the above advice to pregnant women, he insists on the need to "fortify" one's mind against corruption to keep the mind "clear" (40). He also signals general concerns about potentially monstrous generativity, which Sprat later repeats. Salomon's House demands "pure" descriptions of nature, absolutely disallowing, "under pain of ignominy and fines," any portrayal that is "adorned or swelling" or bears any "affectation of strangeness" (297). According to Sprat, the Royal Society maintains "primitive purity" in its descriptions, with a "mathematical plainness" and a "close, naked, natural way of speaking" (113). They share a horror of the "swelling" and figurative generativity that they associate with impurity—and with the language of the "feminine" arts.

A similarly gestational logic structures the way the travelers in *The New Atlantis* receive knowledge about Bensalem—gradually, and on a strictly regimented time scale. When the sailors wash up on the shores of Bensalem, the islanders prescribe several distinct stages of concealment and confinement that the travelers must follow before entering the public space and gaining access to the rituals and knowledge therein. This economy of time echoes Pseudo-Aristotle's timeline of fetal development: "The forming of the child in the womb of its mother, is thus described: Three days in the milk, twice three in blood, twelve days form the flesh, and eighteen the members, and forty days afterwards the child is inspired with life" (49–50). The narrator characterizes the travelers' situation during this waiting period as a space "between death and life, for we are beyond both the old world and the new," a figuratively gestational liminality overlaid with a geopolitical framework (270). That implicitly gestational logic structures the strictly controlled conditions under which they (and we) eventually gain access to Bensalem's public square and gain access to the relation of Salomon's House, Bacon's vision of an ideal regime of knowledge production.

A reproductive framework for understanding knowledge production thus shapes the logic of Bacon's vision. It is significant that the gendered nature of this division resonates with the gendering of public and private spheres, especially when considering the question of how the "citizenship" in "scientific citizenship" should be understood. In *Leviathan and the Air-Pump: Hobbes, Boyle, and the Experimental Life*, historians of science Steven Shapin and Simon Schaffer argue that the Royal Society constructed a new understanding of scientific knowledge by creating a new *social technology* for evaluating knowledge claims, one which appeared to operate as a sort of public square along the lines of Arendt's model, and a new *literary technology* by which the attendant witnesses disseminate their narrative. They point out that the experimental method, now naturalized and widely regarded as *the* scientific method, had to be striven for, argued for, and defended from criticism.

Feminist science studies scholars have shown that the "objectivity" at its center also had to be constructed and naturalized, and that myths of gender provided a foundation. In *Modest_Witness@Second_Millennium.FemaleMan_Meets_OncoMouse*, Donna Haraway deconstructs the "modest witness" figure at the center of the Baconian ideals of the Royal Society, calling attention to the subject position that makes it possible. She points out that the mode of pass-through witnessing that rendered knowledge "objective" was only possible for a small subset of people—white, upper-class gentlemen—and suggests that Shapin and Schaffer's account of the Society's method is limited by their failure to fully unpack the implications of subject position (including gender, race, class, and national origin) on the construction of authority in seventeenth-century experimental science. Certainly, these categories come in and out of view in Sprat's *History*: for example, he emphasizes the importance of elevating "experiences" over "imagination," right after laying out an argument for excluding most people from access to those experiences based on elements of social identity (117). And as Haraway points out, it was precisely these embodied categories of identity that allowed some men's subjectivity to be obscured, thereby producing the authority that we call objectivity.

A View From Somewhere

Enter Margaret Cavendish. The Duchess of Newcastle was an enthusiastic autodidact keenly interested in natural philosophy. As a royalist, her situation during and following the English Civil War and Interregnum heavily influenced the attitudes toward political power and authority that both her fictional and philosophical writings reveal. After returning to England upon the restoration of the monarchy in 1660, Cavendish published (among other texts) *Philosophical and Physical Opinions* (1663), *Philosophical Letters* (1664), and an expansive critical commentary on scientific theory and practice titled *Observations upon Experimental Philosophy* (1666), which was printed together with a short novel entitled *The Description of a New World, Called the Blazing World*, a work of fancy/fiction that served as a companion piece to the serious treatise. Bound together, these two texts represent a gendered dyad, stereotypically masculine and feminine modes of delivering similar central arguments. Like Bacon's *New Atlantis*, Cavendish's *Blazing World* is preoccupied with discourses of natural knowledge and exploring how authority obtains both through relations

302 Citizenship, Science, and Medicine

among people across borders and through relations of knowledge, history, and intelligence.[12] Both feature travel narratives with utopian elements, both follow the adventures of strangers in a previously unknown land, and each explores a society centered upon the production of knowledge about the natural world. But Cavendish's *Blazing World* responds from a self-consciously outsider perspective not only to Bacon's work but to many of the prominent figures and practices of the new experimental methods of natural philosophy.

From the outset, *The Blazing World* evinces a complex relationship with storytelling, gender, and political boundaries. The story opens with a border-crossing that illustrates the implications of being an outsider: "A merchant, traveling into a foreign country, fell extremely in love with a young lady; but being a stranger in that nation, and beneath her in both birth and wealth, he could have but little hopes of obtaining his desire" (154). Rather than a first-person relation, with the narrator purporting to tell his own story, as in *The New Atlantis*, Cavendish gives us a third-person omniscient narrator, adding a degree of removal between the events and the reader. The first person that the narrator mentions is the merchant: we hear about his identity, his desires, his companions, his intentions, his enumerated resources, his plans, and the obstacles in his path. It appears to be his story—until a few pages later when, after abducting the young lady and sailing off with her, he dies of exposure and abruptly exits the tale. It turns out that this is not his story at all; it is hers. While the polar cold kills everyone else on board, the lady survives "by the light of her Beauty, the heat of her Youth"—the same qualities that had incited her kidnapping, suggesting value and virtue entangled in an embodied form of subjectivity that is sometimes erased from agential control (162). After drifting through a small portal that connects the poles of her world and the Blazing World, she encounters a group of Bear-Men, who lift her from the boat and convey her a great distance to the palace, where the Emperor, also taken with her beauty, marries her and grants her absolute power over the Blazing World. To this point she has exhibited no agency at all; her passivity is exaggerated, and her body's status as an object of men's desire—rather than her own subjectivity or intention—moves the story along until she transforms instantaneously from cargo to absolute dictator without ever being simply a participant.

After achieving political power through the only means available to her, marriage, the newly-appointed Empress sets her sights on knowledge, expressing her

---

12 For this multilayered understanding of the term "relation," I am indebted to Frances E. Dolan, whose 2013 book *True Relations: Reading, Literature, and Evidence in Seventeenth-Century England* takes up various connotations of the word—narration, reporting, association, connecting and being connected—to explore how both writers and readers invest texts with meaning, as well as the role that social relations play in constructing truth.

desire "to be informed" (163). Her first act is to establish schools and societies, encouraging her subjects—various races of man-animal hybrids—to engage in academic occupations according to their "nature" (163). She solicits briefings on their religion and politics—like Bensalem, the people of the Blazing World are enthusiastic monotheists, monarchists, and patriarchists—and she commands "true relation[s]" of natural phenomena, synthesizing and adjudicating the diverse perspectives that the various "vertuosos" provide (165). Unlike Bacon's, this model depicts knowledge-making as discursive, situated, and relational, while also highlighting the role of political power in producing authority over truth claims. The story portrays the dissemination of knowledge as similarly fraught. When the Empress feels she's discovered (read: decided) enough about the natural world, she resolves to publish a book of knowledge and asks the spirits that live in her world to find her a learned scribe. When she suggests a series of celebrated philosophers—Newton, Helmont, Descartes, etc.—the spirits remind the Empress that these men would never agree to record a woman's knowledge, and they instead nominate the Duchess of Newcastle (Cavendish's semi-autobiographical avatar; for clarity, I will continue to refer to the author as Cavendish and will reference the character as the Duchess). Far from erasing the authorial function of narrative-making, Cavendish writes herself into the story as a border-crossing, fourth-wall-breaking character who travels between her own world and the Blazing World to serve as the protagonist's scribe, best friend, and sidekick. The two begin a sprawling series of negotiations and adventures that lead them in and out of various social and political situations, culminating in an invasion of the Duchess's world (using submarines for stealth), where the Empress burns cities to the ground in order to establish her native "ESFI"—a nod to Charles II's kingdom of English, Scotland, France, and Ireland—as "absolute monarchy of all that world" (241). While Cavendish's story nakedly advocates for the indispensability of a singular final authority—monarchism, monotheism, monism—it is full of scenes of consultation and collaboration, in which the Empress relies on intelligence reports from her subjects as well as counsel and reasoned discourse. It also calls repeated attention to its narrator being both a disembodied voice and an immutable human body. The Blazing World explores limits that exist both physically and conceptually over knowledge production, especially the ineluctable body.

In her critique of the "modest witness" figure, Haraway unpacks the gendered history of "modesty," showing that this word connoted different qualities in men and women. Masculine modesty implied gentility and sophistication, an inclination in public to subordinate one's private self. This kind of modesty served to establish credibility for the gentlemen of the Royal Society: Sprat boasts of their "fair, and equal, and submissive way of registering nothing but histories and relations"—claiming authority through this purported passivity (116). Feminine modesty played out differently: it was about staying out of masculine realms, being

304 Citizenship, Science, and Medicine

relegated to the private domestic sphere—a physical erasure rather than a rhetorical one. In Bacon's *New Atlantis*, the narrator recounts in exhaustive detail the ritual Feast of the Family, which honors any man in Bensalem who can boast "thirty persons descended of his body": during the Feast, this patriarch is paraded before the crowd "with all his generation or lineage" for an excessive display of pomp, the florid description of which encompasses a significant portion of Bacon's text. Toward the end of a breathless description of this extravagant ritual, the narrator mentions, briefly and in passing, that "if there be a mother, from whose body the whole lineage is descended, there is a traverse placed in a loft above ... where she sitteth, but is not seen" (283). In publicly addressing "his" descendants during the celebration of his social impact on Bensalem's community, the father refers to himself as "the man by whom thou hast breath and life," while the mother, her influence confined to her private body, is relegated to silence and invisibility in the rafters (283). This scene effects a clear distinction between the function of public and private spheres, and unlike Cavendish, Bacon does not call further attention to that erasure in his narrative.

Their fictions, the texts subordinated to secondary "feminine" status, help to complete the picture of their respective views on philosophy, providing missing vantage points that reveal how "objectivity" requires erasure. Their inclination to imagine a shift in methodology through a rupture of political and geographic borders, with the travel narrative genre, underscores the inherently political logic of knowledge making. And it is intriguing that both Bacon and Cavendish use the utopian form, in particular, to sketch out their visions: *Utopia* means "no place," and the genre is freighted with implications of impossibility, naïve idealism, and self-conscious attention to artifice. It is striking that these serious natural philosophers, who also wrote technical and scholarly works, chose to explore these ideas through this specific mode. Like Salomon's House's elaborate artificial trials of nature, speculative fiction allows for experimentation in a controlled environment: an imaginative "what if?" exercise. Whereas Bacon carefully glosses over the authorial role in that thought experiment—having his unnamed protagonist stumble upon it and report back—Cavendish openly paints herself as the inventor of both the Blazing World and her philosophy, creating and forming them into being "[out] of the most pure ... rational matter" of her mind, not hesitating to reveal the manifold marks of her own authorship (*Blazing World* 250). She is transparent about the formative power of the storyteller as maker and about narrative's implicit dual function of relation and invention[13]. Utopia's denotation of "no place" also serves as a fictional illustration for the topological fiction that Haraway critiques as the impossible "god

---

13   For a close look at the connection between these two fictional texts and changing understandings of "invention" at this time, see Frédérique Aït-Touati, "Making Worlds: Invention and Fiction in Bacon and Cavendish."

trick of seeing everything from nowhere" in science's construction of objectivity ("Situated Knowledges" 581). Bensalem's almost-magical geographical situation and its strict maintenance of a one-way flow of intelligence that figures them always at the center are rehearsed in the Royal Society's claim to special authority: Sprat invokes Bacon's *New Atlantis* by name in claiming for London the natural right to serve as the "constant place of residence for that knowledge, which is to be made up of the Reports, and Intelligence of all countries" (87). He argues that Nature has uniquely positioned English gentlemen to produce a "universal intelligence," as evidenced by the "situation of England ... in the passage between the northern parts of the world, and the southern" (85). This pronouncement encapsulates the un-self-conscious absurdity of "objectivity": England only lies between the north and south from the perspective of England itself. Cavendish pushes against this kind of claim in her *Observations*. In discussing Robert Hooke's experiments with microscopy, in which he notes that different lighting conditions and angles produce wildly different images, Cavendish asks, "which is the truest light, position, or medium, that doth present the object naturally as it is?" (17). This inquiry gets at the crux of the problem of so-called objectivity: the authority to decide which perspective offers the most accurate view constitutes the power to decide what is true. It is now commonly accepted that knowledge is always partial and situated, thanks to scholars like Harding, Keller, and Haraway, but Margaret Cavendish was spilling it out into view and fretting over it in multiple genres and forms as early as 1666, using fiction to show truths that "nonfiction" obscures. Long before terms like "sociology of scientific knowledge" or "situated knowledges" began circulating, she was reflecting on positionality and interrogating the social and political conditions of natural knowledge production.

From the very beginning of *Observations*, Cavendish calls attention to the way that knowledge production depends upon access and authority. The preface bluntly acknowledges gendered differences in access to the resources of knowledge production, apologizing for the shortcomings of her prose, which she attributes to gender inequity in education: "many of our sex may have as much wit, and be capable of learning as well as men; but since they want instructions, it is not possible they should attain to it: for learning is artificial, but wit is natural" (11). Cavendish's ideas were not particularly marginal,[14] but her body still functioned to alienate her from the "learned body" and revealed the limitations of their purported commitment to diversity of perspective. This is not to suggest that Cavendish's fiction manages, or even attempts, to make visible all of the implications of individual subjectivity in

---

14   For an analysis that corrects earlier characterizations of Cavendish as an anti-experimentalist whose views on natural philosophy were fundamentally at odds with the Society's, see Emma Wilkins, "Margaret Cavendish and the Royal Society."

knowledge production, nor to suggest that it advocates for democratization or equity: it is fundamentally a conservative vision centered on patriarchal and absolutist ideals. However, both Cavendish's *Observations* and her playfully satirical fiction offer a stranger's perspective that helps to complete the picture precisely because her analysis, as Eve Keller points out, is "spoken from outside the discursive and institutional forums it explores" ("Producing Petty Gods" 450). Cavendish enacts in *The Blazing World* the same unpacking and disrupting of the Utopian mythology that Haraway's "god trick" and "view from nowhere" critiques will perform; the intransigence of bodies serves to reveal much of what Bacon's tale obscures about how knowledge production really operates: it is messy, partial, politically fraught, and unable to maintain stable boundaries. Where Bacon's fiction attempts to erase subjectivity and obscure the centrality of the body, Cavendish answers this with a focus on the impossibility of disembodied knowledge: she shows how reporting and inventing are inextricable, and that a story can never really be told from the outside by someone who is themselves inside that story, as humans are inside of nature. Precisely because of her familiarity with exclusion, Cavendish offers a portrait of knowledge production that is more honest about the forms of erasure that keep outsiders out, and about the messiness—connections, shortcuts, partiality—of what goes on inside. Her layering of worlds and narrators performs a metafictional exploration of the permeable boundary between imagination and reason that also rehearses her critique of the selectively permeable boundary that purports to uncouple "science" from philosophy. As the outsider, she provides a missing vantage point that makes visible the relationship between outsiders and insiders and highlights the ways in which the Baconian vision relies on erasure and exclusion.

This essay has sought to show how anxieties about the provenance of knowledge, and especially the embodied nature of its synthesis and reproduction, pervade the Royal Society's overtly political autobiography. These same anxieties surface in Bacon's and Cavendish's fictions, both of which narrate models of ideal knowledge production in strikingly political terms, with an otherwise unsupportable obsession with political border crossing and defense. Both stories enact and reflect these connections and offer insight into the construction of what institutions have since naturalized as a disciplinary border constituted by method rather than identity and the body. The extent to which border crossings and political negotiations drive each story underscores how questions of who belongs on which side of a boundary, who controls that boundary, and by virtue of which embodied qualities, have always been central to establishing scientific authority. This kind of self-erasing witnessing, and the implied transparency of certain bodies, were crucial to the way that the burgeoning scientific community at its inception established the boundaries that continue to define scientific inquiry and regulate what counts as objective truth to this day. The limiting conditions of "objectivity" (and by extension, one's fitness to practice scientific citizenship) remain tied to the body and its relationship to inherently political boundaries. In elevating what they called a "masculine" method, the Royal Society attempted to naturalize a rationale by which wealthy English men make uniquely competent scientific citizens, their unmarked identities permitting the "universal modesty" that makes some private bodies transparent.

Sprat was correct when he posited "an agreement, between the growth of learning, and of civil government": making knowledge, whether citizen science or scientific citizenship, runs into the same body-centered boundary policing as voting, jury service, and other citizenry functions (29). Enlightenment political ideals and the experimental program of the new sciences both relied on discursive erasure of how regimes produce citizens primarily by excluding based on the body. Calls to democratize knowledge, diversify access, or attend to issues of identity and subject position and the political conditions under which knowledge is produced sometimes draw accusations of "politicizing science"—as if a self-selecting community claiming to report objectively from No-Place were not already inherently political. Knowledge production and political power have always been intertwined, and both derive their authority through narrative-making. The scientific community will need to recognize and confront those connections as we struggle with a multitude of challenges that require their participation and leadership, as many of the threats currently facing the global community constitute a test not only of our sciences but also of our willingness to reimagine our relationship to boundaries.[15]

Works Cited

Aït-Touati, Frédérique. "Making Worlds: Invention and Fiction in Bacon and Cavendish." *Palgrave Handbook of Early Modern Literature and Science*, edited by Howard Marchitello and Lyn Tribble, Palgrave, 2017, pp. 493–503.

Arendt, Hannah. *The Human Condition*. Chicago UP, 1958.

Bacon, Francis. *The New Atlantis* (1627). Reprinted in *Paper Bodies: a Margaret Cavendish Reader*, edited by Lorraine Sylvia Bowerbank and Sara Heller Mendelson, Broadview Press, 2000, pp. 264–299.

—. *The New Organon [Novum Organum]* (1620). Edited by Lisa Jardine and Michael Silverthorne, *Cambridge Texts in the History of Philosophy*, Cambridge UP, 2000.

Benhabib, Seyla. "The Embattled Public Sphere: Hannah Arendt, Juergen Habermas and Beyond." *Theory*, vol. 90, 1997, pp. 1-24.

Calhoun, Craig. *Habermas and the Public Sphere*. MIT Press, 1992.

---

15 See Amina Touzos's chapter, "'You're My People Now': *The Last of Us* Series on the Question of Human Belonging and Citizenship during the Age of Pandemics," for a look at how video game studies is engaging with one such threat to humanity and the complications it presents for citizenship and belonging.

Cavendish, Margaret, Duchess of Newcastle, 1624?-1674. *Observations Upon Experimental Philosophy* (1666). Edited by Eileen O'Neill, Cambridge UP, 2001.

—. *Philosophical and physical opinions written by.. the Lady Marchioness of Newcastle.* London, Printed by William Wilson, 1663. *Early English Books Online* via ProQuest, https://www.proquest.com/books/philosophical-physical-opinions-written-lady/docview/2240955156/se-2?accountid=14505.

—. *Philosophical letters, or, Modest reflections upon some opinions in natural philosophy maintained by several famous and learned authors of this age, expressed by way of letters / by the thrice noble, illustrious, and excellent princess the Lady Marchioness of Newcastle.* London, s.n., 1664. *Early English Books Online* via ProQuest, https://www.proquest.com/books/philosophical-letters-modest-reflections-upon/docview/2240875599/se-2?accountid=14505.

—. *The Description of a New World, Called the Blazing-World* (1666). Reprinted in *Paper Bodies: a Margaret Cavendish Reader*, edited by Sylvia Lorraine Bowerbank and Sara Heller Mendelson, Broadview Press, 2000, pp. 151–251.

"Citizenship." *Glossary on Citizenship and Electoral Rights.* San Domenico di Fiesole: Global Citizenship Observatory/Robert Schuman Centre for Advanced Studies/ European University Institute, 2020, https://globalcit.eu/glossary/.

Dillon, Elizabeth Maddock. *The Gender of Freedom: Fictions of Liberalism and the Literary Public Sphere.* Stanford UP, 2007.

Dolan, Frances E. *True Relations: Reading, Literature, and Evidence in Seventeenth-Century England.* U of Pennsylvania P, 2013.

Eliade, Mircea. *Myth and Reality*, translated by W.R. Trask, Harper & Row, 1963.

Foucault, Michel. *Power/Knowledge; selected interviews and other writings.* Edited by Colin Gordon, Longman, 1980.

Fraser, Nancy. "Rethinking the Public Sphere: A Contribution to the Critique of Actually Existing Democracy." *Social Text*, no. 25/26, 1990, pp. 56–80.

Gal, Susan, and Kathryn Ann Woolard. *Languages and Publics: the Making of Authority.* St. Jerome Publishing, 2001.

Gieran, Thomas F. "Boundary-Work and the Demarcation of Science from Non-Science: Strains and Interests in Professional Ideologies of Scientists." *American Sociological Review*, vol. 48, no. 6, 1983, pp. 781–795.

Habermas, Jürgen. *The Structural Transformation of the Public Sphere.* 1962. MIT Press, 1989.

Haraway, Donna Jeanne. *Modest_Witness@Second_Millennium.FemaleMan_Meets_ OncoMouse: Feminism and Technoscience.* 1995. Routledge, 2018.

—. "Situated Knowledges: The Science Question in Feminism and the Privilege of Partial Perspective." *Feminist Studies*, vol. 14, no. 3, 1998, pp. 575–599.

Harding, Sandra. *The Science Question in Feminism.* Cornell UP, 1986.

Harkness, Deborah E. *The Jewel House: Elizabethan London and the Scientific Revolution.* Yale UP, 2007.

Isin, Engin F. "Theorizing Acts of Citizenship." *Acts of Citizenship*, edited by Engin F. Isin and Greg Marc Nielsen, Zed Books, 2013, pp. 15–43.

Keller, Eve. "Producing Petty Gods: Margaret Cavendish's Critique of Experimental Science." *ELH*, vol. 64, no. 2, 1997, pp. 447–471.

Keller, Evelyn Fox. *Reflections on Gender and Science*. 1985. Yale UP, 1995.

Landes, Joan B. *Feminism, the Public and the Private*. Oxford UP, 1998.

Latour, Bruno. *We Have Never Been Modern*. Translated by Catherine Porter, Harvard UP, 1991.

McKinnon, Catharine. *Feminism Unmodified: Discourses on Life and Law*. Harvard UP, 1988.

"History of the Royal Society." *The Royal Society*, royalsociety.org/about-us/history/#timeline. Accessed 1 Nov. 2020.

Scott, Joan Wallach. *Gender and the Politics of History*. Columbia UP, 1988.

Shapin, Steven. *A Social History of Truth: Civility and Science in Seventeenth-Century England*. U of Chicago P, 1994.

—, and Simon Schaffer. *Leviathan and the Air-Pump: Hobbes, Boyle, and the Experimental Life*. 1985. Princeton UP, 2018.

Shapiro, Barbara J. *A Culture of Fact: England 1550–1720*. Cornell UP, 2000.

Smith, Pamela H. *The Body of the Artisan: Art and Experience in the Scientific Revolution*. U of Chicago P, 2004.

Sprat, Thomas. *The History of the Royal-Society of London, for the Improving of Natural Knowledge*. Printed by T.R. for J. Martyn, at the Bell without Temple-bar, and J. Allestry at the Rose and Crown in Duck-lane, Printers to the Royal Society, 1677. *Google Books*, play.google.com/books/reader?id=g3OOAAAAQAAJ.

Wilkins, Emma. "Margaret Cavendish and the Royal Society." *Notes and Records of the Royal Society of London*, vol. 16, no. 3, 2014, pp. 245–260. https://doi.org/10.1098/rsnr.2014.0015.

Wood, P.B. "Methodology and Apologetics: Thomas Sprat's *History of the Royal Society*." *The British Journal for the History of Science*, vol. 13, no. 1, 1980, pp. 1–26.

"You're My People Now"
The Last of Us Series on the Question of Human Belonging and Citizenship during the Age of Pandemics

Amina Antonia Touzos

Introduction

Typically, when we think of video games, we might associate them with popularized discourses about aggression levels in players or the fear of an increasingly isolated society glued to their screens. However, as the academic field of video game studies has established over the last decade, video games are not only a cultural, even economic, capital but also narratives which deserve to be explored and experienced (Bourgonjon and Soetaert 2013; Domsch 2013). Video games' role in society extends further than their mere entertainment stereotype, as they could also be dubbed a communal culture—as demonstrated by MMORPGs (massively multi-player online role-playing games) or other forms of online play. The communities which are formed here often reach beyond the online spaces from which they originate (Mäyrä 172), while the narratives presented by the games could also be interpreted as communal narratives themselves. Video games, as both a genre and a lifestyle, seem to achieve this notion of communal belonging in two ways: on the one hand, the "shared playful activities experienced ... promote the formation of close and long-standing friendship bonds between a player and the other members of their online community that are not traditionally found in other mediated channels" (Kowert 96),[1] on the other hand, at the core of most narrative-based games lies a conflict of belonging which the players experience through their characters' continuous struggles to achieve a state of security and stability.[2] One could argue that

---

1   However, it should be noted that online-offline spaces originated from online multiplayer games are sometimes also toxic environments (Hilvert-Bruce and Neill 2020).

2   Most role-play games (RPGs) are narrative based. However, one could argue that other forms of gameplay, such as first-person shooters (FPS), also follow a narrative structure which involves the players' *and* characters' fight for survival and a community which grants them stability. For instance, FPS like *Call of Duty: Modern Warfare* (2019) mainly feature team-based combat, while the different missions primarily focus on the players by securing hostages and loca-

the players' *and* their characters' challenges surrounding communal survival and ensuring their own as well as others' safety is also a matter concerning citizenship.

In this regard, a player's expression of citizenship, for instance, becomes valuable to the socio-cultural understanding of "video games ... [as] both an activity and a space where the practices of ... people are analyzed" (Bourgonjon and Soetaert 3). An intersectional reading of video games and video game culture(s) through the lens of both video game studies and citizenship studies can provide useful insights on how citizenship is conceptualized in online and offline spaces and what impact this might have on our understanding of citizenship as a whole. I argue that video games contribute to ongoing debates around the (re)conceptualization of citizenship by exploring the participatory relationship between characters within the game and players on the outside. Here, aspects of community and citizenship become relevant in a multitude of ways, as a game's structures and narratives can and should be read alongside their probable impact on players—the participatory, intersectional audience *behind* the controller.

In this chapter, I look at how representations of citizenship and their ambiguous characterization are employed in the game series *The Last of Us* (2013–2020) by Naughty Dog, specifically in relation to the medicalization of civic rights as well as the trauma narratives at the core of *The Last of Us* and *The Last of Us: Part II* (Isin and Turner).[3] Both games explore stories of people's survival during and after a pandemic apocalypse, caused by a fungal infection, quickly wreaks havoc on the North American continent where the series takes place. The fight for resources is one of the central aspects of the series' portrayal of new civic life, with communities hoarding and battling each other over supplies, locations, and even citizens' status, as communal affiliations and constitutions vary drastically, from military structures to religious sects to the representation of democratic values.

The characterizations and portrayals of citizenship within *The Last of Us* series generally seem to follow, though conflicted and ambiguous in their narrative execution, internationalized Western conceptions of citizenship, primarily coined by the UN charter on the *Universal Declaration of Human Rights* (1948) and cumulative legal documents such as the charter on *The Rights of Non-Citizens* (2006). The latter, as published by the Office of the United Nations High Commissioner for Human Rights, defines a citizen, and, in turn, a non-citizen, as follows:

---

tions to ensure their own (teams') as well as non-playable characters' (NPCs) safety. In this regard, *Call of Duty: Modern Warfare* features both online and offline accounts of community—and citizenship—as players from all over the world engage in online combat against and with each other.

3   For short: *Last of Us I* and *Last of Us II*.

> Citizens are persons who have been recognized by a State as having an effective link with it. International law generally leaves to each State the authority to determine who qualifies as citizen. Citizenship can ordinarily be acquired by being born in the country (known as *jus soli* or the law of the place), being born to a parent who is a citizen of the country (known as *jus sanguinis* or the law of the blood), naturalization or a combination of these approaches. A non-citizen is a person who has not been recognized as having these effective links. (5)

Although the apocalyptic setting in *The Last of Us* series has effectively dismantled all previously known forms of State and (international) State law, its portrayal of new judicial and communal structures seems to be informed by current systems: in the series, members of a community can technically acquire citizenship by being born into it, or having a parent in this community, or by naturalization.[4] However, although *The Last of Us* games seem to build upon this definition of the acquisition of citizenship, these seemingly established "links" between person and State are overruled by one crucial factor: a person's health status. In *The Last of Us* series, citizenship status is granted only to those who are not contaminated with the fungus, regardless of *jus soli*, *jus sanguinis*, or naturalization processes. Here, I argue that *The Last of Us* series narrates citizenship as an ongoing conflict by conceptualizing citizenship, and in turn, its recognition, as a status tied to someone's medical(ized) humanness, whereby humanness means "being human" and to "be human" means one must be uninfected. In turn, being and/or passing as uninfected not only grants human status but also (communal) citizenship, whereas being infected classifies a person as non-human and thus renounces citizenship status. Consequently, citizenship is not granted easily: people who have just been contaminated, immediately receive the status of "non-human" and are either killed or exiled from their communities to prevent infectious outbreaks. In this regard, the games utilize medical terminology to define and redefine what it means to be both human *and* citizen. The recognition of citizenship is thus not only linked to the individual's health status but also their correlating humanness. In this paper, I will continue to differentiate between humanness and humanity: whereas humanness describes the condition of a person being "human" (as in, of the human race), humanity refers to a person's benevolence as part of their identity as a "human." In some of the research referenced here, these two terms are used interchangeably, however, in my analysis of *The Last of Us* series, I wish to maintain their differentiation to further contrast the games' use of both as origins of (oftentimes) traumatic conflicts for the characters and the players. Here, the series' protagonists represent border existences, as they progressively deviate

---

4 This alludes to my argument above that video games cannot and should not be read separately from the structures they exist within (meaning our societies and communities) but are instead informed by and comment on these very structures.

from their world's definition of medicalized "humanness" and its correlation to citizenship which gives rise to conflict over their *humanity*. In turn, the player is assigned a specific role in the games' narratives and beyond, reshaping questions of humanity, humanness, and, consequently, citizenship yet again.

Of particular interest for this paper will be how the series' main characters, Joel and Ellie, navigate their individual yet correlated processes of citizenship and its recognition, with regard to other characters and the players. As the narratives unfold, it becomes apparent that each character's citizenship status is both reliant on but not innately tied to their community's recognition of citizenship. Instead, the characters are forced to relearn their varying states of citizenship as embodied as well, going beyond the seemingly fixated link between citizenship and health status. Here, the traumatic experiences the characters go through, inform their perception of citizenship as they—and thus the players—are repeatedly forced to overthrow their previous sense of community and its affiliated civic status, to instead replace it with their own definitions of belonging. This creates central moments of conflict for the characters and shapes the way *The Last of Us* series conceptualizes the dissonance between citizenship and individuality in relation to the characters' traumatic experiences. Moreover, these conflicts put the player in a peculiar situation, as they at once cause and determine the characters' precarious citizenship status, while themselves reflecting on their own citizenship status outside the game.

Methods and Literature Review

Reading *The Last of Us* series as located at the intersection of citizenship studies, video game studies, and narrative medicine grants a multi-faceted outlook on the correlations between citizenship and its medical as well as non-medical determinators, while also analyzing the consequences of such correlation for our own understanding of a person's (and a people's) humanness and humanity.[5] Rita Charon defines the field of narrative medicine as "the work that has ... potential to help move an impersonal and increasingly revenue-hungry healthcare toward a care that recognizes, that attunes to the singular, and that flows from the interior resources of the participants in encounters of care" (2). Beyond this, narrative medicine is also a methodology which reads health and illness narratives through a lens of care, rather than cure. Thus, in this paper, when I analyze *The Last of Us* series with the help of a conjunction between modern citizenship studies and narrative medicine, I wish to uncover the

---

5   Mita Banerjee's chapter from this volume, "'What the Eyes Don't See': Medical Citizenship and Environmental Justice in Monda Hanna-Attisha's Medical Memoir," provides further analysis of the intersection between narrative medicine and citizenship studies as they relate to environmental racism in the context of the Flint Water Crisis.

underlying structures which have defined our views of human beings and citizens alike, while also being able to offer an alternate approach as to how we can find redefinitions of both in the games—and beyond.

Even though unraveling apocalyptic crises like that in *The Last of Us* series may seem fantastical, the Covid-19 pandemic has shown that there is need for a discussion on core social values and how we perceive of ourselves as (global) citizens. The game series hereby offers a narrative exploration of individual(ized) emotional versus civic duties, which, in turn, could shed light onto our own relationship with these aspects: "Video games have the ability to tackle one of the primary obstacles to developing the citizenship identity by utilizing fictive worlds to help players imagine a larger community and see their relationship in it" (Davisson and Gehm 42). Thus, while investigating how citizenship is established in the game series, this paper will also join discussions on inclusivity and displacement in conversation with "digital technology, ... [which makes] the format [of video games] a unique rhetorical tool for imagining oneself as citizen and acting out that imagination" (40).

The modern discourse on citizenship is centrally concerned with an endeavor to expand the term and its associations, moving away from exclusively legal and political/politicized conceptions of citizenship to include

> [c]hanging patterns of mobility and connectivity, migration and transnational cultural interconnections ... [C]itizenship today is at the same time associated with old and ineffective protocols, which continue to produce exclusion, and yet is also 'in the making', moving into a position beyond the given ... At its best, this ambivalent performance of citizenship has the capacity to rearticulate or reinvent citizenship, to link old and new figurations of citizenship ... across given thresholds of legal and political institutions, social conventions, disciplinary competencies and discourses, ascriptions and attributions of race, class, culture and gender. (Hildebrandt and Peters 3)

In this ambivalent space, the field of video game studies becomes especially useful to the examination of *performances* of citizenship, as video games act both as a medium to be spectated and a performative space (Fernandéz-Vara 2009). Citizenship in this regard is not only enacted within the narrative by the characters, but also through the player engaging with the narrative as an active participant: the game's plot can only unfold when the player interacts with its interface, while games like *The Last of Us* series also aim to include their players not only on a mechanical level but on a narrative level as well. Here, the players engage with "old and new figurations of citizenship" (Hildebrandt and Peters 3) through the characters they navigate and are meant to form an emotional bond with (Brookes 2011). By integrating the players into the characters' traumatic and conflicted journeys around their varying states of

Analysis

Ethical and Emotional Imperatives of Health-Related Citizenship Statuses

The series begins by showing its audience the collapse of the world as they and the characters know it: the first outbreak of a fungal infection on the North American continent in 2013 forces people to flee their homes in a hurry, while the US military desperately tries to control the quickly escalating situation. Here, the series' first main character Joel is introduced, who tries to escape with his daughter Sarah, but is stopped by soldiers. Unsure about whether he is being confronted with two newly infected citizens, one of the soldiers shoots at Joel and 12-year-old Sarah who, fatally wounded, dies in Joel's arms. This beginning sequence of *Last of Us I* confronts the player with the series' themes of medicalizing people and the traumas that result from the sudden instability of citizenship and its processes of recognition for the first time.

Last of Us I introduces its audience to a new charter of citizenship statuses, granted as protective status of a person *and* a community's body and mind as related to medical determinators. The most important distinction here is the differentiation between humans and the Infected, who are depicted as non-human monsters: "They might still look like people, but that person is not in there anymore" (*Last of Us I*). The Infected are the enemy; they cannot be reasoned with and they attack any living being upon sight—thus, once a human has been infected, they "turn" and need to be eliminated to ensure the survival of those still uninfected. *Last of Us I* and *II* do not often feature people turning, however, and if they do, the correlated cut-scenes also portray the emotional conflicts arising from losing someone to the infection and, in turn, having to make the dire decision to kill them. In this regard, the series correlates the emotional effects of the pandemic and its aftermath, with the impact on characters' social behavior and their survival strategies. The medical knowledge the characters, and, hence, the players, have of the infection is limited since not a lot is known or revealed to them about the intricacies of the infection aside from it spreading quickly and being lethal to the person's humanity *as well as* their humanness and, consequently, their life. In limiting scientific knowledge, the games instead lead their players to focus on individual and family fates, as well as on the humanity of those who are still human. The fight for survival is thus emotionally connotated and is not processed by the characters in a primarily medicalized manner, in the sense that they perceive of the infection and its consequences as an "illness" to be cured. Instead, the characters fear and dread the infection particularly because of what it might do to themselves and their community. The infection is defined through its traumatic consequences and experiences for the characters: They lose their loved ones twice; first, because the infection "kills" the conscious aspects we define as "human" in a person, and second, because the now inhuman being needs to be killed to ensure *human* survival. The games' narrative and visual depiction of despair and loss are hereby directed towards those still alive; their status as "humans" and as "citizens" is defined by their *lacking* medicalization. If a character is not infected and thus rendered as "healthy," there is no need for others to question their status as citizen/human, whereas once someone leaves the state of "healthy" by means of an infection, their humanness and consequently their status as citizen are immediately revoked, regardless of their communal affiliation.

Herein, the games create a dissonance between the medicalized view of the Infected on the one hand, and the emotional perspective of humans on the other hand. While fighting Infected in the games, the players are constantly confronted with the medicalized perception of these beings, marking them as visually and narratively inhuman(e) and thus worth, even necessarily, being killed by the players during combat to ensure both the character's and the player's survival.[6] Herein, the Infected are not designed to make the player feel guilty about killing or using violence—in contrast, the narratives and varying combat sequences relating to *human* characters do intend this affect, especially in *Last of Us II*. Particularly interesting here, is that in stripping the Infected of their humanness, they are rendered as objects (as opposed to subjects) which complicates the series' depiction of citizenship. By portraying the Infected as non-human beings, their medicalized characterization as "ill" simultaneously renders them as *inhumane* and dangerous. Similar to the way Robert Williams (Lumbee) traces the concept of the "savage" to white supremacist citizenship culture which labels various peoples as inhuman(e) and therefore uncivilized, *The Last of Us* series constructs the Infected as "savages" to contrast human and non-human, citizen and non-citizen, friend and foe: "Alien and exotic, threatening and subversive, the savage has long been imagined as a familiar, diametrically opposed figure throughout the history of the West, helping to define by counterexample and antithesis a distinctive form of Western civilization" (9). This binary between "us" and "them," framed by Western notions of citizenship, in turn not only enables *The Last of Us* series' depiction of the Infected as "savages" but as non-citizens as well (due to their being uncivilized), whereas human characters are "diametrically" marked as civilized and thus citizens.[7] Moreover, the objectifying, medicalized view

---

6   If the played character (the avatar) is killed in the game, the player is forced to replay the sequence.

7   See Vanessa Evans's chapter in this volume, "'You've Heard it Now': Storytelling and Acts of Citizenship in Cherie Dimaline's *The Marrow Thieves*," for a look at how Indigenous Peoples reimagine citizenship and belonging through storytelling after apocalypse.

on the Infected is amplified by some of the games' apocalyptic environmental settings, which often feature abandoned hospitals or crashed ambulance cars. When such eerie medical surroundings are featured in the series, they almost always develop into combat sequences against Infected, reiterating the latter as both emotional and medical enemies to characters and players. The Infected are hereby not only characterized as uncivilized monsters needing to be killed to secure one's survival/health status, but they also represent the emotional extents of the pandemic: humankind as we know it has been destroyed, there is no hope left, and those who were lost are better off dead than turned into "those things out there." (*Last of Us I*)

At the same time, however, the series does—though only subtly—problematize certain interactions with Infected. In a scene during *Last of Us II*, one of the protagonists encounters a military stronghold which has purposefully captured Infected to use as bait, target practice, or subjects of torture simply for fun. The degradation that the Infected suffer in this sequence marks the ultimate denial of any humanness within them—to the human military group the Infected are not even considered post-human any longer, and instead become objects of violent desires and cruel fantasies. This then raises the question to the military group's own *humanity* as well as their *civility*—to invoke Williams again: "the Western world's most advanced nation-states continue to perpetuate the ... images of ... savagery ... to justify their ongoing violations of the most basic human rights" (8f.). This, unfortunately, is only commented on shortly while players are given the option to kill the Infected who have been captured or engage in their torture, potentially creating ethical dilemmas for the players as well:

> The nature of what it means to be human functions as a primary theme to the game's [*The Last of Us*] narrative. This becomes juxtaposed against the larger question of what it means to be moral in a world where all previous structures imposed to govern morality—courts, jails, an organized central government, and even communities—have fallen away. (Green 747)

Nonetheless, by refraining from commenting on the player's own ethical (or unethical) desires to act (in)humane against the Infected, and even leading players to objectify them—herein possibly encouraging the players to engage in their torture—the game not only remains ambiguous in its portrayal of non-human non-citizens, but also remains (questionably) ambivalent in its depiction, even choice, of humanity. Although *The Last of Us* series largely remains within the binary boundaries of (oppressive) Westernized notions of citizenship (us vs. them), the games complicate their own citizenship narratives with questions of humanity by confronting players with these ethical dilemmas. In doing so, the games insinuate the very conflicts around non-citizens and their protection in our society outside the games: "If non-citizens are lawfully deprived of their liberty, they must be

Amina Antonia Touzos: "You're My People Now" 319

treated with humanity and with respect for the inherent dignity of their person. They must not be subjected to torture or to cruel, inhuman or degrading treatment or punishment, and may not be held in slavery or servitude" (Office of the United Nations High Commissioner for Human Rights 15).

Moreover, by positioning their players in these types of scenarios, *The Last of Us* series complicates its overall portrayal of citizenship and its processes of recognition: on the one hand, due to the crass differentiation between humans and Infected, little room for a multi-faceted ethical exploration of humanness, citizenship, and humanity is left. On the other hand, the players are often thrown into emotional paradoxes, in which the lines between "healthy" and "ill" (infected), "citizen" and "non-citizen" are blurred and moreover, emotionally loaded. The following scene from *Last of Us I*, in which the protagonists Ellie and Joel encounter two brothers, Sam and his older brother Henry, demonstrates the extent of this paradox:

[Ellie goes to wake Sam up and discovers that he is contaminated and turning into an Infected. Sam attacks Ellie—Joel tries to intervene and prepares to shoot Sam; Henry, however, stops him by drawing his own gun.]
[Henry, shoots a warning shot at Joel] "That's my fucking brother!" [Ellie is heard screaming in the background, struggling against a turning Sam.]
[Joel] "Screw it!" [He reaches for his gun again. Henry shoots at him first, but then turns to shoot his little brother in the chest. Sam dies, while Ellie is left free and unharmed.]
[Henry, miserable] "Sam … " [He breaks down crying, while still holding his gun. Joel walks over to him, worried.]
[Joel] "Henry!"
[Henry, sobbing to himself] "Henry, what have you done?!"
[Joel approaches slowly] "I'm gonna get that gun from you, ok?"
[Henry, points his gun at Joel] "It's your fault!"
[Joel] "This is nobody's fault, Henry!"
[Henry, crying] "It's all your fault!" [Henry suddenly shoots himself in the head. He is dead immediately.] (*Last of Us I*)

This scene exemplifies the emotionally laden ethical paradoxes *The Last of Us* games push players into: for one, the lines between life and death, citizen and non-citizen, seem to be clearly drawn in accordance with a person's health status—Sam has been contaminated thus he needs to die. After all, once infected, a person is marked as "ill" and practically considered dead;[8] therefore, they can be rightly stripped of their

---

8   Herein, the games also invoke the notion of "social death," describing the way society renders the yet living or already deceased physical body as "dead," or having experienced "a series of losses," including "a loss of social identity; a loss of social connectedness; and losses associated with disintegration of the body" (Borgstrom 5).

citizenship to protect those who remain "healthy," meaning being alive, human, and thus citizen still.

Scenarios like these, however, also create difficult ethical imperatives: anyone who has been officially declared dead, *must* in fact die, regardless of their (emotional) relation to others which is why Henry ultimately decides to shoot his own brother. Interestingly, although the scene also depicts the pain and trauma of such an act, as Henry sees no other way but to end his own life as well, his suicide does not alter the established acts of recognition of humanness *and* citizenship as directly related to health and health status. Instead, civic responsibility overrules emotions in all aspects, even if it requires one's own death. Having witnessed this, the players are then confronted with the ultimate paradox: Ellie.

The Last of Us series centers its main narratives on Ellie, protegee daughter of Joel, who is the only known human being to survive an infection and thus become immune which renders her neither human nor Infected. By placing the players in the role of Joel in *Last of Us I*, and then Ellie in *Last of Us II*, leading them to care for Ellie, the series uproots its own principle of "civic responsibility over emotions." In *Last of Us I* this reality ultimately climaxes in Joel's rescue of his protegee daughter from a surgery that would have ensured a vaccine for humankind but also would have resulted in Ellie's death—a choice Henry, or anyone else for that matter, was not allowed to make for his family.[9] In turn, in *Last of Us II*, Ellie's immunity is meant to be kept secret, so not to reveal her non-human, non-citizen identity and instead ensure her human citizenship, even if it means disregarding the established rules over health, humanness, and citizenship status to maintain everyone else's safety. The ways in which Ellie's role complicates the series' depiction of citizenship and citizenship recognition, as well as civic responsibilities, will be analyzed in the coming pages.

By creating paradoxes like these, *The Last of Us* series continuously unravels and destabilizes its own (un)ethical narratives and subsequently, the role of their players, as the lines between good and evil, right and unjust, emotion and civic responsibility, are constantly blurred: is Joel in the right for saving his daughter's life despite her non-human non-citizen status? And is Ellie in the right for protecting her own citizenship status above all else, despite the established rules? In a sense, though the series remains conspicuous here, *The Last of Us* games offer their audience a multi-layered perspective on the very conflicts and ethical dilemmas of citizenship, health, and health status we face in our modern-day society:

---

9   This is particularly problematic with regard to the fact that Henry and his brother Sam are African American, whereas Joel and Ellie are white. However, for sake of continuity, I will abstain from a detailed discussion here.

The most typical public health ethical conflict is in deciding upon how to balance the needs of "the many" against the rights of "the individual." Classic examples of this dilemma are who should be saved if not everyone can be saved and how can an individual's privacy and liberty be respected whilst still protecting and promoting the health of others? When addressing these questions, "trade-offs" inevitably occur; however, in order to ensure that these are fair and just, one must be able to assess the duties and rights of all the parties involved. (Stapleton et al. 4)

Meta-Citizenship: Rights and Responsibilities

Although *The Last of Us* series' protagonist Ellie is characterized as occupying a border existence in the games' exploration of health, humanness, and citizenship status, which brings about its own traumatic challenges for her and those around her, Ellie, nonetheless, remains an able, white, queer woman, who passes as "healthy" and thus as "citizen." The obstacles she faces due to her immunity, e.g., Ellie having to keep her immunity secret so not to lose her ambiguous citizenship status, can generally be overcome and often do not even pose an imminent threat to her safety—both regarding her citizenship recognition as well as her humanness recognition. Here, the series does not seem to be able (or does not want to) push the limits of traditional Western conceptions of citizenship too far, as if to remain within the bounds of what has established itself as the (white supremacist) social norm: even though the games position Ellie as the only other non-human non-citizen next to the Infected, she is no "savage." Ellie is no antithesis to be degraded, instead, her unique medical status as the first (known) person to be immune to the infection ultimately renders her as the first of a new kind of human—and citizen. In transcending the established definitions of humanness by tying it to a person's medical "health" status, Ellie destabilizes the existing norms of regulating citizenship through medical determinators. In this sense, Ellie's position could be correlated to the term "patient zero," typically describing "a person identified as the first to become infected with an illness or disease in an outbreak" (Merriam-Webster). In *The Last of Us* series' post-pandemic scenario, Ellie is no "patient zero" in the traditional sense. However, she could be described as "citizen zero," since her health status as neither human nor Infected surpasses any previously established forms of humanness and thus citizenship. Ellie has no "rightful" claim to any citizenship within her world: the recognition processes of both humanness and citizenship status as tied to distinct medical categories (healthy equals human and grants citizenship vs. ill equals not human and revokes citizenship), are not only *not* applicable to Ellie but undermined by her as well, due to her distinctive (un)humanness. In turn, just like "patient zero" marks the first existence of a new ill human, Ellie's existence marks the first instance of a new (un)healthy human—a "meta" human—forcing those around her to reevaluate previous definitions

322   Citizenship, Science, and Medicine

of health and humanness. Consequently, in her medical novelty, Ellie also marks the emergence of new forms of citizenship, overriding the seemingly stable frames for determining humanness through medical factors, which, in turn, grant citizenship. Hence, in her meta humanness, Ellie could be dubbed a "meta citizen" as well.

Respectively, Ellie is set apart from those around her because of her medical and civic duality. For some, Ellie represents the only hope left for humankind's survival, for others, she signifies a risk too great to take, as her ambiguity threatens the (though fragile) stability of society prior to her appearance:

> [Ellie has joined Joel and his partner Tess shortly before the following sequence. Joel and Tess are protecting Ellie, who is fleeing the military, trying to reach the rebel group Fireflies; Joel, however, follows this plan reluctantly. As the military follows them after a conflict, the three seek shelter in an abandoned government building.]
> [Tess] "I'm not ... I'm not going anywhere. This is my last stop."
> [Joel, baffled] "What?"
> [Tess] "Our luck had to run out sooner or later."
> [Joel] "What are you going on about—" [He approaches Tess and tries to take her arm.]
> [Tess jumps back, panicked] *"No don't*—! Don't touch me."
> [Ellie approaches slowly] "Holy shit. She's infected."
> [Joel looks back and forth between Tess and Ellie. He scoffs, visibly hurt, and takes a few steps back.] "Let me see it."
> [Tess pulls her shirt back and reveals the bite mark on her neck. Joel huffs in shock.] *"Oh, Christ!"*
> [Tess suddenly walks up to Ellie and grabs her arm.] "Give me your arm!" [She pulls up the sleeve and shows Ellie's old bite mark to Joel demonstratively.] "This was three weeks. I was bitten an hour ago and it's already worse. This is fucking real, Joel!"
> ... [Tess walks up close to Joel] "Look, there's enough here that you have to feel some sort of obligation to me. *So, you get her to Tommy's.*"[10]
> ... [The military has arrived and begins to approach the building. A decision needs to be made.]
> [Ellie] "You want us to just leave you here?!"
> [Tess] "Yes.... I *will not* turn into one of those things."
> ... [Ellie and Joel reluctantly leave Tess behind, who sacrifices herself to buy them some time.] (*Last of Us I*)

Interesting here are the different emotions towards Ellie and her immunity, specifically regarding Tess and Joel's conflict about a civic, even humanitarian responsi-

---

10   Tommy is Joel's brother and plays a crucial role in the whole series, as he is one of the few people to know of Ellie's immunity and acts as her protective family as well.

Amina Antonia Touzos: "You're My People Now" 323

bility towards themselves, and the world they live in. Ellie's condition is, though unraveling, also something that inspires hope even for those whose situation is hopeless—like Tess's infection. Therefore, when Tess urges Joel to feel "some sort of obligation" to her, she is not only referring to an obligation to her as Joel's partner, but also to her as a human being. Tess's human death is inevitable; the infection will spread and turn her into an Infected, which not only strips her of her human consciousness, but ultimately renders her non-human and thus non-citizen as well. However, what matters most to Tess here is the value of her life as a human being, which ultimately results in her decision to end it by sacrifice before she turns into an Infected. Tess *consciously* chooses her humanness in her death, and in doing so, her humanity, by trying to hold onto the remaining fragments of agency over her life. In framing her sacrifice as "an obligation" to be fulfilled by Joel, Tess asks him to choose her humanness with her, to value her sacrifice as a human being rather than dwelling on the loss her death represents.[11] By reminding Joel of his responsibilities as a human being, Tess also reminds him of his responsibilities as a citizen to and of this world: in *The Last of Us* series, citizenship is granted as a protective status by an individual's community—the civic responsibilities tied to this recognition process, in turn, involve ensuring and reinsuring the (medically) determined humanness of each individual, including one's own. Particularly interesting in this regard, is how Tess then not only uses these established definitions of civic responsibilities,

---

11 This commentary on the fragile relationship between life and death, humanness and humanity, citizen and non-citizen is a reoccurring theme in *The Last of Us* series. For instance, this relationship can be observed in the scene with Henry and Sam, as referenced above: Henry perceives of himself as *inhumane* for killing his little brother, even though his act signifies the enactment of a civic responsibility (Sam is now an Infected, hence, he must die). The *obligatory* fatal violence against his brother's quickly vanishing humanness then symbolizes a violation of Henry's humanity—meaning that Henry's capacity for acting as an empathetic human being dies the second he kills Sam. The aforementioned "civic responsibility over emotion" thus also has significant consequences for Henry's emotional integrity. Nonetheless, *Last of Us I* also resolves this ethical and emotional paradox for the players: Henry, by killing is brother, not only upholds his civic responsibilities, but also reinstates his agency as a *humane* human being, by killing himself, too. In his suicide, Henry restores the balance between life and death, humanity and humanness: if he cannot be humane, then he also cannot be human, thus, he must die. Even more so, Henry's and Sam's processes of citizenship recognition remain intact as well since their deaths are in accordance with the rules of this world. Sam is rightly stripped of his citizenship status by becoming infected and then killed, whereas Henry remains a citizen, even in death. The whole scene, though unsettling, hence not only reinforces the "lawful" enactments of citizenship and civic responsibilities but also restores the emotional balance for the players, who, as with Tess, witness the ultimate sacrifice: to die for the sake of sustaining humanness, humanity, and citizenship—not only for oneself, but for others, too.

to determine her own actions and predetermine Joel's actions, but to redefine these responsibilities as well.

By sacrificing herself to ensure Ellie and Joel's survival, Tess reevaluates previously fixed relations between humanness, humanity, and citizenship through medical determinators: not only can Tess remain an active agent of her own unraveling non-human, non-citizen, soon-to-be inhuman existence, but she can also ensure the success of Ellie's unraveled existence. Ellie, whose meta status as non-human non-citizen would technically require her death and/or social exile, is now protected by Tess's small, yet impactful redefined communal structure—her sacrifice, in turn, becomes a civic act of responsibility for this renewed community. By urging Joel to equally recognize Ellie's importance and require her protection, as the girl's immunity exemplifies the hope that the horrors of the pandemic might soon be over, Tess also claims Ellie's meta human existence as a lived reality: "This is fucking real, Joel!"

Ultimately, Tess's sacrifice is more than a personal choice to merely avoid "turning into one of those things." Instead, Tess acknowledges that by protecting Ellie, she is enabled to choose a better life for everyone else as well, while reestablishing her civic integrity as a human being despite her sinister past: "[Joel] This is *not us*.' [Tess scoffs] 'What do you know about us? About me?' ... 'Guess what, we're shitty people, Joel. It's been that way for a long time.' [Joel, angrily] 'No, we are *survivors!*' [Tess, desperate] *'This* is our *chance*—!'" (*Last of Us I*). Tess understands her role as part of a bigger civic and humanitarian scheme because she recognizes Ellie's importance as well as the centrality of her own decisions to ensure Ellie's success (in whatever form). Hence, for her sacrifice not to be in vain, Tess urges Joel to follow her example. Here, Nuraan Davids writes that

> human flourishing is possible only if we begin to act in ways, which not only recognize our mutuality, but if we are prepared to put in place the measures to sustain that mutuality. Citizenship ... provides us with a language to negotiate renewed understandings and practices of civic engagement and disagreement; it is up to us to accept this responsibility. (190)

This new practice of citizenship and citizenship recognition based on an understanding of mutuality, which Davids refers to here, is not only exemplified by Tess's behavior but also signifies an overall theme in the game series. Tess understands that she is not exempt from the fate of getting infected, despite the measures she has taken in the past to secure her safety. She is not a "survivor" anymore, as Joel calls them; instead, in her changed position from human to "soon-to-be-Infected," she begins to comprehend that no one is safe, until a different solution to the pandemic is found. Hereby, Tess finds a mutuality with others before her and, in turn, accepts Ellie's special role in changing the future for the better. In voicing her developing perspective and, eventually, by sacrificing herself, Tess practices a

Amina Antonia Touzos: "You're My People Now" 325

citizenship based on kinship with Ellie as meta citizen and meta human, as well as those before and after her.[12] Ellie's existence proves to her that change is indeed possible—Tess may have been "shitty people" but in accepting her responsibilities as a *citizen to humankind*, she takes the "measures [needed] to sustain that mutuality" of which she is now a part (Davids 190).

After Tess's sacrifice, the players consequently experience a change in Joel's behavior as well, as he not only agrees to help Ellie but soon grows to care for her. By letting the players take the role of Joel in *Last of Us I*, the game makes them a part of redefining the established recognition processes of humanness and citizenship alike. In doing so, the players not only get to work towards the specific objective of "saving humankind" by protecting Ellie, but they are also asked to reflect on the established frames of defining humankind and, in turn, citizenship in a highly medicalized world. Here, *The Last of Us* can not only be read as commentary on our own society and its medicalized humanness/citizenship recognition processes (Isin and Turner), but also as an example of "the ways that video games can encourage modes of engagement that develop into a player's imagination of citizenship" (Davisson and Gehm 42), humanness, and humanity.

At the same time, however, this is where the series takes a dramatic turn in its portrayal of Ellie and her supposed role in the narrative. Even though Ellie is treated as meta citizen or "citizen zero" by those who know of her immunity, Joel abstains from doing so, herein leading the player to do the same. Joel's relationship with Ellie is not based on feelings of civic responsibility because of her condition; rather, Joel begins to feel an emotional responsibility for Ellie because he cares for her as a *human* being. In Joel's mind, Ellie is not meta, no *wunderkind*, or "citizen zero" to be protected at all costs for the sake of humankind; she is to be protected because of her own innate humanity as an aspect of her distinct humanness. This is also the reason for Joel to save Ellie from the rebel group Fireflies, who want to perform a lethal surgery on her to extract a vaccine. As Joel, however, cannot bear to see his protegee daughter die, he kills the entire medical team to save Ellie's life and, thus, rescue her humanity as well.

As the players follow Joel's, and in the second game, Ellie's point of view, they are led to empathize with Joel's decision to save Ellie's life and, analogously, Ellie's continued struggles over Joel's acts in *Last of Us II*. Here, the games' narratives draw Ellie as a human in her own right: she makes mistakes, is emotional and inhumane at times, whereas her immunity and its potential do not transcend her into a position of godliness. Instead, she is repeatedly confronted with the limits of her own humanness as well as her humanity, as Ellie struggles to accept the weight of her

---

12 See Marcus Llanque and Katja Sarkowsky's chapter in this volume, "Citizenship of the Dead," for more on how the dead enact their obligations to the living, thereby contributing to community and belonging.

meta status, while at the same time, wishing to be of help: "[Ellie to Joel] Back when I was bitten—I wasn't alone. My best friend was there. And she got bit, too. We didn't know what to do. So... She says, 'Let's just wait it out. Y'know we can be all poetic and lose our minds together.' I'm still waiting for my turn!" (*The Last of Us* I). Nonetheless, the games' narratives deny Ellie the chance to become a martyr, fully in tune with her supposed civic responsibilities towards humankind. Throughout the series, Ellie struggles to maintain a "willingness to engage ... from another's perspective ... [to broaden her] own lived experiences and vantage points, and hence ... [her] capacity to act with compassion and empathy" (Davids 189). In opposition to Tess's decision to sacrifice herself, and in doing so, reclaiming her humanity, Ellie never gets to make that choice—her humanness, her humanity, and her status as citizen, even as a human being *per se*, always seems to be at the mercy of others.

Trauma and Citizenship

In *The Last of Us* series, the conflicts arising from Ellie's ambiguous identity are not purely limited to a medical(ized) discourse focused on the infected versus non-infected body, but also involve both characters and players in emotionally challenging and traumatic experiences of and around citizenship—or, even more elemental, of what makes a being human. The following scene in *Last of Us II* demonstrates the series' overall themes of citizenship trauma as well as the conflicting attempt to maintain one's human(e) identity:

[While being attacked by an Infected, Ellie's face mask breaks and she is forced to reveal her immunity to Dina, her partner and lover. This moment is interrupted by more Infected approaching, leading the two women to seek shelter in an abandoned theater.]
[Ellie] "You wanna tell me what's going on with you?"
[Dina] "What going on with me? Ellie... I just saw you breathe spores." [Dina is visibly shaken.]
[Ellie, timidly] "I told you... I'm immune."
[Dina, frustrated] "Okay. You're immune? Come on."
[Ellie] "I was bitten a long time ago..."
[Dina] "What the fuck are you talking about?"
[Ellie, forcefully] "I was bitten, and nothing happened." [Ellie shrugs her shoulders.]
[Dina, while looking at Ellie's arm] "The chemical burn..."
[Ellie] "... Tommy and Joel are the only ones who know... [pauses] Knew. Now you know."
[Ellie hesitates and looks nervously at Dina] "I can't... get you infected if that's what you're worried about. [sighs] I can't make you immune either."
[Dina sobs and does not look back at Ellie.]

[Ellie] "Can you say something?"
[Dina, now crying] "Ellie... [She looks up] I think I'm pregnant."
...
[Dina] "I didn't know—[sighs] I wasn't sure, okay? I didn't wanna be a burden..."
[Ellie, angrily] "Well you're a burden now, aren't you?"
[Dina looks deeply hurt at Ellie.]
[Ellie looks away and takes a few steps back.] "I'm gonna... make sure this place is secure. You just rest." [The cut-scene ends, and the player is back online navigating Ellie.] (*The Last of Us II*)

This scene demonstrates the complexities of how citizenship as a "source and marker of social identity" (Isin and Turner 5)—and in this case, not only social identity but *human* identity as well—correlates with traumatic experiences around establishing one's identity and how the people who one has perceived of as one's community, one's family, shape one's perception of self. Again, this sequence shows how profoundly Ellie's ambivalent medical and thus civic status influence her continuous struggles at attempting to find a congruent identity. The traumas she has experienced from having to (seemingly) settle on the perception of her immunity as something special but in need of protection, and thus having to be hidden, have a significant influence on Ellie's relationships with others and particularly those close to her. She knows of the expectations others have towards her because of her condition: "I can't... get you infected if that's what you're worried about. I can't make you immune either." Here, it becomes evident that Ellie has been indoctrinated into her society's mindset of understanding health status as tied to specific civic responsibilities, whereas Ellie's own indefinable health status renders her civic responsibilities as obscure as well. As the world's failed "citizen zero," Ellie is constantly torn between feeling guilty over her inability to be of use and her desire to live a "normal" life. However, Dina's pregnancy also demonstrates to her how fragile this perception of "normalcy" and lived reality is: no one's identity is stable; change, loss and death are integral parts of Ellie's world as "the law of identity *has* been rewritten. The terms of the self and of the real have been renegotiated, demonstrating that they are not fixed but fluid, susceptible to reopening" (Spencer 314; emphasis original). The traumas, in turn, that come with having to accept one's own and others' instability in relation to their bodies, minds, and identities, are deeply rooted in the characters, as we have seen in Tess, but also in Dina, who are genuinely uncertain over how to handle their changing body in a world that is not stable and regards changing bodies as "ill." Regarding citizenship, this instability also lies at the core of not only the characters' personal narratives but also the game series' narrative as a whole: "On the one hand, citizenship ensures access to participation in society. On the other hand, it implies an ideology of ableism, namely the assumption that citizens ought to be healthy and exercise productive social roles" (Waldschmidt and Sépulchree 27).

328   Citizenship, Science, and Medicine

Within the games' construction of an ideology of ableism, meaning that the community's relational perception of health defines who is rendered "healthy" and thus "able," or "ill" and thus "disabled," Ellie's role is as unraveling as it is stabilizing. On the one hand, the communities Ellie encounters are constructed as (medically) vulnerable, since they need peer protection from the Infected as well as the infection *per se*. On the other hand, Ellie, in her ambiguous meta identity, disrupts the established distinctions between protecting those who are considered "healthy" but vulnerable, and those who are considered "ill" and a threat. As she is neither healthy nor ill, neither vulnerable nor a threat, neither abled nor disabled, Ellie inhabits a liminal space. In turn, her meta existence also makes her vulnerable and in need of protection, as we have seen with Tess and Joel protecting her (and her secret immunity) as part of their civic as well as emotional responsibility. Moreover, Ellie's own traumatic experiences which are both resulting of and enhanced by her identity crisis, shape the way she perceives of herself and is perceived of by other characters and the player: "[Ellie to Joel] I was supposed to die in that hospital! My life would've fucking *mattered*. But you took that from me!" (*The Last of Us II*).

Interestingly, in her resentment of what she believes as her failure as "citizen zero," Ellie redefines the construction of citizenship and its processes of recognition within the series altogether. Citizenship now also represents an embodied, innate though changeable sense of self, rather than a status granted by others according to external factors. Ellie is human, humane, and citizen just by way of being a body (and mind); she "at once ... [inhabits] the sphere of humanity (the human as the subject of rights) and that of the border (the citizen ... as the subject of rights)" (Kesby 116).

Conclusion: Allies and Avatars

In the series "the very idea of citizenship is ... charged with the ... burden of survival" (Petryna 37), while surviving also becomes a matter of redefining the perceived relationship between humanness, humanity, and citizenship for both characters and players. By repeatedly charging the players with Ellie's survival, in *Last of Us I* as Joel and in *Last of Us II* as Ellie herself, the series makes their players an ally to Ellie, as they are the only ones (besides Ellie) who can virtually engage with the world of the games, without risking infection. Hence, the players' status is unique but also aligns them with Ellie's narrative: she is most akin, most citizen-like to what the players know outside the world of *The Last of Us*. In this sense, both the players and Ellie could be rendered as meta: Ellie, because of her immunity, and the players, because they are "naturally" immune due to them not being "inside" the game. Moreover, players are granted an even higher meta-level of (embodied) citizenship, as they are enabled to control and decide over Ellie as a *body to be governed*.[13] Here, the players almost become institutions of government themselves as they grant Ellie citizenship in her *inhumaness* twofold: one, because Ellie is a citizen of the immune community (her and the players), and two, because Ellie is, *within* this community, not a human in the first place—she is a fictional combination of pixels. In this regard, Ellie, again, is pushed into an ambiguous citizenship space: she is not "fully" human and thus not "fully" citizen inside or outside the game. At the same time Ellie also embodies a new form of citizenship, one that is, at least within the games, seemingly autonomous from established external determinators, such as bodily health. In this sense, Ellie functions as a narrative anchor for the players to experience the fragility of a system based on an ideology of binaries (healthy vs. ill, human vs. Infected, abled vs. disabled, etc.). Hence, by witnessing as well as taking part in Ellie's traumatic experiences as a result of her social and internal struggles, the players are repeatedly asked to reevaluate the connections between humanness, citizenship, and humanity with her. Ellie is human, humane, and embodied citizen because of everything she has experienced—moreover, she *is* (all these things), because the players recognize her as such. The players, as integral part to the games' narrative gameplay, thus stabilize Ellie's ambiguous identity and existence as embodied citizen (without an actual body outside the game) because they recognize her actions, her feelings, and her fallibility as relatable: "The avatar [the character played] is not simply a means of access to desired outcomes ... Willingly inverting self-other distinctions, players ... [and] gameplay ... [toy] with unstable categories of identity, presence, and subjectivity" (Rehak 107). In a sense, the players make Ellie a "citizen zero" after all, because she is (ideally) recognized as the first of a new form of humane human citizens. Finally, Ellie is reliant on her innate though conflicting aspects of humanness, humanity, and citizenship status, *as well as* others' recognition of these aspects—inside and outside the games: "So much of ... [*The Last of Us* series] is about how everything we do impacts other people, ... Ellie goes on this journey and the consequences aren't just other people's health and safety. It's also their mental well-being. It's also their future. It's also their ability to love" (Gross qtd. in Takahashi).

In this space, *The Last of Us* series positions itself (among others) through narrative medicine, as the players also explore the characters and their stories through an emotional bond. Here, the overall narratives function as gateways to process the

---

13   However, players do not have unlimited authority over the games' world or characters, as each player is still required to follow given narratives and cannot make content-related decisions, e.g., not killing a person. (This stands in contrast to minor decisions being granted to the player during combat; these decisions, however, do not alter or disrupt the games' narratives in any way). In turn, formal inactivity, meaning not hitting the control keys to, e.g., kill a person, would result in the gamers' inability to resume gameplay overall.

themes of health and illness, medicalization and citizenship, as well as the importance of one's story for these discourses:

> While at times fantastical, our agency in these polygonal environments allow us to emotionally and cognitively feel as if what we are subjected to in-game is also what our experiences would be in the flesh. There is no distinction between real and virtual. We react to the narratives, spaces, and characters based on our own subjectivities. In doing so, play becomes intensely personal. (Luc 92)

Consequently, the discussion of the medicalization of citizenship also becomes a personal one, asking every player of *The Last of Us* series to reflect on their own civic status regarding their emotional and medicalized identities. Video games can hereby offer us an opportunity to look within ourselves and our society through the stories we tell, as we become aware of our patterns inside and outside the online space: "Accounting for the self becomes not an autonomous act but a relational one, accomplished through experimental and creative contact with the stories of others" (Charon 6). The Covid-19 pandemic, possibly more than any other event in the last century, has shown us with full force how reliant we are on the contact with others and their stories, and, at the same time, how fragile our implemented systems we assumed to be stable truly are. In a fascinating yet slightly disturbing way, *The Last of Us* series has foreshadowed a world full of uncertainties, in which humanness, humanity, and citizenship are constantly questioned and redefined. Here, intersectional approaches of reading and analyzing text—be those texts video games or novels—has proven to be useful to understanding our evolving perceptions of health, illness, and what it means to be human. Therefore, even before but especially now in this age of pandemics, video games finalize proof of their value to the narratives we engage with on- and off-screen, whereas the question of who we are and want to be as a people remains more relevant than ever.

Works Cited

Borgstrom, Erica. "Social Death." *QJM: An International Journal of Medicine*, vol. 110, no. 1, 2017, pp. 5–7. doi: https://doi.org/10.1093/qjmed/hcw183.

Bourgonjon, Jeroen, and Ronald Soetaert. "Video Games and Citizenship." *CLCWeb: Comparative Literature and Culture*, vol. 15, no. 3, 2013, pp. 1–10.

Brookes, Sarah. *Playing the Story: Transportation as a Mediator of Involvement in Narratively-Based Video Games*. 2010. Ohio State University, Master's Thesis.

Charon, Rita. "Introduction." *The Principles and Practice of Narrative Medicine*, edited and written by Rita Charon, et al., Oxford UP, 2017, pp. 1–12.

Davids, Nuraan. "Covid-19: Undoing our 'Normal' to Find Humanity." *South African Journal of Higher Education*, vol. 35, no. 1, 2021, pp. 178–191.

Davisson, Amber, and Danielle Gehm. "Gaming Citizenship: Video Games as Lessons in Civic Life." *Journal of Contemporary Rhetoric*, vol. 4, no. 3/4, 2014, pp. 39–47.

Domsch, Sebastian. *Storyplaying: Agency and Narrative in Video Games*. De Gruyter, 2013.

Fernández-Vara, Clara. "Play's The Thing: A Framework to Study Video Game Performance." *DiGRA '09–Proceedings Of The 2009 DiGRA International Conference: Breaking New Ground: Innovation In Games, Play, Practice And Theory*, September 1–4 2009, London, UK, *Digital Research Game Association*, 2009, http://www.digra.org/wp-content/uploads/digital-library/09287.52457.pdf.

Green, Amy M. "The Reconstruction of Morality and the Evolution of Naturalism in The Last Us." *Games and Culture*, vol. 11, no. 7–8, 2016, pp. 745–763.

Hildebrandt, Paula, and Sibylle Peters. "Introduction." *Performing Citizenship: Bodies, Agencies, Limitations*, edited by Paula Hildebrandt et al., Springer International Publishing, 2019, pp. 1–13.

Hilvert-Bruce, Zorah, and James T. Neill. "I'm Just Trolling: The Roles of Normative Beliefs in Aggressive Behavior in Online Gaming." *Computers in Human Behavior*, vol. 102, 2020, pp. 303–311. doi: https://doi.org/10.1016/j.chb.2019.09.003.

Isin, Engin F., and Bryan S. Turner. "Citizenship Studies: An Introduction." *Handbook of Citizenship Studies*, edited by Engin F. Isin and Bryan S. Turner, Sage, 2002, pp. 1–10.

Kesby, Alison. *The Right to Have Rights: Citizenship, Humanity, and International Law*. Oxford UP, 2012.

Kowert, Rachel. "Social Outcomes: Online Game Play, Social Currency, and Social Ability." *The Video Game Debate: Unravelling the Physical, Social, and Psychological Effects of Video Games*, edited by Rachel Kowert and Thorsten Quandt, Routledge, 2015, pp. 94–115.

Luc, Andrea. "Exploring Agency and Female Player-Character Relationships in *Life is Strange*: What Choice Do I have?" *Feminist War Games? Mechanisms of War, Feminist Values, and Interventional Games*, edited by Jon Saklofske et al., Routledge, 2020, pp. 91–100.

Mäyrä, Frans. "Exploring Gaming Communities." *The Video Game Debate: Unravelling the Physical, Social, and Psychological Effects of Video Games*, edited by Rachel Kowert and Thorsten Quandt, Routledge, 2015, pp. 153–175.

Odmalm, Pontus. "Populism, Citizenship, and Migration." *The Handbook of Citizenship and Migration*, edited by Marco Giugni and Maria Grasso, Edward Elgar Publishing, 2021, pp. 377–390.

Office of the United Nations High Commissioner for Human Rights. *The Rights of Non-Citizens*. United Nations New York and Geneva, 2006.

"patient zero." *Merriam-Webster.com*. Merriam-Webster, 2021.

Petryna, Adriana. *Life Exposed: Biological Citizens After Chernobyl*. Princeton UP, 2013.

Rehak, Bob. "Playing at Being. Psychoanalysis and the Avatar." *The Video Game Theory Reader*, edited by Mark J. P. Wolf and Bernard Perron, Routledge, 2003, pp. 103–128.

Spencer, Danielle. *Metagnosis: Revelatory Narratives of Health and Identity*. Oxford UP, 2020.

Stapleton, Greg, et al. "Global Health Ethics: An Introduction to Prominent Theories and Relevant Topics." *Global Health Action*, vol. 7, no. 1, 2014, pp. 1–7. doi: 10.3402/gha.v7.23569.

Takahashi, Dean. "Naughty Dog's Narrative Lead Explains the Story of Last of Us II." *GamesBeat*, 12 July 2020, https://venturebeat.com/2020/07/12/naughty-dogs-na rrative-lead-explains-the-story-of-the-last-of-us-part-ii/.

The Last of Us. Naughty Dog, 2013. Sony PlayStation 3.

The Last of Us Part II. Naughty Dog, 2020. Sony PlayStation 4.

Waldschmidt, Anne, and Marie Sépulchre. "Citizenship: Reflections on a Relevant but Ambivalent Concept for Persons with Disabilities." *Disability and Society*, vol. 34, no. 3, 2019, pp. 421–446.

Williams, Jr. Robert A. *Savage Anxieties: The Invention of Western Civilization*. St. Martin's Press, 2012.

Appendix

Contributors

Mita Banerjee is Professor and Chair of American Studies at the Obama Institute for Transnational American Studies at Mainz University. Her research interests include postcolonial literature, issues of naturalization and citizenship, and medical humanities. She is the author of six monographs, including *Color Me White: Naturalism/Naturalization in American Literature* (2013) and *Medical Humanities in American Studies* (2018). She is a Principal Investigator in the Research Unit "Human Differentiation" and co-speaker of the research training group "Life Sciences, Life Writing: Boundary Experiences of Human Life between Biomedical Explanation and Lived Experience," which is funded by the German Research Foundation.

Erika Canossini is a PhD candidate in Sociology at the University of Toronto. Her research interests lie at the intersection of the sociology of punishment and socio-legal studies. Specifically, she is interested in exploring individuals' life experiences after coming into contact with the criminal justice system. Her dissertation research on the Canadian pardon and record suspension program asks what clemency means for applicants, recipients, and grantors and explores the relationship between the power to punish and the power to forgive. She holds a B.A. in Foreign Languages and Literature from the University of Bologna, a B.A. in Sociology from Queen's University (Kingston), and a M.A. in Sociology from the University of Toronto.

Vanessa Evans is a settler scholar and Assistant Professor of Indigenous Literatures at Appalachian State University. Her current research is interested in the ways diverse and distinct Indigenous novels from North America, Oceania, and South Asia represent resurgence through storytelling, language, and relationship with land. Her essays appear in *The Palgrave Handbook of Incarceration in Popular Media* (2019), *Studies in the Novel* (2022), and *The International Journal of Online Pedagogy and Course Design* (2022). Vanessa is also an Associate Managing Editor for the *Journal of Transnational American Studies*.

Mitchell Gauvin is SSHRC Postdoctoral Fellow in English Literature at Johannes Gutenberg University Mainz. His interdisciplinary research examines citizenship and literature with particular focus on the rhetorics of political, legal, and nationalistic conceptions of personhood in fiction and literary theory. Concentrating on Anglo-American and British contexts, his research comparatively analyzes both literary and legal texts to unravel how literary works engage with, circulate, or protest exclusionary forms of political subjecthood, with emphasis on issues of governmentality, state management, and nationalistic imaginings of citizenship in the contemporary period and the long-eighteenth century.

Sonja Georgi is a Lecturer in American Studies at Johannes Gutenberg University in Mainz, Germany. She received a Master of Arts degree in American Studies, Applied Linguistics, and Economics and a doctoral degree in American Studies from the University of Siegen, Germany. Her research and teaching interests are ethnic literature, African American studies, science fiction and film studies. She is currently working on a book project that investigates African-Native American literatures, histories, and cultures in the context of transnational American Studies.

Jessica Hanselman Gray is a Lecturer in the English Department at the University of California, Davis, where she also completed her PhD in Literature with a designated emphasis in Science and Technology Studies. She received her M.A. in English Literature at Wright State University in Ohio and her B.A. in English at the University of North Florida. Her current project focuses on intersections of literature, experimental science, metaphors of the reproductive body, and the construction of authoritative knowledge in the seventeenth century.

Nina Heydt received both her B.A. in American Studies and French and her M.A. in American Studies from Johannes Gutenberg University Mainz. Her theses explored ethnic representations in American literature and popular culture. Currently, Nina is a PhD candidate and lecturer (wissenschaftliche Mitarbeiterin) at JGU's Obama Institute for Transnational American Studies. Her PhD project focuses on the intersection of law, literature, and popular culture in US prison narratives. In her teaching, she also explores images of gender and ethnicity in US literature and culture. Further research interests include African American Studies, Whiteness Studies/ Critical Race Theory, and crime fiction.

Marcus Llanque holds the chair of Political Theory at Augsburg University. He is the co-founder of the journal *Zeitschrift für Politische Theorie*. Research interests: history of political ideas, especially the history of democratic thinking and the political theory of republicanism. He recently completed a research project on the conflict structure of Sophocles' tragedy *Antigone* (together with Katja Sarkowsky).

Contributors   337

Scott Obernesser is currently Assistant Professor of English at Del Mar College in Corpus Christi, Texas. He received his PhD from The University of Mississippi in 2018 and taught at the Obama Institute for Transnational American Studies in 2019. His research includes "What It Means to Be On The Road: Mobility and Petrocultures During the Mid-Twentieth Century," published in *ISLE Journal*, and "'So Many Strange Plants:' Race and Environment in John Muir's *A Thousand-Mile Walk to the Gulf*," published in *Ecocriticism and the Future of Southern Studies*.

Kaitlyn Quinn is an Assistant Professor of Criminology & Criminal Justice at the University of Missouri-St. Louis. Her research explores the work of volunteers and non-profit organizations in the criminal justice domain in Canada, England, Scotland, and the United States. Her work has been published in the *British Journal of Sociology*, *Punishment & Society*, the *British Journal of Social Work*, *Voluntas*, *Criminology & Criminal Justice*, and the *British Journal of Criminology*.

Anah-Jayne Samuelson is an English Instructor at Red Deer Polytechnic in Red Deer, Alberta. Her teaching and research interests include children's and young adult literature, Indigenous literatures, and the intersections between activism and literature. She has been published in *International Research for Children's Literature*, *Studies in the Novel*, and collections on Neo-Victorianism and Space and Identity within Children's Literature.

Katja Sarkowsky holds the Chair of American Studies at Augsburg University. Her research and publication foci include life writing, Indigenous literatures in Canada and the United States, and literary citizenship studies. In collaboration with political theorist Marcus Llanque, she recently completed an interdisciplinary project on the conflict structure of Sophocles' tragedy *Antigone* and its relevance for understanding how modern reworkings of the play negotiate contemporary political conflicts.

Kristen Smith earned her PhD from York University in 2023 with an intermedial dissertation that examines the multifaceted presence/absence of sound in varieties of visually-oriented poetry from the 1950s to the 2010s. Her academic work has been published with the *International Journal of Media and Cultural Politics*, Interdisciplinary Discourses, Inter-disciplinary Press, and Somatechnics. She has two chapters forthcoming in separate anthologies with Cambridge Scholars Publishing and an article in the special issue "New Sonic Approaches in Literary Studies" with *English Studies in Canada (ESC)*. In both her academic and creative work, she is interested in how art is created in community, connection, and collaboration.

Nasra Smith is a PhD candidate in English at York University. In 2021–2022, she was a Visiting Lecturer at the Obama Institute for Transnational American Studies at Johannes Gutenberg University Mainz. Her dissertation focuses on Eastern African literatures and Indian Ocean Studies, centralizing coastal nations and their archipelagoes from Eritrea to Mozambique. In addition to *Cultures of Citizenship* and *African Studies Quarterly*, she has forthcoming articles in *Studies in Canadian Literature: Black Lives Matter* and *Aquatic Cartographies: Oceanic Imaginaries, Histories, and Identities* (Ethics Publishing).

Malaika Sutter is a PhD student at the University of Bern. She studied English Languages and Literatures and Contemporary History at Bern and earned a second master's degree in English from the University of Rochester NY as a Fulbright grantee in 2019/20. She received a four-year grant from the Swiss National Science Foundation for her interdisciplinary doctoral thesis project "Crafting the Needle: Text(ile)-Image Constellations in Contemporary North American Fiction and Art," which is supervised by Gabriele Rippl and Janet Catherine Berlo.

Amina Touzos is a PhD candidate in the doctoral research program "DIAPASON – Digital Information Landscape and Its Impact on Student Learning" at Johannes Gutenberg University Mainz. She is also a research assistant at the Obama Institute for Transnational American Studies at JGU and she holds a Master of Education in both English and Philosophy from JGU (2021). Her studies and areas of interest primarily include video game studies and medical humanities, with a specific focus on disability studies and trauma studies, gender and queer studies as well as education sciences.

Julia Velten is an Assistant Professor at the Obama Institute for Transnational American Studies at Johannes Gutenberg University in Mainz. She received her doctorate from JGU in 2021. She was a member of the DFG Research Group "Un/doing Differences: Practices of Human Differentiation" from 2016–2019 and was hosted as visiting PhD student at the Trent Centre for Aging and Society in 2017. Her research focuses on aging, medical humanities, and cultures of knowledge in the North American context. Her book, *Extraordinary Forms of Aging: Life Narratives of Centenarians and Children with Progeria*, was published with transcript in 2022.

[transcript]

PUBLISHING.
KNOWLEDGE. TOGETHER.

transcript publishing stands for a multilingual transdisciplinary programme in the social sciences and humanities. Showcasing the latest academic research in various fields and providing cutting-edge diagnoses on current affairs and future perspectives, we pride ourselves in the promotion of modern educational media beyond traditional print and e-publishing. We facilitate digital and open publication formats that can be tailored to the specific needs of our publication partners.

OUR SERVICES INCLUDE

- partnership-based publishing models
- Open Access publishing
- innovative digital formats: HTML, Living Handbooks, and more
- sustainable digital publishing with XML
- digital educational media
- diverse social media linking of all our publications

Visit us online: www.transcript-publishing.com

Find our latest catalogue at www.transcript-publishing.com/newbookspdf